The Hebrew
Messiah

*The Glory and
Triumph of Israel*

Allan Russell Juriansz

המשיח העברי

התהילה והניצחון של ישראל

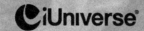

THE HEBREW MESSIAH
The Glory and Triumph of Israel

iUniverse books may be ordered through booksellers or by contacting:

iUniverse
1663 Liberty Drive
Bloomington, IN 47403
www.iuniverse.com
1-800-Authors (1-800-288-4677)

ISBN: 978-1-4917-7211-9 (sc)
ISBN: 978-1-4917-7212-6 (hc)
ISBN: 978-1-4917-7210-2 (e)

Library of Congress Control Number: 2015912614

Print information available on the last page.

iUniverse rev. date: 09/02/2015

Copyright Permissions

Other Books by Allan Russell Juriansz

The Fair Dinkum Jew: The Survival of Israel and the Abrahamic Covenant

King David's Naked Dance: The Dreams, Doctrines, and Dilemmas of the Hebrews

Colonial Mixed Blood: A Story of the Burghers of Sri Lanka

To Desmond Ford—theologian, scholar, and teacher; disciple of Ha-Mashiach.

CONTENTS

PREFACE

Karl Marx, the Jewish philosopher, said, "Religious misery represents at once the expression of and the protest against actual misery. Religion is the moan of the oppressed creature, the heart of a heartless world, the sense of senseless conditions. It is the opium of the people." (See *Critique of Hegel's Philosophy of Right.*) This tells us how deeply Marx felt the miserable condition the world is in. This man also knew the pathos of the unhappiness of God at the devastation humanity is in from disobedience. He probably was thinking mainly of the Judeo-Christian religion when he likened religion to an opium fix. Marx had a deep understanding of the human condition. People think he derided religion. He called it "the heart of a heartless world, the sense of senseless conditions." That is not derision. But he was so wrong in his analogy. Opium brings only a transient high, a fleeting release ending in a greater frustration at that misery. The thrill of greatest value and the eternal release in Judaism is the Messiah, who restores perfection and immortality to end all misery. Marx had lost his vision of the Messiah. All Jews who live without the Messiah confine themselves to continued misery.

The great modern scholar Peter Schafer, with deep perception of the Jewish situation and a wide knowledge of the Jewish literature, sees no uniform expectations of the Messiah in the Jewish tradition. However, he concludes that it is the hope for the restoration of the Davidic kingship. It is the inauguration of a new king from the house of David, who will govern the reunited northern and southern kingdoms of Israel and Judah. He describes a savior king at the end of time who will usher in a new era entailing the ultimate victory over Israel's enemies, the rebuilding of the temple, the gathering of the exiles, and a period of peace and prosperity. (See *The Jewish Jesus* by Peter Schafer, p. 223.)

I perceive he correctly sums up the majority feeling in Jewry. There is no mention of the messianic atonement, judgment, and resurrection, and no hope expressed for perfection and immortality, in his above statement.

The Messiah I hope to qualify will be defined by the Tanak. Some paraliterature will be cited, but the definition will be governed only by the Tanak. In other words, non-tanakian views will not be allowed to define the Messiah of Judaism. That Messiah must fit into a strict monotheism. The Lord our God is one. Blessed be He.

The blueprint for the Messiah is found in the Tanak. That there is such a guide in a book of forty-nine different writings scrolled over one thousand years is a great wonder. God has spent one thousand years trying to show us redemption by the Messiah. Is it a unified messianic picture, or are there major discrepancies and contradictions? In this book I undertake to search out the answer to this question. I have the assurance from the Talmud that "*every prophet prophesied for the Days of the Messiah*"(Ber. 34b), so the rabbinic sages knew where the answers were. And I believe, with Moses at Sinai, that the key to the understanding of the messianic provision is the garden of Eden, where God and humanity were entwined in primitive devekut, and where the great wrenching separation occurred. And Moses at Sinai elaborated and enshrined that messianic redemption proclaimed at the gates of Eden. The earthly tabernacle temple, a copy of the heavenly temple conceived by God, established the plan of that redemption. The mechanics of redemption contained the disposal of sin (disobedience to law), by instituting repentance, forgiveness, and atonement. It was available to individuals on a daily basis. As well, the Day of Atonement, celebrated yearly, centered in the Most Holy Place, signified the cosmic restoration of perfection and immortality.

My lifelong realization of my own mortality and imperfection of being has found me vulnerable. My resultant dedication to the sacredness of the Tanak has energized me, and the pondering of the messianic concept has thrilled my daily living. It stems from my devout belief in God and the challenge God has offered in my contemplation of His marvelous creation and redemption of humanity. The Tanak has led me to regard redemption as His main current and distraught occupation. It is His longing pleasure. This has anchored my hopes and expectations within His plans and has given me a positive and secure outlook for the future.

In the Tanak, messianic expectation is central. Messiah is the focus of all important recorded events. (See *Il Messia* by David Castelli, pp. 202–209.)[1]

Judaism 101, available online, can be considered a valiant effort on behalf of modern Jewry to explain to the world the messianic concept:

The Messianic Idea in Judaism

Belief in the eventual coming of the Mashiach is a basic and fundamental part of traditional Judaism. It is part of Rambam's 13 Principles of faith. In the Shemoneh Esrei prayer, recited three times daily, we pray for all the elements of the coming of the Mashiach:

1. Ingathering of the exiles
2. Restoration of the religious courts of justice
3. *An end of wickedness, sin, and heresy*
4. *Reward of the righteous*
5. Rebuilding of Jerusalem
6. Restoration of the line of King David
7. Restoration of the Temple Service[2]

The above elements, with the exception of numbers 3 and 4, are eminently achievable today without Mashiach. But the end of wickedness, sin, and heresy, and the achievement of the reward of the righteous, which is the expected perfection and immortality, are *massive tasks* and will need intervention by deity. According to the Tanak, these come with messianic atonement, the apocalyptic collapse of history, judgment, resurrection, a total eradication of disobedience, and a restoration of perfection and immortality. Otherwise, the status quo will be left in perpetuity. Also, King Messiah ben David cannot be a transient one human lifetime figure if He is looked upon as the defined eternal King of Glory dreamed about in the Tanak. Such a Mashiach must be divine and is eminently fulfilled by the Ha-Mashiach functionality of Elohim. This is the definition of the true Son of David.

There is a willingness in Jewry to embrace a great and mighty political kingdom in which the Messiah reigns in the eternal future. But there is a great neglect to recognize the divinity of Messiah ben David, who provides messianic redemption from sin and the eternal kingdom.

There are many Talmudic utterances of messianic redemption. See the following:

- *Midrash Tanhuma,* Section *Mas'e,* Paragraph 4
- *Midrash Bereshit Rabba,* ed. Theodor, p. 445
- *Midrash Shir ha-Shirim Rabba,* VI, 10
- *Sanhedrin 97 a; Exodus Rabba,* XXV, 16
- *Midrash Tehillim* to Psalm 45:3; *Sanhedrin 98a*

These are all quoted by Gershom Scholem in his book *The Messianic Idea in Judaism* in support of messianic redemption.

The Tanak describes and defines the Ha-Mashiach as a functionality of Elohim to achieve both freedom from sin and provision of an everlasting kingdom. There is major adoration of Mashiach in Psalm 45 and the Talmud raptures over its messianic application:

> You are fairer than all men;
> Your speech is endowed with **Grace;**
> Rightly has God given you an eternal blessing.
> Gird your sword upon your thigh, O hero,
> In your splendour and glory;
> ***Your divine throne is everlasting;***
> Your royal scepter is a scepter of equity.
> (Ps. 45: selected verses, emphasis added)

The commentary in the margin of *The Jewish Study Bible* (p. 1332) makes the primary application of these words to kings Saul and David, and even Egyptian kings who were handsome! But their kingdoms were transient. The Talmud exults in this Psalm as a messianic application of grace, splendor, glory, and equity, and the declaration that the Messiah has a divine throne that is everlasting

(*Midrash Tehillim to Psalm 45*). How can we doubt that Messiah is deity in the face of these tanakian declarations and rabbinic adorations? How can we squeeze Him into the straitjacket of a mere mortal human lifetime?

My use of the words "function" and "functionality" in this book is by necessity. These words are needed in the protection of my essential belief in monotheism. I am not alone in this endeavor. As far as I know, these words are original with me in my application of them; that is, I have not come across them in the context of my use of them in my "wide" reading. But I find a kindred spirit in this idea in the writings of Joseph Klausner. His concept of the Godhead (synonymous with "Father," "Jehovah," "Adonai," and "Elohim") is challenging. Why does he need the term "Godhead"? Would not the word "God" suffice? "Godhead" implies a multiplicity of deities with a "head boss," or at least a delegation of function within God Himself. Klausner tries to accommodate "Shekina," "the voice of God," "the Holy Spirit," "the bath qol," "the Ma'mar" (cf. "Logos"), and "the first-born of God" within the scope ("power") of the "Godhead." This is because of his own tenacious dedication to monotheism. He sees a multiplicity of God's activities, assigning them personalities, to accommodate what God will do. He attributes the idea of "the first-born of God" to Philo. But he had forgotten that this idea is embedded in the Tanak. David (Ps. 2:7, 12), Isaiah (Isa. 9:6), and Daniel (Dan. 3:25; 7:13, 14), among others, already subscribed to it. I clearly see in Klausner's ideation that he is hard put to accommodate all God's manifestations toward humanity into one identity obedient to monotheism. He uses the words "powers," and "Godhead" to do this. Compatible with his ideation perhaps, is my own desire to express the Ha-Mashiach and the Ruach Hakodesh "powers" of the "Godhead" as "functionalities." The term to me demands and embraces the "substantial (One Substance) presence of God Himself" in His functions as Mashiach and Holy Spirit, rather than in the abstract "powers," which Klausner likens to the sun and its rays. He prefers the word "powers" to "emanations."[3] I believe my idea of functionalities eliminates the Christian tendency to treat God, Messiah, and Holy Spirit as "God in three persons," "the Trinity." This Christian idea incites the accusation of "three

Gods" despite Christians not believing in three Gods. But use of the term "functionality" preserves monotheism. The Lord our God is one; blessed is He. But in this ideation I do not restrict God from manifesting Himself as the promised human manifestation of Himself in the Mashiach. Geza Vermes goes through great pains and contorted gymnastics of logic in his attempt to isolate the concept of God from the concept of Messiah. (See *Christian Beginnings* by Geza Vermes pp. 106–114.) But Messiah is prominently deity in the Tanak, and the Talmud both enthusiastically and halfheartedly agrees.

In this, my third publication on Judaism, *The Hebrew Messiah: The Glory and Triumph of Israel,* I seek to define the messianic dream outlined in the Tanak. I will be faithful to the Tanak in describing the Ha-Mashiach but will do everything possible to involve the talmudic and modern scholarly opinions in this description. The great rabbinic sages expressed strong messianic dreams in the Talmud, and though highly varied and divisive, and sometimes at variance with the Tanak, they will be extracted and described. Congruency with the Tanak will be sought, and incongruent ideas and concepts will be labeled as such and discarded. The reader must be warned that the talmudic sages did not agree among themselves in their ideas and dreams of the Messiah and the Messianic Age. But Gershom Scholem sees a good discussion in the Talmud. At the outset he says,

> Classical Jewish tradition is fond of **emphasizing the catastrophic strain in redemption.** If we look at the tenth chapter of the tractate Sanhedrin, where the Talmudists discuss the question of redemption at length, we see that to them it means a colossal uprooting, destruction, revolution, disaster, with nothing of development or progress about it.[4]

I will show the unity of definition and concept of the messianic idea in the Tanak. I believe that messianic intervention to bring about the redemption of humanity is the most compelling, satisfying, exciting, and thrilling part of the tanakian religion called Judaism. It is the anchor of body and soul in this mortal life. Its contemplation is the most edifying experience possible. It is the restoration of perfection and immortality and the close companionship with God, which were all lost in *Gan Eden*. It assures us of a future after this life. Gershom Scholem defined it as "Acute Messianism." In my opinion he is Israel's modern giant in the understanding of Messianism and the future of the planet earth.

The messianic idea throughout the history of Israel has a double accomplishment as defined in the Tanak:

1. Redemption from sin and death, and provision of perfection and immortality to a redeemed humanity.
2. Restoration of the Davidic kingdom in an earth made new where King Messiah ben David reigns forever and ever.

Whenever Israel was in trouble, their longings for the Messiah intensified. More often than not these longings were triggered by their political vicissitudes rather than by their spiritual condition per se. Their forays into idolatry caused those vicissitudes. But their spiritual decadence alone, with the exception of the prophets, did not motivate those messianic longings. They did get warnings from the prophets, but they were mostly spiritually blind and deaf. When they were in exile, desire for the Mashiach was eminently motivated to implement return to the homeland. The prophets who ministered to them always addressed both the political exilic misery as well as their spiritual decadence. Joseph Klausner has written perceptively about this. He has divided the prophets' messages into those applying to Israel's idolatry and political limbo miseries, and those applying to "The End Time" or "End of Days" or the "Messianic Age," these embodying the process of redemption.[5]

Isaiah primarily addressed how Messiah forgave their spiritual depravity and provided atonement for sin. To Isaiah, Messiah was God Himself. And he was emphatic about the messianic kingdom in an earth made new. Daniel was in total agreement. Jeremiah and Ezekiel dealt primarily with their political limbo and expanded the messianic apocalyptic and eschatological "End of Days." All the prophets prophesied for the restoration of perfection and immortality. I do not want a temporary messiah to provide another transient "Golden Age" as existed in King David's tenure. I want an eternal one in which I can share eternally! That is what the Tanak has promised.

In summary, Rabbinic Judaism is a by-product of the discussion between the sages through the ages of the diaspora after the second temple was destroyed. Current Rabbinic Judaism is not the primitive redemptive Judaism of Sinai. Rabbinic Judaism presents several variants in respect to Messianism. Many sages endorsed the apocalyptic eschatology. True primitive redemptive Judaism was established at Mt. Sinai and has not become obsolete. *Shechinah, law, mercy, and blood* remain the mighty bulwarks established at Sinai. They were predictive of messianic atonement, the Messianic Age, and the King Messiah ben David. Ruach Hakodesh and Ha-Mashiach will bring the redemption. In this unifying common thread, discarded by many eminent modern Jewish scholars, Israel and all humanity have a glorious future.

The Jews cannot argue for a total dedication of messianic energy and activity to restore their own terrestrial political and national agenda in the status quo and stop there. These ambitions are allowable and necessary to enable the fulfillment of the Abahamic covenant. The Zionists of the last two hundred years with the eminent leadership of Herzl, Weizmann, Jabotinsky, Ben Gurion, Netanyahu, and others have achieved national and political status without the appearance of a messiah. I see God's hand in this mighty national restoration. But political and national independence must be used to achieve fulfillment of the Abrahamic covenant. A New Age without perfection and without immortality is the stale status quo and is meaningless alone. The old Davidic kingdom is only a figurative type of the dynamism of Mashiach ben David's kingdom. The inexorable apocalyptic Mashiach Ben David will arrive and rule eternally.

In this book I have arranged the prophets in what I perceive is their most likely chronology, starting with the earliest. This is not a universally accepted chronology. I also recognize the split chronology of some of the writings, especially of Isaiah, Ezekiel, and Daniel. This approximate chronology, the multiple authors, the so-named editing, and the assumed and probable interpolations do not diminish the messianic message and the sacredness of the Tanak. The Tanak is a wondrous document and is the legitimate and true revelatory foundation of Judaism.

There is significant repetition in this book, as the great concepts of the Tanak and the essence of *Judaism as embodied in the Most Holy Place of the Temple* are discussed in reference to various persons, times, and places.

I am prone to emphasis in this book since I wish to "speak" the book rather than present a passive message in writing. I apologize to the reader who might be irritated by it.

I use the synonyms which apply to the Redeemer interchangeably, namely Mashiach, Messiah, and Ha-Mashiach. I also use Holy Spirit and Ruach Hakodesh synonymously. I love all these nominal appellations of Elohim. Blessed be He, the Lord our God is one.

Allan Russell Juriansz

ACKNOWLEDGEMENTS

I acknowledge with gratitude the editorial assistance by iUniverse.

I have dedicated this book to Desmond Ford, eminent theologian, scholar, and author. I did not have the privilege to sit in his classes as a student when he was professor and chairman of the Department of Theology at the prestigious Avondale College in Australia. But since I first met him transiently in 1957, he has been a great influence on me. His dedication to and exposition of the Ha-Mashiach in the primitive redemptive Judaism of the Tanak opened my eyes to this wondrous document, wherein lies the plan of redemption of the Jews and all humanity. It is the triumphant hope of the world. Our continued friendship since then despite our living in different parts of the world has been inspirational. It has motivated me to write this book. As my guru he may not agree with all my ideas, but that is his prerogative. (See the biographical sketch on Desmond Ford at the end of this book.)

A major part of the discussion in this book is dependent on the authors cited in the bibliography. They are inspirational, and their knowledge and research have provided me with many of the opinions on which I have settled. But the major influence in my expressed opinions has been the basic theology of the Tanak. I regard the Tanak as an inspired and sacred document, the very vital and revealing conversation of God with Israel. The Talmud is Israel's esteemed discussion among themselves and is often argumentative and full of disagreements, which is a natural outcome of a brilliant people who have led the way in defining our relationship with God.

Since my youth I have regarded the painting *Sacrifice by Abraham* by Rembrandt as being a messianic enactment. That appreciation has been greatly strengthened by the discussion of the event by Geza Vermes. I thank him for this. That messianic depiction, which occurred on the temple mount so long ago, has a clarity that was not well perceived by the rabbinic sages.

I wholeheartedly acknowledge Israel's right to exist and defend itself as a nation. The precarious position of modern Israel as an island in the raging sea of contemporary sectarian and violent Islam is calamitous. The poorly perceived and chaotic Jewish orientation to the imminence of the eternal messianic kingdom is also calamitous. The tanakian messianic hope is Israel's mission to the world and is the fulfillment of the Abrahamic covenant. It is Israel's absolute moral right to existence. And the messianic perception by Israel is imperative. For this function Israel's destiny is secure. Israel cannot and will not be wiped off the face of the earth. The prophetic apocalyptic is inexorable.

My study is based largely on the *Jewish Study Bible: Tanakh Translation.* I greatly desire to give my book a Jewish perspective and find it very appropriate to use a translation exclusively made by Jewish scholars. All quotes of the Holy Scriptures are from this translation unless otherwise acknowledged. Occasionally scripture is quoted as found in the author cited, though that author may or may not credit a particular translation.

INTRODUCTION

The Ha-Mashiach is the primary, central, and dominant theme of the Tanak. The anatomy of the messianic concept as perceived by all the prophets is a mixed but coherent and unified picture when carefully deciphered. The great mistake many Jewish and other scholars make in writing about the Messiah is to consider the messianic concept as an evolutionary item in the Hebrew milieu (e.g., see *The Messiah: Developments in Early Judaism and Christianity*, edited by James H. Charlesworth, 28 authors). An understanding of Messianism may be something that evolved in Jewish minds, but Messianism must be viewed as well established in God's mind in eternity. It was made known to Moses and the prophets and involved God's creation and redemption of our world. The Edenic story tells it all, even if it is accepted only as metaphor.

The Talmud often lacks coherence, and it can be contradictory, but it also has some brilliant concepts congruent with the Tanak (e.g., the recognition of the messianic nature of Isa. 9:6, the stupendous *"the Mighty God, planning Grace."*) The prophets of the Tanak were so awed by the prospect of the coming Mashiach that they let the messianic functions run together. The massive redemptive work of the Mashiach lacks a clear chronology, as the accomplishment of atonement and the restoration of perfection and immortality are mixed simultaneously. The kingly function and the everlasting kingdom cannot be established without prior atonement. With many rabbinic sages and Jewish scholars, *atonement is not perceived*. They magnify politiconational reinstatement and aggrandizement.

I am mindful that many books have been written in the last two hundred years about the Mashiach. I have read many of them. The accounts that I principally value are (1) *The Messianic Idea in Judaism*, by Gershom Scholem; (2) *The Messianic Idea in Israel from its Beginning to the Completion of the Mishnab (Mishnah)*, by Joseph Klausner; (3) *The Messiah according to the Jews*, by David Castelli; (4) *The Jewish Messiah*, by James Drummond; (5) *The Star of Redemption*, by Franz Rosenzweig (a very remarkable work, written with more than a touch of mysticism); (6) *Everyman's Talmud* by Abraham Cohen; (7) *The Abomination of Desolation in Biblical Eschatology*, by Desmond Ford, (which brings a clear understanding of the apocalyptic). (7) *The Messiah – Developments in Earliest Judaism and Christianity* edited by James H. Charlesworth, is the result of a symposium held by both Jewish and Christian scholars. Papers presented by 28 authors were compiled in this valuable work. It does not present a unified theology of the Messiah. Instead it presents a significant spectrum of messianic ideas in a discussion of the Tanak and parallel literature.

In my previous work of defining tanakian Judaism, which I titled *King David's Naked Dance: The Dreams, Doctrines and Dilemmas of the Hebrews*, I restricted my discussion to primitive redemptive tanakian Judaism. I write from the conviction that the Tanak is the sole ancient sacred canon of the Hebrews and that Rabbinic Judaism is mostly an argumentative discussion, with massive attention to law and Halakah. The primitive redemptive Judaism of Abraham, Jacob, and Moses is not the prime concern of the rabbinic sages. The Tanak must define the true Messianism of the Hebrews. The Talmud and the vast other noncanonical works tend to confuse many modern Jewish scholars who write on the topic of messianism. Most ignore the redemptive plan of the Almighty. Their writings constitute a blurred politico-national Messianism, mainly conceived within a continuation of the status quo. This book, I hope, will be based on the tanakian witness, and I will take advantage of the Talmud, Apochrypha, pseudepigrapha, and Tannaitic and Amoraitic writings, as the opportunity arises. With regard to the Tanak, I agree wholeheartedly with the talmudic dictum that

> **Every Prophet only prophesied for the days of the Messiah and the penitent** (Ber. 34b)[6]

and the similar sentiment seen here:

> **Great is repentance, for it reaches to the Throne of Glory. Great is repentance, for it makes the Redemption (by the Messiah) to come near.** (Joma 86a *et seq*).

The highly esteemed Gershom Scholem described acute Messianism as the energy that brings about the Utopian state of the world:

> *We have been taught that the messianic idea of the progress of the human race in the universe, is achieved by man's unassisted and continuous progress ... Traditionally however, the messianic idea in Judaism was not so cheerful ... History would reach its terminus, and the new state that ensued would be the result of a totally new manifestation of the DIVINE. In the prophets this stage is called "The Day of the Lord" ... If we look at the tenth chapter of the Sanhedrin, where the Talmudists discuss the question of redemption at length, we see that to them it means a colossal uprooting, destruction, revolution, disaster, with nothing of development of progress about it. "The Son of David" will come ... liberation of Israel in essence; but it will march in step with the liberation of the whole world.*[7]

This means that the talmudic sages credited the prophets of the Tanak for the focus on an apocalyptic messianic redemption. The Hebrew Bible is a dialogue between God and His people primarily about achieving redemption. Scholem here recognizes Messianism as a "*DIVINE*" intervention, "a totally new manifestation of the Divine." Undoubtedly, the inference by necessity has to be that the Messiah is divine.

This book I present to you, *The Hebrew Messiah: The Glory and Triumph of Israel,* will be solidly structured on the blueprint in the Tanak.

Joseph Klausner says in his preface dated 1926 that he hoped his book named above would be a scientific work, which he defined as

> A book which arranges the Messianic beliefs and opinions in all times and periods according to historical evolution, and shows their connexion with and attachment to historical events ...[8]

He includes the Apocrypha, pseudepigrapha, the periods of the Tannaim and Amoraim and continuing. My view is that such a work only traces a developmental history within scholarly considerations, which eventually arrives at an opinion, which may be "scientifically" contrived but is certainly not necessarily the theological truth. In my opinion the truth about Messianism resides in the Tanak and need not be deduced from other works, which complicate and confuse it.

Messianism cannot change with every invented or deduced opinion from now till doomsday. New insights are valued, but *the Messiah of the Tanak is the Redeemer of the world and is available for redemptive understanding now*. It is quite distressing to me that Klausner perceives the term "Messiah" as a nomenclature for the kings and priests of the Tanak who were anointed with oil. He disregards the eternal preexistence of *Messiah the Redeemer,* who restores perfection and immortality, first enunciated terrestrially at the gates of Gan Eden in the redemptive story of the "enmity" between Eve and the Serpent. The murder of Abel is implicit with messianic redemptive structure, which cries from his blood spilled on the ground. Klausner's first perception of Messiah is in the apocryphal Fourth Book of Enoch. This is a pitiful lack of discernment and disregards the redemptive messianic theology spelled out by Moses.

A discussion of messianic theology in Judaism must be given a framework.[9] This requires the recognition of the great concepts of the Tanak. There must be recognition of God as Creator and the subsequent history of the fall of humanity as outlined by Moses. His great accomplishment was the written Torah from the Oral Torah that had passed down from Adam, through the line of the great patriarchs to Abraham, Jacob, and finally to himself. We owe to Moses the description of the history of the world from the beginning in Gan Eden, where disobedience and death devastated the planet and shattered immortality. We owe him for the deliverance of an uncouth, idolatrous, unruly, and suffering people from Egyptian slavery and for bringing them to the borders of the Promised Land. We owe to him everything that was beamed from Sinai, and especially the messianic temple service, where Shechinah, law, mercy, and blood mightily *comingled* in the redemption of humanity.

Moses documented the foundation of Judaism, within which was laid God's agreement with Abraham and the favored ethnicity of Israel. The Abrahamic covenant, mightily reinforced with Jacob, must be recognized as the great foundation of the Jewish nation where land, Torah, and Messiah are the vital points of the covenant. Circumcision is merely the ritualistic hallmark instituted as the sign of the covenant with God. As a ritual, the removal of the *foreskin* is a committal to the task of the Abrahamic covenant. But it is not as important as the choice of a woman's *womb* to bring the Mashiach to the planet, to implement the redemptive "God with us." The prophets spoke of this quite clearly. This will be discussed in detail later.

Abraham transplanted himself from Ur of the Chaldees to the Promised Land. Jacob, the great patriarch, solidly laid down commitment to the Abrahamic covenant, the magnification of the role of Ha-Mashiach, and the prophetic primacy of the royal line of Judah. Moses credits Jacob with the enunciation that Judah is chosen as the royal line to beget King David and Messiah ben David. Mashiach is thus the most dominant and powerful factor in Judaism. Mashiach would provide redemption from disobedience and death, and bring back perfection and immortality to the human race. Mashiach would wipe the world clean and set up the new heaven and new earth, where He is an eternal King. This ideation in the Tanak is crystal clear.

Jacob's contribution to Messianic Judaism is grossly underestimated, and undervalued. Jacob's dream at Bethel and his struggle at the brook Jabbok were enactments of interaction with the Mashiach. Subsequently Moses carefully documented his understanding of Mashiach. The Passover was full of the messianic meaning of deliverance. At Mt. Sinai, the law was given, and messianic deliverance from sin—the breakage of that law—was enshrined in the symbolic sacrifice of the animal without blemish. This was the enactment of the *daily* expiation for sin and the *yearly* Day of Atonement, *for God knew well that we all break the law.* He remembers that we are dust (Ps. 103:14). The slaying of Abel by Cain highlighted the command for the sacrifice of messianic blood. Cain's substitute was not accepted. The sacrifice of Isaac by Abraham on Mt. Moriah was the great enactment of messianic atonement. We owe the recording of all this to Moses.

Messianic theology in the Pentateuch is full of symbols and typology stemming from redemptive elements. The lamb without blemish initiated in Eden was a symbol of the messianic atonement for sin. The earthly temple was a type of the heavenly temple. The blood of the Passover lamb, splashed on the lintels and doorposts brought messianic deliverance from death. The 'daily' sin offering in the Temple brought forgiveness and atonement. The sacrificial blood splashed on the Ark of the Covenant and the Mercy Seat in the Holy of Holies by the high priest on the Day of Atonement was a symbolic messianic atonement for all Israel. Many hierarchical persons in Israel were messianic types by anointing with oil: kings, prophets, judges, warriors, and others. King David saw himself as a type of the Messiah and so did Moses. David understood the messianic penetration of humanity by divinity as the great condescension and debased himself in the portrayal of the naked dance. Many scholars see the nation of Israel as the 'servant' in Isaiah. The Abrahamic Covenant of which circumcision was a mere sign was Israel's task for the blessedness of all nations.

The writer of the apochryphal Jewish document 1 Enoch took this typology very seriously. He borrowed heavily from the Pentateuch, Isaiah, and Daniel. In the Similitudes he fashioned a very reasonably constructed titular symbolic nomenclature:

1. The Righteous One
2. The Anointed One
3. The Chosen One
4. The Son of Man

Professor J. C. Vanderkam has made an excellent study of this (see *The Messiah* pp. 169-191). In the framework of creation and redemption the writers of the Tanak treated these titles in both typologic and messianic manner. All four titles have been applied to the Messiah as an 'individual.' This very strongly culminated in the "the root" and "the branch" of Messiah ben David.

J. J. M. Roberts (see *The Messiah* pp. 39-51, in his essay *The Old Testament Contributions to Messianic Expectation*) has done an excellent study compiling numerous Tanakian passages he analyzed for messianic meaning. He has classified these as "Ex Eventu Prophecies," "Enthronement Texts," "Restoration and Dynastic Texts," "Jeremiah, Ezekiel, and Related Texts," and "Postexilic Texts." In contrast, by his criteria, he rejects several passages which the Rabbinic sages down through the ages have long considered highly messianic. He errs in not seeing an atoning Messiah behind the typology. Presumably he discounts the Eden story which he does not even mention. He strongly supports the messianic intent of the following: Isa. 1:21-26, 10:27, 11:1-16, 14:25, 32:1-8; Zech. 9:1-10; Amos 9:11-12; Jer. 23:5-8, 30:8-9, 33:14-26; Ezek. 17:22-24, 34:23-24, 37:15-28; Mic. 5:1-5; Hos. 3:5.

After the destruction of the second temple, Rabbinic Judaism chose to walk away from redemptive Judaism and Mashiach was abandoned as sole Redeemer, the restorer of perfection and immortality. Instead, a focus on law-keeping and benevolence as being salvific was substituted. There is no doubt that Torah is the very texture of God's will,[10] but Torah was disobeyed in Eden, and the damage caused by this disobedience must be healed. The Ha-Mashiach is the instrument to do this. Instead, Mashiach became the hope for terrestrial politiconational independence and freedom, on a local monarchical basis, a desire that pales in comparison with the eternal messianic kingdom, which follows the Judgment and the Resurrection.

The political and national history of the Children of Israel found its zenith in the great reign of King David. National and political considerations became Israel's priority and great preoccupation. National status is important for the propagation of messianic redemption, but national status is not the end game. Solomon's reign was a disaster. It was downhill all the way until AD 1948. The national history was punctuated by various "political" messiahs, whose attempts to bring Israel out of national limbo could be considered merely skirmishes and not messianic triumphs. Bar Kochba and Sabbatai Zevi are examples. Yeshua of Nazareth was rejected because he was not concerned with national politics and because he identified himself as the Son of Man of Daniel 7. Israel went through devastation after devastation with imposed diasporas and great loss of life. No other people have been treated as badly as have the Jews. The Tanak outlines their history from Moses to Malachi. Scholem states it very clearly:

> In this context the Bible [Tanak] is not understood as the historical record ... Here I am thinking of the Bible [Tanak] as a canon of authoritative religious statements ... and to the whole of which religious authority was ascribed by Judaism in the course of its historical crystallization.[11]

The Tanak identifies idolatry and loss of focus on the Abrahamic covenant as the causes of Israel's devastations. The two great temples, which represented the essence of Israel's redemptive Judaism, were allowed by God to be destroyed because the Israelites had desecrated them. Read again Malachi's indictment and condemnation of Israel. The pagan oppressors had assisted in this desecration. God could not stomach the corrupt temple's illicit sacrifices anymore. The great dynasty of prophets and reformers of this long, miserable, and tragic history from David to Malachi had only one dominant theme. That theme was the messianic deliverance, which was available to them if only they could return to redemptive Judaism.

But Mashiach was not understood, and *the pretence that Israel could achieve perfect law-keeping became their religion.* Josephus called it "Inviolable piety":

> We've [the Jews] introduced the rest of the world to a very large number of beautiful ideas. What greater beauty than inviolable piety? What higher justice than obedience to the Laws?[12]

What inviolable humbug! Humanity breaks God's laws every day by sins of commission and omission. Simon Sebag Montefiore quotes Rabbi Yohanan ben Zakkai in the Talmud: "We have another atonement. It is acts of loving kindness." This "another atonement" is a substitution of the redemptive Judaism established by Moses at Sinai. Simon Montefiore himself goes on to say,

No one realized it at this time, but this was the beginning
of modern Judaism – without the Temple."[13]

Humbug Indeed! Can Sinai be set aside? Mashiach became only
a hoped for politiconational salvation. Abraham's covenant with
God and the messianic mission for the restoration of Gan Edenic
perfection and immortality were lost.

The framework in which we see God's exertion to save His people
Israel, and through them all humanity, by messianic intervention
must not be lost. Thank God the Day of Atonement is still observed.
There is no other atonement.

Elohim's Mashiach functionality was the remedial prescription
for the restoration of perfection and immortality. The Ruach
Hakodesh provided *devekut* and repentance. Forgiveness, atonement,
and mediation were provided by the Ha-Mashiach. These were the
functionalities of Elohim and account for the plurality of His name.
Blessed be He. "Hear O Israel, the Lord our God is one Lord" (Deut.
6:4). Together this work of redemption would accomplish restoration
of perfection and immortality. Gershom Scholem detailed this
denouement of God's plan as the classical, restorative, and Utopian
factors of acute Messianism.[14]

This book is designed to define and describe the great messianic
miracle in the Tanak. *Mashiach will be traced from Creation to re-
Creation.* Messianic deliverance is the dominant theme expressed
throughout the pages of the Tanak. As pointed out already, the Talmud
states, *"Every prophet only prophesied for the days of the Messiah"*
(Ber. 34b).[15] Every Jew should repeat this statement every day.

The Ha-Mashiach has been and is the great longing in the heart
of every Jew. Therefore, it is incumbent on every Jew to diligently
search the Tanak for the qualifications, recognition, and work of the
Ha-Mashiach.

Moses Maimonides (Rambam) attempted to do this task and
set a standard, or blueprint, for the Messiah and when He should
appear.[16] In modern times Joseph Klausner has performed a most
arduous and meticulous task in sifting the evidence for and against
a certain specific messiah.[17] But the giant in modern times who has

laid down the rules within the framework of the panoramic picture of the Creation and the history of the world is Gershom Scholem. He has defined this as acute Messianism.[18] His work is encased within a strictly Jewish milieu. He does pay a lot of attention to Sabbatai Zevi as a contender. He severely criticizes Kabbalism and Hasidism for the "neutralization of Messianism." They do not believe in the catastrophic apocalyptic of the Tanak, which ushers in the messianic atonement, judgment, and resurrection in the Messianic Age.

The anxiety that seizes us when worrying about identifying the Mashiach will not distress us when we correctly identify Him in the Tanak. The Ruach Hakodesh will guide us. The important outcome of our research should and must be the congruency of the Mashiach we build with the blueprint in the Tanak. We cannot use any other source as the foundation for this research, as the Tanak is Israel's historical sacred canon and supreme guide. The Talmud may be useful in understanding the opinions of the rabbinic sages in their conversations with each other, but they cannot trump the views in the Tanak beamed from Sinai.

Gershom Scholem is the modern-standard bearer of Messianism in Israel. He looked to the Tanak and discovered that the Mashiach was central not only to the Tanak but also to Israel's future as a people. He magnified the arrival of Mashiach. He clearly became excited by the eschatology and apocalyptic of the Tanak. He decried the corruption of Israel by false ideas of Mashiach and false messiahs. I will discuss his writings at length in this book.

Desmond Ford is the most outstanding non-Jewish writer, to my knowledge, who clearly describes the tanakian Ha-Mashiach. In his writing he has outlined clear and concise definitions:

- Eschatology = the doctrine of the "Last Things"
- Apocalyptic = the sudden catastrophic intervention of God in the affairs of earth to right all wrongs and terminate history
- Mashiach = part and parcel, the very substance of God Himself

Ford relates tanakian eschatology and apocalyptic to Ha-Mashiach very succinctly and dramatically.[19]

Gershom Scholem predates agreement with these definitions.[20] He sees the Messiah as a catastrophic intervention in civilization resulting in the collapse and total destruction of history.

This book will trace messianic definition and the apocalyptic of the Tanak and will focus on the redemptive Judaism of Moses the patriarch. The redemptive work of Ha-Mashiach is implicit in the writings of Moses. I will base the discussion on the evidence in the Tanak, and I will use the Talmud and other noncanonical writings where I see congruence with the Tanak.

The Jewish Study Bible: Tanakh Translation is the mainstay of my study. I occasionally quote the commentators in this translation. This will reassure my Jewish readership. I also use other translations of the Tanak. I love the King James Version for its literary brilliance. I treat the Tanak as the Jewish canon. It will become apparent that my admiration for Gershom Scholem is extreme because he regards the Tanak as the conversation of God with the Hebrews and uses the Talmud for reference only. His ideas of Messianism are definitely tanakian.

The terms "Mashiach," "Ha-Mashiach," and "Messiah" are used in my book variously and synonymously. All three names are rich with meaning. "Holy Spirit" and "Ruach Hakodesh" are also used synonymously.

The dates quoted in the contents are only approximate. There are scholarly disputes about all of them.

I dogmatically assert that the Tanak is the ancient and closed Jewish canon. I also assert that multiple authors, revisions, editings, and interpolations known to me in no way diminish the message of the dominant concepts of Creation and Redemption.

This book is written primarily for the Jewish people, but its application is intended for all humanity. I rejoice in the magnificence of primitive redemptive Judaism, God's unit concept embracing Creation, Redemption, and Glorification.

CHAPTER 1

Modern Jewish Scholarly
Attitudes toward Judaism

It is characteristic of the Jewish scholarly world of the last two hundred years to present Judaism as a philosophic, dynamic, and evolving religion. Its modern wide scope, variety, and the plethora of the various religious subsets are freely admitted and, in fact, lauded. *The Cambridge Guide to Jewish History, Religion, and Culture*, published in 2010, is perhaps representative of the thinking of the majority of modern Jewish scholars:

> Over the past two and a half centuries, many individuals born to Jewish parents ... *found innovative ways to reshape their religious beliefs and practices* in response to the modern world creating a range of Jewish religious movements.[21]

This claim is expressive of the resilience and preservation of the Jews in their persecuted and murderous diaspora, which I heartily endorse as having taken place. This survival is presented as a monument to the Jewish people. But I am disturbed by this indefinite status.

I have read 'exhaustively' in the writings of modern scholars (e.g., Theodor Herzl, Gershom Scholem, Martin Buber, Franz Rosenzweig, Joseph Klausner, Abraham Cohen, S. Y. Agnon, Walter Benjamin, Claude Montefiore, Simon Sebag Montefiore, Jacob Neusner, and Solomon Schechter, who are Jewish). Most of these scholars shone in the radiant exuberance of German-Jewish religious and literary revival. There is no doubt that the Jews in Germany in the nineteenth and first half of the twentieth centuries produced many German-Jewish scholars who brought a fresh radiance into Germany. These scholars also sought to understand, interpret, and reshape Judaism into a modern setting. Modern Zionism rose out of this intensely rich milieu. Max Weber and James Drummond were non-Jewish scholars who also enriched this era.

My own intense interest in Judaism goes back to my youth, which was saturated with Seventh-day Adventism, which evolved from the Protestant religious upheaval of the nineteenth century. The study of Judaism and its dominant aspect of Messianism has further fully occupied my retirement from active surgery in 2005. The discovery that I have some Jewish genes in my blood has increased my motivation. My great regret is that I am not schooled in the Hebrew language. Nonetheless, the study and definition of the "ancient" or "primitive" redemptive Judaism of Moses and the prophets is my priority. I strongly agree with Gershom Scholem, who stated

> Christianity as a historical phenomenon bears virtually no resemblance to original Christianity as a religious phenomenon … **The Judaism of today, too, is not the Judaism of Moses.**[22]

Kenneth Seeskin is very discerning in his excellent chapter titled *Jewish Philosophy* in *The Cambridge Guide*, where he differentiates between the "God of the Philosophers" (Rabbinic Judaism) and ha-Levi's "God of Abraham, Isaac, and Jacob" (primitive redemptive Judaism). Judah ha-Levi (ca. AD 1075–1141) greatly resented and railed against refashioning Judaism without the temple. Seeskin's recognition of the change to a "more modern philosophic Judaism" as a debate that is "still with us" presents a dichotomy between Moses's Judaism and what is being embraced today by the large majority of Conservative and Reform Jewish camps.

The Hebrew Bible, the Tanak, is acknowledged by the majority of Jewish scholars as the revelatory foundation, and at least the "starter document" of Judaism. *The Cambridge Guide* further states,

> Finally, no one can attempt to understand the Jewish experience without considering *the centrality of the written word* and its interpretation in all of Jewish religious

life, history and culture. Traditionally Jews believed that each of the books that make up the Hebrew Bible reflected **God's revelation** in some way, and they looked to this *"Written Torah"* for guidance in every aspect of human life.[23]

Emmanuel Levinas, of Lithuanian Jewish ancestry, who is looked upon as a great twentieth-century French philosopher, is quoted by the editors of *The Cambridge Guide*:

> Consecration to God: his epiphany, beyond all theology, and any visible image, however complete, is repeated in the daily **Sinai** of sitting before **an astonishing book,** ever again in progress because of its very completeness.[24]

And again, Marc Zvi Brettler, one of the contributors to *The Cambridge Guide* makes a strong stand that a key feature of Judaism is that the Hebrew Bible constitutes *revealed scripture.*[25].

This is a definite, albeit in some few cases grudging, acknowledgment that the Tanak is a unique document containing ideas in the mind of God. Although it is not defined as God's thoughts expressed through the inspiration of human intermediaries, I believe this is implicit in the words emphasized in the above quotes. I believe the word "inspiration" has often been deliberately avoided by some Jewish scholars. There is no doubt that *the Tanak is a terrestrial document,* written over a period of one thousand years, edited and reedited, that includes alleged interpolations. It has some "flaws" as a human product, and this the authors of the document quoted above have described laboriously, emphatically, and quite clearly.[26]

In his book *Ancient Judaism,* Max Weber shows in detail the changes that occurred to the Pentateuch and the Prophets during the Israelite confederate, kingly, exilic, and post-exilic periods. This was particularly apparent with the Pentateuchal books of Leviticus and Deuteronomy, and also noted with the authorship of Isaiah and Daniel. My perception is that not all Weber's conclusions are correct. Irving M. Zeitlin, in his book *Ancient Judaism: Biblical Criticism from Max Weber to the Present*, brings some clarity to the subject. However, I strongly assert that despite these edits, revisions, interpolations, and "flaws," *the Tanak remains the authentic conversation between God and the Hebrew people* and constitutes the true status of the existence of humanity on the planet. Martin Buber saw the Tanak as a document of conversation with God, which was made very personal in his "I and Thou" terminology. He collaborated with Franz Rosenzweig in this effort to bring a clearer Jewish understanding to their translation of the Tanak into German. (See *Martin Buber's Biblical Translation* by Benjamin Ivry in *The Jewish Daily Forward*, October 16, 2012.) Buber stated clearly, "Israel understood – or rather, lived – life as being-spoken-to and answering, speaking to and receiving answers." (See *Schriften III* p. 742, quoted by Gershom Scholem in *On Jews and Judaism in Crisis*, pp. 154–156). Thomas Cahill, in his book *The Gifts of the Jews*, speaks eloquently to the fact that the Jews came up with the wondrousness of the Tanak as a spiritual document in their conversation with God.

The events since Creation trace and define the Almighty's plans conceived in eternity about the destiny of humanity. These plans were well understood and expressed by Moses the patriarch. *There is no contradiction or flaw in the conceptual expression of God's plan.* The devout Jew believes implicitly in Elohim as Creator and Redeemer. Martin Buber saw humanity hemmed between Creation and Redemption and God's involvement as one complete action of the Almighty. (See Martin Buber's *Prophetic Faith*, pp. 349–461.) God has miraculously guarded His conversation with us so that His plan of Redemption is well preserved and shines through. I see it as perfect in Moses's expression of it. Redemption can be seen clearly in the structure and function of the temple's Most Holy Place.

If Sinai is invoked, as is so well expressed by Levinas, it behooves us to understand what was expressed at Sinai, in order that we may state it clearly, protect its integrity, and follow its guidance. *There can be no denial of Sinai.* The essence of Sinai is manifest as Shechinah, law, mercy, and blood, reposited in the Most Holy Place of the tabernacle sanctuary. These elements were combined as the energy of the Almighty to reclaim His Creation that was spoiled in Gan Eden. The Eden account powerfully describes the commencement of life on the planet. The vicissitudes of *Homo sapiens*, regressive and progressive, must be viewed as a reality, even if the Eden story is to be regarded as a metaphor. Without acceptance of God as Creator and Redeemer, Rabbinic Judaism, no matter how erudite, is empty and meaningless. Religion that does not accept God as Creator and Redeemer makes no sense. Messianic atonement is implicit in Redemption. Such a belief must therefore exclude all do-it-yourself (DIY) methods of salvation.

We know the Almighty as Elohim, who spends His energy as Ruach Hakodesh and Ha-Mashiach, which are His functionalities, working to realize His plans of Creation and Redemption. We know nothing about Him except as revealed by these functionalities. This realization is central to Judaism. The conversation of God with the Hebrews that took place in the Tanak eminently shows these plans, and *we must not annul these foundations of Judaism.* We must not substitute a philosophy in its place. An erudite philosophy can evaluate and define Judaism in modern times and terms, but this *cannot dismiss God's plan* to deal with disobedience, the sin problem, and mortality.[27]

Jewish philosophy has sometimes been defined in terms of the influence of the ideas of the Greek philosophers (Aristotle et al.). The writings of great thinkers such as Philo, Spinoza, Kant, Moses Mendelssohn, Abraham Cohen, Hermann Cohen, Franz Rosenzweig, Joseph Klausner, Emmanuel Levinas, and Gershom Scholem have brought some modern clarity to the theology and ethics in Judaism. But they cannot displace the essential work of Ruach Hakodesh and Ha-Mashiach, who seek to restore perfection and immortality to humanity in God's plan. Elohim's energy as Ruach Hakodesh and Ha-Mashiach in the Tanak will effect our salvation. Without this restoration, humanity faces a dismal future. Moses saw this clearly, and his definition of God's plan at Sinai cannot be set aside.

In his essay on Jewish philosophy, Kenneth Seeskin does come to a superbly wondrous point. In summarizing Franz Rosenzweig's ideas, Seeskin powerfully states,

> **With the experience of being loved** [by God] **comes the sense of having sinned ...** With a confession of sin comes repentance and forgiveness ... "Loved only by

God, man is closed off to all the world and closes himself off." Like God, a person must reach out to something beyond the self and become a being in relation. This can only be accomplished by accepting another fundamental commandment, "Love thy neighbor."[28]

In summarizing Kant and Hermann Cohen, Kenneth Seeskin says,

... the moral law, which commands us to treat all of humanity as an end in itself, is primary ... Simply put, God is the being who makes it possible for us to fulfill the moral law *and who is ready to forgive us when we fall.*[29]

These ideas brilliantly emphasize God's intent at Sinai, in the Most Holy Place of the temple. Repentance, forgiveness, atonement, and intercession are all accomplished for Israel in the Most Holy Place *when we fall.* Therefore, *we must trust Sinai.* The provision of forgiveness when we fall wondrously resides in the Most Holy Place, where *the sprinkled blood in the presence of the Shechinah activates the triumph of mercy over justice.*

Primitive redemptive Judaism continues to beam from Sinai to save the world. We cannot trust in philosophy and reason alone. The Nazi Holocaust tells us that. (See *FDR and the Jews*, by Richard Breitman and Allan J. Lichtman. Also see *Nazi Germany and the Jews 1933–1945*, by Saul Friedlander). The so-called "moral high ground" and "logic" of the Allies was damnable. The brilliant but precarious situation of the Jews in Germany before World War II illustrates that their enrichment of German cultural life was not endorsed by the German people. Jewish brilliance did not save them. The continuing oppression of people confirms that philosopy, logic, intended compassion, and reason are not protective.[30]

Because the second temple was lost in AD 70, we cannot set aside what it stood for in God's plans. The Hebrews replaced the tabernacle temple constructed in the wilderness with Solomon's temple. When that was destroyed, it was rebuilt and renovated as the second temple. And because this was also destroyed, we cannot change Judaism. If we do, *it is a colossal and outright capitulation to the wicked powers* that have repeatedly destroyed our temples, and we also capitulate to our *unsaved idolatrous condition*, which led God to allow the destruction. The Jews are rightly quick to identify anti-Semitism. This is a homegrown anti-Semitism evolved in Jewish minds that seeks to annul Sinai.

The temple on earth, which is an ideational duplication of the heavenly temple, is the key to the plan of God. The rituals that were expressions of the principles that defined *repentance, forgiveness, expiation by the blood, and redemption* cannot and must not be set aside. Shechinah, law, mercy and messianic blood constitute the essence of the Judaism of Sinai, present when God elected to formally dwell with Israel. These facts are basic to Judaism and apply to all humanity. We *cannot* and *must not invoke Sinai* without proclaiming and protecting these verities. The third temple must be built, and Shechinah, law, mercy, and blood must be restored as *the vital essence in Judaism*. This is not a call to restore animal sacrifices. There is a mighty reason for this, and it is the subject of my mind's final publication for the future. Today, the symbolic ideation of animal sacrifice alone suffices. The necessity for preserving its symbolism is understood. The Passover and Day of Atonement as currently magnified are the great monuments to the essence of this Sinai Judaism and are sufficient to emphasize repentance, forgiveness, expiation by the blood, and redemption, *without slaughtering more animals*. Animal sacrifice was the type. Messianic redemption is the antitype. The Tanak and the Talmud make it clear that Ruach Hakodesh and Ha-Mashiach are the functionalities of Elohim to reclaim humanity to His bosom. The catastrophic apocalyptic of the Tanak is *inexorable* and cannot be avoided.

Many talmudic utterances support this ideation. Gershom Scholem proclaims,

> I must preface a word intended to correct a widespread
> misconception. I am referring to a distortion of historical
> circumstances ... which lies in denying the continuation
> of the apocalyptic tradition in rabbinic Judaism.[31]

Scholem accuses Martin Buber and Franz Rosenzweig of denying the apocalyptic of the Tanak. (See *On Jews and Judaism in Crisis*, by Gershom Scholem pp.159–171.) There is a great effort made by many Jewish scholars to seek modernity in their adjustment to and annulment of the basic primitive Judaism of Mt. Sinai, which, I allege, has been deserted by Rabbinic Judaism. The *Cambridge Guide,* quoted above, eminently promotes this effort to bring in modernity:

> Yet, a religion based upon static texts [the Tanak] however holy, cannot easily adjust to the ever-varying conditions of human existence … In every era, expositors of the divine message [rabbinic Judaism and "Oral Torah"] have discovered new meanings in the Torah and demonstrated their relevance to an ever-evolving Jewish community …
> **As editors, we resist the temptation to suggest that such a rich and constantly evolving history, religion and culture can be explained by ONE COMMON UNIFYING THREAD.**[32]

I assert that these scholars are furthering the cause of assimilation by promoting such an orientation. Semiṭism in Judaism must include Sinai. Denial of Sinai in favor of a replacement is a drastic anti-Semitism, more lethal than any overt persecution. Of the twenty distinguished contributors to the *Cambridge Guide*, all are still in the diaspora—a voluntary diaspora of their own—except Harvey E. Goldberg, who is domiciled in Israel. The others all hold prestigious professorial chairs in North American universities. Now, there is nothing innately wrong with continuing in a voluntary diaspora. I hold the opinion that the continuing voluntary diaspora of the Jews in the West in modern times is a boon to the security of Israel as a nation and country. We celebrate Esther every year at Purim.

These professors are influential in the USA and contribute to maintain support for Israel. I am a continuing Zionist, and Israel must be solidly established and protected as a strong nation. Zionism has had its Jewish detractors in the past.[33] Anti-Semitic Semites currently wield influence. Miko Peled (author of *The General's Son*, published by Just Worlds Books) and other Jewish anti-Zionists seek to destroy modern Israel in our time. Modifying and setting aside

Sinai is the *most subtle and devastating form of anti-Semitism and assimilation.* As long as the USA is a strong ally of Israel, Israel is less vulnerable to her avowed foes waiting to annihilate her. But I see the almost seven million Jews in the USA, the majority of who are of the Reform and Conservative factions, well on the way to assimilation. I am not alone in this opinion. Thomas Friedman and others seem to agree.[34]

Reform Judaism in the USA (see Emet Ve-emuneh: Statement of Principles) has gone further in setting aside Sinai:

> One of the first things that the early Reform rabbis did was *cut out any reference to the theological belief in the Messiah ... Resurrection ... [and] rebuilding of the Temple in Jerusalem.* In the 19th century, these early Reform Rabbis found these beliefs in the supernatural to be too fantastic to be true.[35]

We need to relearn lessons already noted in the past. Jewish anti-Zionism posed as part of the Jewish modification of Sinai. Walter Laquere took umbrage to the freelancing anti-Zionist liberal trend of Jewry: "If the American and British liberals [Jews] were concerned with the political implications of Zionism, the Germans [Jews] took it more seriously, trying to analyse and refute its philosophical roots. Felix Goldman, an anti-Zionist Rabbi, regarded Jewish nationalism as a child of the general chauvinist movement which had poisoned recent history but which would be swept away in the new era of universalism." (See Walter Laquere's *Thursday's Child Has Far To Go*; also see *World Security Network* for Dieter Farwick's interview of Walter Laquere, February 20.) Liberal German Jews carried on an active persecution of their Zionist fellow Jews, who retaliated with "If German, French, and British Jews nevertheless chose to stay in their respective countries, it was because they longed for the fleshpots [of Egypt] rather than the Messiah." (See *History of Zionism* by Walter Laquere pp. 396, 397.) Back in 1887, an American Jewish Rabbi convention in Pittsburg declared, "We consider ourselves no longer a nation but a religious community. And therefore expect neither a return to Palestine ... nor the restoration of ... the Jewish State." (See

Ibid p. 402). In 1920 the Central Conference of American Rabbis declared, "… Israel was not a nation, Palestine not the homeland of the Jewish people – the whole world was its home" (See *Ibid* p. 403).

In a lecture delivered at the plenary session of the World Jewish Congress in Brussels, August 2, 1966, Gersholm Scholem addressed this "revisionist" attitude of modern Jewish scholars. The lecture was titled "Germans and Jews" and sought to explain what went wrong with the German-Jewish relationship that led to the Nazi Holocaust of the Jews. He blamed the German-Jewish liberals for their "decisively progressive Jewish self-dissolution." This self-abnegation of the Jews was viewed by Germans as evidence of their lack of moral substance. Scholem saw it clearly:

> We have clear documentation to show that the disdain in which so many Germans held the Jews *fed on the ease with which the upper cultural stratum of the Jews disavowed its own tradition. For what could a heritage be worth if the elite of its chosen heirs were in such a rush to disavow it?* (See *On Jews and Judaism in Crisis* by Gershom Scholem, Essay titled "Germans and Jews" pp.71–92, emphasis added).

What has happened and is continuing to happen in North America is a virtual duplication of this disavowal, a total departure from Sinai, and a loss of tanakian Messianism.

As a rebuke to all these above revisionist statements by the *Cambridge Guide,* the Emet *Ve-emuneh: Statement of Principle of Conservative Judaism* of the Reform Constituency of American Jews, and the errant anti-Zionist rabbis referred to above, *what can be more supernatural and fantastic to be true than the existence of God and His Creatorship?* Could it be that Reform Judaism has ceased to believe in God and His Creatorship because these "beliefs in the supernatural [are too] fantastic to be true"? It is preposterous that Mt. Sinai can be set aside by a plethora of philosophical rabbinic and neoscholarly reinterpretations. If the cruel enforced diaspora was responsible for this, aliya must now reverse this trend and return to the despised "*one common unifying thread"* of primitive redemptive

Judaism, bequeathed to us at Sinai. God has not changed His mind since Sinai. God does not change His plans conceived in eternity to suit the vicissitudes of human whims and fancies, and modern scholarly revisionist mind gymnastics. Shechinah, law, mercy, and messianic blood *are still Elohim's eternal and powerful plan for reclaiming humanity.* The Jews are on the earth for a purpose that was foreordained from eternity. This purpose is Sinaiatic revelation to the world of messianic redemption. Again, I am not alone in this idea.

Gershom Scholem, in his usual cool, logical, and tanakian orientation, identifies the major theological basis in Judaism. In his essay "Reflections on Jewish Theology," he states,

> There are four questions which today are central to me in discussions of this kind ["position and possibilities of Jewish theology"]:
>
> (1) The question of the *authoritative sources* on which such a theology can draw: in other words, the question of Revelation and Tradition as religious categories which can constitute the foundation of a Jewish theology.
> (2) The question of the *central values*, or of the ideas underlying such values, that can be established from such sources and from the conviction that God exists.
> (3) The question of the *position of Judaism* and its tradition in a secularized and technologized world.
> (4) Finally, the question of *the meaning*, in this context, for our life and thought as Jews, of the decisive and subverting events of Jewish history in our time, that is, of the catastrophe of the Holocaust and everything connected with it, as well as the establishment of a Jewish commonwealth in Israel, the Judenstaat.[36]

Scholem discusses these four questions extensively within the consideration of the following: Orthodoxy, the divine origin and character of the Torah, moral theology in a secularized world, the sources of the Bible (Tanak) as canon, rabbinic tradition, Kabbalah, and the synagogue. He discusses the so-called paradoxes, contradictions, and speculations existing in the theology of modern Judaism. He deals with the difficulty of multiplicity of interpretations and the danger of the freedom that comes with the liberty of multiple interpretations. But when he discusses revelation as Sinaiatic revelation and revelation of the Torah as a whole as *mattan Torah* (giving of the Torah) and the quality of revelation as *Torah min hashamayim* (*"the Torah from Heaven"*) he invests the Sinai experience with an authority that cannot be set aside.

In summing up messianic theology, Scholem describes a trilogy:

> It seems to me particularly notable that *the Messianic idea*, the third element in that trilogy of Creation, Revelation, and Redemption, exercises unbroken and vital power even today. *Creation, so closely linked to the conviction of the existence of God, has to an extraordinary extent receded or vanished from contemporary [Jewish] consciousness.* Outside the fundamentalist minority, Revelation persists only in enlightened or mystical reinterpretations which, no matter how legitimate they may be, no longer possess the original vehemence which promoted its enormous influence in the history of religion. *Yet the Messianic Idea has maintained precisely this vehemence … It has become the centre of great visions in the present age.*[37]

The gifted German Jewish thinker Franz Rosenzweig describes the Jews as a people who live with God; who have an existence with the Father, an existence stemming from Eden and the commissioned Abrahamic covenant. This cohabitation was implemented cosmically at Sinai when the Shechinah came to dwell in the Most Holy Place of the tabernacle temple. But it must be admitted that there has been an estrangement in that "existence with the Father," and that Ruach Hakodesh and Ha-Mashiach are "the Father's" functionalities to bring us back to the true "existence with the Father," the original devekut.[38]

Rosenzweig's own hopes for the future were concentrated in his ideation of Creation, Revelation, and Redemption. His theology of Judaism was dominated by *redemption by personal piety* obtained from law-keeping. Rosenzweig has his own code of theological language and is sometimes difficult to follow. However, in the summation of his book *Star of Redemption* he states quite clearly,

> But the Redemption would then have to occur in the relationship of the "remnant" [the pious Jews] to the "Law." How is this relationship conceived? What does fulfilling the Law mean to the Jew? How does he conceive it? Why does he fulfill it? ... Every one of his deeds, every fulfilling of a commandment, achieves a portion of this union. To confess God's unity – the Jew calls it: to unify God. For this unity is as it becomes, it is Becoming Unity. And this Becoming is enjoined on the soul and hands of man. Jewish man and Jewish law – nothing less than the process of redemption, embracing God, world, and man, transpires between the two. The fulfilling of the commandment is inaugurated and stamped as an act which brings redemption nearer, with a formula in which the individual elements, such as they are absorbed into this last One, once more resound individually: the "holy God" who has given the law, the "Shekhina" which he expropriated from himself to the remnant of Israel, the "awe" with which this remnant turned itself into the dwelling place of God, the "love" with which he thereupon proceeded to fulfill the law, he the individual, the "I" which fulfills the law, yet he "in the name of Israel" to which the law was given and which was created through the law. The most constricted has all expanded into the whole, the All, nay better: has redeemed itself for the unification of the One. The descent into the Innermost has disclosed itself as an ascent to the Highest. The merely Jewish feeling has been transfigured into world redemptive truth. In the innermost constriction of the Jewish heart there shines the Star of Redemption.[39]

This difficult lengthy definition of his summary of the mechanism of redemption looks masterful but makes no mention of the Mashiach. In my mind the striving in law-keeping has more meaning in the realm of sanctification and devekut. But *terrestrial human Law-keeping is never perfect,* although striving after it is extremely laudable and is incumbent on every Jew. But God does not accept as perfect anything less than 100 percent, which none of us attain. Isaiah labeled our best piety as "filthy rags." Therefore we must return to the Most Holy Place to plead for mercy and atonement by the blood to be sprinkled on the law and the mercy seat in the presence of the Shechinah. The Shechinah is there to assure and ensure us of mercy and pardon as the messianic blood is splashed on us. Rosenzweig has forgotten in this summary to mention the mercy seat and the messianic blood, which were also present in the Most Holy Place along with the law. He singles out the law and sees humanity saving itself by keeping the law. *This is a great fallacy.* Show me one Jew who has kept the law perfectly! If such exists, he bypasses the Day of Atonement! Humanity cannot redeem itself with imperfect lawkeeping.

The Jews have had four thousand years of existence to try to achieve perfect piety. Sadly, although setting high standards, Israel as a nation has, since Abraham, demonstrated idolatry, secularism, and halakic ritualistic extremism. The young Martin Buber rightly railed against halakah as an instrument of redemption. Scholem noted that Buber had a deep aversion to the law, to halakah in all its forms. Buber saw halakah as hostile to life and redemption. Instead, Buber called Sinai "Innermost Judaism," "Genuine Judaism," "Primordial Judaism." (See Buber's *On Judaism* pp. 77–109). Halakah certainly has its part in lifestyle, but Buber did not see it as redemptive. And who in Israel keeps the law perfectly? Let the Jew without blemish stand up. Isaiah proclaims that all we have to offer is "filthy rags." Our collective true condition is described in Isaiah chapter one. The Abrahamic covenant can find fulfillment only with Mashiach redemption.

Gershom Scholem understood well the import of Rosenzweig in this above definition of redemption. In a discussion of Rosenzweig's book *Star of Redemption*, Scholem states,

Whether or not the attempt to deduce the two possibilities
for theocratic modes of life in Judaism and Christianity
from the dialectics of the concept of redemption could in
fact determine the true place of each one may remain in
dispute, though this is one of the principal points in the
Star, which most unavoidably calls for serious analysis ...
To be sure, by his use of the doctrine of the anticipation of
redemption in Jewish life, a concept as fascinating as it is
problematic, Rosenzweig took a decided and hostile stand
against *the one open door* in the otherwise very neatly
ordered house of Judaism. He opposed the catastrophes
contained in Messianic apocalyptic which might be
considered the point at which even today theocratic and
bourgeois modes of life stand irreconcilably opposed.
The deep-seated tendency to remove the apocalyptic
thorn from the organism of Judaism makes Rosenzweig
the last and certainly one of the most vigorous exponents
of a very old and very powerful movement in Judaism,
which crystallized in a variety of forms ... Apocalyptic
as a doubtless anarchic element, provided some fresh
air in the house of Judaism; it provided a recognition
of the catastrophic potential of all historical order in an
unredeemed world ... For a thinker of Rosenzweig's rank
could never remain oblivious to the truth that redemption
possesses not only a liberating but also a destructive
force – *a truth which only too many Jewish theologians
are loathe to consider and which a whole literature takes
pains to avoid.* Rosenzweig sought at least to neutralize it
in a higher order of truth.[40]

While giving the distinct impression that redemption will be
achieved by law-keeping without messianic intervention, Rosenzweig
did occasionally throughout his book resort to more than a touch of
Messianism and apocalyptic, as in the following statement below. But
it must be admitted that in his title *Star of Redemption*, the redeeming
Star was the law and not the Ha-Mashiach. He stresses Shechinah,
law, and mercy *but ignores the blood*, which the high priest carried

into the Most Holy Place in cosmic silence and splashed on the ark of the covenant, which contained the law and held the mercy seat above it. That *act of sprinkling blood* has tremendous significance and cannot be ignored in Judaism of any stripe. That blood dripped for centuries on the most holy spot in Judaism, the temple mount, where Abraham sacrificed Isaac. Rosenzweig forgot that God's mercy triumphs over His justice because of our inability to keep the law perfectly. Listen to a brief but unmistakable flash of messianic apocalyptic from Rosenzweig:

> Thus the soul must pray for the coming of the kingdom. God once descended and founded His kingdom. The soul prays for the future repetition of this miracle ... The soul cries out: *Oh that YOU would part the heavens and descend.*[41]

What a fantastic admission by Rosenzweig! The Redemption descends from above and is not acquired below by lawkeeping. And again there is another flash! But this statement from Rosenzweig totally credits the Mashiach with salvation, and has more than a tinge, nay, a enormous mountain of the apocalyptic. It also clearly enunciates the great truth that the Mashiach is eternal and not mere man. No one can say that Rosenzweig believed in a Messiah who would be just "a mere human with extraordinary talents":

> Yet no one knows better than he that being dear to God is only a beginning, and that *man remains unredeemed* so long as nothing but this beginning has been realized. Over against Israel, eternally loved by God and faithful and perfect in eternity, *stands he who is eternally to come*, he who waits and wanders, and grows eternally – *Messiah*. Over against the man of earliest beginnings, against Adam the son of man, stands *the man of endings,* the son of David the king. Over against him who was created with the stuff of the earth and the breath of the mouth of God, is *the descendant from the stem [Isa. 11:1] of anointed kings;* over against the patriarchs, *the latest offspring;*

over against the first, who draws about him the mantle
of divine love, *the last, FROM WHOM SALVATION
ISSUES FORTH to the ends of the earth;* over against
the first miracles, *the last,* which – so it is said – *will be
greater than the first.*[42]

Rosenzweig sends mixed signals in his book, but the prominent
doctrine he advanced is redemption by the piety of keeping the law.
The greater part of his book stresses redemption by lawkeeping
and not by Mashiach. Gershom Scholem perceived this and did not
approve of Rosenzweig's antiapocalyptic stance, but we can see
this was not solid as a salvific element. In Rosenzweig's book *Star
of Redemption*, the Messiah of the apocalyptic occasionally breaks
through. Such a statement as the above overwhelms any disbelief in
the apocalyptic messianic redemption.

In my first publication, *The Fair Dinkum Jew: The Survival of
Israel and the Abrahamic Covenant*, I tried to identify the Jew who
understood and accommodated the Abrahamic covenant. I showed
that the covenant also constituted the favored ethnicity and the
divinely endowed legitimacy of the Jewish race as a chosen minority
people. I identified the Tanak as the canon of primitive Judaism. I
defined it as the primitive and original Torah, which was conveyed
in an oral medium from Gan Eden until written down by Moses the
patriarch at Mt. Sinai. I further defined it as the Hebrew people's
conversation with God. In that conversation, which must necessarily
be entered into for our enlightenment and redemption, the preeminent
principle should be sustained by the concepts and precepts He is
presenting, and the reasons why. The context of these concepts and
precepts in the Sinai experience must be strictly obeyed and cannot
be set aside. Sin was dealt with in connection with the shedding of
blood. There is no doubt that this was indeed a type. The rabbinic
sages always insisted that only God can forgive sins. God thus does
so by the shedding of His own messianic blood. That is what enables
mercy to triumph over justice.

In my second publication, *King David's Naked Dance: The
Dreams, Doctrines, and Dilemmas of the Hebrews*, I sought to
define and describe primitive tanakian Judaism. I qualified this as

the primitive redemptive Judaism of the Tanak, which was practiced by Adam, Noah, Abraham, Jacob, Moses, and David. It gelled at Sinai. Moses was given *more than the law* at Sinai. He was given the symbolic messianic sacrificial system of the animal without blemish, in the machinery of the Aaronic priesthood. This sacrificial system had been first instituted outside the gates of Gan Eden. This primitive Judaism was indeed a redemptive religion. I pointed out that modern Judaism has evolved as a multifaceted philosophy since the loss of the second temple in AD 70. The arrival of the Talmud as a "religious conversation among the Jews" (in contrast to the Tanak, which was a conversation with God) has changed Judaism. Dedication to the Talmud in the diaspora by the rabbinic sages and schools, before and since AD 70, has resulted in the formulation of a loose and variegated Rabbinic Judaism. This has hardly any resemblance to the primitive redemptive tanakian Judaism of Sinai.[43] Gershom Scholem is absolutely right: "*The Judaism of today is not the Judaism of Moses.*" Who, indeed, are these people who propagate a Judaism foreign to Sinai? Do they not perceive that they advocate the most subtle and vicious forms of anti-Semitism and assimilation?

The authors of *The Cambridge Guide* are remiss in their attempt to give Judaism a modern whitewash. Modernity cannot replace primitive redemptive Sinaiatic Judaism. In reality, in Israel and the diaspora, modern Judaism is a plethora of religious camps with much enmity and antagonism between the subsets. This divisiveness has the potential to destroy Israel. Sectarian genocide is destroying Islam and the people who practice it. Islam has also developed an arm of extremist jihad that is attacking Israel and the West. The disunity in Jewry is creating havoc in Israel, preventing a concerted and united future religiously, politically, and nationally. It is feared that the mission Abraham undertook from God, where land, Torah, and Messiah were bestowed and embraced, will not be carried out. Israel, it is feared, is one lost war away from another possible annihilation as a nation. To be sure, there is a place for pluralism in nonessentials, as possible in ritual and lifestyle halakah, but when it comes to Creation and Redemption, the plan has been established from eternity. Ruach Hakodesh and Ha-Mashiach are not for changing. Their redemptive power cannot be expunged.

Primitive redemptive Judaism of the Tanak embodies Creation, Redemption, and Glorification. This describes the perfect and immortal creation of humanity, the disobedience to God's law, and the loss of that perfection and immortality. Messianic redemption was prescribed by God to reverse this catastrophe. Elohim sought to accomplish this plan by the functionalities of Himself, in Ruach Hakodesh and Ha-Mashiach functions. The Lord our God is one; blessed be He.

Since monotheism is absolutely essential to Judaism, Ruach Hakodesh and Ha-Mashiach must be viewed as functions of Elohim, His almighty plurality, functioning to cope with humanity and its problems. Yahweh, Ruach Hakodesh, and Ha-Mashiach cannot be viewed as three different Gods, but as manifestations of the outreach powers of Elohim in functional spheres. The "Fatherhood of God" and "the Godhead" are terminological human ways of expressing this functional unity. This is the "Us" Moses utters in the beginning of the book of Genesis.

The Hebrews have accepted the Ruach Hakodesh function of Elohim as within Himself, and God in verity. The Ruach Hakodesh functions in devekut and provides repentance. The Ruach Hakodesh speaks to every human heart. This is a full-time job, humanly speaking. But most rabbinic sages have been reluctant to define, qualify, and endorse the redemptive function of Elohim in the Ha-Mashiach medium, wherein forgiveness, atonement, mediation, and kingship *in the eternal kingdom of Messiah ben David* are provided—also a full-time job! The description of the Ha-Mashiach in the Talmud is predominantly confused, is variant, and lacks unity. This needs correction, and Scholem goes a long way to do that. He does so by emphasizing the inexorable nature of the eschatologic catastrophic apocalyptic of messianic arrival, which makes an end of history as we know it by atonement, judgment, resurrection, and the establishment of the Utopia—the eternal kingdom of Messiah ben David, Isaiah's new heaven and new earth.

Mention must be made of another modern scholarly attempt to treat the Messiah in the Tanak as a nonessential and evolutionary development in Judaism. It may be an unintentional conclusion in the production of the symposium that resulted in the production of the book *"The Messiah." There is no cohesive unity in these essays by both Jewish and non-Jewish scholars. Messiah is not treated as the solution to the sin problem.* Certain authors attempt to whitewash Judaism. I particularly single out R. A. Horsley's essay *'Messianic Figures and Movements in First- Century Palestine.'* which relegates 'messianic' and 'Messiah' as insignificant in this period. He totally relies on Josephus for messianic trends in this period. This is a travesty to the Jewish longing for the Messiah in every generation of Jewish existence, which expressed itself clearly in the Temple rituals, despite Temple corruption. Messianic expectation was strong enough for many to accept Yeshua of Nazareth as the Messiah. Until the Temple was destroyed in AD 70 the 'daily' sin offering and the yearly Day of Atonement and Passover festivals were grand symbolic allusions to the Messiah of Judaism. The latter two continue to be though many Jews are blind to it.

In summary, the attempt of some modern Jewish scholars to give Judaism a new look is out of order. Sinai can be understood better but cannot be changed or updated. Ruach Hakodesh and Ha-Mashiach are still there to effect the Redemption planned from eternity.

Max Weber described the God of confederate Israel as a war god. I take issue with this conclusion, as my view is that God intended proselytism as a mechanism to acquire land. While His messianic redemption is provided, God prefers to save His children. When Weber summarized the great qualities of Yahwe, he concluded that *Yahwe always was and remained a God of salvation and promised redemption.* In *sefer ha berith* (*"Book of the Covenant"*), *Berith* with Abraham, Jacob and Moses constituted that guarantee, the blessedness of all nations. (See *Ancient Judaism* by Max Weber, pp. 118–154.)

To abrogate Sinai is to *deny Creation and set aside Redemption.* It is a subtle and lethal form of anti-Semitism, assimilation, and atheism, *the denial of the existence of God.* It also renders the Jews *of no consequence*, God forbid.

CHAPTER 2

The Eternal Preexistence
of Ha-Mashiach

I believe that before Elohim created a perfect world, He foresaw the occurrence of disobedience and death and the need for *the functions of Ruach Hakodesh and Ha-Mashiach in Redemption,* which functions existed within Himself. These functionalities had effected Creation and now would effect Redemption. I believe this is implicit in the Tanak and the Talmud. The ideas of Creation and Redemption were one unit and had been in God's plan from eternity. Space in the cosmos is limitless, and eternity has no beginning or ending. In this cosmic sense Redemption was not just an afterthought. This belief excites dangerous conclusions: Where is God's omnipotence to prevent disobedience and its ugly results of *human suffering?* Did He indulge in a callous strategy? Is there no pity with the Almighty that we should suffer all this mostly self-inflicted pain? Is it because He wanted a very expensive voluntary worship from us? Expensive indeed, with both human and divine costs. God's inexplicable allowance of the catastrophe of disobedience and death is beyond the edges of our human understanding at present.

The Talmud grapples with this idea but does not resolve it. It is revealed in the rabbinic discussion of God's collaboration with the angels before embarking on Creation. Peter Schafer discusses this subject eruditely in his book *The Jewish Jesus,* in the chapters titled "Angels" (pp. 160–196) and "The Suffering Messiah Ephraim" (pp. 236–263). He has researched rabbinic discussion in writings dated late Tannaim and early Amoraim. The source of the discussion is the Bavli. (See BerR 1:3; 3:8; 8:3, 4, 8; PesR 14:9; Sanh 38b, 98b.) Schafer also draws from the Dead Sea Fragments (4Q541, 4Q274–11Q31, 4Q471B, and 4Q491 in *The Dead Sea Scrolls Study Edition*), researched also by other writers. Ostensibly, in the Bavli account, God consulted with the angels and they advised Him not to proceed with Creation because they foresaw the resultant mayhem of disobedience and death. Some rabbis believed that God punished some of these angels for their "adverse" advice and willfully proceeded anyway with Creation. God is portrayed as stubborn and self-indulgent in this decision.

More importantly, God also emphasized that *His messianic suffering* would occur in the preplanned redemption. This idea that Messiah must suffer in the Redemption is a major consideration in this rabbinic discussion. The Pesiqta Rabbati uses Psalm 22 to outline this suffering. Indeed, messianic suffering is not a Christian invention. It belongs in eternity, and its first terrestrial comprehension is in primitive Judaism. It is a major consideration in Rabbinic Judaism as well. Daniel Boyarin emphasizes this primacy in his book *The Jewish Gospels*. (See chapter 4, pp. 129–156). He states unequivocally: "Gospel Judaism was straightforwardly and completely a Jewish movement." (See also Martin Hengel's book *The Beginnings of Christianity*, p. 85, Jerusalem: Yad Ben-Zvi Press). Psalm 22 and Isaiah 53 were accepted by the sages as the basic tanakian proof of messianic suffering to come. (See my discussion on this subject in my chapter on the talmudic Messiah).

I embrace the concept that a suffering messianic deliverance has been a provision in the mind of God from eternity—a firm principle in the Tanak and strongly asserted in the Talmud. It is expressive of God's deep love for humanity. We know God only as the Great Spirit. But it appears that He has a basic ingrained desire and need to love humanity, anthropomorphically speaking.

Messianic existence before Creation is well established in the Talmud:

> Seven things were created before the world was created: Torah, Repentance, the Garden of Eden, (i.e. Paradise), Gehinnom, the Throne of Glory, the [heavenly] *Temple* and the name of *Messiah*.
> (Pes. 54a, emphasis added).

And again:

> From the beginning of the Creation of the world King
> Messiah was **born**, for he entered the mind (of God) even
> before the world was created.
> (Pesikta Rab.152b, emphasis added)[44]

I interpret the Talmud here as saying that God had these provisions for effecting redemption—Torah, repentance, the temple, and Messiah—in His mind from eternity. The remple embodied the mechanism of redemption.

The "birth of King Messiah" enshrines the doctrine of the penetrance of humanity by messianic divinity as a "Birth," primarily defined by Moses, and prominently elaborated by David, Isaiah, Micah, and Daniel. And every prophet who spoke about Messiah intoned this doctrine. He already "existed in the mind of God" and was God Himself as Creator and Redeemer. Messiah would be born on the planet.

The eternal preexistence of Ruach Hakodesh is assumed in Judaism as God Himself, and manifests as a powerful identity. The rabbinic sages never questioned this belief. This was not considered a binitarian view. The academic question is therefore allowable: Is Ruach Hakodesh a "hypostasis" of God that implicates a binitarian view? The answer is a definite negative, as we embrace Ruach Hakodesh as God Himself. Hypostases of God are not allowed in the strict monotheism of Judaism, although some of the Babylonian sages appear to have subscribed to it.

Many Jewish scholars insist on a purely human Messiah, but some Babylonian sages discussed Messiah as a "Hypostasis of God" who makes an appearance in eternity (as in the discussion of "Son of Man" in Daniel 7). Messiah is described in tanakian writings as God Himself but separate from Ruach Hakodesh. However, there is a major reluctance in Rabbinic Judaism to allow the Ha-Mashiach to be of the same status as Ruach Hakodesh—that is, God Himself.

The Tanak and the Talmud teach that Ruach Hakodesh speaks to every human mind and performs the redemptive work of gifting repentance. Repentance motivates the penitent one to come to the temple. The sin offering in the temple effects forgiveness and atonement.

It must be admitted that in the Aaronic priestly work of the temple instituted by Moses, the sacrificial "Animal Without Blemish" is the symbol of messianic atonement. This idea is firmly established by the shedding of its blood, defined clearly and emphatically by Moses at Sinai (Ex. 24; Lev. 16). Thus the blood of the sacrificial animal without blemish effects atonement and forgiveness in the daily cleansing from sin, which follows on from the work of penitence. As well, there was the mighty ritual of the yearly cleansing on the Day of Atonement. In this ritual, the blood of the animal without blemish was carried into God's presence in the Most Holy Place and splashed on the law and mercy seat, making God's mercy triumph over His justice. The Mashiach blood must therefore be admitted to function for forgiveness and atonement. According to the prophets, Messsiah is born, suffers, and dies to provide this.

The rabbinic sages exulted in God's mercy triumphing over His justice. They called Him Rachmana ("the merciful") and taught that the world is judged by grace (Aboth III. 19). The attribute of grace exceeds that of punishment by five-hundredfold (Ex. 20:5; Joma 69b; Tosifta Sot. IV. I; Pes. 87b; Ber. 7a: A.Z. 3b; Pes 119a p. Kid. 69d). The messianic redemption therefore provided eternal life by God's grace, an escape from eternal death. The resurrection was Israel's only hope of eternal life.

So why is there a reluctance in Rabbinic Judaism to accept the preexistence of Messiah as God in eternity? Primitive redemptive Judaism does indeed exult in this in the Tanak.

Ruach Hakodesh and Ha-Mashiach are thus inseparably bonded in the provision of repentance, forgiveness, and atonement, which result in perfection and eternal life for humanity. No Jew true to Sinai can deny this. It is a mighty concept, conceived by God in eternity, that humanity should be redeemed by Him through His functions termed as Ruach Hakodesh and Ha-Mashiach. There can be no redemption without repentance, forgiveness, and atonement. Sinai Judaism is thus massive in its clarity and power.

Moses tells in the Pentateuch the story of Creation, when Elohim said, "Let *Us* make man in *Our* own image after *Our* likeness" (Gen.1:26 KJV). In "Us" and "Our" God was including His own functionalities of Ruach Hakodesh and Ha-Mashiach. He was speaking of the perfect humans and world He was about to create, *and would subsequently redeem.* This is an idea, a reality, that makes the human mind dizzy—and for some, very perturbed. As already mentioned, some rabbinic sages tried to explain this as a collaboration with the angelic host; some of whom strongly opposed it because of its foreseen messiness and suffering.

Messiah and the Holy Spirit were eminent in Creation. Moses stated clearly that Creation was wrought by the *Word of the Lord* and the moving of the *Spirit of God*. Philo accepted the Word (Logos) as eminently present at Creation. By the Word of the Lord the heavens were made, and all their host by the breath of His mouth. (Ps. 33:6–9) *The Word and the Holy Spirit were as integral with God as His own breath and existence.* Many rabbinic sages who accepted Philo as an authority admitted rather tangentially that the Word and the Ruach Hakodesh were present and effective at Creation. In the Tanak, Moses and the prophets unequivocally teach that they are also together in Redemption. Despite accepting Word and Holy Spirit in Creation and Redemption, the sages were reluctant to recognize the existence of the "Us" as three Gods. Most sages recognized the Holy Spirit as God Himself but were unsure what status to assign the Word. If Word represented the Messiah, some were confused, as they expected Him to be only human, so could not place Him in Creation. But Messiah was recognized to be preexistent and with monumental tasks to perform in redemption. The mechanics unmistakably included human birth, suffering, and death. The Bavli accepted this. (See references above regarding the provision of grace).

As stated at the outset of this chapter, we must admit that God foresaw the great disobedience. But He ensured the future for the *perfect repair* of the fall of Adam and Eve by His Ruach Hakodesh and Ha-Mashiach functionalities. The cost of that insurance would be very great; it would be Himself. And if Messiah was to be born on the planet, into a sinful world, there could be *no greater condescension for deity*. The plan for messianic condescension and suffering have therefore existed from eternity. The provisions for redemption resided in God's complex self, His Holy Spirit, and His messianic capacities. I take it as a given, therefore, that God was manifest at Creation and in Redemption as Ruach Hakodesh and Ha-Mashiach functionalities, both existent in eternity within God and as God Himself.

25

I have discussed "Hypostasis," "Word," "Wisdom," and "Logos" extensively in the chapters titled "Messiah in the Wisdom Literature," "Ezekiel's Mystic Messiah," and "Daniel's Messianic Visions" in this book.

Isaiah, who stressed that *messianic birth was a visit to earth of deity,* spoke of Redemption as equivalent to Creation in that the darkness of the fallen state was to be replaced by the marvelous light of Redemption.

> The people that walked in darkness have seen a great Light; On those who dwell in a land of gloom Light has dawned ... For a Child has been born to us, A Son has been given us (Isa. 9).

To repeat, the concept of "hypostases" of God is not allowed. Monotheism is an absolute axiom of Judaism. Multiple gods cannot and do not exist in Judaism. But the pluralism of God's constitution (or fabric or substance) in the Tanak cannot be denied. Elohim defines Himself as the Creator and Redeemer in the name "Us."

In the Tanak, there are some landmark allusions that some scholars have interpreted as *"Hypostases of God"* manifest as a "voice" in a "fiery" setting:

❖ The burning bush experience of Moses took place at his first visit to Mount Sinai while he was grazing Jethro's sheep. Allegedly, here is an appearance of a hypostasis (Ex. 3). Moses is visited by *"an Angel of the Lord"* in a blazing fire. This "Angel of the Lord" was none other than *"God [Who] called to him out of the bush."* This *"voice"* claims the name *"I Am"* and describes Himself as "the God of your father, the God of Abraham, the God of Isaac, and the God of Jacob." The record states that Moses hid his face because he was afraid to look at God. *The Jewish Study Bible* commentary (p. 110) states that this "Angel of the Lord" is a manifestation of God that takes the form of fire, a substance evocative of the divine.

❖ Another instance of a hypostasis of God as perceived by scholars appeared as a *"voice,"* again at Mount Sinai, and again in a very fiery context (Ex. 19). This took place at the giving of the Decalogue, the major event in Israel's contact with God.

❖ The appearance of a "hypostasis" occurs again as a "*voice*" from a fiery manifestation in the heavenly temple in Ezekiel's first vision (Ezek. 1, 2). But this time it comes from the "semblance of a Man" who has the appearance of the "semblance of the Presence of the Lord" and He is seated on the "semblance of a throne." This picture resembles Daniel's vision of a fiery scene where the Ancient of Days sits on a throne and "One like a human being" (Son of Man) is given "dominion, glory, and kingship ... that shall not pass away" (Dan. 7). There is also a linkup with David's Psalm 110, where "The Lord says to my Lord ..."

It can be safely insisted that these "hypostases" making appearances on earth in the "fire" and "voice" media are not multiple gods up in heaven but indeed are God's functionalities, active in Creation and Redemption. Ruach Hakodesh and Ha-Mashiach existed within God in bygone eternity, but not as three Gods. There is only one God; blessed be He. One cannot excise Mashiach (Word) and Ruach Hakodesh (Holy Spirit) from Creation and Redemption without devastating God's very substance and plans in eternity. As humans, we give them individuality, personality, and independence. Are we entitled to do so? We try to separate them from a "Godhead," which indeed they are not. This nomenclature is of our own human devising, created so that we can comprehend and explain a complex situation. Moses expressed it very wisely as "Us." Moses comprehended the power of creation and redemption and expressed it as being effected by *Elohim*, or *Us*.

Moses worshipped only one God.

Returning to the discussion of God in eternity, why He went ahead and created humans who he foresaw would be disobedient is beyond our understanding at present. The legacy of the suffering and shame that has befallen humanity is immense. Messiah is also predicted to suffer immensely. The idea that Messiah must suffer as God's own outlay of Himself in this redemption must be considered catastrophic. *The messianic agony* outlined by the prophets, which He must go through to redeem humanity, *is colossal.* Was there equivalence between our suffering and His impending condescension and agony? The divine condescension was wondrously greater—an illustration of His great love for us. As Isaiah predicted, *He would be crushed to save humanity.* Crushing is a total catastrophe. This is understandable only in the light of the satisfaction God obtained in creating and redeeming His greatest loved object in the entire multiverse and in His entire eternity. He wanted spontaneous love, not the love exacted from puppets. God is the origin and source of love, and when He said He would make man in His own image, He was referring to the ability to love of a free will. Love is the supreme and dominant emotion in the multiverse. God is love, and humanity is most like Him when we love Him and our fellow humans. God is a spirit, and His love is very real to us who feel His love and believe that He exists.

Since God planned Creation and Redemption in some stage of His eternity, He would execute both acts Himself. Therefore, in the required ideal and vital axiom of monotheism, *creating and redeeming cannot be delegated tasks.* Redeeming would be the more difficult task. There is no Holy Spirit or messianic suffering known to us in the act of the creation of humanity. But both would suffer in the mechanics of Redemption. (See Isaiah 53, describing "travail of soul" and "anguish"; Lamentations 1:16; Lam. R. I. 45, describing Ruach Hakodesh "weeping." Read Psalm 22 used by the *Midrash Pesiqta Rabbati.*). Again, Ruach Hakodesh and Ha-Mashiach would be the functionalities of Elohim and as such must be deity and divine by definition, very God Himself. Franz Rosenzweig had a remarkable insight here, connecting Creation and Redemption:

> But God's redemptive function assumed a special importance even within this knowledge that is manifest to us. Redemption is His day of rest, His great Sabbath, the day which is but adumbrated [foreshadowed] in the Sabbath of Creation.[45]

Rosenzweig firmly grasped Isaiah's declaration:

> He shall see of the travail of His soul [and] shall be satisfied;
> by His knowledge shall My righteous servant justify many;
> for He shall bear their iniquities. (Isa. 53:11 KJV)

The Jewish Study Bible translates this verse as follows:

> Out of His *anguish* He shall see it: He shall enjoy it to the
> full through His devotion. My righteous servant *makes*
> *the many righteous, It is their punishment that He bears.*

Messianic anguish begets His enjoyment. What a marvelous Sabbath the Almighty enjoyed in Creation! Redemption is implicit in Creation; it is God's business, and He will enjoy His special Sabbath when Redemption is accomplished. Perfection and immortality are implicit in both. Having created, God then concentrated all the power of the multiverse, which He embodied in Himself, into the work of the Redemption. The "Word" and the "Spirit of God" were active in Creation and are active in Redemption. If God could be described as an octopus, *Ruach, Hakodesh, and Messiah are His strong grasping tentacles* to effect redemption. In Psalm 91 David exults in God's redemptive power by describing it as a *powerful bird* providing refuge "Under His wings." God would empty heaven of its most powerful resources in the rescue of humanity. This is perfectly compatible with the great conceptual layout of the Tanak, a layout first explained in the Pentateuch by Moses and repeatedly clarified in the rest of the Tanak.

I use the word "clarified" advisedly. The writers of the Tanak frequently mixed up their contemplation of the Ha-Mashiach atonement, the Messianic Age, the Judgment, the Resurrection, and King Messiah ben David's eternal kingdom. Its brightness dazzled their deciphering of its details, chronology, and apocalyptic. They frequently mixed the functions of the Messiah. Though inspired, they were terrestrial beings with feet of clay. Gershom Scholem voiced this as a complaint against the Biblical prophets:

> To be sure, the predictions of the prophets do not yet give us any kind of ***well-defined conception of Messianism.*** Rather we have a variety of different motifs in which the much emphasized utopian impulse – a vision of a better humanity at the End of Days – is interpenetrated with restorative impulses like the reinstitution of an ideally conceived Davidic kingdom.[46]

Scholem interprets the messianic atonement as a restoration and reinstitution, and the subsequent satisfying sequel at the end of days as Utopian. This is the outcome of the very real machinery of Redemption. The Talmud envisages Mashiach, pangs of Mashiach, and the Messianic Age, all conceived within the envelope of messianic arrival. These elements are all there in the Tanak, as fruit in a fruit salad—not neatly packaged, labeled, and dated, as Scholem and everybody else would have liked it. But it does follow logically and clearly: God's functionality of Ha-Mashiach restores perfection and immortality by the atonement, described as a "crushing." Then, apocalyptically, with the Judgment and Resurrection, Isaiah declares that He wipes out sin from the multiverse and creates a Gan Eden–like new earth, which endures forever. The eternity of the new earth or Messiah ben David's kingdom demands an eternal messiah. *Nowhere in the Tanak is there a description of a human-only, one-lifetime messiah.* The miracle of re-Creation is the same as Creation, and only deity can do it. No human-only messiah, no matter how gifted, can accomplish what is expected of Messiah ben David. It does require a divine messiah who is already preexistent, because He is God Himself and will eternally rule as king. A strictly human-only messiah will not last forever. Just as God lived with Israel as the Shechinah, so will God live with the Redeemed as Messiah ben David in the eternal kingdom. This topic will be taken up again and again in this book.

Because the Talmud has a great variation in the ideas of the Ha-Mashiach expressed within its pages (see *Everyman's Talmud,* by Abraham Cohen, pp.346–356), I admit that there is a mixed-up picture that needs careful deciphering. The Talmud's most variant and errant idea is that *Ha-Mashiach is a created being, an exceptional human, who will perform a "one-human-lifetime task,"* expected to bring Jewish politiconational dominance in the world, which will last forever. If that status is believed, death will have to be assumed as the human Mashiach's end after his one lifetime. This is incompatible with the tanakian concept. The primitive redemptive Judaism of Abraham, Jacob, and Moses has been invaded here by Rabbinic Judaism, Kabbalah, Sabbatianism, Hasidism, and other devised messianic concoctions. The clear concept of Mashiach in the Tanak was thus lost to modern philosophical Rabbinic Judaism. The massive task of restoring perfection and immortality to humanity demands that *Messiah be eternal and divine, God Himself.* The Tanak does not predict a temporal Israeli domination of the world in the status quo by an exceptional one-lifetime, human-only, extraordinarily gifted messiah. The Messiah ben David establishes an eternal kingdom where there is perfection and immortality. It clearly takes place after atonement, Judgment, and the Resurrection.

The importance of Torah must be emphasized here. Torah has existed from eternity. *The Torah is the government of God in the multiverse.* Disobedience occurred somewhere in the celestial space in the origin of evil, a contagion that spread to the earth.[47] Disobedience to Torah in Gan Eden was the great original terrestrial catastrophe. Moses gave us a clear understanding of this when the two great corrective proclamations were beamed from Mt. Sinai:

1. The Ten Commandments, written in Hebrew, carved by the finger of God on the tables of stone, embodied the Torah. This was the essence of His law for terrestrial (fallen human) purposes.
2. In His great prescience, God knew humanity would be disobedient and He prescribed the Aaronic priesthood. This priestly machinery encapsulated Ruach Hakodesh repentance and Ha-Mashiach forgiveness of sin, atonement, and mediation, in the sacrificial system of the temple.

This sacrificial system is labeled as cultic by many erudite scholars. Today the word "cult" implies a religion or religious sect generally considered to be extremist or false. There is nothing cultic about the symbol of messianic suffering and sacrifice, ordained from eternity. The sacrificial system is not a pagan ritual and was not borrowed from any surrounding civilization (e.g., the worship of Mithras, Herakles, Jupiter, or Apollo), as the intellectual scholar A. N. Wilson implies.[48] Geza Vermes also repeatedly calls the sacrificial system cultic. This does damage to the symbolism of the redemptive act. He repeatedly denies the eternity of the Messiah. (See *Christian Beginnings*, by Geza Vermes, pp. 99–133.) The origin of the sacrificial system in Judaism was first implanted outside the gates of Eden after the great disobedience (Gen. 4; Lev. 16, 23). God instituted the "Animal Without Blemish" as the symbol of "Messianic Atonement" for sin. Because the animal whose blood was to be shed symbolized the Messiah, that animal *must be without blemish*, for it symbolized the role of Mashiach in God's redemptive power. The blood was shed not for the appeasement of a pagan deity but for the propitiation of messianic intervention to reverse eternal death. Eternal death must be conquered by God Himself. God alone can do it. That is what Moses taught. The law and the messianic sacrifice were beamed from Sinai at the same time to the multiverse. Neither should be diminished or ignored. A. N. Wilson and Geza Vermes are so wrong to diminish the messianic symbolism in the sacrifice of the animal without blemish. It is implicit from God's eternity that the Messiah must suffer and die as an atonement that reinstates perfection and immortality to the human race.

Because the Torah had been disobeyed, repentance and atonement became absolute prime requirements. The Day of Atonement, which foretold and enacted the messianic functionality of God to redeem, brought the law, God's mercy, and the Shechinah together for the splashing of the blood, symbolic of messianic provision. This cannot be denied by any Jew faithful to Sinai.

Modern Rabbinic Judaism runs with the law and forgets the other great provision of the Ruach Hakodesh and Ha-Mashiach—mercy. Mercy saves the sinner who has broken the law. Both law and mercy were powerfully beamed from Mt. Sinai *at the same time.*

There is no doubt that the Ha-Mashiach of primitive tanakian Judaism is God Himself, the Redeemer, and that He is eternal and divine. All Jews hail Mashiach as the Redeemer. The deity and divinity of Ha-Mashiach is seen in the synonymous definition of God and Redeemer displayed in the Tanak. This is presented as follows:

- YHVH is the *"Divine Goel,"* redeeming His people (Isa. 63:16).
- YHVH is *"El Shaddah, Adonai,"* Saviour in the escape from Egypt (Ex. 6:2,3).
- YHVH is *"Ga'a-leta,"* the Redeemer who delivers Israel from "the clans of Edom" who seek to destroy them (Ex. 15:13).
- YHVH is *"yom'ru G'uley y'h asher G'alam mi Yad-tzar,"* the Redeemer who gathers Israel from the ends of the earth in judgment (Ps. 107:2,3).
- YHVH is *"ha-dur,"* majestic in the role of deliverer (Isa. 62:11; 63:1).
- YHVH is *"goali,"* Vindicator, Redeemer, a judge, conducting judgment at the latter day upon the earth (Job 19:25).
- YHVH is *"Haggoel,"* the Redeemer (Job 19:25; Ps. 19:14).
- YHVH is *"Goel,"* the Kinsman, Redeemer (Num. 5:8).
- YHVH is *"Goel, Yisrael,"* the Redeemer of Israel (Lev. 25; Ps. 39:7).
- YHVH is *"Goel, Haddam,"* the Avenger of blood (1 Sam. 6:20).
- YHVH is *"Adonai Tsuri v'go'ali,"* the Lord my rock and my Redeemer (Ps. 19:14).
- YHVH is *"Tsidkenu (Sid-qe-nu),"* the Lord our Righteousness (Jer. 23:5, 6).
- YHVH is the *"Ancient of Days,"* whose functionalities present as Ha-Mashiach and Ruach Hakodesh (Dan. 7, Ps. 2, Isa. 9, Mic. 5). Ha-Mashiach manifests as the Son of God in eternity, and the Son of Man in the divine penetrance of humanity.
- YHVH is *"Immanuel, God with us"* (Isa. 9:7). The sonship of Ha-Mashiach is so expressed as a terminology we use for our own understanding of the functionality of God. If a divine child is being born into an earthly setting, then in earthly language, we call God His Father.

The conclusion drawn from the above is that God, Ruach Hakodesh, and Ha-Mashiach are one and the same unity of substance, and not three Gods. In the apocalyptic of Daniel and Isaiah and indeed all the prophets, Ha-Mashiach is Redeemer and King. God's functionality seen in the expression of Ruach Hakodesh and Ha-Mashiach cannot be denied. The concept is embedded in the Tanak, Israel's sacred canon. It is the record of their conversation with God. The Talmud is the record of their conversation with each other.

Franz Rosenzweig has this most thrilling realization to share:

> What God, the true God, may have been before Creation thus defies the imagination. Not so that which He would be after redemption. True, here too our living knowledge tells us nothing about God's essence beyond the Redeemer. *That He is the Redeemer is the last thing we learn by our own experience: we 'know that He lives' and that our 'eyes will behold Him.'* But God's *redemptive function* assumed a special importance even within this knowledge that is manifest to us ... Redemption is His day of rest, His great Sabbath, the day which is but adumbrated in the Sabbath of Creation.[49]

That God Himself is the Redeemer is wonderfully proclaimed by Isaiah:

> And there is no God else beside Me, a just God and *a Saviour,* there is none beside Me. *Look unto Me and be ye saved,* all the ends of the earth; for *I am God and there is none beside Me ...* The *Word* is gone out of My mouth in righteousness, and shall not return, that unto Me every knee shall bow, every tongue shall swear. Surely, shall one say, *in the Lord have I righteousness and strength ... In the Lord shall all the seed of Israel be justified,* and shall glory. (Isa. 45:21–25 KJV, emphasis added)

The following adoration of Messiah ben David in Psalm 45 is beautiful:

> Thou art fairer than the children of men; **grace** is poured
> into thy lips; therefore God hath blessed thee forever ...
> And in thy majesty ride prosperously because of truth and
> meekness and righteousness ... Thy throne, O God, is
> forever and ever ... Thou lovest righteousness, and hatest
> wickedness; therefore God, thy God, hath anointed thee
> with the oil of gladness above thy fellows. (Ps. 45:3,4,7,8
> KJV, emphasis added)

The great Jewish philosopher Ibn Ezra, in AD 1089, applied this psalm to both David and Messiah ben David. (See *The Jewish Study Bible*, p. 1332.) Rabbi David Kimchi (Radak) agreed. (See CHABAD. org.) *Messiah's throne* is addressed as "Thy throne, O God, is forever and ever." But then Messiah gets the approbation of "God, thy God." To me this appellation indicates *God's own exultation* in the plan of redemption by His messianic functionality. David emphasizes this again in Psalm 110. It also resonates with Son of Man and Ancient of Days in Daniel 7 and in Ezekiel's Kavod. And my conclusion is that God and Messiah ben David are one and the same. God is allowed to exult in His own accomplishments. He exulted over Creation. "He saw that it was good." Now He exults over Redemption. "He shall see of the travail of His soul and shall be satisfied." He has accomplished both acts. Rosenzweig marks Sabbaths celebrated by Elohim over both events. Who am I to question God's great satisfaction in the redemption? He is the eternal messianic functionality as the great I Am That I Am of the burning bush experience of Moses. (See Exodus 3), of the fiery *voice* when God came down on Mt. Sinai at the giving of the law and mercy, and of the voice in the fiery vision of Ezekiel where he saw the "semblance of a Man." The redemption is accomplished by Mashiach in the garb of humanity so that God can indeed exult, "Thy throne, O God, is forever and ever," when referring to Messiah ben David, who rules in the eternal kingdom, very God in substance.

The Creation and Redemption of humanity have been with God from eternity. They are expressed from eternity as the functionalities of Elohim in the manifestations of Ruach Hakodesh and the Ha-Mashiach. They are what He does in Creation and Redemption. The Lord our God is one; blessed be He.

These concepts are abundantly declared in the Tanak. In the Talmud, the great rabbinic sages embraced the Ruach Hakodesh as deity without compromising monotheism. But they balked at accepting Ha-Mashiach as deity. They knew He would be born on the planet. They supposed Him to be an ordinary human, albeit a very talented one. The reason appears to be the fleshly appearance of Ha-Mashiach. But "the fleshly appearance" is clearly a tanakian doctrine, explicitly well supported by Abraham, Jacob, David, Isaiah, Micah, and Daniel.

Divine fleshly appearances of God are well noted in the appearance of God to Abraham and Sarah under the terebinths as "the Lord" (Gen. 18), and His appearance to remove Lot forcibly from Sodom (Gen. 19). God appeared to Jacob at the Brook Jabbok: "I have seen God," He is "human and divine" (Gen. 32), and to Moses at the "Burning Bush" as the great "I AM THAT I AM" (Ex. 3). Daniel and Nebuchadnezzar saw Him "like a Divine Being" in the fiery furnace (Dan. 3:25), and as the Son of Man being commissioned by the "Ancient of Days" and "coming with the clouds of heaven" (Dan. 7). There is only one divine being in heaven in monotheistic Judaism, and He is Elohim. So here we have God appearing transiently on this earth in the guise of a human. He also makes appearances in heaven as such. The conclusion is that God can do what He likes and appear as He likes when He likes, in any form He chooses.

But He also comes in an epochal manner in the messianic birth. This birth is not a temporary or transient appearance but *a messianic human life*, via the womb of a woman, to live a memorable life that accomplishes the atonement. We cannot avoid this reality.

To David, in this messianic birth, God is the Father: "*You are My Son, I have fathered You*" (Ps. 2). And again, "*From the womb, from the Dawn*" (Ps.110)

To Isaiah, the young woman bears a Son to be called "*Immanuel, God with us*" (Isa. 7:14). And again the "*Child is born [as] the Mighty God, the Everlasting Father*" (Isa: 9:6 *KJV*).

To *Micah*, the city of His birth is a real place: "O Bethlehem Ephrath ... From you One shall come forth to rule Israel for Me – *One whose origin is of Old from Ancient Times ...* He shall wax great to the ends of the earth" (Mic. 5:1, 2).

These are all considered messianic references by the rabbinic sages. These all predicted a fleshly human appearance of God.

Thus, as eternally planned, when God penetrates humanity as Ha-Mashiach to provide the atonement, He enters as a newborn (Isa. 9:6). This medium was promised to Eve outside the gates of Gan Eden, and God would keep His promise. Eve ardently hoped to be the mother of the Messiah. It is fair to say that every woman born in the line of Judah, the son of Jacob, hoped to be the mother of the Ha-Mashiach. He would come as Messiah ben David. It was a solid and solemn promise made by God to Eve, to Sarah, to Jacob, to Judah, and to King David. And all the prophets trumpeted it, and every Jew has lived "for the days of the Messiah." It is the great longing of every Jewish heart on the planet. That longing was to be realized through a birth from the womb: *Immanuel, God with us.*

Micah makes a clear enunciation of Messiah's eternity in the announcement of His penetrance of humanity:

> One who will be Ruler over Israel,
> ***Whose origins are from of Old,***
> ***From Ancient Times.*** (Mic. 5:2, RSV, emphasis added)

"From of Old," "Ancient of Days," and "Ancient Times" are regarded as the eternal attributes of God. This concept of Micah has been regarded as the enunciation of the eternal kingdom to be set up by Messiah ben David. He comes from eternity and goes on into eternity.

To many rabbinic sages and scholars in Israel who solidly believe in monotheism, as I indeed do, the taking on of fleshly human form, determined from eternity in the redemption of humanity, is a challenge to monotheism. There is an extensive discussion of this in the chapter of this book on the Messiah in the Wisdom Literature, specifically regarding the books of Proverbs and Ecclesiastes. Briefly, Proverbs chapter 8 is a description of the eternity of messianic ideation in the mind of God as His messianic redeeming functionality. The names "Wisdom," "Reason," "Word," and "Logos" bring this to light. Philo interpreted these in lofty phrases as "Image of God," "Name of God," "Firstborn Son," "Chief Logos of God," "The Second God," and

"Angel of the Lord." Philo went as far as to say that God gives the title of "God" to his Chief Logos. Philo speaks of "Two Gods." (See *Agriculture 51; Dreams 1.230; Questions on Genesis 2.62; Changing of Names 87; Dreams 239*, quoted from the C. D. Yonge translations of Philo titled *The Works of Philo*. See also *The Jewish Jesus*, by Peter Schafer, pp. 173–178, for a discussion of Philo's ideas. See also the essay by P. Borgen *There Shall Come Forth A Man – Reflections on Messianic Ideas in Philo* in the book *The Messiah*, pp. 341-361).

Some of the rabbinic sages interpreted Wisdom to be a "hypostasis" of God. Others had been grappling with this ideation and had discouraged such thoughts because of the challenge to monotheism. Such ideation is indeed a challenge to monotheism if a second God appears on the scene. But the matter is easily solved if it is accepted that Messiah is indeed God's functionality to effect redemption, and not a second God up in heaven. The human Messiah, owning deity and a cosmic mission, becomes the human vehicular substance of Elohim to effect redemption. Placing God on the earth does not mean that He is therefore absent from heaven. God is omnipresent and is not harnessed to one area or one function. This indeed is difficult to understand and accept. But we must accept this if we want redemption. How God does it causes consternation in our thinking. It is a miraculous mystery. But then the Creation is just as big a miraculous mystery, which we gladly accept because we know our God and believe in Him and love Him. Gershom Scholem unhesitatingly stated, "I am a religious person because I am sure of my belief in God." (See *On Jews and Judaism in Crisis*, by Gershom Scholem, p. 46.) We must accept the eternally planned messianic redemptive functionality of Elohim as being God Himself, and there can be no "Second God" or "Divine Hypostasis." In primitive redemptive Judaism, Messiah is God and God is Messiah, one and the same eternal God. Philo is wrong to use the title "Second God." The Lord our God is one; blessed be He.

In summary: Elohim planned in eternity that He Himself would be Creator and Redeemer. At the Creation He declared His plurality (Us). This "Us" included His functionalities – the Word and the Holy Spirit effecting the Creation. Why would not the Word and the Holy Spirit be God in effecting the Redemption? That is precisely what was

His declared intention from eternity. This idea is eminently supported by many rabbinic sages (see BerR 8:4f; b Sanh 38b; BerR 1:4; PesR 34. 36. 37). In fact the Rabbis suggested that God threatened to withdraw His **Combination Plan** for the Creation and Redemption unless His messianic functionality was respected.

Purportedly, the creation of humanity was opposed by the angels with whom He collaborated. Peter Schafer very tenderly states, "God ... relies solely on the willingness of the Messiah to take upon Himself the burden of sin of all humankind." By this Schafer gives the Messiah personality and independence. He further quotes from Arnold Goldberg's book *Erlosung durch Leiden* (Frankfurt am Main e.V., 1978, p. 186): *"In a unique way the Messiah is put [here] into the centre of Creation; all future life depends on Him."* (See *The Jewish Jesus*, by Peter Schafer, p. 246, 247.) The Rabbis actually make Creation and Redemption the crucial responsibilities of God's messianic functionality. We know from the Tanak that in the Redemption the Ruach Hakodesh provides the gift of repentance and the Mashiach provides forgiveness and atonement. Thus perfection and immortality are restored. But God has declared repeatedly that He is the Redeemer. So basically Messiah and Holy Spirit are God Himself seen in the redeeming functionalities.

We must look to the description of the Messiah as the prophets perceived Him. There is no doubt that the Tanak contains the messianic penetration of humanity to attain the redemption. Although "Son of Man" and "Son of God" are sometimes used in the Tanak as generic terms referring to non-messianic individuals and kings who were anointed, we have a wealth of references to the Messiah as "Son of Man" and "Son of God." It is evident that the production of this relationship between God and His messianic functionality was spoken about in eternity, and it was a predicted earthly reality, as was the messianic birth. It would occur as the penetration of God into humanity. Therefore, *we are out of order* when we seek to establish a messianic presence as an actual hypostasis "begotten" in eternity as a "Son of God" or "Son of Man." The Sonship is the anthropomorphic human description that starts on the penetration of humanity by divinity. This use of the Father–Son relationship serves to help humanity to understand the messianic God coming to earth to effect the Redemption. Here the plurality of Elohim is again on display. Messiah thus is very God and not a preexistent offshoot hypostasis. Isaiah 9 declares this plainly. The Holy Spirit and the Mashiach will remain as God the Great Spirit in plurality after Redemption.

The next chapter deals with the promise of that messianic Sonship as the *Seed of the woman Eve.* Unwittingly or not, the rabbinic sages raptured in this event and trumpeted it thus:

> Blessed (ashrei) is the hour in which he was created,
> Blessed is the *womb* from whence he came,
> Blessed is the generation whose eyes behold him,
> Blessed is the eye which waited for him …
> Blessed is the eye which merits seeing him,
> Since *the utterance of his tongue is pardon and Forgiveness for Israel.*
> (PesR, S 8; Braude, PesR, p. 689; Arnold Goldberg's *Erlosung durch Leiden*, p. 274)

None of the above could be applied to any anointed king of Israel, except typologically in a generic application. King David rejoiced in this Messiah and jubilantly relished being a type of his Lord.

The Holy Spirit is God indeed, pervasively moving as the mighty wind in Creation. Now in the Redemption, this functionality of God will pervasively convict of sin and gift repentance to humanity.

Messiah is God indeed, the Word in Creation (Logos, "as in the thing we speak." This functionality will appear in human form in the Redemption, born from the woman's surrogate womb to provide atonement.

These mighty acts were *both planned by God from eternity.* The inquisitive mind must ask the question, did God always exist in His eternity as *Elohim, the plural "Us,"* as Moses expressed Him in spelling out the Creation and the Redemption, or was the event of Creation the first expression of God's functionalities?

Since evil did exist before the Creation of the world, its origin and correction by God needs to be addressed. Since God is love and His motivation is activated by love, did He love the fallen angels whom

He had created, and did He take action to redeem them? The answer is a resounding affirmative. The origin of evil is well recognized in the Tanak. (See chapter on the origin of evil in my book *King David's Naked Dance*). I believe that God's functionalities of Messiah and Holy Spirit were active in the Creation and Redemption of the fallen angelic host. The Ruach Hakodesh was active in convicting fallen angels of sin and gifting them with repentance. And Mashiach was active in providing expiation and atonement for them as Michael the great prince, who some discerning rabbinic sages and others recognized as the archangel. The title "archangel" is rich with meaning. It therefore is logical that Elohim did exist as the mighty *"Us"* way back in eternity, when the angels sinned. It is perfectly logical to assume that the messianic functionalities of God gifted repentance to and made atonement for the fallen angels. *Why not? Indeed, why not? Was He to become "archman" in the same capacity as He was "archangel?"*

Since we believe that God is omniscient, omnipotent, and omnipresent, it is very logical to assume that He has always existed as Elohim, the plural "Us." But then, when did He come to exist as the Son of Man, the child that is born as "the Mighty God planning Grace" and "the Everlasting Father, the Prince of Peace?" How does this "child" qualify to be born as His own "father" unless they are both one and the same? At what stage in eternity can we apply David's discerning "Thou art My Son, this day have I begotten Thee?" And at what stage in eternity can we apply the foretold suffering Messiah of Psalm 22 and Isaiah 53? From the terrestrial viewpoint, the actual event of the *birth* of the Messiah will need to be used as the *point of application* of the "begotten sonship" and the "assumption of Fatherhood" for this Son when He is born on the planet. That is the point when deity penetrates humanity in the great condescension. But then we must admit that Elohim as "Us" *contained* Mashiach and Ruach Hakodesh long before that earthly event. The when and where of that *containment* in eternity is a question we cannot answer now. It came into our awareness with the provision of our redemption. Perhaps it will remain conjecture till God tells us, since He has always been there in His eternity. The Lord our God is one. Blessed be He.

CHAPTER 3

The First Terrestrial Messianic Promise

In his treatment of the so-called development of Yahwistic theology, Max Weber, in his book *Ancient Judaism*, sees parallels and contrasts to ideas in Egyptian, Canaanite, Babylonian, and Indian religions. He emphasizes borrowings, interpolations, and revisions of the Pentateuch. There is some evidence for interpolations and revisions. ***But Sinai stands dramatically as the source of the concept of Creation and Redemption as one unit in Judaism.*** Weber is correct in his account of the influence of the Levitical priesthood established by Moses, in enforcing the Pentateuchal theology and guarding it from heathen influences, thus gifting Israel and the world with a superb theology. He freely admits that the Mosaic creation account stands out as "***the end product – the unsurpassed majestic, but quite unplastic story of Creation in the present first chapter of Genesis, is an accomplishment of priests***" (see *Ancient Judaism*, pp. 168–263). Moses is the source of the Creation and Eden account, and Weber states that it was tweaked by some Levitical priests. Here the account of the disobedience and fall of humanity was guaranteed a reversal. Despite his praise for the majestic story of Creation, Weber failed to see the messianic reclamation by God enshrined by the Levitical priesthood as the cosmic destruction of sin and death. This reclamation occurs in the Most Holy Place of the heavenly temple, of which the tabernacle temple was the type. (See Isaiah 6.) This was enshrined in eternity in the presence of the almighty God in the heavenly temple.

Since the great disobedience that came about in Gan Eden was the disobedience to the Torah, it is necessary to define "Torah" for Gan Eden. Obedience to Torah determined primal fitness to be with God. It is the Torah in the primitive Judaism of Moses, constituted by the utterances of God, that commenced in Eden. Adam and Eve experienced it in pure primal devekut with God. Torah in Eden was constituted by one commandment: "Do not eat of the Tree of Knowledge of Good and Evil." Edenic Torah as affected Adam and Eve was passed on in the oral medium through the Patriarchs to Moses. This, plus the mighty revelations at Sinai, he wrote down at Mt. Sinai as the Pentateuch. But God's conversation with Israel continued through all the inspired prophets to Malachi. The Tanak was the final work, which came together, concluded, and was closed by the Sanhedrin.[50]

Meir ben Gabbai, in his "Avodat Ha-Kodesh," described the Torah as follows:

> The highest wisdom [the *sofia* of God, which is the second *sefirah*] contains as the foundation of all emanations pouring forth out of the hidden Eden, the true fountain from which the Written and the Oral Torah emanate …[51]

Here I register an objection to the inference that the Talmud is the further proclaimed "Oral Torah," being included in the "highest wisdom." I argue that the Tanak is a conversation with God and is the highest wisdom, whereas the Talmud is an argumentative discussion among the rabbinic sages. There is no "Thus saith the Lord" in the Talmud. To repeat, the Tanak is Israel's canon, which does not include the Talmud.

The Talmud credits the Ruach Hakodesh with inspiring all the authors of the Tanak. I embrace this concept. Abraham Cohen sums it up thus:

> Of the Hebrew prophets, Moses was pre-eminent and stands in a class by himself … His comprehension of the divine message was more intimate than theirs. The revelation granted to him was the source from which all the later prophets drew. "What the prophets were destined to prophesy in subsequent generations they received from Mt. Sinai" (Exodus R. 28:6) … It followed from this that nothing spoken by a later prophet could in any way be in conflict with, and add to or detract from, the writings of Moses. "Forty eight prophets and seven prophetesses

43

spoke prophecies for Israel, and they neither deducted from nor added to what was written in the Torah [Pentateuch], with the exception of the law to read the Book of Esther on the Feast of Purim" (Meg. 14a) … "The Holy Spirit which alights on prophets does so by measure …" (Lev. R xv.2). "When the latter prophets Haggai, Zechariah and Malachi died, the Holy Spirit departed from Israel" (Sanh. 11a). The supreme message of Hebrew prophecy was the call to erring men and women to retrace their steps to God. Every prophet only prophesied for the Days of the Messiah and the penitent" (Ber. 34b). "It shall come to pass afterward that I will pour out My Spirit upon all flesh; and your sons and daughters shall prophesy, your old men dream dreams, your young men shall see visions" (Joel 2:28, Num. 15:25).[52]

It seems obvious from the above passages from the Talmud that the rabbinic sages *were averse to adding or subtracting from Moses.* This therefore precludes any statement, belief, or modification of Mosaic Judaism that the Talmud itself contains. It is very gratifying indeed that many rabbinic sages emphasize that *the supreme message of the Tanak is messianic Redemption.* In the chapter in this book titled "The Messiah of the Prince of Egypt," I list talmudic utterances in Halakah that are deemed to be attempted additions to Moses, besides the allusion above to the law to read the book of Esther on the Feast of Purim, which is an exception. This will be discussed later in this book.

There was a cessation of the flow of prophets after Malachi, about 400 BC. This was interpreted by many who wept sadly that "the Ruach Hakodesh had departed from Israel." The "Bath Kol" was invented to claim a small measure of continuing inspiration.[53] But Malachi had clearly declared that Elijah, the forerunner, and Messiah were imminent. There was no need to lament or to invent a "Bath Kol." The Holy Spirit is always around us and has never been withdrawn. The Tanak attests to that.

Since it is logically concluded that the document that evolved into the Tanak became the compact Torah, viewed by the Sanhedrin as a complete Torah, we can proceed to decipher the messianic proclamation in it. Torah is simply the governing vehicle to define the fitness necessary *to be again with God in primal devekut.* This fitness could only be achieved by *messianic provision* of the perfection and immortality required to be again with God. Messiah would provide the perfection by His *redemptive righteousness,* and Messiah would conquer sin and eternal death by the *atonement,* bringing back immortality. This no mere ordinary human can do. Sinai declared this and embodied it as the essence in Judaism, deposited in the Most Holy Place of the temple, where dwelled the Shechinah, law, mercy and messianic blood.

Is God two-faced in His application of Torah? In his book *Ancient Judaism,* Max Weber goes to great pains to portray Yahwe as the "War God" in the time of confederate Israel, eminently showing His "cruelty" in the conquering of the Holy Land by Abraham's progeny. Weber relies on the song of Deborah and the *Amarna letters,* which are rich in imagery. He also uses the so-called riotous sexual victory ecstasy of winning soldiers to try to prove his thesis. Weber is so wrong. There is a colossal anthropomorphism employed here that assigns to God the war deeds of Israel and the natural calamitous catastrophes of the cosmos. While it is true that terrestrial land acquisitions by waves of marauding peoples in history have been accomplished by cruel acts of war and genocide, whether perpetrated by bows and arrows, knives, guns, chariots, tanks, bombs, missiles, or chemicals, these are the inventions of humans. Weber's image of confederate Israel's "War God" is wrong. It is incompatible with redemption. God's creation was marred by disobedience, which cannot exist eternally on the planet, because that same Creator ordained Redemption in His eternity. Weber's young "War God" is a description conjured out of Israel's wars of land acquisition.

I strongly contend that *war is a human device* generated by misinformation, greed, and desperation. "Holy Wars" are not holy, nor the plan of Yahweh. God has a two-stage plan to deal with disobedience. *God* is "angry" and "brokenhearted" about His lost pleasure with humanity in primal devekut. The eminent rabbinic tradition admirably portrayed God as praying that His own mercy may gain the upper hand over His "wrath!" (See Ber 7a; A.Z. 3b;

Pes. 119a; p. Kid. 61d; Sanh. 39b; Aboth III. 19; Gen. R. XII. 15; Gen. R. VIII. 4. These are all quoted in Abraham Cohen's description of God's justice and mercy). God provides messianic redemption. This is not forced on anyone but offered as a choice to avail or not avail of messianic redemption. The tanakian eschatology does predict an eventual annihilation of those rejecting redemption. It is disobedience that does not avail of God's mercy and grace that results in eternal death, no matter how that death is described. What is most satisfying is that God's planned redemption for all humanity in His eternity has vanquished eternal death. That redemption is available to all who desire it. No one needs to die eternally.

The final consequence of disobedience is eternal death. Messianic provision was God's plan to vanquish death. This was eminently instituted by Moses in the establishment of the tabernacle temple, where the law was enshrined. Here, disobedience resulting in death was vanquished by mercy, the mercy seat, where between the cherubim the almighty Elohim made His abode. The Day of Atonement required the splashing of messianic blood on the law and the mercy seat to effect God's mercy. This is *the most stupendous contribution* of the religion called Judaism. Messianic blood atones.

God is not two-faced. I contend that conversion of the idolatrous hordes of Canaan to the Redemption of Yahwe was God's intention. They were to be proselytized by Israel to the Redemption that was installed in the Holy of Holies of the temple. Repentance, forgiveness, and atonement were designed as the powerful antidote to eternal death, not only for Israel but also for all humanity. This was the ideation that has often been expressed as "God is on our side." We place ourselves "On God's side" when we choose messianic atonement. The eradication of idolatry and land possession by the crime of war was the human substitute, made to look God-ordained. Samuel erred first in anointing Saul as king, because Saul was not of the tribe of Judah. Then he erred in demanding Saul to annihilate all enemy life in his wars. The Abrahamic covenant was the agreement to be the blessedness of all nations. Israel was severely punished by the consequences of her own idolatry and neglect of the covenant. God allowed her temples and people to be destroyed and devastated. But that should never have happened. This history does not give

Israel's enemies the right to continue efforts for her annihilation, and Israel has every right to defend herself. This right must be interpreted as enjoined with the task of the covenant, the effecting of the blessedness of all nations in messianic Redemption. Israel must offer the world a redeeming Messiah.

With this understanding of God and His application of Torah we now examine His dealings with the sinful pair. Mercy now is His dominant theme.

The very first messianic proclamation followed immediately after the great disobedience, after the confession of Adam and Eve. God did not delay in making the promise. We are not to suppose that messianic Redemption had been left to the last minute to be declared by Abraham or Moses. Adam and Eve were depressed and saw only death ahead. God gave them the cosmic promise of readmission into Gan Eden and pure primal devekut with Him, from which they were just ejected. God *addressed the promise to Eve*, perhaps for two reasons: Firstly she was the one who was deceived. Adam went into sin willingly. Secondly, and stupendously, woman would be the vessel that would be the *organic surrogate link* between divinity and humanity to bring the Mashiach to earth as a divine penetration of humanity. Moses recorded it thus:

> Then the Lord said to the Serpent, Because you did this, more cursed shall you be ... I will put *enmity* between you and the woman, and between your offspring and hers; They shall *strike* at your head, and you shall *strike* at their heel. (Gen. 3: 14–15)

This is translated more aptly "Between thy seed and her Seed" by the KJV. The KJV not so aptly translates the word "strike" as "bruise." A bruise is much too gentle and innocuous a wound to be inflicted by the two antagonists. Some translations use the word "crush," which is much greater in severity. The crushed head would cause death, but the crushed heel would not be as deadly, because the Messiah would take up His life again. Still, this was a gross understatement about the messianic part God would play. Isaiah described it more severely as a crushed Mashiach *leading to death, which He would overcome, because He was divine; Messiah would be God Himself* (Isa. 53). David described it as a rising from Sheol (Ps. 16:10).

The part played by the Serpent should not be minimized. Abraham Cohen quotes explicitly from the Talmud:

> Satan [the Serpent] performs three functions: he seduces men, he accuses them before God, he inflicts the punishment of death (B.B. 16a). He is the seducer *par excellence,* and his methods are well exemplified in his conduct toward the first patriarch.[54]

The great Edenic disobedience was a cosmic catastrophe. An evil influence had spoiled God's perfect relationship with His Creation and His greatest known pleasure. We must not get diverted into an argument about the deception by the serpent. If we believe in the presence in Gan Eden of the Tree of Life, we must accept that the presence of the Tree of Knowledge of Good and Evil as the alternate choice, which exercised the free will granted to humanity to worship God. The Serpent beguiled the woman.

A tit-for-tat confrontation is described here. In the translation of *The Jewish Study Bible*, the important word "offspring" refers to the Serpent's progeny, and "they" refers to Eve's offspring, who will inflict a head wound to the Serpent. The pronoun "you" is the reference to the Serpent, who will inflict a heel wound to the "offspring" or "seed" of Eve. The Hebrew Masoretic text renders Gen. 3:15 thus (provided for those fluent in Hebrew): "w'eyvah ashiyt Beyn'kha yveyn haiSHah uveyn zarakha uveyn zaraH hu y'shuf'kha rosh waTah T'shuf'kha rosh w'aTahT'shufeNu aqev."

In a discussion of charismatic Judaism, Geza Vermes draws attention to Gen. 3:15. (See *Christian Beginnings*, by Geza Vermes, p. 23.) This discussion was in connection with Rabban Hanina ben Dosa, who was bitten by a poisonous serpent while reciting the Tefillah. The serpent died, while Hanina survived (Tosifta. Ber. 3:20). A similar story is present in the Jerusalem Talmud, where a snake died on biting Hanina. The moral of the story here is "Woe to the man who meets a snake, but woe to the snake that meets Rabban Hanina ben Dosa" (Jerusalem Talmud Ber. 9a). Here is perhaps a unwitting depiction of the encounter that would take place between the promised Seed of Eve and Satan. It does not quite conform to the encounter between Mashiach and the Serpent. They both die. But Isaiah declares that Mashiach takes up His life again because He is divine (Isa. Chap. 53). Sadly, Vermes misses the point that here God is promising to come as the Mashiach to redeem the world. It is implicit in Isaiah. The Serpent dies as a result of the Mashiach's conquest. But Mashiach has the power to take up His life again.

Genesis 3:15 is the promise that Eve's "offspring" would inflict a lethal (head) wound on the Serpent, a final end to sin and mortality. It would be a "crushed" head indeed! The use of the plural word "they" in reference to the Seed or Offspring of the woman has been interpreted by some as being, necessarily, a reference to the divinity of the redeeming "Offspring" being none other than deity. Elohim would do it Himself. The "Us" and "Our" who created would also be the "Us" and "Our" to redeem. In the various translations, the pronouns used to refer to the "offspring" or "seed" are "he," "his," and "it." The translators of *The Jewish Study Bible* use the plural "they," and it is quite appropriate, as the Ruach Hakodesh and the Ha-Mashiach are included in the "Us" and "Our." The cosmic promise made by God to Eve was that the messianic deliverer, present in God's mind from eternity, was Himself, and He would come as a human, as *Eve's Seed*. That same promise was made to Abraham in the covenant thus: "… and in **thy Seed** shall all nations of the earth be blessed." (See *Il Messia*, by David Castelli, pp. 37–38.)[55] There is no doubt that the great Italian Jewish writer David Castelli recognized the messianic redemption implicit in the Abrahamic covenant's "thy seed."

This pronouncement from the mouth of God to Eve is very important, and we must draw out its core meaning. It is the first terrestrial announcement of redemption. It is understandable that Eve, from the depth of her despair, sought forgiveness for the great disobedience and loss of immortality. She desperately wanted to get back into Eden and primal devekut with God. She was ready to grasp at any straw of hope that might be offered, and she was given the Messiah. The fruit of her womb was the great hope that God held out to her. Her offspring would deal a lethal blow to the Serpent who had trapped her. The flaming sword wielded by the angel at the gates of Eden was no longer intended for her, but now would kill the Messiah, exacting the penalty of the disobedience to Torah. The gates of Eden were never shut. But the sword of death was placed there to exact messianic death, as humanity's substitute. Messiah would be Eve's substitute in her endeavor to go through those gates. As eternal death it was her lot, but now she had a substitute. She could now walk through those gates unimpeded, to be restored to immortality and pure primal devekut with God. As she passed through those gates, her feet would be wet with Mashiach blood as He lay there at Eden's gate, bleeding and dying for her. The fiery sword contained the promise of redemption. The sword would be spent on the Messiah at those gates. His blood would be carried into the Most Holy Place and splashed on the law and the mercy seat, activating the triumph of mercy over Justice. That is the mighty redemption God offered.

So this "enmity," these mortal blows, that God was placing between Eve's divine-human seed and the evil power was a tremendous hope. In considering this balm to Eve's soul, she clearly saw the offering of messianic provision, which God had in His mind from the days of eternity gone by. The Talmud is insistent that Mashiach was a provision long before the Creation. (See Pes. 54a.)[56] What other meaning is there to God's offer that Eve's offspring would deal the Serpent a lethal blow? Will any Jew or anyone else challenge this messianic miracle God Himself offered to Eve?

God's functionality as the Ha-Mashiach power must suffer a major blow in the encounter. Since God would come as a divine penetrance of humanity, it would cost His human death. A "heel wound," if indeed it could be measured, was how He measured the agony He must go through to reclaim His greatest love object in His entire multiverse and eternity. As already pointed out, it was a fantastic underestimation by Elohim of the condescension it would cost Him. (It was like the Australians say, "No worries mate!" when one responds to a good deed done at some significant cost.) But Elohim had the power to take up His life again. The meaning understood by Eve is the key to the message in these words of God. When she gave birth to her firstborn son, her words were messianic:

I have gained a male child with the help of the Lord.
(Gen. 4:1b)

The infant came in a package labeled "Help of the Lord." The Hebrew Masoretic Text is translated as follows:

I have gotten a man from YHVH.

The *God's Word Translation* states it in very dramatic messianic language:

I have gotten the Man that the Lord promised.

The *God's Word Translation* of the Bible has had little publicity. It was pioneered by the scholars William F. Beck, Elmer Smick, Erich Kiehl, and Phillip B. Geissler. Five other associates, Hebrew scholars, assembled Hebrew, Aramaic, and Koine Greek Texts for guidance. They had seventeen technical reviewers and four language reviewers. In my opinion, this wording above is a magnificent translation.

Eve proclaimed the child Cain was the Messiah, a gift from God. She hoped against hope that the great misfortune of her miserable disobedience could be rectified immediately. For a time, her son Cain was perceived as the Mashiach. When Abel was born, there was no messianic pronouncement or fanfare. The record simply states that she bore Cain a brother who became a keeper of sheep (Gen 4:2).

Imagine her chagrin—nay, her broken heart—when Cain murdered his younger brother. Not only were her two gorgeous sons taken from her, but her messianic hopes were dashed as well. What could be more devastating to a woman's soul? But she loved her God tremendously and continued to hope to conceive the promised Messiah. When Seth was born, she joyfully and hopefully cried out, again in the dreadful pain of childbirth:

God has provided me with another *offspring* ...
(Gen. 4:25)

The KJV renders it as follows:

"For God hath appointed me another *seed* ..."

Poor, pitiable, lamentable, and disappointed Eve! We do not know the circumstances of her old age and death, but she went to the grave with the great assurance that she would one day be able to walk back through the gates of Eden into pure primal devekut and the loving embrace of her God. In her old age she totally depended on another woman in Israel to give birth to the Messiah. Since Jacob on his deathbed blessed Judah with being progenitor of the Messiah, every woman in that tribe hoped her womb would be the fortunate privileged one (Gen. 49:8–12). She could well have said, "Blessed is the womb from whence He comes."

Did Moses see it when he wrote those words about the "enmity" between Eve and the Serpent, and the "head" and "heel" wounds? He certainly knew the symbolism of the sacrificial animal without blemish as the symbol for the messianic sacrifice for sin. If you ask the "two Isaiahs" if they knew about it, they would answer, "Read the ninth chapter of our book and then the fifty-third chapter." The book of Isaiah certainly extolls the promised human Messiah as a penetration of humanity by divinity, ready to bear the penalty for sin; substitutive in suffering, He actually dies, but He continues as an intercessor. (See Adolf Neubauer's *The Fifty Third Chapter of Isaiah According to the Jewish Interpreters*, 1877, archival).

Ah! If only Eve were to have lived in Isaiah's time, she would have exulted in it. If only she could hear Isaiah's words, she would rejoice exceedingly. The babe she had hoped to carry in her womb qualified for those words:

> For unto us a Child is born, unto us a Son is given.
> And the government shall be upon His shoulder.
> And His name shall be called Wonderful, Counselor,
> *The Mighty God, The Everlasting Father,* the Prince of Peace.
> (Isa. 9:6 KJV)

Isaiah was assured that the Mashiach would be God Himself. Would Eve, in her wildest dreams, have been able to understand

Isaiah's suffering Servant and the death He was to die? Ah yes! She would. She witnessed her son Abel's murder at the hand of his brother who rejected the symbol of the messianic redemption in favor of fruits and vegetables, the sweat of his own brow. She knew that the sacrificial lamb without blemish was the messianic symbol:

> Therefore will I divide him a portion with the great, And he shall divide the spoil with the strong, Because he hath poured out his soul unto death, And he was numbered with the transgressors, And he bore the sin of many, And made intercession for the transgressors. (Isa. 53:12 KJV)

Only the *messianic functionality of Elohim* is qualified to bear the sins of others. *Messiah is Elohim's substance. Elohim is the Creator and He insists on being the Redeemer.* The rabbinic sages firmly believed that only God could forgive sins. And so it is! No human-only Messiah could pay such a high price. It was planned from eternity. Isaiah knew he was describing the messianic Redeemer. So did Eve understand the power and fulfillment of that "enmity" described to her outside the gates of Eden! What a major disastrous and devastating disappointment to her it must have been that she could not be the woman to bear Him, as she had hoped! She would have to wait for messianic salvation to be fulfilled down the corridors of time. She would wait in the grave. The words "Rejoice greatly, O daughter of Zion, Shout O daughter of Jerusalem. Behold they King cometh unto thee. He is the righteous Saviour" were written for her, the mother of all peoples, and also for all the daughters that were borne through her. How downtrodden have women been since the dawn of time! Ah! They have every reason to rejoice. Their King Messiah ben David would come to earth by *a chosen woman's surrogate womb.* What a glorious cosmic adoration for all downtrodden women, downtrodden by the chauvinistic male species! In my opinion, the surrogate womb accommodating the penetrance of humanity by divinity far surpasses the significance of circumcision as a surgical ritual witness to the Abrahamic covenant.

Rabbi Judah the Prince saw the crushing of the suffering Servant, whom he interpreted as the Mashiach. (See Sanh. 96b, 98b, Ber. 5a.)[57]

Primitive redemptive Judaism patiently waits with Eve for atonement, judgment, resurrection, perfection, and immortality. What a marvelous and exciting religion is redemptive Judaism! What a stupendous atonement is in store for Israel! What a resurrection it would enable! Daniel said that we shall shine as the stars of the morning! That was the very substance of the realization of Gershom Scholem, Israel's giant expounder of catastrophic acute Messianism.[58]

CHAPTER 4

The Murder of Abel

When Abel was born, Eve did not exclaim any messianic expectation. She already lived in the hope of Cain as the Messiah. Adam and Eve were good parents. They had told their children the story of Creation and their marvelous experience of pure devekut with God in Gan Eden. There was nothing more thrilling than loving God and feeling His love for them. The great magnetism of love starts with God. That love grew ever stronger as He effected their redemption. They shed bitter tears as they recounted the story of the loss of immortality by the great disobedience to Torah. They instructed their sons that one day they would walk back through the gates of Gan Eden and take them with them. They often took their young sons for walks to the gates of Eden to show them the prize they had lost. It was still a part of their bitter world of folly, regret, and tears. They shamefully recounted how they had been driven out. The record that God rejects disobedience is unbelievable but true. But He left those gates wide open.

Can you imagine God chasing the terrified weeping pair as they ran naked through the gates to the outside world? The angel brandishing the flaming sword still stood there at the gates to prevent their reentrance. The boys would ask, "Why was the sword being brandished? Was it threatening them? Would they be killed with it if they got too close or tried to enter?" The gates were still wide open, but the sword was there to exact the price of readmission. Those gates were never shut. Adam and Eve reassured their children that that sword would one day inflict a death wound on the Mashiach, and then they would be allowed back in. Mashiach had to approach the garden gates *from outside,* although He was God Almighty and dwelled inside. That is why He had to be born as a human—so He would be on the outside of the garden, *sharing the lot* of Adam and Eve, and all sinners, including all pious Jews. He had to be Adam and Eve's *substitute*. That is why they offered the lamb without blemish—a symbol of the Mashiach, who would *release* them from the death they had brought on themselves.

They did not yet fully understand what death meant for them personally, but they saw the lamb without blemish die before their eyes, because they killed it. The boys cried on seeing the poor blameless lamb's throat being cut. They watched the pumping blood escape in the agony of a death struggle as the little blameless lamb writhed in anguish. Their tears and shrieks were not for nothing. Eve herself cried quietly and gulped her choking sobs as she beheld the boys' innocent weeping. It was brutal. She comforted them as best she could with her own trembling hugs. The enormity of her disobedience wrenched a sorrow in her bereaved soul. Even Adam's tight embrace of her aching heart could not console her. Eve looked at Cain with sorrowful eyes as she envisioned his future messianic death, but there was hope in her brain.

As she contemplated her sadness, the enormity of God's love for her far exceeded the enormity of her guilt, blame, and sorrow. Mercy triumphed over Justice for her at those Gates, but Mashiach must die. The messianic death was the measure of her great God's colossal love for her, and the enormous, stupendous, and mighty messianic restoration of immortality. The messianic atonement was the only balm that soothed her wounded heart. She had been the only privileged woman to have the purest primal devekut with God. The hope that Cain was that man-child who would qualify to be the Mashiach that God had promised grew and thrilled her soul. Ah! Would Cain have to die by that sword brandished at the gates? Would she have to witness his death struggle at the gates when the angel cut his throat with that sword? Would she have to watch as his writhing gave way to the stillness of death? Did she really understand it? Could she be his substitute? For after all, it was all her fault. But *God had reserved that death for Himself.* He told her that it had to be her "Seed." No human had died as yet. But as the blood from the carotid arteries of the lamb's throat she had slit spurted on her, she knew the cost she and Adam had incurred. She realized that that death could only be accomplished by the Ha-Mashiach who was promised to her. When would Cain step forward to claim that function? How would it unfold? There were questions in her mind, and she built up a great deliverance in the expectations of her tender, inexperienced human psyche, now tormented by the regret for her sin.

They had taught their sons to present a sacrificial animal without blemish as a burnt offering, symbolic of the Ha-Mashiach expiation. The substitution of the symbol was easy to understand, but it was inexplicable in its denouement. It is still inexplicable to her Hebrew progeny who were entrusted with the Abrahamic covenant. But it is the only God-given solution planned from eternity. There is no other expiation, no other atonement; and no substitute will be entertained in God's immutable counsels. "Great is Jehovah the Lord. Mighty is His power. 'Tis heard in the whispering breeze, in the green scented forests." Listen to it. It is the Ruach Hakodesh convincing you of your need for the Ha-Mashiach salvation, offering you the gift of repentance. He pleads. It is His job allotted in eternity, the responsibility of God Himself.

Adam and Eve were somewhat at a loss, as they saw Cain was not religious as he grew up. When he moved out on his own, he did not offer any burnt sacrifice for the expiation of his sins. He would argue with them about the atonement: "Why would a just God decide to die for us when we were the ones to blame?" It was their fault, and they should suffer the consequences for their wrongdoing. Cain laughed it off when his mother told him that he was the Mashiach. Eve was greatly disappointed and cried herself to sleep on many a night. One day Cain told her that he did not feel divine. He was not the penetrance of humanity by deity. He felt he certainly was not the candidate. He thought it was absurd and impossible. He told them he was not going to be murdered at the gates by that angel and that they had better look elsewhere for a Mashiach. Their hopes for him grew dim and were extinguished. He was the prototype of Esau, who refused the birthright. Adam and Eve had already been looking at Abel, wondering quietly if he would fulfill their hopes. Despite Cain's rejection of the messianic candidacy imagined for him by his parents, the idea that Abel might be a stand-in Mashiach had made Cain intensely jealous. So Adam and Eve spoke to him one day. He was invited to their collective family worship. Perhaps they could encourage him on his spiritual pathway.

Cain was an agriculturalist and had beautiful orchards, vineyards, and vegetable gardens. Abel was a shepherd. There was no altar in Cain's garden, and he felt no need for any messianic hope. He had shared much of his produce with his parents. He was always uncomfortable when they spoke to him about spiritual matters. He wondered if there was any truth to this story of what had happened to them in Gan Eden. Gan Eden had disappeared while he was still a lad, and he began to think back as if it were a mystical dream. He did not like his parents' emotional outbursts when he found them weeping about a past that seemed totally unreal. "Grow up, Mom and Dad" is what he would say to them. But it bothered him that there was no other explanation for life on the planet. It bothered him to see his brother excitedly listening to his parents' stories about their devekut with God. Abel had carefully memorized all they told him and would spend time in meditation and prayer. He would go back on his own to where the gates of Eden had been. He made the spot a private tryst between himself and the promised Mashiach. Abel thrilled when His lamb without blemish on whose head he had made confession and whose throat he had slit would be consumed on the altar with fire that came out of the heavens. In those early days God was very close. Abel had a very firm belief in his redeeming God.

In an effort to influence Cain to godliness, Adam and Eve invited him to their home for a joint offering to God. Abel had a lamb without blemish. Adam had several lambs without blemish available. Cain arrived without a lamb. Instead he brought a beautiful basket of luscious fruit and vegetables. Adam had built four altars in their yard when the children were boys. Now they each placed their lambs on their altars, except for Cain, who shockingly placed his fruit and vegetables on his altar. His father remonstrated with him, informing that they had told him many times that God had requested an animal without blemish, because it was God's symbol of the Mashiach. Cain was intransigent. He bluntly told them that God could take it or leave it. His produce was the product of the sweat of his brow and that God should respect him by accepting his gift. Adam was beside himself in trying to persuade Cain to offer a spare lamb he had in readiness. But he refused. He called on God in a loud voice as he looked up into the heavens: "This beautiful produce I offer you as a fitting emblem of the sweat of my brow. These are my good works! You had better accept it! I have obeyed your laws, worked hard all week, and kept your Sabbath. I have done many benevolent deeds. So my effort to please you is on this altar, a witness to my hard work."

Adam and Eve were heartbroken as they stood by after confessing their sins over the sacrificial animal without blemish and slitting its throat to let the blood gush out. Abel had done the same. Within minutes, lightning bolts from the sky consumed their sacrifices, while Cain's produce lay untouched on the altar, a witness to his own disavowal of the messianic sacrifice. Cain was furious. How dare God not respect his efforts to earn salvation by the sweat of his brow. He felt he had not broken any laws. He stormed off in a rage. The record says,

> The Lord paid heed to Abel and his offering, but to Cain and his offering He paid no heed. Cain was much distressed and his face fell. And the Lord said to Cain: Why are you distressed, and why is your face fallen? Surely, if you do right, there is uplift. But if you do not do right sin crouches at the door. Its urge is toward you, Yet you can be its master.
> (Gen. 4:4b–7)

The next day, Abel wandered by Cain's fenced-off lush property. He was leading a flock of sheep to a distant pasture. Cain was pruning his grapevines and saw him. He went out to talk to him. Abel was a quiet, humble fellow and approached Cain and gave him a hug. Cain shoved him away with the words "So you think you are better than I because God accepted your dumb lamb offering?" Abel got up from the ground a bit ruffled and faced his angry brother. In a quiet voice he said, "The lamb without blemish represents the Mashiach who will one day atone for our sins. That is why God requires it. We cannot substitute for the Mashiach. He is our Redeemer. The lamb is a fitting symbol. His blood atones for us." At that, Cain grabbed his brother's crook and bashed him to death. He was shocked at his deed and ran into his tent while Abel lay on the ground and bled to death.

When Abel did not return home that night, Adam and Eve went in search. They were shocked to see his lifeless body in a pool of blood, in the field outside Cain's property. They took the body home and washed it; and the next day, they buried Abel. The planet had experienced its first human death, its first murder, *the first attempted substitute for the Mashiach,* and the first great devastation of parents' hearts. And in the cosmic scene, a greatly distressed Elohim took refuge in the Most Holy Place of the heavenly temple and bowed His head in silence while His tears flowed as expansively as the River of Life. The multiverse stood still in shock. Adam and Eve wept bitterly as they saw the truth of God's Torah and the fruit of their disobedience. Cain's disobedience had caused his brother's death. He came out and faced his heartbroken parents. He had no repentance in his heart, as he still harboured the anger he felt against God for not accepting his offering. He now feared God would come after him and went into hiding. But God found him.

> The Lord said to Cain, Where is your brother Abel? And he said, I do not know. Am I my brother's keeper? Then He said: What have you done? Hark! Your brother's blood cries out to Me from the ground, which opened its mouth to receive your brother's blood from your hand. If you till the soil, it shall no longer yield its strength to you. You shall become a ceaseless wanderer on earth. Cain said to the Lord, My punishment is greater than I can bear … I must avoid Your presence and become a restless wanderer on earth …"
> (Gen. 4:9–13)

The Law of Moses would exact life for life as the commandment declared: "Thou shall not kill." But God did not sentence Cain to death. The commentators of *The Jewish Study Bible* aptly say in the margin, "***The man who could not tolerate God's inscrutable Grace, now benefits from it.***"[59]

Cain had broken the two great commandments in the Torah. He did not love his God with all his heart; nor did he love his brother as himself. There is no substitute for messianic expiation for these sins. God created and God insists on redeeming. He will not allow any competition, as He is a jealous God, and this fully extends to His act of redemption. Any form of substitution is the abomination of desolation spoken of by Daniel the prophet (Dan. 12:11). It is the grossest idolatry conceived. God will not tolerate it. No fruits or vegetables are accepted; no benevolent acts or deep study of Torah. Only His messianic blood is accepted as He pours out Himself to save humanity, His most loved object. Those who think their own best efforts post Eden are acceptable to God without messianic intervention are sadly mistaken. Messianic redemption is entrenched from eternity. God will not shift over to make room for benevolent acts or the deepest study of Torah as substitutes. Only His own blood will suffice. God will die to redeem. He is the Redeemer from eternity, long before the foundation of the world. Abel was a witness to it and Cain could not deny it. Those who try to substitute the messianic redemption will be like Cain. They avoid God's holy presence in His holy temple. They become restless wanderers on earth.

But like Cain, take heart. Sinners benefit from God's inscrutable grace—unmerited messianic redemption. This is an expression of the most beautiful and compassionate religion that is primitive redemptive Judaism. There is nothing comparable, nothing more reassuring, nothing more satisfying, nothing more electrifying, and *nothing more saving*. It is the expression of the great love of God. It will carry us back through the gates of Gan Eden, into immortality and into the embrace of our almighty God. Mashiach accomplishes it at the gates of Eden. The angel at the gates brandishes the sword only for Mashiach, not for us sinful mortals. We have a substitute. We can view His body as we pass by, lying on the ground in a pool of blood at the Gates of Gan Eden. Our feet will get wet with that blood on the ground. But Mashiach does not lie there dead for long. Elohim created and Elohim redeems. Elohim glorifies. "Out of His anguish He shall see it, He shall enjoy it to the full through His devotion" (Isa.53:11a).

As the sin-bearer of Isaiah 53 there are consequences of terrible suffering to God's Ha-Mashiach functionality—actually, a suffering that is God's alone:

> Is it nothing to you, *All ye that pass by?* Behold, and see
> if there be any sorrow Like unto my sorrow, which is done
> unto me, With which the Lord hath afflicted me In the day
> of His fierce anger. (Lam. 1:12 KJV)

This scripture has many applications. Some scholars attribute
the Lamentations to Jeremiah. Others point to a 586 BC date and a
different unknown author mourning the destruction of Solomon's
temple. The suffering of the Jewish people is another application.
But God is also very angry with sin, and Ha-Mashiach the sin-bearer
bears the consequence, because as Isaiah says, *God crushed Him.
God crushed Himself because He is our sole Redeemer.*

The Jewish Study Bible renders this verse thus:

> May it never befall you,
> All who pass along the road –
> Look about and see:
> Is there any agony like mine,
> Which was dealt out to me
> When the Lord afflicted me
> On His day of wrath?
> (Lam. 1:12)

The Messiah speaks here in human tones. But the agony is God's
own. Perhaps the writer is quoting from Psalm 22, or is it Isaiah 53?

The Jewish Study Bible margin commentary[60] points to the previous
verse, which talks about the terrible famine in Jerusalem. But it then
picks up on "His Day of wrath" and applies the scripture to the messianic
Day of the Lord and connects it with Isa. 13:13, Joel 2:1, Amos 5:18,
and Obad. verse 15. These are all considered messianic scriptures:

> Ah! You who wish for the Day of the Lord!
> Why should you want the Day of the Lord?
> It shall be darkness, not light! –
> As if a man should run from a lion
> And be attacked by a bear;

Or if he got indoors,
Should lean his hand on the wall
And be bitten by a snake!
Surely the ***Day of the Lord*** shall be
Not light but darkness,
Blackest night without a glimmer!
(Amos 5:18–20, emphasis added)

Amos thus deduces that *there is no escape for the Mashiach* on the Day of the Lord. It is the day the Mashiach lays down His life. It is the day His blood trickles, nay, flows as the River of Life. Then why is it dark and gloomy? Because it is the day of Mashiach agony. It is the cost of sin. Its consequences were planned from eternity. *It is the Redemption!*

Blow a horn in Zion,
Sound an alarm on My holy mount!
Let all dwellers on earth tremble,
For the ***Day of the Lord*** has come!
It is close –
A day of darkness and gloom,
A day of densest cloud
Spread like soot over the hills.
A vast enormous horde –
Nothing like it has ever happened,
And it shall never happen again
Through the years and ages.
(Joel 2:1–2)

The Messianic intent of Joel in this scripture cannot be disputed.

Therefore shall heaven be shaken,
And earth leap out of its place,
At the fury of the Lord of Hosts
On the Day of His burning wrath.
(Isa. 13:13)

On Isaiah's day of the *crushing* of the Mashiach, the earth will leap out of its place! The murder of Abel illustrates that *God intends to fully undertake all that is involved with redeeming His people.* He *will not* entertain any other modality. God is our redeemer. The Lord our God is one. Blessed be He. He is the lamb without blemish whose blood is splashed in the Most Holy Place to cause mercy to triumph over justice. The rabbinic sages were right to call God *Rachmana*:

> **While believing, therefore, that He is the Judge of the Universe, the Rabbis delighted in calling Him Rachmana (the Merciful), and taught that "the world is judged by Grace."** (Aboth 111. 19)

The Day of the Lord also brings doom to those who do not avail of messianic Redemption. In the final Day of Judgment, God will call into account those who sought redemption by their own devices. It will be their blackest night, without a glimmer.

CHAPTER 5

Does God Have a Plan?

The promise to the first family and their expectation and longing for the Mashiach is briefly covered in the previous two chapters. Questions must be asked: We know that God has a plan conceived in eternity. Is it a fixed timetable He has in mind? Or is His plan contingent on certain conditions? Why did He not redeem the human race early in the history of the world? Why did He not prevent a lot of heartache, suffering, and wickedness in our history by effecting His messianic functionality early in planetary history? These are perfectly viable and valid questions. The "enmity" between the Serpent and Eve has been inordinately prolonged in its denouement. What is involved with the "wounds" to be inflicted? What chronology is involved in the battle between the Serpent and the "Offspring" or "Seed" of the woman?

The whole world has been in misery since the fall of humanity. The history of Israel shows the great agony that the Hebrews have endured. They have lived hostage lives and died sorrowful deaths, or been murdered en masse in several countries down through the ages. The national devastations, diasporas, persecutions, concentration camps, gas chambers, and death ovens have been cruel past the breaking point. That mound of human ash in Poland piled up outside the Nazi gas chambers and ovens cries out to God: "Bring the kingdom!" God made a major statement concerning Abel's blood that was crying from the ground. So cries all the spilled Hebrew blood. There have been similar tribulations other races have endured, but none so devastating. The whole of humanity groans with feelings that cannot be uttered. Every death on the planet is a travesty of God's plan, and He takes refuge in the heavenly temple and sheds His own private tears as He agonizes in His eternity. The questions asked are not questions of presumption. Humanity is in tribulation with the wickedness and inhumanity expressed on a daily basis on the earth, not to mention the wars and the genocides. The questions are as legitimate as they are difficult to answer. We all feel like saying, "Please hurry up, God. We cannot endure anymore!"

Does God have any remorse? Is He blind to the longing in our hearts for Ha-Mashiach? Can He not see the suffering? Does He feel any of the pain we bear? Is He too busy elsewhere in the multiverse to notice our pitiful and painful plight? We admit that we are mostly the cause of our own condition and destiny, although many innocent ones suffer.

More questions, all very valid, are on the agenda. Many have lost their way by pondering these questions. When Job, whom the scriptures define as a righteous man, was at the height of his suffering, his wife advised him to "curse God and die" (Job 2:9 KJV). *The Jewish Study Bible* translates it "You still keep your integrity! Blaspheme God and die!" Many shortsighted pitiable ones have done just that. God understands and forgives. The Tanak and the Talmud attempt to answer some of these questions.

The Tanak emphasizes that God wants to save all born on the planet. Mashiach does not come for Israel alone; He comes for all humanity. Every individual is very special to God. Every one of us is a valued and precious Gilad Shalit in God's sight. God wants every last Jew and Gentile freed from sin and death. Some in Israel wanted to be too special in their own conceit, but the Tanak declared that being special and chosen was for a task. The wise rabbinic sages in the Talmud voted for inclusiveness, not exclusiveness, although some squabbled about the inclusion of the Gentiles (Ber. 61a; ARN xxxvi; Tosifta Sanh. X111; Hil. Teshubah 111. 5).[61]

The Abrahamic covenant was made for such a plan. Land, Torah, and Messiah were in the equation for the "blessedness of all nations," not simply to provide national and political independence for the Jews. Kings and governments have caused headaches and corruption in almost every instance, especially in the history of Israel. Solomon, reputed to be the wisest man, was also the most stupid. He massively established idolatry in the land.

Hosea has recorded some of God's heartache and longsuffering. "Ephraim is joined to his idols, let him alone" (Hos. 4:17 KJV) is a heartrending cry from the Almighty. Can you not hear Him? Hosea's wife left him on adulterous forays five times, but he forgave her each time and took her back. God used that as an illustration of His forgiveness and longsuffering with Israel. Moses, the originally reluctant leader of Israel in slavery, would not entertain God's impatience with Israel after the worship of the golden calf for even a moment. He was a type of messianic intervention and determination:

> And the Lord said to Moses, I see that this is a stiff-necked people. Now, let Me be, that My anger may blaze forth against them and that I may destroy them, and make of you a great nation. But Moses implored the Lord his God, saying, Let not Your anger, O Lord, blaze forth against Your people, whom You delivered from the land of Egypt with great power and a mighty hand ... Turn from Your blazing anger and renounce the plan to punish Your people. Remember Your servants, Abraham, Isaac and Israel, how You swore to them by Yourself ... Now, if You will forgive their sin, [well and good]; but if not erase me from the record which You have written.
> (Ex. 32:9–35, selected passages)

God's frustrations with Israel are well documented in the Tanak. *But He has a plan.* The Talmud records a harrowing story of the sadness God feels as He weeps in His desperate longing and loneliness:

> ... it is related that after the Destruction of the [Second] Temple, the Emperor Vespasian dispatched three ship-loads of young Jews and Jewesses to brothels in Rome, but during the voyage they all threw themselves into the sea and were drowned, rather than accept so degraded a fate. The story ends with the statement that on beholding the

harrowing sight: The Holy Spirit wept and said, For these do I weep." (Lam. i. 16; Lam. R.I. 45)

The Holy Spirit is God indeed, and weeps over every such cruel infliction. In the chapter dealing with the Patriarchal Era we see God in a state of deep sorrow:

And the Lord regretted that He had made man on earth, and ***His heart was saddened.*** (Gen. 6:6)

God has a plan. He certainly does, and it was carefully put in place in the years of bygone eternity. His powers of functionality to provide the return to perfection and immortality were expressed in Ruach Hakodesh and Ha-Mashiach. He would work simultaneously to provide repentance and atonement. These would have to precede the Utopia. Malachi vehemently predicted it. According to the predictions of Daniel and Isaiah, God would penetrate humanity first and pay the price He Himself had named. Then history would end catastrophically and the graves would be opened to immortality. That is the plan. There would be the element of surprise in the timing, but He told us clearly what to expect. It is all in the Tanak and needs to be carefully deciphered and extracted. Its tanakian authors were awed by it so much that they presented it, as I have said before, like a rich fruit salad. He will penetrate humanity, provide the atonement, and then establish the messianic kingdom. He will be King of Kings and Lord of Lords and reign forever. It is all in God's plan. *He created, He will redeem, and He will glorify.* The Lord our God is one. Blessed be He.

How will we cope with His delays?

And the Lord answered me, and said, Write the vision, and make it plain upon tablets, that he may run that readeth it. For the vision is yet for an appointed time, but at the end it shall speak, and not lie; though it tarry, wait for it, because it will surely come, it will not tarry.
(Hab. 2:2–3 KJV)

The psalmist advocates patience and trust as we urge the Lord to hurry up:

> O Lord, You have been our refuge in every generation.
> Before the mountains came into being,
> Before You brought forth the earth and the world,
> From eternity to eternity You are God ...
> You have set our iniquities before You ...
> All our days pass away in Your wrath;
> We spend our years like a sigh ...
> Turn O Lord! How long?
> Show mercy to your servants ...
>
> O you who dwell in the protection of the Most High ...
> He will cover you with His pinions;
> You will find refuge under His wings.
> (extracts from Ps. 90 and 91)

Faith is the answer to our impatience and groanings. "The just shall live by his faith." God will take advantage of our faith to implement His plan.

CHAPTER 6

The Patriarchal Messiah

Scholars begin the patriarchal era with Adam. There are two peaks of estrangement from God in this period: the Flood and the Tower of Babel. The patriarchs were Seth, Enosh, Kenan, Mahalalel, Jared, Enoch, Methuselah, Lamech, and Noah (Gen. 5). It is possible—and very likely, according to some scholars—that some patriarchs have been left out. There may have been several generations between those named. It may be that only the God-fearing ones are mentioned.

Eve's messianic hopes at the time of Abel's murder were still high, and when Seth was born, she again exclaimed, "God has provided me another *offspring* instead of Abel ..." (Gen. 4:26). This reveals that she had substituted Abel for Cain as the Messiah, in the hope that she could still beget the Messiah. But it was not to be. Eve understood perfectly that the promised "Seed" of deliverance and re-entry to Eden was the Messianic Redeemer. Seth had a good influence on society because the record says, "Then began men to call upon the name of the Lord" (Gen. 4:26 KJV). The impression we get is that Adam and Eve had many children unnamed in the Tanak who populated the earth rather quickly. The ones that ardently hoped of reentering Gan Eden are the ones named. They were the spiritual leaders. Seth was a good influence on his relatives and urged them to turn to the Lord. How soon they had forgotten! How did Seth do this, and what did he tell them? It had to be the message of hope for the Mashiach. The information provided tells of their ages, the sons who were heirs in the succession of religious leaders. There must have been run-of-the-mill patriarchs in the succession.

One of the patriachs was outstanding. He was Enoch, a deeply religious man, very close to God, for the record states, "And Enoch walked with God, and he was not, for God took him" (Gen. 5:24 KJV). What a wonderful fate, to be taken by God alive. Did Enoch bypass the Mashiach and attain paradise with God? Was he granted

70

provisional immortality? Was God guilty of favoritism? What does "walked with God" mean? Adam and Eve had done that in Gan Eden, because God used to come around "in the cool of the day" (Gen. 3:8 KJV). *The Jewish Study Bible* translates it as "the breezy time of the day." Our great God is a Spirit, and this is a very apt description of His visitation with the first couple. Ruach Hakodesh is a very fitting name for the Holy Spirit, likened to the wind, the breeze. It was devekut time for Adam and Eve, until that fateful day when they heard His footsteps at the appointed time for devekut. They had hidden themselves from Him because they had sinned, in the way that most of us hide from Him when we have deliberately sinned against Him. Even worse, we ignore Him.

Enoch knew and trusted His God and was very close to Him. Had Enoch reached perfection of character to qualify for reentry into Gan Eden? God had not put a sign up outside the gates of Gan Eden that said, "Come back and gain reentry if you keep the law perfectly. I will let you back in if you show Me you are 100 percent perfect." God knew that was impossible. The sign outside the gates of Eden was a sword requiring the shedding of messianic blood. Enoch was not always righteous, according to the Bavli, not even in heaven. He committed a misdemeanor according to the rabbis. (See b Ber 7a; b Hag 15; 3 Enoch; Hekhalot Rabbati, and Merkavah Rabbah). Rabbi Ishmael b. Elisha (Aher) accused Enoch of pretending to be YHWH, and not, as he was, an "exalted angel." Pretending to be God is a massive sin. According to the Bavli story, Enoch was flogged in heaven for this pretension. The question must be asked: why was he not dispatched forthwith to Gehinnom? We conclude that he was deemed righteous only because he had been forgiven. The only way back was through Mashiach atonement. No other way had been outlined. Enoch was "taken" having obtained a "credit note" from the Mashiach. God indulged Himself. He has His favorites, even though they are blemished! He wanted some "firstfruits" to keep His own hopes up. He missed Adam very much. Perhaps He took Enoch's wife as well. Women have not gotten the equal attention they deserve.

The Tanak has Enoch in heaven with no new status. But some rabbinic sages have greatly elaborated the story of Enoch, creating a "hypostasis of God" out of him. They created the *Metatron*. It is recorded in the Bavli (b Sanh 38b; ShemR 32:4) and Hekhalot literature. Peter Schafer and Daniel Boyarin have written extensively about the Metatron. Schafer describes the rabbinic elevation of Enoch to Metatron according to some sages, as follows: "fully human and was chosen by God to be transformed into a divine being," and "that exceptional human being who ascended to heaven and was transformed into the 'LESSER YHWH'." (See *The Jewish Jesus*, by Peter Schafer, chapter titled "God and Metatron," pp. 138-147; also see *Beyond Judaism: Metatron and the Divine Polymorphy of Ancient Judaism*, by Daniel Boyarin, pp. 323–365). The noncanonical books of First Enoch and Fourth Ezra are used in support of the exaltation of Enoch to being a "Lesser God" to Elohim.

On the basis of these apochryphal books some scholars have tried to transform Enoch into the Son of Man of Daniel chapter 7, and thus as the Messiah himself. This is a theological absurdity (see *The Messiah pp. 145-191)*. At best it may be said that Enoch was a type of the Son of Man, just as Moses and David were. But the author of the Similitudes got carried away with the ascent of Enoch to Paradise, and overstepped the typology and tried to transform Enoch into God Himself. This is grossly un-Tanakian. Enoch's metatron status is totally unacceptable in monotheism and borders on blasphemy. There is controversy among scholars that 1 Enoch is a Jewish document with interpolations. On current evidence I believe it is, and I agree with Professor M. Black, emeritus, of the University of St. Andrews, that its dating is ca. first century BC – first century AD (see essay *The Messianism of the Parables of Enoch* in the book *The Messiah*, p. 162).

I reject the whole tradition of this minority rabbinic doctrine, as I do not accept the idea of hypostases of God. The Metatron is part of the fanciful imagination of some rabbis. It destroys monotheism and is polytheistic and idolatrous. Perhaps here is the reason the Sanhedrin rejected 1 Enoch from inclusion in the Tanak.

The prophet Elijah was also translated to heaven. He too had a "credit note" and was given a special pass on the Mashiach's merit. But the Mashiach had not yet come, and there was an unpaid debt posted in the Bank of Heaven that had to be paid in the future. It has collected a lot of interest. Fancy God being in debt! Enoch and

Elijah were reminders to God of His promise to redeem the world: "Don't forget we are here. You have a job to do down there! Don't get too busy with other projects in the multiverse. You owe us a lot. We want a permanent status here." They remind Him on a daily basis to "Bring the Kingdom."

Neither Enoch nor Elijah was perfect, but they were there in lieu of the messianic atonement. God was using Enoch and Elijah to encourage everyone to trust in the messianic hope, which He showed was real. Messianic hope was the central theme in the patriarchal lineage. Messianic hope is the central hope of every Jew that ever lived. The sacrificial animal without blemish was the symbol of messianic redemption. Will anyone contradict that verity? The Talmud is of the opinion that God also took Moses to heaven (Yoma 4a; Pesiktah Rabbah 20:4).[62] God had to disinter Moses from his grave in Mount Nebo, for he was buried in a little valley opposite the Moabite village of Beth Peor. (Deut. 34).[63] I went to Mount Nebo looking for the grave. My Jewish guide said, "Your effort is wasted; the grave is empty. He has been taken to heaven." These men are up there to constantly remind God that He has an obligation to redeem the human race!

Noah was the final patriarch to be in the limelight in the Tanak. The preamble to Noah was population explosion, prosperity, and preposterously utter wickedness:

> When men began to increase on the earth and daughters
> were born to them the "divine beings" saw how beautiful
> the daughters of men were and took wives from among
> them that pleased them.
> (Gen. 6:1, 2)

Many translations of this chapter do not use the words "divine beings" but instead employ the words "sons of God." The context of this chapter draws a contrast between two classes of people: "Children of God" and "Children of men." There were no such beings with a divine origin—that is, beings invested with deity. Nowhere in the Tanak is there a mention of deity being shared with ordinary created beings. The Ha-Mashiach would come as a penetration of humanity by Elohim Himself. *Deity and Divinity in tanakian Judaism are appellations of God alone.* In monotheism, no one else is divine except God. In the creation story and in the context of the post-Eden disobedience and death, there were no divine deities wandering around the earth having sex with humans and producing children. There were giants, but these were superior only in stature and not invested with divinity. The Nephilim are discussed in Genesis as the offspring of "divine beings" cohabiting with the "daughters of men." The major concept here leading to the wickedness of the antediluvian world is the intermarriage of the "sons of God" with the idolatrous "daughters of men." This intermarriage between the monotheistic children of God with idolatrous daughters of men has perhaps been one of the greatest besetments of Israel, as in the case of Esau and Solomon. They both lost the birthright. Malachi was vehemently upset by such marriages, as they were very prevalent in his day.[64] According to the record, the only family left of the "Children of God" who had not become idolatrous were Noah's family. Immediately after mentioning this intermarriage, which had led to the almost complete apostasy of the antediluvian monotheist community, this is what Moses records:

> The Lord said: My breath shall not abide in man forever …
> [The KJV renders this as "My Spirit shall not always strive with man."] The Lord saw how great was man's wickedness on earth and how every plan devised by his mind was nothing but evil all the time. And the Lord regretted that He had made man on earth, and His heart was saddened. The Lord said, I will blot out from the earth the men who I created … But Noah found favour with the Lord. (Gen. 6:1–8) [The KJV renders this as "But Noah found Grace in the eyes of the Lord."]

After Mashiach was promised to redeem humanity, God indulged Himself and took Enoch yonder. And now He has cancelled Mashiach for the antediluvians. In summary judgment, he sends the antediluvian world to Gehinnom. Ah, but is not His justice greater than His wrath, and does not His compassion exceed His justice? The record brandishes the Mashiach again by offering the *grace* that Noah found. God had Noah preach to the antidiluvians for 120 years before He finally gave up on them. One day we will ask God for His reasoning behind this difficult decision. We will also ask Him about Sodom and Gomorrah.

While the wickedness of humanity exceeds all limits, His mercy is more abundant. God still wants to salvage His most valuable possession in the multiverse. Mashiach was rejected completely by the antediluvian world. The acceptance or rejection of Mashiach will be *the final judgment of all humanity.* The Talmud declares that the big question in the Judgment will be ***"Did you hope for the Salvation of the Messiah?"*** (Shab. 31a).[65]

The Torah will be the standard, but there will be no one there who will measure up one hundred percent to qualify. We all have not kept it perfectly; nor can our sinful "dust of the ground" genetic structure keep it perfectly. But we *all* can appropriate the messianic redemption. That does not give us license to antinomianism. We must all continue to fight tooth and nail to keep the law of God, for that is the proof that we trust in Mashiach.

Had the antediluvian world accepted repentance and believed in Mashiach, they would not have been destroyed. The flood would not have wreaked its destruction. But they were too busy in their own pursuits.

We can escape Gehinnom only by messianic redemption. God created; God must and will redeem. There is no alternative. No fruits and vegetables, no benevolent acts, no deep study of Torah, and no mystic private devekut will suffice as salvific redemptive agents. They all fit into a good sanctified life, but only messianic redemption is salvific. Messianic blood must be shed on our altars. That is basic in primitive tanakian Judaism, and it is implemented in the Most Holy Place.

God is constantly on the lookout for humans He can engage to carry out His will. And He found Noah. Noah's preaching was the vehicle for warning the antediluvian world. Noah's first act after the flood was to offer a lamb without blemish, signifying messianic deliverance. Noah's sons Shem, Ham, and Japheth repopulated the area. But their progeny again forgot God. They feared the danger of another flood. Instead of trusting Mashiach for their future, they built the Tower of Babel to escape the Judgment of God. This was another blatant substitute for the Mashiach, another abomination:

> They said one to another: Come, let us make bricks and
> burn them hard … Come, let us build us a city, and a tower
> with its top in the sky, to make a name for ourselves …
> (Gen. 11:1–9)

And God confounded their language. Bricks and mortar and tall towers are no safeguard in the Judgment. They are not messianic substitutes or escapes.

Abraham, the last patriarch before the Jews were inaugurated as the chosen people, relied totally on the Mashiach.

CHAPTER 7

Abraham's Messiah

As a young man, Abraham held a deep commitment to his patriarchal Oral Torah. It took shape as an emotional conversation with his God. It commanded the entire plan of his life. It led him to smash the idolatrous livelihoods of his father and grandfather. They had become idolaters whose existences had been totally given over to ignoring the worship of YHVH. Was he a lone voice in the idolatrous world of Ur of the Chaldees, a part of the civilization of Sumerian Mesopotamia? He was not that far removed from Noah, being born from the Arphaxad line of Noah's son Shem. Abraham's father and grandfather bought and sold idols. Obviously they had decided that the coming of the Mashiach was a figment of the imaginations of their forefathers. Messianic expectation was of no value to them. Their modern world was one of making money and enjoying wealth and luxury. Their idol worship was titillating and involved immorality. Their civilization, not so far removed from the destroyed antediluvian world, seemed to have no memory of that destruction. They had become just as depraved. Mashiach had long since been forgotten as the redemption planned for them by God to restore them to immortality and Gan Eden. God had designed Mashiach for them from the days of eternity. But it had been discarded in preference for indulgence of the lusts of the flesh in Ur of the Chaldees. They were trapped in its thrall.

It is a great wonder what had inspired this vibrant young man to have committed the oral Torah to memory and had given him the determination to be an instrument in the hand of God Almighty. God found him to be a refreshing experience and had become quite dedicated to him, as he had to God. God loved him deeply. He was like a lotus flower blooming from the filthy mud that was Ur, with which his father and grandfather had become synonymous. Abraham had come to God's rescue, and God loved him for it. The relationship with Abraham became God's preoccupation as the Almighty devised

His *Chosen People plan to redeem the world.* The calling of the Chosen People was not the cunning device of convenience, concocted by the Jews for their own selfish aggrandizement. They were the plan devised by God with Abraham, who was perhaps the only one who knew the Oral Torah, apart from Melchizedek, king of Salem, with whom God also had a special relationship. Here were the only two leaders who carried the banner of Mashiach in the entire world. God had certainly been reduced to poverty in His influence in the world He had created and desired to redeem. In human words, God had gone to bed frustrated and depressed every night for years, weeping like a jilted lover till blissful sleep gave Him some relief. Or was He sleepless with worry? *"He who keepeth thee will not slumber. Behold He who keepeth Israel shall neither slumber nor sleep"* (Ps. 121:3,4 KJV). God remembered the rainbow promise He had made to Noah, and He was loathe to consider destroying "lost" humanity again for not accepting Mashiach. Abraham and Melchizedek brightened His eternity again. Such was the cost of bestowing free will to humanity. God had not desired a forced or fixed love. So as He had enlisted Noah, He now enlisted Abraham.

At this point it is of value to consider this person *Melchizedek.* Moses describes him as "King of Salem, and Priest of the Most High God." (See Genesis 14.) King David described him as a messianic type. He was the lone witness to Elohim in the wild land of Canaan:

> Thou art a priest forever after the order of Melchizedek.
> (Ps. 110:4 KJV)

> You are a priest forever, a rightful king, by My decree.
> (Ps. 110:4)

Psalm 110 is one of the greatest messianic psalms. The Talmud states so (Midrash Book One, 19, 29; Midrash Rabbah Gen. LXXXV, 9; Numbers XVIII, 23; Midrash Yelamdeim). Rabbi Ovadiah ben Sforno is quoted to assert that Psalm 110 is dedicated to King Messiah.[66] I will discuss it again when I present the messianic understanding of King David. This psalm is a link with Daniel 7. Suffice it now to note the gist of this totally messianic psalm:

The Lord said to my Lord,
Sit at My right hand while I make your enemies your footstool.
The Lord will stretch forth from Zion
Your mighty sceptre: hold sway over Your enemies!
Your people come forward willingly on Your day of battle.
In majestic holiness, from the womb, from the dawn,
Yours was the dew of youth."
The Lord has sworn and will not relent.
You are a priest forever,
A rightful king by My decree.
(Ps. 110:1–3)

There are several observations to be made here:

1. "The Lord said to my Lord" is a soliloquy, and David, as the speaker and interpreter, is naming God as "The Lord" and the Ha-Mashiach functionality as "My Lord." God tells His messianic functionality to sit at His right hand, interpreted to mean God is telling His messianic functionality to act strongly. As His Ha-Mashiach functionality He is about to penetrate humanity to perform the work of redemption. God is about to act to redeem, and the Psalmist is writing it in human terms. There is a definite parallel in the book of Daniel, where the Ancient of Days commissions "One like a human being" to whom is given "Dominion, glory and kingship … An everlasting dominion that shall not pass away." (Some scholars see a hypostasis of God in this Psalm.)
2. Mashiach would be born "in majestic holiness *from the womb*" on the planet earth." Divinity has penetrated humanity. Why else use the word "womb" here in messianic context? God had planned this penetrance *from the dawn.*
3. God's Mashiach functionality was instituted "from the dawn" of His plan for Creation, devised in the eternity of God's mind. He is delighting in His plan to procure the redemption Himself. He does not share the Worship of humanity, the Creation of humanity, and He will not share the implementation of the Redemption of humanity.

The talmudic rabbinic sages did not comprehend the penetration of humanity by divinity but still regarded this psalm as messianic, which it certainly is.

4. The "dew of youth" is fleeting. The dew sparkles like the grandeur of diamonds but evaporates, majestic nonetheless. A messianic sojourn on the planet earth in human form would be a very transient one in this context. But it would be resplendent like the morning dew and establish an everlasting redemption.

These aspects will be discussed further when considering David's understanding of the Mashiach.

Returning to Abraham and Melchizedek, we note that *The Jewish Study Bible* omits the reference to Melchizedek in this psalm, preferring to translate verse 4: "The Lord has sworn and will not relent, You are a priest forever, a rightful king by My decree." The KJV translates it as "The Lord has sworn and will not repent, Thou art a priest forever after the order of Melchizedek."

It is worthwhile for those who know the language to look at Psalm 110:4 in the Hebrew: "Nis'Ba y'hwah w'lo yiNachem aTah-khohen l'olam al-Div'rany mal'Kiy-tzedeq."

The margin of *The Jewish Study Bible* on page 1408 comments that despite translating the words "mal'Kiy-tzedeq" (interpreting and translating it as two common nouns) as "rightful king" or "king of righteousness and justice," it can also be translated as the personal name "Melchizedek." In this case there is a definite allusion to Genesis 14:18. The messianic Psalm 110 is more in tune with this reference of Moses to Melchizedek, a messianic figure.

The talmudic discussion of Melchizedek names him as a Semite, and as such being "present in Noah's Ark in the loins of his forefather" Shem.[67] The translation "Melchizedek" is indeed more appropriate in this psalm. Melchizedek is described as priest of the Jerusalem temple in the Talmud, Midrash, and Targum. This is also present in Chazalic literature.[68] Chazal, or Hazal, is derived from *Hakhameinu Zikhronam Liv'rakha*, literally "rabbinic sages, may their memory be blessed." Chazalic literature assumes the authority to be the final interpreter of the Tanak, from which there is no dissent. Specifically the Targum Jonathan, the Targum Yerushalmi and the Babylonian Talmud writings are in this declared jurisdiction.[69] The Jerusalem Targum also records this lineage of Melchizedek as a Semite, monotheist, king of Salem, and priest of God Most High. Strangely, he disappears from view after rejoicing in Abraham's victory over the kings who had sacked Sodom and the cities of the plain and taken Abraham's nephew Lot captive. Melchizedek rejoiced in that victory, prepared a feast for the victors, and gave Abraham presents. Abraham himself paid tithes to Melchizedek, thus acknowledging him as a superior priest and messianic figure. (See Genesis 14.)

With this talmudic information, it is difficult to obviate the name Melchizedek when translating this messianic psalm (Psalm 110). His disappearance after purportedly bequeathing Salem to Abraham is unresolved. Salem was that parcel of land that was the future capital, the Holy City. An unknown Jewish writer in the Epistle to the Hebrews[70] made Melchizedek extremely important, naming the Messiah as a "priest after the order of Melchizedek." The Aaronic priesthood was not yet ordained, but the prototype is here enshrined. The Mashiach is accented here as a "High Priest" and "Intercessor" for humanity before God. The inference here is that Mashiach is not only the symbolic sacrificial lamb without blemish, but also the High Priest who takes the blood into the Most Holy Place and sprinkles it on the ark of the covenant and mercy seat in the presence of the Shechinah on the cosmic Day of Atonement. In the heavenly temple, Mashiach offers His own blood as the sacrificial victim and is the mediator (cf. Michael standing in the Most Holy Place of the heavenly temple, Ber. 4b; Ex. R. 11. 5).[71]

Abraham would offer his son to God on that hill in Salem called Mt. Moriah, today's temple mount. This topic will be discussed further later.

Back to the story of the young man Abraham in Ur of the Chaldees. He had a vision of the Messiah after he destroyed the idols of his father and grandfather. God wanted an agreement with him, and that is when the Abrahamic covenant was made. Its sole aim was to give the world the benefits of messianic Redemption. In the contract, Israel would become the Chosen People to whom would be given the Promised Land. They were also to be the keepers of the Torah:

THE ABRAHAMIC COVENANT

The Lord said to Abram,

> Go forth from your native land
> And from your father's house
> To the land I will show you.
> I will make of you a great nation,
> And you shall be a great blessing
> I will bless those who bless you
> And curse him who curses you;
> And all the families of the earth
> Shall bless themselves by you.

(Gen. 12:1–3)

No one, Jew or Gentile, will argue regarding the messianic intent of this covenant and mission entrusted to Abraham. It was not primarily to provide Israel with a piece of land on which to build a nation, although that was part of the accrual of its benefits. It was to give the world the gift of the Messiah, who would provide atonement for sin (sin was disobedience to Torah) and usher in the messianic kingdom and the restoration of perfection and immortality. There would be restoration of Gan Eden and pure devekut with God. That was promised to Eve, Abel, all the patriarchs to Noah, and now to Abraham and his progeny. The covenant contained Land, Torah, and Mashiach. Mashiach was the culmination of the covenant. Circumcision was instituted for male Jews as a sign of the covenant. Israel got "side-tracked" with circumcision so that it became the important ritual and the covenant it signified was forgotten.

When the covenant was made with Abraham, he had no children, but in faith he believed God and made his journey with Sarah and all his flocks and herds from Ur to Hebron. There Abraham and Sarah grew old. Abraham even purchased the Cave of Machpelah for their bones to be buried in. Sarah was barren. She thought she was doing the practical thing, but she was running ahead of God by getting Abraham a son from her handmaid Hagar. God was not happy with this arrangement and visited them *in fleshly human form* (under the terebinths) to insist that it would be the fleshly child of both Abraham and Sarah. "Sarah laughed" with the prospect of getting pregnant in her old age, but God reprimanded her. When she did get pregnant, she likely felt like Eve and looked forward to begetting "a man from the Lord." Did she wish or wonder whether it would be the Mashiach? Surely she did understand the messianic import of the covenant. She may have been showing a little scepticism as she had no son to start a chosen people in the Promised Land. After Isaac was born, as the cantankerous old mother she then demanded that Abraham send Hagar and Ishmael away, and God sanctioned it. So Abraham reluctantly sent them away into the wilderness. In this deed God was showing that there is no atonement except through the "Promised Child." *"In thy Seed shall all the nations of the earth be blessed"* was a promise. Mashiach would come through their loins.

The Akeda (The Binding of Isaac):

The big and magnificent emphasis on messianic redemption came when Abraham was asked to offer the wondrous child of his old age as a sacrifice. God was making a cruel and unreasonable request. This incident in the history of the Jews has had no satisfactory explanation from the rabbinic sages. They were bewildered by it. There is, however, a plethora of modern authors who expound on it, fascinated by the unreasonable nature of God's request. God's request appears to have tinges of heathenism in it, and that may explain the paucity of rabbinic opinion on it. There is a rebellion of opinion from some scholars presenting an alternate story, insisting that Abraham was in fact disobedient to God and refused to sacrifice Isaac. Moses expressly forbade human sacrifices with the direst punishment. God did not want their children to be sacrificed. They were instructed to sacrifice only the animal without blemish as a symbol of messianic sacrifice.

Omri Boehm, a professor of philosophy in the New School of Social Research, a university in New York City, has drawn significant attention to it. He wrote about it in the *Vitus Testamentum*[72] and released a book entitled *The Binding of Isaac: A Religious Model of Disobedience*.[73] His bibliography reveals that many writers have discussed the story in recent times. In summary, he sees in Genesis 22:1–19 a brief "original" story in which Abraham disobeys God because God was being unreasonable. He sacrifices a ram caught in a thicket and goes home. Boehm postulates that this "original" story in Genesis was expanded by two interpolations, inserted at separate times. He sees the "proof" of this in the stylistic variations of the interpolations and the use of two different names of God in the story: "Elohim" and "Yahweh". He notes that Maimonides was uncomfortable with the story in Genesis 22 and believed that the binding of Isaac did not take place in reality but only in Abraham's unconsciousness. (See *Guide to the Perplexed II*, by Moses Maimonides p. 42.) Boehm states that Maimonides believed the Akeda was intended to make known two basic principles of the Torah: (1) the extent to which the limits of love for God and fear of Him might reach, and (2) that prophets consider as absolute truth whatever "comes to them from God" (*Guide to the Perplexed II*, p. 24). If, in fact, these postulated interpolations were inserted, my belief is that this story including these interpolations emphasizes the messianic suffering and death discussed in the Pesiqta Rabbati. (See chapter "The Messiah in the Talmud" in this my book). There the centrality of the suffering and death of the Messiah as a sacrifice for sin is painted as a scene taking place between God and the Messiah in heaven. There can be no tinge of heathenism in that scene in heaven. Messiah, the functionality of God Himself, couched in earthly terms as a son, undertakes to agonize and die for the sins of the human race. In Omri Boehm's postulation, I see a veiled political motivation in his wish to establish a "religious model of disobedience." He is opposed to the Zionist vision of the State of Israel. Omri Boehm's political views are well advertised. I do not endorse his political views or his view that the original story here is one of disobedience. It is not so in the Tanak which gives a very plausible story.

The friendship and understanding between God and Abraham is a wondrous thing. Did they really understand each other so well as this dreadful request implies? I view this event as a dare between them. God dared Abraham, so Abraham took God at His word and dared Him back. What a wondrous thought, but it was more than a dare for God. Messiah was the functionality of the Almighty, fashioned in the days of God's eternity, in His mind, and promised to Israel as the Messiah, the redemption. Some rabbinic sages agreed with this dictum. (Pes. 54a; Pesikta Rab. 152b).[74] God would create and God would redeem His fallen creation. His functionality would atone for lost humanity. He would be the sacrifice for sin. He would thus wipe the multiverse clean of disobedience to Torah. This messianic redemption was well established long before the Creation, and at Sinai Moses carefully outlined the messianic redemption first proclaimed outside the gates of Gan Eden. No one will detract from the significance of the murder of Abel in defending the symbol of messianic sacrifice. The rejection by God of Cain's substitute "fruits and vegetables" was the reason Cain murdered Abel.

And here God impressed on Abraham what the Mashiach would do. What a mighty concept—completely and utterly beyond our comprehension, but wondrous just the same! It was the greatest manifestation of God's love for us. The Jews were given to understand in the human idiom that Messiah would be born on the planet as God's Son. Did Abraham understand the full significance of God's request? "*Take your son and sacrifice him at a place I will show you*" was the grim and horrible request (Gen. 22:1). It was just as grim and horrible up in heaven when that burden was upon God. It is noble indeed that a man lay down his life for his friend! There is no tinge of heathenism in that. God made His point to Abraham. The suffering and death of the Messiah extolled in Psalm 22 and Isaiah 53 shows that God would indeed sacrifice His own Son.

Where was Melchizedek in this whole event? Had he disappeared, leaving Mount Moriah in Abraham's possession? This dreadful deed was to be perpetrated on the central spot in Salem, Melchizedek's domain. This deed would seal the property as the sacred and holy spot where the temple of Solomon would be built with the Most Holy Place upon it. Isaac's blood was to be shed here on this spot. Throughout the hundreds of years of the duration of Solomon's temple, and after its destruction and rebuilding, and after Herod would make it grander than Solomon's, *the Most Holy Place would stand on this sacred spot*. And on this spot stood the ark of the covenant and the mercy seat and the Shechinah for most of that time. And on this spot would the blood of the animal without blemish be splashed over a thousand years, *on the Day of Atonement*. This is the bloodiest spot in the entire multiverse, stained with the blood of the messianic sin offering.

This spot is what makes Jerusalem the Eternal Holy City. Our Jewish private guide through the rabbinic tunnels underneath the Western Wall stopped at a certain place. He said, "You are standing underneath the spot on which stood the Most Holy Place of the second temple." I stood there electrified by the great religion that is primitive redemptive Judaism. The roof of stone above us had been soaked with a thousand years of blood that had dripped down off the ark of the covenant and mercy seat, splashed there by the High Priest in silence on the Day of Atonement.

Then Abraham and his hapless son left the two servants behind with the words "We will worship and we will return." With the emphasis on the word "we," Abraham showed that if he gave his child to the Lord, the Lord would give him back to him. What great faith! So they journeyed to that place. Isaac asked, "Here is the rope, the wood, the knife, and the fire, but *where is the lamb without blemish?*" And Abraham made the soft but thunderous answer *that reverberated throughout the multiverse,* silencing the myriad heavenly beings as they collectively held their breath. That answer sounded in the highest decibels in God's ears: Abraham said, "God will provide." Indeed, the Almighty would provide, as *that was His prerogative and His plan from eternity. He was coming Himself* as His messianic functionality to provide redemption. No one could, and nothing would, be a substitute. Did Isaac understand what his father intended to do to him as he carried the load of wood on his back? Did he try to run away? The record says that he willingly submitted himself. What a mighty enactment of what would be the messianic atonement! Looking ahead in eternity, God never shrank from, nor will He ever shrink from, providing the redemption Himself. His human penetrance "willingly submits Himself." It is no small abomination to try to substitute His redemption.

Why are not all Jews enthralled by this spectacle? The rabbinic sages for millennia have been wondering why Moses recorded this story. None appear to have come to a satisfactory conclusion about its meaning. Why did not the rabbinic sages see this view? Why were they bewildered? Why is the Talmud not replete with its discussion and vaunting of its holiness and wonder?

Abraham Cohen, in his book *Everyman's Talmud,* discusses the Abrahamic sacrifice of Isaac under the heading of "God and the Universe," in the subsection of "Angelology." The Talmud labels Satan as a "fallen angel," one who repeatedly challenges God. The following explanation in the Talmud best illustrates, from the rabbinic point of view, Abraham's handling of God's "unreasonable" request:

> The Scriptures relate, "Abraham made a great feast on the day that Isaac was weaned" (Gen. 21:8). On this verse the Talmud tells: "Satan said before the Holy One, blessed be He, 'Sovereign of the Universe! Thou didst graciously bestow offspring on this old man [Abraham] at the age of a hundred years; and of all the feasts he made [at the weaning] he did not offer a single dove or pigeon [the cheapest of sacrifices] unto Thee!' He [God] replied to him, 'Did he not do it all for the sake of his son? If I were to tell him to sacrifice his son unto Me, he would immediately obey' (Sanh. 89b). Having in this way been responsible for the test, Satan proceeds to make it fail in its purpose. Samael came to see our father Abraham and said to him, 'Old man, old man, have you lost your senses? Are you going to slay a son who was granted to you when you were a hundred years old?' 'Certainly,' said Abraham. 'And should God impose still severer tests upon you, will you be able to endure them?' 'I will,' he answered, 'even stronger than this one.' 'But tomorrow He will say to you, Shedder of blood! You are guilty of having shed the blood of your son!' 'Even so,' said Abraham, 'I must obey.'
>
> Seeing that he [Satan] could not succeed with him [Abraham], he went to Isaac and said, 'Son of an unhappy mother, your father is going to slay you.' Isaac replied, 'Nevertheless I must submit.'
>
> Then Satan said, 'And all the beautiful garments which your mother made for you will pass into the possession of Ishmael, the enemy of your house; do you pay no attention to that?' Although the whole of it did not enter (Isaac's mind), part of it did; so it is written, And Isaac spoke unto

Abraham his father and said, 'my father' (Gen. 22:7).
'Father' is mentioned twice, indicating Isaac's wish that
Abraham should be filled with compassion toward him.
(Gen. R. LVI. 4)

This story from the Talmud is a tantalizing altercation between
God and Satan, taking place possibly in some level of heaven or the
nether region. But the Talmud misses the divine significance there is
to Abraham's sacrifice of Isaac.

Belatedly in Jewish history, Geza Vermes has made an excellent
effort to elucidate the theological significance of this story of the
sacrifice of Isaac by Abraham. In his book *Scripture and Tradition
in Judaism: Hagadic Studies* (1961), he offers a full messianic
explanation. But instead of crediting Isaac's willingness to lay down
his life as symbolic of the messianic redemption, Vermes attempts
to make Isaac the Redeemer of Israel, of whom he was only a type.
Vermes found the story in the Fragmentary Targum that comments
on Genesis Chap 22. In the event, which is labeled "The Binding of
Isaac," Isaac asked Abraham, "Where is the Lamb for the sacrifice?"
"And Abraham said, "The **Word** of the Lord shall prepare a Lamb
for Himself. If not, my son, you shall be the burnt offering. And they
went together with a quiet heart." The Targum says, "The eyes of
Abraham were turned to the eyes of Isaac, but the eyes of Isaac were
turned to the angels of heaven ... *and saw the Holy One*" (emphasis
added). Indeed, Isaac looked into the heavens and saw the Holy One,
the *messianic Redeemer* of Israel, Philo's Word, Logos, of whom he
was a type.

Vermes then cites Pseudo Philo's *Liber antiquitatum Biblicarum,*
Josephus, and *IV Maccabees* and some Midrashim, to connect
Genesis 1:22, Genesis 22, Job 3:18, Psalm 8:5–8, and Isaiah 53. I
strongly agree these scriptures he cites are messianic. Vermes calls
Isaac's willing sacrifice in allowing himself to be bound a martyrdom.
Vermes contends that it was as acceptable as the atonement for
sin, even though his blood was not actually shed. The shedding of
sacrificial blood was needed to expiate for sin, as Moses required in
Leviticus 16. Vermes accepts the symbol of Isaac as if his blood were
spilled in reality. Vermes then invests "The blood of the binding of

Isaac" as the efficacious blood of the Passover Lamb in Egypt and the blood of the evening and morning lambs killed for the daily sin offering in the temple. There is no doubt that Vermes concludes that Isaac's willingness to be the burnt offering makes him the actual messianic martyr who expiates the sins of all Israel. In disagreement with Vermes, I contend that Isaac was *not Israel's Messiah.* But he is indeed a *symbol of the Messiah.* I totally disagree that Isaiah was intimating (as Vermes implies) that the child to be born as the mighty God, the everlasting Father (Isa. 9:6), and the suffering Servant (Isa. 53) was retroactively referring to Isaac. Moses never did point to Isaac as the Messiah. The blood of the Lamb Without Blemish must be spilled in death for the expiation for sin. This was established at Eden and Sinai. Jacob never viewed his father Isaac as the Messiah. Jacob saw that his father, Isaac, had escaped the death the Mashiach would suffer. Isaac reassured his sons that the ram in the thicket was the symbol of the messianic sacrifice that he and his father, Abraham, had offered that day on Mount Moriah. Isaac never intimated to his sons that he was the actual Messiah. Moses saw the Messiah down the corridors of time, the "Prophet like unto himself," a messianic figure, symbolic of the one who was to come in the future.

I also point out that the Targum Fragment uses the language ***"The Word of the Lord shall prepare a Lamb for Himself,"*** and again, ***"Abraham worshipped and prayed the Name of the Word of the Lord."*** The use of "the Word" in the Targum Fragment is highly compatible with the Wisdom Literature, where the active messianic functionality—the Word, the Logos—effects both Creation and Redemption. (See chapter 13, "Messiah in the Wisdom Literature.") I strongly endorse the binding of Isaac as a symbol of the messianic expiation. But Isaac was not the Messiah in reality providing redemption for the whole world. This idea is extremely farfetched and unbiblical. Nowhere in Isaiah is there such an intimation. Isaac had a sheltered and pleasant life and was not the suffering Servant of Isaiah. Isaac was not the Messiah. Vermes sullies his own reputation as a Biblical scholar in this conjured interpretation.

God had determined that He would die in atonement in His "Begotten Son" penetration of humanity. Couched in human terms: ***"I will save your son, Abraham, but My Son must die!"*** This is coincident with the central role to be played by the Messiah as the suffering one of Psalm 22, used in the Midrash Pesiqta Rabbati. That is the gist of the messianic atonement for sin. But that is not all the Messiah has been designated to do in the eternity of God. Did Abraham understand it? The animal without blemish was provided as he unbound his son, and they worshipped together, offering up the messianic symbol of atonement. The entire universe burst into song. God had made His point. He Himself would condescend in the "Penetration" of humanity. He would sacrifice Himself, providing the human race with their redemption. The Lord our God is one; blessed be He. One day, Abraham's bones, now concealed in the Cave of Machpelah, shall arise clothed with perfect flesh and immortality because of messianic atonement.

Indeed, Geza Vermes has made a very admirable study of the sacrifice of Isaac by Abraham. He sees the messianic nature of the event quite clearly, as I have written above. (See also *Christian Beginnings* by Geza Vermes, pp. 99–103).

I was smuggled into the Arab Palestinian area of the Cave of Machpelah in Hebron, which is the principal section of the tomb. I was told by an Arab guide that only a few feet under the locked entrance to the underground cave, above which I stood, were the bones of Abraham and Sarah, Isaac and Rebekkah, and Jacob and Leah. My whole being thrilled as I stood there, and the panorama of the sacrifice on Mt. Moriah passed before my eyes. I saw Abraham place his son on that altar. I grasped the grandeur and condescension of the almighty God Elohim, in the functionality of Ha-Mashiach, which He had planned from the days of eternity. I trembled with the comprehension. I saw Abraham raise the knife to slay his son. And I realized that God spoke of Ha-Mashiach when He said, as translated by *The Jewish Study Bible*: "***You are My Son, I have fathered you this day***" (Ps. 2:7b). This is a human expression of the great and only penetrance of humanity by divinity as a divine birth. And it is for the Redemption.

God had offered King Ahaz a sign, anywhere from "down to Sheol or up to the sky." But Ahaz refused a sign, implying the futility of testing the Lord. Isaiah retorted impatiently:

Listen, House of David
Is it not enough for you to treat men as helpless
That you also treat my God as helpless?
Assuredly, *my Lord will give you a sign*
Of His own accord!
Look, the young *woman is with child*
And about to give birth to a son
Let her name him *Immanuel*
[Meaning with us is God].
(Isa. 7:10–14, emphasis added)[75]

Abraham's greatest thrill had to be the offering of Isaac, which prefigured the messianic sacrifice. God divested that great act of Abraham of any tinge of heathenism that the request ever implied. He intends to save all our children from the devilish act of human sacrifice. In the prophet Daniel's terms, the old man Abraham "sacrificed" his son Isaac as would the Ancient of Days commission the Son of Man. That spot on the temple mount would be the bloodiest spot on the planet. We will extoll the significance of "The Binding of Isaac" and his willingness to be sacrificed. He was indeed sacrificed in symbol—the symbol of the messianic expiation. With the gift of the precious son Isaac came the gift promised at the gates of Eden—Immmanuel, God with us. Blessed be the Lord God of Abraham; the Lord our God is one. God is not helpless with the sin problem. He comes Himself in our earthly thinking as "God's Wisdom." He demonstrates His mighty power in the redemption planned in eternity.

Jacob's Dream painted by Rafael

CHAPTER 8

Jacob's Messianic Dream

The dislocation of a hip is a very rare complication of a wrestling match. When it happens it is usually the result of a preexisting congenital malformation of the hip socket in its articulation with the head of the femur. Jacob had wrestled with God so tenaciously that God had to dislocate Jacob's hip to get away from him. Jacob has to be the most lovable figure in Israel's history. His disablement by God has a parallel later, when the nurse caring for Mephibosheth—the five year-old son of Jonathan, the son of King Saul—dropped him on her flight to save his life from David's pursuing army. But she picked him up and ran all the way to Lodebar, east of the Jordan, and hid him there. He suffered a greater injury than Jacob did, becoming a paraplegic. Both these injuries have a cosmic significance, as I shall show.

Jacob was the son of Isaac, a twin born to Rebekkah. He came out of her womb after Esau. The whole story of Jacob's deception and his stealing of the birthright from his slightly older brother was unnecessary. Esau had disqualified himself for several reasons. There is a similarity of the brothers Jacob and Esau with those other famous brothers, Cain and Abel. Jacob was a religious man, but Esau was not. Jacob was a shepherd, and Esau was a hunter. Jacob was a homebody, but Esau fell in love with idolatrous Canaanite women and was hardly ever at home. Jacob had memorized the Oral Torah and had sworn allegiance to the Abrahamic covenant. Esau never gave it a thought. Jacob would pick wives from his monotheist clan who worshipped YHVH, but Esau worshipped idols and had rejected the Abrahamic covenant and could not care less about the Mashiach. He had his own agenda and timetable and was preoccupied with sex. Esau was not a candidate to whom the Torah and the Covenant were to be entrusted. True, he needed its remedial application in his life. But he was having a lot of great sex and could not care less. Jacob was a dreamer and pledged his life to the mission of the Covenant and the Mashiach.

An attitude of God has been recorded by the prophet Malachi, which some have found hard to understand or accept. Some even allege that Malachi misspoke the words that were in God's mouth:

> I have loved you, saith the Lord. Yet ye say, In what way
> hast Thou loved us? Was not Esau Jacob's brother? saith
> the Lord; yet I loved Jacob, and I hated Esau ...
> (Mal. 1:2, 3 KJV)

Malachi's message is contextually hinged to the condemnation of Israel's offering of "tainted" bread, "blemished" sacrificial animals, stealing of tithes and offerings, and marriages with idolatrous heathen women. The animal without blemish was symbolic of the Mashiach, perfect deity, God Himself. And yet Israel brought what they knew was inappropriate, which they would discard as garbage. How dared Israel do this? It was illogical and irreligious thinking, a form of "saving money." After all, the animal was to be slaughtered and burned, so who cares if it was blemished? God was painted as being too fussy and devaluing the disabled. Esau is in the conversation here, in Malachi. He was totally engrossed with sex, and this had led him into idolatry to please the women he loved. His erectile mechanism was his total preoccupation, and he did not have time for Torah. Solomon should also have been castigated here for leading Israel into idolatry as a result of the women he kept. Esau did not bother to find repentance, which comes before the offering of sacrifices. He could not bother with symbolic animal sacrifices. He was the "fool who said in his heart: No, God" (Ps. 14:1). *The Jewish Study Bible* translates this more succinctly: "The benighted man thinks God does not care." Esau did not care enough even to bring a hypocritical sacrifice devoid of repentance. Esau showed a gross form of pride, and God abhors pride. It was his uncaring attitude that God was criticizing through Malachi. God hated Esau's attitude.

The parallel with Cain and Abel is strong. God's requirement of an animal without blemish, symbolic of Ha-Mashiach, *has no substitute.* After all, it was the symbol He had chosen to represent

Himself in the redemption of humanity. Fruit and vegetables, the produce of our own works, our meticulous observation of ritual, and our good deeds of benevolence are all good for sanctifying us, but they are not salvific and will not save us. As redemptive agents, these measures are an affront to God. The blood of the sacrificial animal without blemish is all that matters. It is the symbol of messianic redemption (Lev. 16). Jacob believed that with all his heart and soul. That is why God loved him. But this needs clarification.

The great imponderable here is not why God "hates Esau," but why He "loves Jacob." The reason God loved Jacob so much is that despite all his unworthiness, Jacob earnestly desired to be, and grasped the fact that he would be, the ancestor of the Mashiach. He wholeheartedly embraced the Abrahamic covenant, and that was his whole life, his all-consuming passion.

Esau and Jacob both knew that their grandfather Abraham had raised the knife to kill their father, Isaac, on Mt. Moriah. Jacob saw in that act the supreme sacrifice that God Himself would make to save all humanity. That was the overwhelming factor in Jacob's life. Isaac told his twins that story over and over again. They would come and beg to be told it. Jacob thrilled to recall that event—how their father had been so excited to make that trip with his father; how he had carried the wood for the sacrifice; how he had questioned their grandfather of the need for a sacrificial animal; how he suddenly realized that he was to be the sacrifice; how he was bound with the rope so nervously by his father, so that he could not run away; and how his father had pulled out the knife and raised it to cut his throat. The twins shuddered listening to the story. They trembled with fear on hearing about their father being tied up. They screamed in terror when they heard that the knife was raised to cut his throat. Nevertheless, they wanted to hear that story over and over again. Isaac always ended the story the same way. His father had spared him because God intervened to stop him. But one day in the future, the Mashiach, perhaps as one of their sons or one of their son's sons, God would come down from heaven and be born on earth. God Himself, as the Mashiach, would be their sacrifice for sin, to eradicate sin from the multiverse. And that knife that symbolized the end result of sin would be permitted to cut His throat, and He would die for all humanity so they could live eternally. He would do this because He was God and had the power to take up His life again.

And when the nights were too hot to sleep in the tent, they loved sleeping under the stars. They would ask where heaven was up there and from where among the stars the Mashiach would come down to be the sacrificial lamb. Jacob did not have to lie and deceive to get the birthright. It was his because he understood the longing in God's heart to reclaim His lost treasure. Humanity was and is God's greatest love object, His preferred love object in the entire multiverse. Jacob wept with the sadness that came over his deepest emotions when he recounted the near-death experience of his father. He sorrowed for God's great agony in the redemption. Isaac kept that knife that had nearly cut his throat as a keepsake of that epochal moment. The twins were allowed to view it. It reminded them that sin means death. It reminded them that one day the Mashiach would be "crushed" for the remission of the sins of the whole world. God's great love could not have been greater in their minds. As time went by, Esau ceased to care as his raging hormones took over and all his energies were spent in pleasuring his sexuality. But wherever he went, Jacob thrilled when thinking of the near-death experience of his father Isaac.

Indeed, Jacob's religion was a redemptive one. At Brook Jabbok, when he thought Esau was about to kill him, he quaked with the fear that the Abrahamic covenant was in danger were he to die. He clung to God so tenaciously for salvation that God had to dislocate his hip to get away from him. God changed his name to Israel on that spot: "And He said, thy name shall be called no more Jacob, but Israel; for as a Prince hast thou power with God and with men and hast prevailed" (Gen. 32:28 KJV).

Jacob's awesome position in the plan of God to restore the lost Eden overwhelmed him. He carried that conviction to his deathbed, where he prophesied of the Messiah. There was no one in Israel that had the vision and foresight of the messianic role as Jacob did, not even Moses. Moses magnified the Torah and meted out punishment for disobedience. Moses certainly felt the quake of Sinai as he instituted the symbol of the messianic sacrifice and the Aaronic Priesthood to administer it in Israel. But Jacob saw his redemptive God as the ladder to heaven and immortality. How marvelously privileged were Abraham, Jacob, and Moses! How sacred is the Abrahamic covenant! These men were pivotal in the powerful plans of the almighty Elohim—the plans that from the days of eternity were in His mind.

Jacob lived in the experience of the sacrifice of his father. It is possible that he had the rich legacy of the hugs of his grandfather Abraham, who had faced the killing of his own son before he had understood what exactly was involved in his calling by God. It was not just to have a homeland, a place to live in the world, although that was very vital. It was not just to repeat the Torah and make his children memorize it, although that was essential to the propagation of God's law. They all realized that they could not keep the law perfectly because of the weakness of the flesh. They grasped the provision that their sins would be forgiven and they would be reconciled to God through the messianic gift. Redemption was necessary to restore Gan Eden. That was the plan that existed before the foundation of the world. Jacob knew more than anyone else that he was pivotal in those powerful plans of the Eternal God. He dreamed about it at Bethel. He grasped it with all his tenacity at Jabbok. He faced his murderous brother with the assurance that God would not allow him to be killed. O that Israel today may be like Jacob and realize they are "princes" with God because of Jacob. But they need to be as dedicated to the Abrahamic covenant as he was.

Jacob had been a conniving liar and thief. He did not have to be, because Esau was not interested in the covenant or in comprehending the messianic mission. Esau also had screamed in terror as a child when Isaac told the story. But in his maturity he had said no to God. Having sex with idolatrous women and worshipping their idols was not compatible with propagating a messianic mission. He traded the birthright for a mess of pottage. Jacob had run ahead of God and adopted unnecessary measures to fulfill God's plans. His grandmother Sarah had set a bad example. She had assessed herself as old and barren, and in her humility she thought of herself as an impediment to God's great covenant made with her husband. She had tried to get a son from Hagar. This was a desperate attempt to facilitate God's plan. Rebekkah similarly aided and abetted Jacob's deception. There was now trouble between the twins. The peaceful home life was shattered. Esau determined to kill Jacob as soon as Isaac was dead, and he leaked his intention. He merely wanted to inherit all his father's possessions, all the riches that Abraham had left his father. So Isaac and Rebekkah packed Jacob off to her brother Laban in Padan-Aram. He voluntarily left all Isaac's possessions to be inherited by Esau and never contested the posthumous inheritance of Isaac's possessions. He could work for Laban and find a wife there from among her monotheistic relatives. God would materially prosper him. But listen to the farewell blessing that came from his father's lips as he said good-bye to this son he would never see again. Jacob practiced no deception for this blessing:

> And God Almighty bless thee, and make thee fruitful, and multiply thee, that thou mayest be a multitude of people; And give thee the blessing of Abraham, to thee and to thy seed with thee, that thou mayst inherit the land wherein thou art a sojourner, which God gave unto Abraham. And Isaac sent Jacob away. (Gen. 28:3–5 KJV)

Jacob realized then that his father was no longer deceived and had given him the birthright. The future of the covenant was far more important to him than his father's material possessions. He fled his home in fear of a murderous brother.

> And he came to a certain place and tarried there all night, because the sun was set; and he took of the stones of that place, and put them for his pillows, and lay down in that place to sleep. And he dreamed, and behold a ladder set up on earth, and the top of it reached to heaven: and behold the angels of God ascending and descending on it. And behold the Lord stood above it, and said, I am the Lord God of Abraham, thy father, and the God of Isaac: the land whereon thou liest, to thee will I give it, and to thy seed; and thy seed shall be as the dust of the earth ... **and in thy Seed shall all families of the earth be blessed** ... And Jacob awakened out of his sleep, and he said, Surely the Lord is in this place! This is none other than the house of God, and

> this is the Gate of Heaven ... And he called the name of
> that place Bethel ... And this stone I have set for a pillar,
> shall be God's house. (Gen. 28:1–22 KJV, emphasis added)

Jacob stood at the gates of Eden, and in his mind's eye he saw the angel with the brandished sword standing there. Did he wonder whether that sword was poised for him or for the Mashiach? Here is the Abrahamic covenant being reinforced with him. Here is *land, Torah, and Messiah.* God stood at the top of that ladder, and He wanted all humanity back in paradise. Jacob now felt the liability for the covenant. The dream of connecting earth and heaven through the Mashiach of the Abrahamic covenant would energize him for the rest of his life. O that modern Israel might understand the Abrahamic covenant and the messianic mission to restore humanity to paradise.

There is not the slightest shadow of a doubt that Jacob's religion was a redemptive one. He built altars and sacrificed animals without blemish. Did he see the perfection and deity of the Mashiach in that requirement for an animal without blemish? Why else would that be necessary? Mashiach was his ladder to heaven. Repentance came with the conviction of sin; confession, forgiveness, restitution, and atonement followed. Access to heaven was totally guaranteed by Ruach Hakodesh and Ha-Mashiach.

Jacob worked hard for his uncle Laban for fourteen years, accumulating two wives, two concubines, and several children, including eleven sons. One more son would be born later. And then he had another dream: "And the angel of God spoke to him in a dream ... I am the God of Bethel, where thou anointedst the pillar, and where thou vowed a vow unto Me: now arise, get thee out from this land, and return to the land of thy kindred" (Gen. 31:11–13 KJV).

On his journey back he built altars along the way and sacrificed at Bethel and at Shalem. He bought a piece of land at Shalem and called the altar Elelohe-Israel ("the mighty God of Israel"). (See Genesis 33:17–20 KJV.) His parents were now dead, and there was no homecoming. The fear that he would be murdered by his brother Esau remained.

Jacob sent messengers to Esau with a peace offering. They came back with the information that Esau was on his way to meet him with four hundred armed men. He was greatly distressed and filled with the fear of impending death. He strategized as a coward by sending the whole family ahead with all the flocks and herds he had accrued in Padan-Aram. Perhaps Esau might take pity on the women and children. At the very front he placed the peace offering he had prepared for Esau, thinking perhaps Esau might be placated by the offer of a rich present. He positioned himself at the end of the retinue, thinking that if the family was destroyed, he could still run away! He did not realize yet that God was planning to disable him so he could not rely on himself to escape death at the hands of his brother. Was running away his foolish idea? Quaking with fear, he hid himself in the gully in which flowed the brook Jabbok. As the night was falling, he was exhausted by worry and the lack of sleep and fell into a fitful slumber. He awakened when a man wrestled him into a stranglehold. At first he thought Esau had found him and was about to kill him:

> Jacob was left alone; And a Man wrestled with him until the break of dawn. When He saw that he had prevailed against Him, He wrenched Jacob's hip at the socket ... Then He said, Let Me go for dawn is breaking. But he said I will not let you go, unless You bless me. Said the Other: What is your name? He replied "Jacob." Said He, your name shall no longer be Jacob, but Israel, for you have striven with beings Divine and Human, and have prevailed. Jacob asked, Pray, tell me Your name. But He said, you must not ask My name! And He took leave of him there. So Jacob named that place Peniel, meaning, I have seen a *divine* being face-to-face, yet my life is preserved. (Gen. 32:24–30)

The KJV renders this last sentence as follows:

> For I have seen God face-to-face, and my life is preserved.

The Hebrew word translated as "God" here is "Elohim" (meaning "the majestic God," a plural word). Down the years ahead, Moses was denied seeing God's face: "Thou canst not see My face; for there shall no man see My face and live" (Ex. 33:20 KJV). Because of this awesome statement and the prohibition of seeing God, *The Jewish Study Bible* translates it in keeping with the ideation of Moses not being allowed to see God's face, since no mortal sees God's face and survives. Adam and Eve were the last to do that in Gan Eden, but they lost the privilege when they became mortal. God came disguised as a human when He visited to assure Abraham and Sarah of the promised fleshly son. So the translators of *The Jewish Study Bible* gave this altercation with Jacob the meaning of "close encounter." But the Hebrew word is "Elohim" in both verses 28 and 30 in the Masoretic text and must be translated as "the majestic God." The other very important factor here is that the being with whom he wrestled was described as a "divine and human" being. The translators of *The Jewish Study Bible* used God's plural name correctly, translating it as two natures in functionality, divine and human, an extremely important designation of the Ha-Mashiach. When God penetrates humanity He does it to provide redemption. On Mt. Sinai, He did not penetrate humanity, but His presence was there as the awesome fiery God of eternity, the Great Spirit. Using the "Talmudic" application, this is the correct terminology of the coming Messiah: He would be "divine and human." This signifies the lowly *"condescension" of the Ha-Mashiach to humanity.* This is highly compatible with the penetration of humanity by Divinity, which David, Daniel, and Isaiah specifically describe as follows:

> You are My Son, I have fathered you this day. (Ps. 2:7)

> One like a human being (son of man) Came with the clouds of heaven. (Dan. 7:13)

> A woman with child ... a son ... Immanuel, God with us. (Isa. 7:14)

> a Child is born ... a Son is given ... the Mighty God ... (Isa. 9:6)
> a man of suffering ... cut off from the land of the living. (Isa. 52, 53)

These excerpts from the Tanak are perfectly conceptually congruent. The Ha-Mashiach is expected here on earth as the divine penetration of humanity, so it makes perfect sense.

Jacob had placed himself at the back of the retinue. Now he limped up the bank of the brook Jabbok in complete dependence on God to save him from death at the hands of his brother. He could not run away. Now Jacob had the courage to limp to the head of the pack in front of the gift he had prepared for Esau, trusting totally in God to appease Esau's anger and prevent death at his hand. He had won the wrestling match with God with more tenacity than strength and now knew he had divine protection. His lameness was his assurance. His sins were forgiven by messianic sacrifice. He now had superhuman strength to take the Promised Land away from Esau. Protected by his Ha-Mashiach, he was now *invincible.* In accepting the Messiah, we must admit our lameness, paraplegia, and total helplessness. We will then be invincible, just as Jacob was:

> Looking up Jacob saw Esau coming accompanied by four hundred men … He himself went on ahead and bowed low to the ground seven times until he was near his brother. Esau ran to greet him. He embraced him and, falling on his neck, he kissed him, and they wept.
> (Gen. 33:3, 4)

Abraham was the great advocate of monotheism and gave the Jews their ethnicity, their special place, and their destiny. But Jacob was the inspired pivotal person who gave birth to an inspired nation with the mission to show the world the redeeming Mashiach. The vision of Jacob at Bethel and the tenacity of his embrace of God at Jabbok would typify the entire history of the Jewish people. He was no longer Jacob. He was now Israel. He was a prince, the son of the eternal King. That mission of his high calling is not yet complete. Jacob's dream has still to come alive and be realized nationally and globally. Israel must embrace and tenaciously wrestle with their Mashiach. After four thousand years, will that dream come true?

On his deathbed, Jacob pronounced the future of his sons. Surprisingly, some of his predictions were curses. His best future was reserved for his son Judah:

> You, O Judah, your brothers shall praise;
> Your hand shall be at the nape of your foes
> Your father's sons shall bow low to you.
> Judah is a lion's whelp;
> On prey, my son, have you grown.
> He crouches, lies down like a lion,
> Like the King of Beasts – who dares rouse him?
> The Sceptre shall not depart from Judah,
> Nor the ruler's staff from between his feet
> So that tribute shall come to him,
> And the homage of peoples be his.
> He tethers his ass to a vine,
> His ass's foal to a choice vine,
> He washes his garments in wine,
> His robe in blood of grapes.
> His eyes are darker than wine,
> His teeth are whiter than milk.
> (Gen. 49:8–12)

Jacob made assessments, curses, and blessings on all his twelve sons on his deathbed. The blessing on Judah is the best by far, and greatest. It is enormous and was predictive of the Jewish nation and the Mashiach, the Redeemer of the world. Its analysis is extremely important.

The translation above by *The Jewish Study Bible* renders Gen. 49:10 differently from the KJV, which translates it as follows:

> The Sceptre shall not depart from Judah, nor a Lawgiver
> from between his feet, UNTIL SHILOH COME; and unto
> Him shall the gathering of the people be. (Gen. 49:10,
> emphasis added)

In the original Hebrew:

Lo yasur shevet [The Sceptre shall not depart]
M'Y'huda oomkhokek meeveyn [From Judah nor a lawgiver from between]
Raglav ad kee yavo Sheelo [His feet until Shilo comes],
V'lo Yeekatameen [And to Him the people shall gather].

The Aramaic translation known as Targum Onkelos renders this as follows:

God shall uphold His promise to Judah even till the
Royal Figure comes to claim the dominion that is His due.

Many Jewish scholars see in the Judah blessing the glorious King David, and they also look past David to the Mashiach. (See *Il Messia* by David Castelli, pp. 38–41.)[76] Having only the Oral Torah and the Abrahamic covenant, now the covenant reinforced with him by God at Bethel, Jacob is confident in his blessing of Judah. He was clearly pointing forward to the coming of the Ha-Mashiach.

The messianic import of this prediction by Jacob is universally accepted among rabbinic scholars.[77]

Although the identity and mission of the Messiah are topics of significant dissension among the rabbis, they agree these verses definitely allude to Messiah.

Rabbi Zlotowitz stated the following:

The overwhelming consensus of Rabbinic commentary interprets this verse (Gen. 49:10) to allude to the Messiah (See Midrash Rabah).

The following two verses expand the messianic description.

Rabbi Ovadiah Sforno, an Italian commentator of the sixteenth century, stated,

The Messianic King rides an ass rather than a horse because it is God who wages the wars by which he comes to rule, "and He will be the King of Peace". (See Midrash Rabah)

Horses were portents of war, but donkeys were symbols of peace.

Another universally accepted messianic reference among the rabbinic sages was Zechariah 9:9:

> Rejoice greatly, O Daughter of Zion;
> Shout, O Daughter of Jerusalem;
> Behold, thy King cometh unto thee;
> He is just and having salvation;
> Lowly, and riding upon an ass,
> And upon a colt, the foal of an ass.
> (Zech. 9:9)

Jacob's future outlook did not get stymied in the intricacies of establishing a nation. Moses was to do that in God's timetable and His distribution of jobs. But Jacob was awed and overwhelmed with what he saw down the centuries of time to the messianic arrival. Did he see the sacrificial nature of the Mashiach? All Hebrew commentators I have read seem to avoid a deep explanation of verses 11 and 12. Some of them attach these verses to a "time of prosperity" in the Mashiach's reign because of the volume of wine described.

But I see the Mashiach's blood being shed in these verses:

> He washes His garments in wine;
> His robes in the blood of grapes.

I see the agony of the sacrifice in His bloodshot eyes:

> His eyes are darker than wine.

I see the whiteness of His teeth accentuated because of the total drainage of His blood into his robes, shed for the sins of the whole world:

> His teeth are whiter than milk.

It is a gory sight to behold the sacrifice of the Messiah as Jacob saw it. Jacob lingered on his own deathbed as he stared and stared at the sight. He longed to live to see that day of the Messiah. He longed to wrestle again with the Divine-Human God-Man. Isaiah describes that messianic picture of the bloodied mess that Jacob saw:

Why is your clothing so red,
Your garments like his who treads grapes?
I trod out a vintage alone ...
Their life-blood bespattered My garments,
And all My clothing was stained. (Isa. 63:1–4)

The gory sight Jacob saw on his deathbed is what it will take to cleanse the whole world in the final day of messianic atonement. (See the *Pesiqta Rabbati* and Psalm 22, cf. Isaiah 53.) Ah! That bloody spot, stained with centuries of the Day of Atonement blood on the ark of the covenant and the mercy seat, splashed by the High Priest, dripping on the floor in the Most Holy Place, on the temple mount. It is the very spot that Abraham raised the knife to kill his son. The blood has seeped into the rock of the temple mount, staining it forever.

There are unmistakably two descriptions of the Messiah in Jacob's blessing of Judah.

In the first picture He is described as the sacrificial lamb without blemish, soaked in His own blood in the agony of His descent into death, atoning for the sins of the whole world. *Here is the massive redemption to immortality, dispensed for the whole world.* Centuries after Jacob, Isaiah would describe it in detail:

But the Lord chose to crush Him by disease,
That, if He made Himself an offering for guilt,
He might see offspring and have long life.
And that through Him the Lord's purpose might prosper.
Out of His anguish He shall see it;
He shall enjoy it to the full through His devotion.
My righteous Servant makes the many righteous.
It is their punishment that He bears.
(Isa. 53:10, 11)

The Psalmist bears witness:

> But Thou didst not leave His soul in Sheol,
> Nor didst Thou suffer
> Thy Holy One to see corruption
> (Ps. 16:10 KJV).

In the second picture He has overcome death and the grave to bring immortality to the world. In this picture Jacob describes the Messiah as "a lion's whelp" who has fed on prey. He crouches ... like the king of beasts – who dares rouse Him? He has preyed upon the forces of sin and death. He is Shiloh. He now rules the entire world.

Ah, Jacob, dreamer of dreams, if only all Israel would dream your dreams so that they could grasp—yea, embrace—the high calling of *their God-ordained destiny to proclaim Mashiach to the whole world!*

The Holy Temple

CHAPTER 9

The Messiah of the Prince of Egypt

Moses must be recognized as the source of the distinctive ideas in primitive redemptive Judaism. His writings, the Pentateuch, must be lauded. In the Pentateuch we find the revealed science and structure of God and the multiverse. The reality of the existence of life on the planet is vividly described in the creation story. The entrance of evil to spoil that creation and the corrective measures God has undertaken are all there in the Pentateuch.

Modern scholar Thomas Cahill perceptively and correctly states that the Jews, starting with Abraham, were the first people to find a new way of religious thinking, understanding, experiencing, and feeling, when Abraham exited the depraved, chaotic polytheism of the Sumerian context. He credits Moses for its systematization and points out correctly that the Jewish worldview underpins modern western civilization:

> The [Hebrew] Bible is the record par excellence of the
> Jewish religious experience, an experience that remains
> fresh and even shocking when it is read against the myths
> of other ancient literatures.
> (*The Gifts of the Jews*, pp. 5, 6 by Thomas Cahill)

But Cahill greatly errs in discounting Creation and the Edenic experience, which ties Abraham to Adam and Eve and God's great plan of Redemption outlined by Moses. The great Edenic *devekut with God*, which unfallen humanity enjoyed, was to be restored. That was Abraham's inheritance and redemptive destiny, not the idolatrous and sexual religious filth of Sumer. Cahill sadly perceives no promise of Messiah in Eden, in the Abrahamic covenant, or at Sinai. He ignores the *messianic restoration of this primeval devekut*. His brief reference to the Messiah is contained in the dismissive word "daydreaming." This is in reference to the kingdom of Messiah ben David. (See *The Gifts of the Jews* p. 209.) Cahill went astray when he tied Abraham's spiritual origins to Sumer and not to Eden. He forgot that Messiah was planned from God's eternity in the reclamation of His love relationship with the human race. Messianic redemption is God's greatest gift to the human race. It is contained in the Jewish envelope called the Tanak.

The messianic structure and function, the great redemptive energy described by Moses, is in the Holy of Holies of the temple: *Shechinah, law, mercy, and messianic blood.* That mighty essence of Judaism was beamed from Mt. Sinai, and all the prophets ran with it. One day in the future, hopefully not too long, I predict, Rabbinic Judaism will see that it has departed from the heart and soul of this primitive redemptive Judaism, God's gift to the world. Messiah is the way back to the heart of God, since we cannot keep God's law perfectly; however, we should do our utmost to keep His law.

My visit to Egypt was dominated not by wonderment of the pyramids but by admiration for that baby crying in the bulrushes as my cruiseboat dallied at that celebrated spot. In sadness I also observed the drowned Hebrew baby boys floating down the Nile and into the Mediterrenean. Moses was the mighty founder of the nation of Israel, the chosen people of the covenant, bearing Ha-Mashiach redemption to the world. He was God's chosen messenger of the Abrahamic covenant: "***In thy Seed shall all nations of the earth be blessed.***"

Moses's greatest stroke of fortune was that his mother Jochebed was hired to be his nurse by the princess of Egypt who found him in those bulrushes of the Nile. Jochebed and Moses's father, Amram, were monotheists, and despite being slaves they had memorized the Oral Torah. Jochebed instilled the Oral Torah into Moses's brain in those early years. It may have looked like luck, but it was in the plans of YHVH. Moses grew up to be the heir apparent, the crown prince, the next pharaoh of Egypt. He was educated as a royal prince in both the book learning and the sports education of the universities of Egypt, and no doubt in the worship of the multiple idolatrous gods in the temples of the Nile. But he did not succumb to the idolatry of Egypt. The template he laid down in the Pentateuch contained the spirituality, ethics, and health laws for his idolatrous kin. In the Pentateuch we find God's two great and supreme acts: Creation and Redemption.

With the early conviction in his heart that he belonged to the highest authority in the multiverse, he "played his cards" cunningly. *He knew his roots.* The Oral Torah of the Hebrews coming down from Adam constantly rang in his ears. *The story of Gan Eden thundered in his brain.* His conversation with God began early and shaped his thoughts. He also advanced in the education of the time. Hammurabi's works were avidly studied. There is much evidence that his code of behavior and the legal laws he drew up to govern the Israelite slaves were similar to the Code of Hammurabi and the enactments promulgated by Mesopotamian rulers. (See *Ancient Judaism* by Max Weber, pp. 62, 63.) There is no doubt the Code of Hammurabi impressed him, but the Oral Torah governed every avenue of his mind, and he worshipped the God of his patriarchal forefathers. Perhaps a Hebrew synagogue had survived from the days of the good times when Joseph was prime minister of Egypt. The Jewish influence had no doubt shone as a beacon from the land of Goshen. Now they were sordid suffering slaves, harrowingly harnessed and harassed in the massive economy of Egypt. There had to be a trace of Hebrew culture and spirituality in Egypt, but it did not have any national significance at that time.

After three hundred years or more of slavery, the children of Jacob were at their lowest ebb. The lure of heathenism, as well as the idolatry of the temples of the Nile with its enthralling sexual titillations mixed with religious ecstasy, had attracted many of Moses's prolific kin. The "flesh pots" of Egypt were thoroughly enjoyed by the Hebrew slaves. The worship of the "Golden Calf" at Sinai reflected how much idolatry and sexual depravity their sensual and corrupted minds and bodies had absorbed. This was the legacy they brought with them out of the land of Egypt. It was something in which they had profusely indulged. Moses had a massive task of cleansing the riffraff that he had dragged out of Egypt. No wonder he was so strict! There is some evidence that certain Levitical priestly interpolations had occurred to make the Pentateuch even more severe than written by Moses. Precious few had retained the Oral Torah. Many, perhaps most, had left Egypt very reluctantly, since despite the hard slave labor, their lustful bodily desires had been indulged, and there was much illicit sexual pleasure available as an extra 'evil bonus' for their slavery. It is little wonder that Moses magnified the law and summarily punished and eradicated the dross of the Hebrews. The Levites killed three thousand men who had worshipped the Golden Calf on that horrible day of idolatry at Sinai. Can you imagine it? These people were so vile that they had reprimanded Moses and Aaron for bringing them out of Egypt:

> All the Israelites railed against Moses and Aaron. "If only we had died in the land of Egypt ... It would be better for us to go back to Egypt" ... The Lord spoke further to Moses and Aaron, How much longer shall that wicked community keep muttering against Me? ... But your carcasses shall drop in this wilderness, while your children roam the wilderness for forty years, suffering for your faithlessness, until the last of your carcasses is down in the wilderness.
> (Num. 14:2,3b,26,32,33)

God was exasperated. It was no small thing that God was of a mind to destroy the lot and make Moses the source of his chosen people. God's fiery appearance on Mt. Sinai had failed to impress these vile people as they danced in a sexual frenzy around the golden calf. That sexual frenzy was a big part of the activities prevalent on the banks of the Nile that their carnality had enjoyed and still craved.

The Egyptians adored Moses, the young prince. He was a beautiful specimen of manhood, impeccably behaved, his masculinity polished as a prince to the highest degree by his palace tutors. The lure of the pleasures available to a royal son of the palace was enormous. He skillfully resisted these charms and grew up as a shining light in the idolatrous darkness of Egypt. He was a type of the coming Mashiach. But he began to live a double life. In a clandestine effort to help his own people, dressed as an Egyptian, he made private trips around the slave camps and acted incognito on their behalf, in an attempt to lighten their load of cruel slavery. It was on one such foray that he murdered an Egyptian taskmaster who was harassing a Hebrew slave. He hid the body in the sand and raced back to the palace to hide his act of wild justice. (See Exodus 2:11–14.) It took a while for his tachycardia to subside. He was now a murderer.

But he had made his choice. God paid special attention to this beloved son who had determined to serve Him and free his people from slavery. An unknown Jewish writer has penned these words:

> By faith Moses, when he was come to years, refused to be called the son of Pharaoh's daughter, choosing rather to suffer affliction with the people of God than to enjoy the pleasures of sin for a season.
> (Heb. 11:24–25 KJV)

He had a messianic job to save his people from the corruption of sin and slavery in Egypt. There had been much motivation from the entreaties of his mother, Jochebed, to lighten the load of the suffering of his kin. But the Abrahamic covenant was more powerful in his making the break with Egyptian royalty. He saw the Royalty of Heaven, The God-Man his ancestor Jacob had encountered, and Jacob's prediction of the Mashiach so clearly that the throne of Egypt faded and shriveled as an alternative. There was a *Promised Land* to occupy, a *chosen people* to be fashioned, and a *redemptive Messiah* to unleash on this world. He had the big picture in his mind, and it was overwhelming. But he was not yet ready. The wild justice he tried to enforce was not the way to do it. He needed some further education, and it was forced upon him, although his own actions had triggered it. He became a wanted man in Egypt. The taskmaster he had killed was of high rank but was now well hidden in the desert sand. A massive search in the land was underway. A big reward was offered. The very Israelite 'brother' he had helped betrayed him for the reward. He became a fugitive, escaping stealthily at night, by himself, to the land of Midian. The heir to the throne of Egypt fled from Egyptian justice. He found a job tending sheep for Reuel, the priest of Midian (Ex. 2:11–22). He needed to learn shepherding skills before shepherding his people out of Egypt. Out there on the grassy meadows, watching the sheep, he kept hearing the Abrahamic covenant thundering in his ears. His mother had done a good job. She was a chosen woman, highly regarded by God. God had a list of favorite women: Eve, Sarah, Rebekkah, and now the princess of Egypt and Jochebed. Several others would be granted special missions: Esther, Naomi, Ruth, Hannah, Abigail, and other very powerful women.

There was also a thundering in the ears of the God of heaven. The time was ripe:

> A long time after that, the King of Egypt died. The Israelites were groaning under the bondage and cried out; and their cry for help from the bondage rose up to God. God heard their moaning, and God remembered His Covenant with **Abraham,** and Isaac and Jacob. God looked upon the Israelites, and God took notice of them.
>
> (Ex. 2:23, 24, emphasis added)

This was a cataclysmic occurrence—God and Moses, both remembering the Abrahamic covenant and giving their simultaneous energies to it. How could they have forgotten! God had been waiting for Moses very patiently. And now Moses pretended reluctance. He wanted God to twist his arm. Here is a great exposition of the respect God pays to human free will, and His valued use of human talent. Moses wanted a major endorsement, and he got it. His stammering was a gross exaggeration!

In the meantime he had married Zipporah and begotten a son named Gershom (meaning "I have been a stranger in a foreign land"). (See Exodus 2:22.) He had settled down to what he thought was a quiet life. He did not travel far but ventured into the land of Uz, where he became friends with a monotheist named Job. Moses wrote Job's story. The authorship of the book of Job is the subject of controversy. Some scholars believe it is the oldest book of the Tanak, because there are significant affinities between much of the language of Job and the earlier biblical literature.[78] I believe Moses is the author of Job based on that evidence, as well as the theology of the book being totally congruent with the theology of Moses. Some scholars believe that the authorship is of a much later unknown writer because of allusions to later periods. But as we know, down through the ages, there were editors, interpolaters, and revisers of the Pentateuch. I believe there was similar treatment of the book of Job by editors and revisers who added these later allusions. But the unity of the message of Job stands. Based on the present evidence, I credit Moses with its authorship.

The book of Job takes up the subject of human suffering and its possible causes. The prophets blamed the sufferings of the Hebrews as the visitation of punishment by God. The accepted idea was that suffering occurs as a result of sin and is caused by the actions of the person who suffers. God might also allow suffering to occur for His own glory, but with eternal reward in mind. In the case of Job, he suffered as a result of God's argument with Ha-Satan about Job's uprightness and loyalty to God. "Hast thou considered my servant Job?" (Job 1:8) is a boast and a dare. Job's suffering came thick and fast subsequently and was heartrending. His friends discuss the etiology of his suffering. Job summarizes that both the righteous and the wicked do suffer. His big question was "How should man be just before God" (Job 9:1 KJV) in order to avoid suffering? Through all the suffering, Job is steadfast in his allegiance to God. *It is the messianic hope that keeps his faith strong in the Almighty.* His friends Eliphaz, Bildad, Zophar, and finally Elihu present all manner of arguments, but he is not impressed. And then he utters the famous messianic hope: "For I know that my Redeemer liveth, and that He shall stand at the latter day upon the earth; And though after my skin worms destroy this body, yet in my flesh shall I see God, Whom I shall see for myself, and my eyes shall behold, and not another; though my heart be consumed within me" (Job 19:25–27 KJV). "If a man die shall he live again? All the days of my appointed time will I wait, till my change come. Thou shalt call and I will answer Thee" (Job 14:14–15 KJV). There was a solid personal connection between the "Thou" and the "I." In Job's mind, *God and Redeemer were one and the same.*

Unless God allows all human machinations and solutions conjured for the status of humanity are for naught. So now God finally invokes His recreative power into the discussion, firmly connecting Redemption with Creation: "Where wast thou when I laid the foundations of the earth?" God recounts His wondrous works of the Creation. In great awe, Job decides to shut up and eat crow! But God will not accept that attitude. God answers with more wondrous works of the Creation. Job then decides to open his mouth again and accept the challenge of the Creation. All suffering is to end. As God showed His power in Creation, He now outlines His power in Redemption. God stumps all those in this argument about suffering by introducing His own suffering: "*Offer up for yourselves a burned offering*" (Job 42:8b KJV). In the symbol of the burnt offering of the animal without blemish, there is total eradication of the sinful and suffering human condition. *God's messianic self suffers for the expiation*, and by it He ushers in the *eternal kingdom of Messiah ben David*, where sin and suffering are no more.

In the recording of Job's story, Moses shows God is in charge. Suffering is the result of wrong choices and sin. But just as God is powerful in Creation, He is mighty in Redemption. God Himself suffers in that Redemption. God's suffering, symbolized in the sacrifice of the animal without blemish, signified the messianic sacrifice for the expiation. This is the answer to all human woes. God created and He Himself redeems. God's messianic boast is justified, and His dare is vindicated. His messianic redemptive act is just as massive as His creative act. In the book of Job, Creation and Redemption are offered as *one mighty act conceived in eternity.*

The "Burning Bush" experience at Horeb (Sinai) disturbed Moses's tranquility and reminded him of his God-given mission to carry out the Abrahamic covenant. Land, Torah, and Messiah became the active top priorities in his life. He was commissioned by the great I AM THAT I AM. Although he claimed to be "slow of speech," this weakness never showed up once he became activated. We all know the story of how he wrenched the slaves out of the viselike grip of Egyptian slavery. It is figurative of the tremendous job of messianic extrication of His people from this historic world of sin. The details of the removal of Israel from Egypt are dramatic and are well outlined in the biblical story. But in doing the most difficult job in the history of the Jews, his concentrated focus was messianic. Apart from receiving the Ten Commandments from the hand of God, Moses instituted the two greatest bulwarks of Judaism that survive to this day. This he did because he knew the law would be broken. Both are significantly incongruent with the Rabbinic Judaism that evolved out of the Talmud after the destruction of the temples. Despite the great focus of Rabbinic Judaism on the ritualistic Halakah, which magnifies the ceremonial law, these bulwarks have survived as *the greatest landmarks of primitive redemptive Judaism: the Passover and the Day of Atonement.*

Sinai is the legacy of Moses. Sinai is best seen in the Most Holy Place of the earthly tabernacle temple. Law, mercy, and blood, in the presence of the Shechinah, are reflections—yea, mighty bulwarks—of what constitute the Redemption in the heavenly remple and are portrayed by the prophets (e.g. Isaiah [see Isaiah 6:1–7], Habakkuk [see Habbakuk 2:20], Haggai [see Haggai2:6–9], and Malachi [see Malachi 3:1]).

Max Weber has much to say in his book *Ancient Judaism* about the influence of Sumerian philosophy and the influence the Code of Hammurabi had on Moses. I do not agree with many of Max Weber's conclusions, but he points out correctly that pre- and post-exilic theological revisions were made to the book of the covenant, the priestly code, and the holiness code, which are parts of the Pentateuch. (See *Ancient Judaism*, pp. 61–73.) The Talmud also bears record that much in the Halakah was added to Sinai, though not original in the Pentateuch. There is a surfeit of interpolations and revisions injected into the original Sinai document penned by Moses. Abraham Cohen points this out:

> A fundamental issue with the Rabbis was the acceptance of a traditional Torah, transmitted from one generation to another by word of mouth, with the written text. It was claimed that the Oral Torah, equally with the Written Torah, goes back to the Revelation on Sinai, if not in detail at least in principle. *Forty-two enactments, which find no record in the Pentateuch, are described by the Talmud as 'laws' given to Moses on Sinai.* The rest of the Oral Torah was implied in the Scriptural text [of the Pentateuch] and was deducible from it by certain rules of exegesis.[79]

So not everything claimed to have been beamed from Sinai bears Sinai's signature trademark! These non-Sinai proclamations of the rabbis must be discarded if they are not congruent with the messianic message, which dwells in the Most Holy Place. Careful checking and analysis needs to be done. Not all that is stamped "Sinai" is authentic. However the messianic idea of redemption remains intact in the Pentateuch. Later revisions and interpolations must be tested for congruency. It is an abomination to use the 'Sinai stamp' illegally, no matter how erudite or revered the authors may be.

The Passover: Instituted by Moses the night before they left Egypt was a stupendous redemptive pre-Sinai *"blood festival"* event. It is marvelously congruent with Sinai, and it extols the blood of the lamb without blemish. *"I will pass over you when I see the blood."* David Castelli saw the messianic redemptive import of Moses as a messianic figure in the great deliverance from Egypt. He saw it as figurative of the redemption from sin. (See *Il Messia* by David Castelli.)[80]

The Day of Atonement: The other great *"blood festival"* beamed from Sinai was enmeshed with the Most Holy of the tabernacle temple, which itself was instituted after God came down on Mt. Sinai. As with the Passover, the Day of Atonement is *heavy with blood.* (See Leviticus 16, 17.) To all Jews these "blood festivals" are the pinnacle of their religion. No Jew can deny the blood in these festivals. Calling it "cultic" does not diminish or negate it. Blood is not magnified in Rabbinic Judaism. Rabbinic Judaism talks about what Israel can do for God. Halakah is to be lauded as praise for our God. But both Passover and the Day of Atonement are most eloquent about what God can do for Israel. Both prospects are important, but only what God can do for us is messianic, redemptive, and salvific. There can never be a substitute for this redemptive *Judaism of the Blood.* God rejects substitutes for messianic redemption. He rejected Cain's fruits and vegetables. He rejected the ritual climb of the Tower of Babel. He rejects acts of benevolence and deep study of the Torah as 'redemptive agents.' He rejects 'The Enlightenment' as a messianic salvation. God rejects all these as substitutes for His messianic redemption. He wants us to see and admit that He Himself is our Redeemer. Why would He want to penetrate humanity in the functionality of the Messiah if any or all of these substitutes listed above would be salvific? They all have merit in our adoration of God, and in being sanctified, but none are significant in redemption. *He reserves the act of Redemption for Himself.* It is His job, and He will not share it. He created, and He will redeem. In outlining the temple blood ritual, Moses insists on redemption by the blood. Blessed be Elohim; the Lord our God is one. Just as we had no share in our creation, *we have no share in our redemption.* The enactment of it is His prerogative. It is a cosmic re-Creation. We must accept His Redemption without a murmur, and with no attempt to earn it. It does not seem fair that He should take the entire responsibility to save us, but *that is the way He wants it.* He will not let any other god have our worship, and He will not let any idol or other contrived measure save us. Moses is emphatic about this in the temple service.

The great fear in talmudic Judaism is that messianic redemption is too easy, too antinomian. There is always the urge to do it yourself so you can feel that you have done your part. It seems more meritorious, but it is not, for "we are all as filthy rags" (Isaiah 64:6). Halakah sanctifies but cannot save, because we can never attain perfect keeping of the law. An 'atmosphere' of 'perfect law-keeping' can never precipitate the coming of the Messiah; nor can it be proffered in the Judgment as a 'pass,' or hard-earned 'ticket' into paradise. Fortunately, these are not my words. Here are two congruent statements from the Talmud. Abraham Cohen discusses them under the topic "The Doctrine of God":

> The attribute of Grace, it was taught "exceeds that of punishment (i.e. justice) by five-hundredfold" (Joma. 69b) ... "Even in the time of His anger He remembers mercy" (Pes. 87b) ... While believing, therefore, that He is the Judge of the Universe, the Rabbis delighted in calling Him Rachmana (the Merciful) and taught that "THE WORLD IS JUDGED BY GRACE" (Aboth III. 19).[81] (Emphasis added)

Grace is unmerited favor. Despite other variant views in the Talmud, the rabbinic sages stated that one of the big questions in the final judgment is

DID YOU HOPE FOR THE SALVATION OF THE MESSIAH? (Shab. 31a)[82]

Here is a statement from one of the greatest modern voices in Judaism. He is discussing the messianic idea in Judaism:

> If we look at the tenth chapter of the tractate Sanhedrin, where the Talmudists discuss the question of redemption at length, we see that to them it means a colossal uprooting, destruction, revolution, disaster, with nothing of development or progress about it.

And then Scholem quotes from the Talmud:

> The Son of David [Messiah] will come only in a generation wholly guilty or a generation wholly innocent – a condition beyond the realm of human possibility. Or, "the Son of David will not come until the kingdom is subverted to heresy."

> These hopes for redemption always show a very strong nationalist bent. ***Liberation of Israel is the essence, but it will march in step with the liberation of the whole world.***[83]

I will discuss Scholem's ideas and talmudic Messianism repeatedly in this book.

But these statements above, though congruent with tanakian theology, are incongruent with the majority opinion in the Talmud, and with the current ideas of Rabbinic Judaism, as I will show.

To go back to the two great bulwarks of primitive redemptive Judaism instituted by Moses, the common component to the two great festivals is the shedding of blood. We cannot shy away from this topic by calling this arrangement by God *cultic*, as does *The Cambridge Guide to Jewish History*.[84] The authors of this book show a veiled disdain for the "cultic" description of animal sacrifices. Geza Vermes also stealthily labels the sacrificial system as cultic and avoids a discussion of expiation by the blood so essentially and emphatically stressed by Moses (Lev. 16 and 17). This topic needs further elucidation. The shedding of the blood of the animal without blemish was the symbol of messianic sacrifice. There is no other possible explanation. Both these immortal and triumphant festivals involve *blood* and *freedom*. There is *nothing* in primitive redemptive Judaism or Rabbinic Judaism that is more messianic.

The Passover gave them freedom from slavery in Egypt and kept their firstborn from death. In the institution of the Passover Festival, the blood of the lamb without blemish was shed, collected, and splashed on the doorposts and lintels of their homes. When the angel of death passed by during the midnight hour and saw the blood, their firstborn were spared. That is what Passover means:

> ***When I see the blood I will pass over you.***
> (Ex. 12:13 KJV, emphasis added)

Franz Rosenzweig states:

> The Exodus we must first remember, albeit as vividly as if
> we had taken part in it ourselves … [85]

This is good advice. Rosenzweig addressed this dictum to Christians, but it applies extraordinarily to Jews. The flesh of the lamb must be eaten with bitter herbs. Its blood must be splashed on the doorposts and lintels of our lives. It must cleanse us from the heathenism and filth of Egypt. It signifies a cleansing from sin and saves from eternal death, much more surely than it freed the Israelite slaves. Moses was indeed a type of the Messiah when as the only Hebrew who was not a slave in Egypt saved them. So shall the Messiah be the only sinless Hebrew who will save Israel from sin.

The Day of Atonement gave them freedom from the guilt of sin. Sin is ubiquitous in humanity, just as slavery affected all Israel. The blood the High Priest took into the Most Holy Place and splashed on the ark and mercy seat in the presence of the Shechinah gave *all* the people cleansing from *all* their sins.

The rendering of both freedoms is the messianic function. I challenge any Jew who thinks otherwise about these two festivals, the greatest festivals in the Jewish dispensation and in the whole world. There is no doubt about the messianic intent of both, and *there is nothing more powerful in Judaism.* Just as Moses was a messianic figure because as the savior of his people he was the Hebrew who was not a slave in that era of Egyptian slavery, the human penetrance of the Messiah will not be a slave to sin.

This was the Judaism that Moses instituted at Sinai and was practiced and preached by all the prophets and writers of the Tanak. *This primitive redemptive Judaism cannot be set aside* just because the temples were destroyed. Moses certainly laid down the law, and we must do all we can to keep the law. But realizing we all fall short, Moses set up the God-prescribed machinery that gives us freedom from the slavery of sin through messianic redemption. Moses instituted the Aaronic priesthood and built the tent tabernacle. These were illustrative and vital functions of the economy of redemption. The tent tabernacle served as the location for the cleansing and disposing of sin and guilt. On a daily basis the opportunity was afforded for the personal expiation for sin. The Messiah forgives and expiates and removes the guilt. "As far as the east is from the west, so far hath He removed our transgressions from us." (Ps. 103:12 KJV). The sins of the world do not get stored in the temple. They dissolve and vanish once the blood is applied. What happened for the individual on a daily basis happened for the nation on a yearly basis. It was to happen on a one-time cosmic basis for the whole world when God's Mashiach functionality penetrates humanity and presents that sacrifice in the heavenly temple.

On a yearly basis on the Day of Atonement, the High Priest took the blood of the sacrificial animal without blemish into the Most Holy Place and splashed it on the ark of the covenant and the mercy seat, in the presence of the Shechinah. Justice, mercy, messianic blood, and

Shechinah comingled for the accomplishment of the atonement. The shedding of messianic blood is indispensable to the atonement, and there is no substitute. That is the redemption taught by the patriarch Moses. It cannot be set aside. Judaism is a dead religion without this Messianism of the blood instituted by Moses at Sinai. The law sentences us all to death because we all are disobedient. But the messianic expiation restores us all to perfection and immortality. If Jews pretend they keep the law perfectly, they need not partake of the Day of Atonement. Remove all perfect lawkeeping Jews from the synagogue on the Day of Atonement. Messiah is not for them.

Again, that great modern mind in Judaism, Franz Rosenzweig, stated,

> Just so the Day of Atonement, as the day of *the entrance to eternity*, is for our year what the Sabbath means for the week: consummation ... The Day of Atonement became the highest festival of all ... [86]

He saw the true significance of the Day of Atonement where messianic blood was shed and splashed on the ark of the covenant and mercy seat in the presence of the law and the Shechinah. This accomplished repentance, forgiveness, and expiation, and provided perfection and immortality. It is *our entrance to eternity.* Implicit in this statement is the admission that Ha-Mashiach is deity. It cannot be otherwise, because God reserves Redemption as His sole act. How marvelous is the primitive Judaism of Moses established at Sinai! It thrills the soul and invigorates with the reality of eternal life! How can we deny it? *It is our entrance to eternity!* Let us not beam anything else as redemptive from Sinai. If we do, it is tantamount to worshipping the golden calf! It is an abomination. Moses will grind it into powder, mix it with water, and make us drink it. And we will die. It will be an entrance into eternal death.

Let us never forget; God is speaking here through Moses:

> *For the life of the flesh is in the blood, and I have assigned it to you for expiation for your lives upon the altar; it is the blood, as life, that effects expiation.* (Lev. 17:11)

Moses must be congratulated for bringing the slaves out of Egypt and fashioning them into a law-abiding people. They did not make it easy for him, and in fact they had reached the vile state, as had the antediluvian hordes. Moses's greatest attribute, therefore, was messianic. He pleaded with God to spare them, and if not, he was willing to die with them. God respected his wishes and spared the wretched lot. As Abraham was willing to sacrifice his son, Moses was willing to die with his people. What messianic words he uttered: "**Blot me out!**" Messiah elected to be "blotted out." Moses greatly regarded the coming of the Ha-Mashiach. In the spirit of that willingness to die with them, he spoke of the coming Mashiach:

> The Lord your God will raise up for you a Prophet *from among your own people, like myself*; him you shall heed. This is just what you asked of the Lord your God at Horeb [Sinai], on the day of the Assembly, saying, "Let me not hear the voice of the Lord my God any longer or see this wondrous fire any more, lest I die." Whereupon the Lord said to me, "They have done well in speaking thus. I will raise up a Prophet for them *from among their own people, like yourself.* I will put My words in his mouth and he will speak to them all that I command him, *and if anybody fails to heed the words He speaks in My name, I Myself will call him to account.*
> (Deut. 18:15–19, emphasis added)

In this dialogue between Moses, the people, and God, a great fear was expressed by the people in their encounter with God Almighty in His fiery state on Mount Sinai. They found the fiery mountain threatening. They feared the fate of the worshippers of the golden calf. They asked for a mitigated and less threatening human version of God. God replied that that was perfectly understandable and He would send the Mashiach as a human being bearing the stamp "**From your own people.**" Some of the rabbinic sages interpreted this conversation as the promise of the Mashiach.[87] It is well taken. So here is another promise of the human penetrance of the Ha-Mashiach functionality of Elohim. But in this promise there is also judgment. Judgment will be passed on the basis of acceptance or rejection of the Mashiach:

> ... and if anybody fails to heed the words He [Ha-Mashiach] speaks in My name, I Myself will call him to account.
> (Deut. 18:19b)

A discussion of prophets and their credentials follows in the Deuteronomy record. *The Jewish Study Bible* commentary goes into a detailed discussion of prophets in general, as does the biblical record. But it is obvious that the special prophet being sent by God is messianic in that he is a "less awesome, less fiery, less threatening, and a special compatible human version" of God Himself who comes "from your own people." All other prophets were human, and it was taken for granted. But this particular one is special in that there is a guaranty that *He is the same fiery God on Mt. Sinai* but coming as a gentle human. *It is God Himself.* We do not want a fully human Messiah because He will last only one lifetime. We want Him to be immortal and rule us forever and ever. And we want to live with Him forever and ever. Isaiah promised that He would be more than human, with the functionality of Elohim:

> For a Child has been born to us,
> A Son has been given us.
> And authority has settled on His shoulders.
> He has been named
> "The Mighty God is planning Grace;
> The Eternal Father, a peaceable ruler" –
> In token of abundant authority
> And of peace without limit
> Upon David's throne and kingdom,
> That it may be firmly established
> In justice and in equity
> *Now and evermore.*
> (Isa. 9:5, 6 emphasis added)

This child brings a kingdom that is for "Now and evermore." There is no alternative to the divinity of the Ha-Mashiach, since He is for "Now and evermore." That great Jewish thinker Franz Rosenzweig expressed it thus:

> Yet no one knows better than he that being dear to God is only a beginning, and that man remains unredeemed so long as nothing but this beginning has been realized. Over against Israel, *eternally loved by God and faithful and perfect in eternity, stands he who is eternally to come, he who waits, and wanders, and grows eternally – the MESSIAH.* Over against the man of earliest beginnings, against Adam the son of man, *stands the man of endings, the son of David the king.* Over against him who was created from the stuff of earth and the breath of the mouth of God, is *the descendant from the stem of anointed kings;* over against the patriarch, *the latest offspring;* over against the first who draws about him the mantle of divine love, *the Last, from whom salvation issues forth to the ends of the earth;* over against the first miracles, *the last, which – so it is said – will be greater than the first.*[88]

Rosenzweig defines the essence of messianic function in the person of the Messiah. He comes in His eternal divinity as the human version of the fiery God on Mt. Sinai, one that saves them rather than consumes them with the fire of Sinai. There is no doubt that God's functionality as Ha-Mashiach comes as a penetrance of humanity. And God attaches the judgment that comes with the rejection of His messianic witness: *"I Myself will call him to account."*

Franz Rosenzweig has something further to say of the universality of the Ha-Mashiach:

> And man, who is created in the image of God, Jewish man as he faces God … As the beloved of God, as Israel, he knows that God has elected him and may well forget that he is not alone with God, that God knows others whom he

himself may or may not know, that to Egy t and Assyria
too, God says: "My eo le."[89]

Rosenzweig here enunciates the true scope of the mission of the
Abrahamic covenant: That God knows others whom the Jew may or
may not know; that to Egypt and Assyria too, God says, "My people."

What a God! "The Mighty God planning Grace!" It is for the
whole world! Hear, O Israel, the Lord our God is one. Blessed be
He. This is primitive redemptive Judaism at its triumphant height.
This is universal and priceless, the greatest value ever to come
our way. Thank you, Moses, for convincing The Almighty to save
us at Sinai. And thanks be to God for this unspeakably matchless
messianic gift.

To conclude this chapter on Moses, which plainly contains
the messianic intent in the Pentateuch, it must be regarded as the
primitive redemptive Judaism established by him. But this primitive
Judaism has been supplanted by Rabbinic Judaism, which is a far cry
from Sinai. In rightly castigating Christianity in the modern world as
having wandered away from what he calls "Christianiy as a historical
phenomenon," Gershom Scholem declared,

> The Judaism of today, too, is not the Judaism of Moses.[90]

Scholem was echoing Judah ha-Levi (ca. AD 1075–1141), who
asked the question whether Judaism was committed to the God of
the philosophers or to the God of Abraham, Isaac, and Jacob. (See
The Cambridge Guide, p. 385.)

Are the modern Rabbis listening? The Judaism of Moses cannot
be set aside.

CHAPTER 10

Messianic Utterances of Joel

Joel is classed as a "nonspecific" prophet in terms of the history of Israel. Scholars do not have definite evidence from his book to place him in any era of the history of the Hebrews. They feel generally that perhaps he fits into the period of Persian domination, 539–332 BC, and confine him to about 400–350 BC.[91]

The esteemed Joseph Klausner is in agreement with this dating to be about the year 400 BC between Deutero-Isaiah and Zechariah.[92] *The MacArthur Study Bible* places Joel in the time of Elisha, around 830 BC.[93] The arguments among scholars about dating him emphasizes that his message has wide application. Most scholars agree that he appears to address the kingdom of Judah. This favors the later dating.

The book of Joel can be divided into four parts:

1. **Punishment for idolatry:** The punishment of Israel for her idolatry and waywardness is portrayed as a loss of prosperity in terms of food availability. Wheat, wine, oil, fruit, and milk are in very short supply. He blames the locusts for the damage. "What the cutter has left, the locusts have devoured. And what the locusts have left, the grub has devoured. And what the grub has left, the hopper has devoured" (Joel 1:4). The intended meanings of "cutter," "locust," "grub," and "hopper" are obscure. *The Hebrew Study Bible* suggests these represent Babylon, Persia, Greece, and Rome, who all ravaged the Holy Land.[94] This is feasible and outlines the times of devastation by the invaders. Joel sums up the critical situation in 1:12c: "And joy has dried up among men."

2. **Exhortation to repent:** Exhortation comes: "Gird yourselves and lament ... Spend the night in sackcloth ... Solemnize a

fast, proclaim an assembly; gather the elders – all inhabitants of the land – in the House of the Lord your God, and cry out to the Lord" (Joel 1:13, 14). Lamentation then occurs as the situation is presented before God, who is implored for redress. (See Joel 1:15–20.) An appeal is made: "Oh, spare Your people, Lord! Let not Your possession become a mockery" (Joel 2:17). God responds.

3. **Proclamation of the Day of the Lord:** "Blow a horn in Zion, Sound an alarm on My Holy Mount! For the *DAY OF THE LORD* has come!" A military scene is then described. There is a great travail. The Day of the Lord unleashes the implementation of the messianic Redemption. There is further exhortation to repent:

> Turn back to Me with all your hearts,
> And with fasting, weeping, and lamenting.
> Rend your hearts rather than your garments,
> And turn back to the Lord your God.
> For He is gracious and compassionate …

A further exhortation to gather the people together follows, for lamenting and repentance. There is a *"time of trouble"* (cf. Dan. 12) accompanied by revival, where God pours out His "spirit on all flesh … Before the great and terrible *Day of the Lord* comes" (Joel 3:1–5).

4. **The messianic kingdom:** The messianic kingdom follows, but not without the punishment of the nations that afflicted Israel:

> For lo! In those days and in that time,
> When I restore the fortunes of Judah and Jerusalem
> I will gather all the nations
> And bring them down to the Valley of Jehoshaphat
> There I will contend with them
> Over My very own people, Israel.

After the punishment, prosperity is restored to Israel:

> And the Lord will roar from Zion,
> And shout aloud from Jerusalem,
> So that heaven and earth tremble
> But the Lord will be a shelter to His people,
> A refuge to the Children of Israel ...
> And Jerusalem shall be holy
> Nevermore shall strangers pass through it.
> And in that day,
> The mountains shall drip with wine,
> The hills shall flow with milk,
> And all the watercourses of Judah shall flow with water;
> A spring shall issue from the House of the Lord ...
> And the Lord shall dwell in Zion.
> (Joel 4:1–2b, 16–18a, 21b)

What sweet words!: "*A Spring shall issue from the House of the Lord ... And the Lord shall dwell in Zion.*" Here is a mighty reference to the sanctuary, "the House of the Lord," where in the Most Holy Place is messianic redemption, the comingling of law, mercy, and blood in the presence of the Shechinah, *a lifegiving spring of repentance, forgiveness, and expiation.* It is the heavenly Day of Atonement (cf. Isa. 6). There is no doubt that here is a promise that perfection and immortality will be restored and there will be a new heaven and a new earth. And when the new earth is established, the heavenly temple will be planted on earth as a witness to the great redemption accomplished. Will the third temple be the heavenly to be planted on esrth? God, the King Messiah ben David, will celebrate His cosmic creative and redemptive sabbaths in that temple eternally.

The Lord our God is one. Blessed be He.

CHAPTER 11

The Messianic Love Stories of Ruth and Esther

These two books are dealt with together because they were purportedly written by or for women and are messianic love stories of deliverance. One is a romantic love story in which a Gentile contributes her genes to Israel's royal line, which eventuates in King David and then King Messiah ben David. The other love story delivers the diasporic Jews from annihilation by a wicked Gentile enemy. Esther tells the latter story, which provides an allegory of the messianic deliverance of God's people on the planet. The stories of Ruth and Esther will be discussed separately.

Ruth

Ruth was King David's great-grandmother, a converted Gentile Moabite who came from an idolatrous heathen family. Jewish tradition believes the book of Ruth was written by Samuel, although Adele Reinhartz states that its authorship is unknown in her preamble commentary to the book in the *The Jewish Study Bible* (p. 1579). Some scholars place the writing of the book around 450 BC.

The story is so well known that it is superfluous to repeat it here for lack of space. The book of Ruth is read in the synagogues on Shavuot, the Feast of Weeks, the celebration of God's giving the law to Moses at Sinai. Reinhartz states, "This element of the feast is related to the prevalent rabbinic theme of Ruth as the ideal convert to Judaism who takes the Torah upon herself just as the Israelites did at Mount Sinai." Despite the talmudic controversy over whether the Gentiles will partake of the messianic kingdom or not, this is a marvelous admission and celebration in Judaism of the inclusion of the Gentiles in Messiah ben David's eternal kingdom.

The genealogy of David is firmly established here, tracing him from the royal line of the tribe of Judah:

> May the Lord make the woman [Ruth] who is coming into your house like Rachel and Leah, both of whom built up the House of Israel, prosper in Ephrathah and perpetuate your name in Bethlehem! And may your house be like the house of Perez whom Tamar bore to Judah ... This is the line of Perez: Perez begot Hezron, Hezron begot Ram, Ram begot Ammi-nadab, Ammi-nadab begot Nahshon, Nahshon begot Salmon, Salmon begot Boaz, Boaz begot Obed, Obed begot Jesse, and Jesse begot David.
> (Ruth 4:11, 12, 18–22)

King David's lineage from Judah is a scandalous story. In Genesis 38 we have a story almost parallel to Ruth. It concerns Judah's dalliance with and marriage to the Gentile Canaanite woman Shua, presumed to be from an idolatrous heathen family. She bore him three sons named Er, Onan, and Shelah. The record says that Er was wicked and God killed him. He left a childless widow named Tamar. The levirate marriage law required Onan to sire a child with Tamar, but he practiced coitus interruptus with her, and she did not get pregnant. The record says that God took Onan's life also. The third son, Shelah, was still a child, so Judah sent Tamar back to her father's house to await the sexual maturity of Shelah. That time came and went, and apparently Judah conveniently forgot about Tamar. So Tamar, presumed also to be from a Canaanite idolatrous heathen family, decided to trick Judah. She disguised herself as a harlot and enticed Judah to have sex with her. She got pregnant by him, her father-in-law, and bore twin sons. One, who was named Perez, was David's ancestor.

David had no illusions about his DNA, which came from the more authentic maternal female genes, from heathen and idolatrous Moabite and Canaanite blood. Tamar acted as a harlot and had sex with her own father-in-law. Clearly the union was an adulterous fornication. By this adulterous fornication the Gentiles became entrenched in Abraham's seed in their royal line. But it is cleansed and accepted by conversion to Judaism because of the transforming messianic redemption. This is the primary message of this romantic book of Ruth. It is declared by God through the Psalmist, King David himself:

> But I have installed My King on Zion, My holy mountain! …
> You are My Son, I have Fathered You this Day.
> (Ps. 2:6, 7)

The Son of God in this qualification is both generic and messianic. The rabbinic sages of the Talmud regarded this scripture as highly messianic. God's functionality, the messianic Redeemer, is accepted in Judaism as *God's son.* As God's son, there is a penetration of humanity by deity. The rabbis linked this sonship with the prophet Daniel's *Son of Man,* the Messiah. (Dan. 7; see Midrash *Pesiqta Rabbati;* also see *The Jewish Gospels,* by Daniel Boyarin.) God did bless David as His chosen generic son as king, but David knew exactly what God was implying here. David understood and reveled in the idea that he was a type of the Messiah. God is talking about the messianic Redeemer here, His messianic functionality. He is not talking about David alone.

This messianic Redeemer is also here in the book of Ruth, typified by *Boaz, the kinsman-redeemer.* And here again is entrenched the penetration of humanity by deity to redeem. The Messiah comes as a human, our Divine Kinsman. David and Boaz were types of the penetration of humanity by divinity to perform the Redemption. He comes as a human but He also is our Divine Redeemer.

The Israelites at the foot of Mt. Sinai trembled with fear at the awful fiery manifestation of God on the mountain. They wanted a toned-down version of God's presence. So they complained to Moses, asking for a less threatening version of God. Moses reassured them that the Messiah would be human. Moses was also a type of the Messiah:

> The Lord your God will raise up for you a prophet *from among your own people,* like myself … "I will raise up a prophet for them from among their own people, like yourself."
> (Deut. 18:15–18, *emphasis added*)

Bethlehem is the city of Judah, Naomi, Ruth, Boaz, Obed, Jesse, and David, a locus favored by God for Israel's royalty. It is where Messiah ben David arrives. Micah specified it:

> And you, O Bethlehem of Ephrath,
> Least among the clans of Judah,
> From you one shall come forth
> To rule Israel for Me –
> ***One whose origin is from of old,***
> ***From ancient times.***
> Truly, He will leave them [helpless]
> ***Until she who is to bear has borne.***
> (Mic. 5:1, 2, emphasis added)

Isaiah amplified this, clearly proclaiming messianic deity:

> The people that walked in darkness
> Have seen a great light;
> On those who dwelt in a land of gloom
> Light has dawned …
> ***For a Child has been born to us,***
> A Son has been given us.
> And authority has settled upon His shoulders.
> He has been named
> "The Mighty God is planning ***Grace;***
> The Eternal Father, a peaceable ruler" …
> Upon David's throne and kingdom.
> (Isa. 9:1, 5, 6 emphasis added)

King David was under no misapprehension about his "tainted" ancestry. He knew he did not have "purity" of Abrahamic lineage. *David's veins ran thick with once idolatrous Gentile heathen blood.* He had a double complement of female Gentile genes, from both Tamar and Ruth. David, the most illustrious and celebrated mortal 'Gentile-Jew,' the zenith of Jewish royalty, is now dead and gone and lying in the dust from whence he sprung. But the Messiah ben David dramatically takes the limelight. Isaiah declared that the people that walked in darkness are to see a brilliant Light. On those who dwelled in a land of gloom, Light has dawned. He comes as a promise from God. He is God Himself in the functionality of the mighty God planning grace.

How flirtatiously and romantically Ruth bathes, douses herself with perfume, disguises herself in finery, and sneaks in, in the dead of night. She lies down at the *feet* of Boaz. Her heart is tachycardic, pounding with all the Gentile female sexual urges of intense desire and loaded with the enthralling enticements of a woman seeking the ravenous love of a man, like a heat-seeking missile:

> Then she went over stealthily and uncovered his *feet* and
> lay down. In the middle of the night, the man gave a start
> and pulled back – there was a woman lying at his *feet*.

He recoils, but then recognizes her desperate need. She pleads:

> Spread your robe over your handmaid, for *you are a*
> *redeeming kinsman*

So he covers her with his robe and says,

> Lie down till the morning.
> (Ruth 3, emphasis added)

The trembling electric sexuality of this scene is startlingly exciting and titillating. *But for those whose sensibilities are immersed in the pathos of the human condition* and who feel the great desire God has to reclaim us to His bosom in primal devekut (Edenic communion with God), *what a marvelous messianic scene this is!* Here we are in our poverty and bereavement, gleaning in the field the morsels carelessly dropped. We long to be in the bosom of our God, who is rich in the glory of His infinite mercy. In the darkness of our blackest night without a glimmer, we approach in the stealth of our undeserving condition, trying to be attractive to our Lord by having our ritual baths and wearing the threadbare and smelly finery of the filthy rags of our benevolent acts. We uncover the nakedness of His condescension into our debased world and plead for Him to cover our broken and fallen condition. And He graciously covers us with His righteous robe till the morning of our redemption. The Messiah of eternity must recoil, for He is very God indeed and is faced with redeeming us from death. His omnipotent majesty recoils because His humanity must be crushed in the suffering He must go through in that condescension. *But He does it most abundantly!* (Ps. 22; Isa. 53; see *Bavli*: Sanh 38b, Suk 52a, BerR 1:4, 75:6; also see Qumran Fragments 4Q 491, 541.) We lie down with Him in the darkness, now full of the promise of His suffering sacrificial love. His robe and His loving arms are firmly around us. We thrill in the ecstasy of our glorious redemption. *In the morning of His eternal kingdom He pays off all other claims on us,* taking the blame for our inglorious past. He buys the barren fields of Naomi's dead husband and sons, and marries us, the bride He has been fantasizing about since the fall in Eden. In His marvelous redemption we are forgiven and healed and restored to His bosom. This is the messianic message of Ruth. This is the reason the Sanhedrin included this love story in the sacred canon. This is the stupendous portrayal of God's majesty, mystery, and unfathomable love, so powerful in our redemption.

Ruth, as a former Moabite Gentile, spoke words to her mother-in-law, to whom she clung, so she could return with her to the land of Judah. These words must every Gentile speak in spirit to understand messianic redemption, revealed by the primitive prophetic Jewish consciousness:

> And Ruth said, Entreat me not to leave thee, or to turn away from following after thee; for where thou goest, I will go; and where thou lodgest, I will lodge; thy people shall be my people, and thy God, my God. Where thou diest, will I die, and there will I be buried; the Lord do so to me, and more also, if anything but death part thee and me. When Naomi saw that Ruth was steadfastly determined to go with her, then she ceased speaking unto her ... ***So they went until they came to Bethlehem,*** in the beginning of the barley harvest.
> (Ruth 1:16–19a, 22c KJV)

"Salvation is of the Jews," declared Yeshua of Nazareth. Enthralled by these words, Dietrich Bonhoeffer expressed the confidant opinion "With its prophetic hope, Israel stands alone among the nations. And Israel becomes the place at which God fulfills his promise." (See *Christology*, by Dietrich Bonhoffer, p. 62.)

The world must come to Bethlehem, for that is where the Messiah ben David will be. The Messiah of the Jews is the Messiah of all humanity. The Kinsman-Redeemer awaits us there "in the beginning of the barley harvest," when the riches of His mercy are plentiest. We will lie down in the darkness of the blackest night of our glimmerless condition till the Light of the morning of the eternal kingdom of Messiah ben David. The Lord our God is one. Blessed be He.

Esther

Esther, or Hadassah, was an orphan who was brought up by Mordechai, her older cousin, in Shushan, the capital city of the kingdom of Medo-Persia, which extended from Ethiopia to India. Esther and Mordecai were diasporic Jews. Anti-Semitism was rife in the empire. The king was Ahasuerus (Xerxes), and his queen was Vashti. Ahasuerus is said to have ruled from 486 BC to 465 BC. There were 127 provinces in his empire, which likely included the Holy Land, so it is likely that all Jews on the planet were threatened with annihilation.

The story is that Vashti, the queen, refused to appear before the king's drunken feast. She was replaced by the beautiful woman Esther, a Jewess, the top choice of the king. Mordecai was instrumental in preventing a plot to kill the king. He was rewarded by elevation above the wicked Haman, who planned to annihilate the Jews. The king made a preventative edict for the Jews to defend themselves, and so they went on the offensive, killing a very large number of their enemies who attacked them throughout the empire.

The reality of the history of Esther has been deemed questionable. *The Jewish Study Bible* commentary written by Adele Berlin denies the reality of the story. Berlin calls the heroes Mordecai and Esther one-dimensional and unrealistic, despite admitting that the setting of the Persian Court is authentic. Berlin denies that a queen called Esther ever existed. She feels that Esther is best read as a comedy. Rabbinic midrashim seem to have intuited this, and they add to the fun by their preposterous embellishments of the story and its characters, extending in the most unsubtle ways the farce or burlesque inherent in the book with its bawdiness and slapstick humor. (See *The Jewish Study Bible*, pp. 1623–1625; also see *Esth. Rab.* on 1:11).

Berlin admits that the book has a serious side, centered on the diaspora, and addresses the inherent problems of a minority people. She explains it is a prototype of anti-Semitism. She reminds us that Esther is the only biblical book of which no remnant has been found at Qumran.

Berlin is brave to voice these opinions. Some might think she is misinformed. The Jews generally take it as a historical occurrence. They celebrate their salvation from annihilation ("pur," which means "the plot") in the Feast of Purim. Despite the alleged levity, excessive eating, and drunkenness at Purim, it is a celebration of messianic redemption. The redeemed of Israel and of all humanity will be saved in Messiah ben David's eternal kingdom despite being persecuted.

Esther and Mordecai also are messianic figures. Esther was to save her people under the threat of Mordecai that she herself would die as a result of Haman's engineered royal decree. Mordecai's challenge to Esther was as follows:

> And who knoweth whether thou art come to the kingdom
> for such a time as this? (Esther: 4:14c KJV)

In the modern world, where Israel is the strongest minority nation, its security is considered ethereal. There are more Jews still living outside Israel in a now voluntary diaspora. Current diasporic Jews are strong in the Western civilizations. They are needed in the protection of Israel, still to fulfill the Abrahamic covenant. The eschatological apocalyptic events of the Tanak are inexorable. The Jews, despite living constantly in the fear of being annihilated, will never become an extinct people. The Tanak assures us of this. They must fulfill the Abrahamic covenant. It is not enough to be circumcised. They must preserve the world by proclaiming the Messiah as agreed in the covenant, of which circumcision is merely the sign. But Israel herself is vulnerable. Modern diasporic Jews are the modern Esther. They have "come to the kingdom for such a time as this." They must decipher the tanakian Messiah and get ready for judgment and resurrection. The Messiah comes to the kingdom to save the redeemed. "Rejoice, O daughter of Zion, shout O daughter of Jerusalem, for thy King cometh unto thee. He is the Righteous Saviour and He shall speak peace unto the nations." The book of Esther has a secure place in the sacred canon.

The Ark of the Covenant

CHAPTER 12

King David's Messiah for Sinners

The writings of David must be viewed as very sacred. "A text from the Dead Sea Scrolls, MMT*d (4Q397:14-21; C.9-10)* speaks of the books of Moses and the books of the Prophets *and David,* thus indicating its highly esteemed status."[95] Most scholars do not recognize the theological eminence of King David. This source further states that the Psalms is a "collection of collections" of the poetic prayers of individuals. The origins of most of these are said to be obscure. The Hebrew name is *Tehillim,* which means "songs of praise." These are adored and quoted frequently in rabbinic literature. In the Dead Sea Scrolls, a Psalms scroll (11QPsa, lines 4–5) says that David wrote 3,600 Tehillim plus other compositions. There is evidence that the tanakian book of Psalms is an incomplete collection.

The psalms attributed to David are packed with the theology of Judaism and, in particular, Messianism. They are canonical and sacred. The psalms of Solomon are noncanonical and are part of the pseudepigrapha, not included in the Tanak. I do not regard them as sacred.

There is widespread opinion among scholars that David wrote most of the psalms included in the Tanak. Some are ascribed to Solomon, Korah, Asaph, Ethan, Heman, and Moses. The Talmud tells us that David wrote the psalms with the collaboration of ten elders, namely Adam, Melchizedek, Abraham, Asaph, Moses, Heman, Jeduthun, and the three sons of Korah.[96] Joseph Klausner divides the 150 tanakian psalms into two lots: those compiled before and those compiled after the Babylonian exile of 586 BC. This division does not affect the theology, which has its own unity. The theology of the psalms included in the Tanak clearly *defines the doctrines of primitive redemptive Judaism.* Jacob, Moses, David, and Isaiah are the *greatest theologians in Israel's ancient history,* and they are congruent.

Samples of talmudic support for the messianic nature of the psalms are as follows: Midrash Shemoth.par.va-era 8; Midrash Tehillim 21; Sanhedrin 97a; Sanhedrin 38a; Mikraoth Gedoloth; Pesahim 118b; Avoda Zara 3b; Sukka 52a; Zohar, part III p. 307, Amsterdam edition.

David Castelli sees a lot of Judaism's redemptive theology in the Psalms. He sees "The Day of Judgment" and "The Great Messianic Ingathering of God's People" from all the nations to serve the Lord. Psalms 11, 46, 66, 68, and 117 are named as evidence. (See *Il Messia*, by David Castelli p. 76.)[97]

From his anointing by Samuel to be king, David had been possessed by the Holy Spirit (1 Sam. 16). Led by the Holy Spirit, David's understanding of the Messiah stemmed from his ideation of the deity of the Redeemer and also evolved from his own personal spiritual life. He applied the concepts of repentance and expiation, as outlined by Moses in the tabernacle temple, to his own sinfulness. The majesty of the status of his royal election by God as king was overwhelmed by the understanding of the condescension of deity in the sonship of the Messiah. And he saw with perfect clarity of vision that Messiah ben David was to come after him and establish the eternal kingdom. Estranged from God by his sin with Bathsheba, he pleaded with God, **"Cast me not away from Thy presence, and take not Thy Holy Spirit from me"** (Ps. 51:11 KJV). He could not rest till he was right with God.

David's embrace of redemptive Judaism dominated his personal spiritual life as he battled to keep the law but often fell short. He saw his kingly rule (which was the zenith of Israel's national power) as a type of the great eternal kingdom of the King Messiah. In these two roles we see the two functions of the Ha-Mashiach. These, David deciphered, were, first of *salvation from sin in his own life and the reversal of the great disobedience of Gan Eden*, which he expected the Messiah to generate. The second function, the *restoration of the eternal messianic kingdom*, was to be achieved by the resurrection and the induction of perfection and immortality in a new earth. These dual roles he saw would be accomplished by the messianic functionality of Elohim in the penetration of humanity by deity in the forceful concept: "You are My Son, I have fathered You this day" (Ps. 2:7). It applied as generic to him, but he worshipped its messianic application.

In the first role of salvation from sin, he saw its function in the Aaronic priesthood sacrificial system. As the most heinous sinner in Israel recorded in the Tanak, he needed repentance and expiation. His Judaism was the basic redemptive Judaism that had come down from Abel's sacrifice of a lamb without blemish. It intoned the shedding of messianic blood. The mechanics of his understanding of this provision consisted of Shechinah, law, mercy, and messianic blood, in the Most Holy Place of the tent tabernacle. No one in Israel's history was more protective of the tabernacle temple's implementation of the redemptive function. It was his life's greatest desire to build a magnificent temple to his God, a task that went to his son Solomon. The Day of Atonement magnified that expiation and brought cleansing from sin. He wanted to replace the flimsy tent that housed the Most Holy Place, which contained the ark of the covenant, mercy seat, and bloodstains in the presence of the Shechinah. He wanted to give his God a grand structure in which to live on earth. His naked dance was a dramatic demonstration of the condescension of that messianic role for cleansing from sin. David's repentance and cleansing from sin is a model for the restitution of all sinners. (See Psalm 51.)

In the second role he saw his kingly status as the model or type for the messianic kingdom. Mashiach would be King of Kings and Lord of Lords. He recognized his own royal election by God in the blessing of Jacob's son Judah. The scepter he held between his knees while sitting on his earthly throne represented Shiloh, and he thrilled to be the progenitor of this Mashiach, whose blood was shed to cleanse him. That same King Mashiach would rule forever and ever.

He indulged greatly in the enactment of both roles, and God loved him for it. There is no doubt that David saw the two messianic roles clearly as he sang his psalms of adulation. Years later Isaiah rejoiced to proclaim both roles in the same definition. So did Daniel and the other prophets who are completely congruent in the definition of the two messianic roles. David truly understood the expiation by messianic blood in the high priestly ministry of the Day of Atonement established by Moses. (See Leviticus 16 and 17.)

The Penetrance of Humanity by Divinity

The Talmud has repeatedly stressed the Davidic pattern for the Messiah. Many of David's psalms are cited as messianic, as noted above.

David clearly saw the Mashiach as a penetrance of humanity by divinity, long before Isaiah and Daniel spelled it out. No doubt they had been singing his songs of redemption. In Psalms 1 and 2 we find a mixture of the two messianic roles, but they come through in clear functional definition.

Psalm 1 is a spiritual boast, an exultation. How is it that David could be so confident to proclaim himself as "The happy man who has not followed the counsel of the wicked ... Like a tree planted beside streams of water," when he was such a convicted felon? It was because his sins were forgiven by messianic expiation. And he saw himself as a happy man because of his repentance and redemption.

In Psalm 2 he tells how it happened. His Messiah, who "sitteth in the heavens," is defined as follows:

> But I have installed My King on Zion, My holy mountain!
> Let me tell you of the decree:
> The Lord said to me,
> *You are My Son,*
> *I have fathered you this day.*
> (Ps. 2:6, 7, emphasis added)

This declaration is both generic and messianic. It endorses David as king. In the generic model all Israel's kings were named as God's sons. But the human model is superceded. In David's situation the genetics are invalid. The Canaanite Gentile heathen woman Tamar, acting the harlot with her father-in-law, was in his ancestry. David also knew he was the son of Jesse and that his great-grandmother was Ruth, a converted Gentile heathen Moabite. She was not even an Israelite by birth, let alone of the tribe of Judah. Not a drop of her blood had Judah DNA. After all, motherhood was the proof of Hebrew lineage. The rabbinic sages rejected a Messiah who was not a bona fide product of the womb of a woman who was not from Judah. One of the reasons many Jews rejected the short-lived Hasmonean dynasty is because they were not of the tribe of Judah. I contend that David had no illusions about his own DNA, which was so mixed with Moabite "heathen" DNA. He is not only talking about his own anointing as king in Psalm 2. He is talking about the Mashiach when voicing the words of God: "*You are My Son, I have fathered You this day.*" Fatherhood in Israel could not prove lineage. He is deluded if he is talking about his own DNA. Here he is talking about the humanity of the Mashiach. And it did not matter that Ruth's DNA was heathen Moabite DNA. There was no trace of divinity in David's sinful blood. The sages regarded this psalm as messianic. Here Ha-Mashiach would be divine because He would come as a functionality of Elohim, which on the earth in our human idiomatic comprehension is expressed as a Father–Son relationship. So, in human terms, for want of a better way, we describe His coming as God's Son, fathered by the Almighty. But there is no doubt that the messianic origin is God Himself the Redeemer, taking upon Himself humanity, *the great condescension.*

There are three streams of Jewish interpretation of Psalm 2:

1. RaSHI: "Our rabbis have taught that this concerns the Messiah-King, and in harmony with this interpretation it can be applied to David himself ..." We must conclude from this pronouncement that Messiah is indeed God, here expressed as a divine Son fathered on earth. We must also conclude here that David, if he was the designated son, was in no way divine.

2. Ibn Ezra: the "anointing of David as king, for which reason it is written 'This day have I begotten you' or else it concerns the Messiah ..." Ibn Ezra could not resist matching this with the sending of the Messiah. In modern times Daniel Boyarin stresses this definition (the anointing of kings), denying the messianic nature of this Psalm. (See *The Jewish Gospels*, by Daniel Boyarin, pp. 26–31. He finds support for this in the writings of Catholic scholar Joseph Fitzmyer.) But he could not resist a double application to "the notion of a promised Redeemer, a new King David whom God would send at the end of days." By this he cancels his denial.

145

3. Popular expositions, such as the Metsudat David, which stresses that the words "You are My son" (Avoda Zara 3b)[98] refer to Israel. This perhaps is with the reasoning that all humans are sons of God. But it traps Israel into the responsibility of being the Messiah. Israel cannot be her own Redeemer, since redemption is God's avowed sole responsibility. In consideration of this point, with allusion to the rabbinic interpretation that the Son of Man of Daniel 7 is also a reference to Israel, Daniel Boyarin does not agree. In proof he even calls to witness this absurdity the "exegetical and very much to the point" argument of the fourth-century Iranian church father Aphrahat. As well, Boyarin uses J. A. Everton's words: "The act of coming with the clouds suggests a theophany of Yahwe Himself." (See *The Jewish Gospels* by Daniel Boyarim, pp. 39–40.)

Franz Rosenzweig and Martin Buber translated the Tanak into German. Rosenzweig, a German Jew, understood the nuances of both Hebrew and German. The translator of the *Star of Redemption* from German into English, William W. Hallo, admitted his own task was not easy:

> The attempt has been made, albeit within severe limits, to translate identical German words into identical English words, and their derivatives into English derivatives; ... [99]

Rosenzweig, in his essay "Atheistic Theology," published in 1914, expressed an opinion on the messianic penetrance of divinity into humanity. Nahum N. Glatzer wrote thus in the foreword to *Star of Redemption*, commenting on the "Atheistic Theology" essay:

> What is needed is a renewal of "the offensive thought of revelation;" offensive, for it points to ***the divine breaking into (Hereinsturzen) the lowly, human, sphere,*** or, as he called it later (1916), the "intrusion of the spirit into the non-spirit." [100]

Rosenzweig regarded God as the Great Spirit.

N. N. Glatzer explained this statement in Rosenzweig's words as "offensive, for it points to the divine breaking into (Hereinsturzen) the lowly human sphere …"[101] But in the same context Rosenzweig said he was tired of Protestant Christians insisting on the humanity of the Mashiach, as he was of the Jews insisting on Israel being the recipient of the revelation at Sinai. *What Rosenzweig wanted was a renewal of the divine breaking into the lowly, human, sphere….* Besides his desire to have a much closer devekut with God in the knowledge that Jews "were already with the Father," he clearly wanted his Mashiach to be both human and divine. He exalted the power of his Mashiach in *Star of Redemption* to such a degree that he could not accommodate this magnificence and power into a purely human Mashiach who would last only a mortal lifetime. I rejoice to repeat Rosenzweig's immortal words:

> Over against Israel, eternally loved by God and faithful and perfect in eternity, stands he who is eternally to come, he who waits and wanders, and grows eternally – the ***Messiah.*** Over against the man of earliest beginnings, against Adam the son of man, stands the man of endings, the son of David ***the King.*** Over against him who was created from the stuff of the earth and the breath of the mouth of God, is the descendant from the stem of anointed kings; over against the patriarch, the latest offspring; over against the first, who draws about him the mantle of divine love, the last, ***from whom salvation issues forth to the ends of the earth;*** over against the first miracles, the last, which – so it is said – will be greater than the first.[102]

Benjamin Pollock has written extensively on Franz Rosenzweig and may not agree with this interpretation of Rosenzweig's *Atheistic Theology*.[103] But there is no doubt that in Rosenzweig's *Star of Redemption* his Messiah has been forever in eternity and lasts forever as the King Messiah. And this same Messiah has a human existence on earth, appearing "from the stem of anointed kings."

Psalm 16 is regarded as a messianic utterance of David:

> Protect me, O God, for I seek refuge in You ...
> You are my Lord, my benefactor; there is none above You ...
> The Lord is my allotted share and portion; You control my fate.
> I bless the Lord who has guided me;
> My conscience admonishes me at night.
> I am ever mindful of the Lord's presence;
> He is at my right hand; I shall never be shaken.
> So my heart rejoices, my whole being exults.
> For You will not abandon me to Sheol,
> Or let Your faithful One see the Pit.
> You will teach me the path of life
> In Your presence is perfect joy;
> Delights are ever present in Your right hand.
> (Ps.16: selected verses)

The Jewish Study Bible margin comments delightfully list what some of the words might mean in body parts: conscience = kidneys, right hand, and heart; body = flesh = liver—all vital parts of his body, which David wishes to preserve.

This psalm expresses confidence in messianic deliverance from death, and he exults in the prospect of resurrection. Verse 10 is particularly exciting, as it reflects David's own hope of resurrection. But the words he uses are messianic. The Masoretic text indicates a dual application here with the use of the Hebrew word "*chasiyd,*" meaning "Holy One." David considered himself safe in messianic forgiveness, but he also sees his Saviour rising from the grave as "***God's Holy One.***" It connects with Isaiah's "Suffering Servant," who dies and who made His grave with the wicked, but who does not get left in Sheol (Isa. 53:9).

David's concept of the Mashiach is stupendous. Many of the prophets drew from it. Isaiah certainly did.

The tent tabernacle, with all its paraphernalia, represented the mechanics of the religion called Judaism. It was taken from the pattern of the heavenly temple and carefully replicated by Moses. Its dominant theme and essence was messianic Redemption. David was a great king and warrior, but his greatest personal thrill came from his efforts to preserve the messianic elements of Judaism in his actions to protect and glorify the tabernacle temple. He saw the earthly temple as a copy of the heavenly. How dare we walk away from the temple after its destruction by the Romans in AD 70.

King David's naked dance is perhaps his greatest depiction of the Messiah's role as the sin-bearer. Let us look in detail at the great drama that occurred in David's handling of the tabernacle temple:

The ark of the covenant was a box. God commissioned that it be made of acacia wood. It was overlaid with pure gold and had a thick rim of pure gold. The four corners each had a ring of gold to facilitate its carriage by poles of acacia wood overlaid with gold. These were permanently placed on either side through the rings. The two tables of stone with the Ten Commandments written in Hebrew by the finger of God were placed inside the ark.

God also commissioned the mercy seat to be made. It was a platform the same length and breadth as the ark, made of pure gold. Two cherubim of beaten gold were mounted one at each end of the mercy seat, facing each other. Their wings were outstretched, covering the mercy seat.

> And thou shalt put the mercy seat above upon the Ark …
> and there I will meet with thee, and I will commune
> with thee from above the mercy seat between the two
> cherubim …
> (Ex. 25:21a, 22a KJV)

The mercy seat was above the ark. This indicates that mercy was more powerful than the breakage of the law. The ark and the mercy seat were placed in the mobile tent tabernacle, in the Most Holy Compartment. It was here that the fiery presence of the Shechinah dwelled between the cherubim. This fulfilled the desire God had to "dwell among" the Israelites (Ex. 25:8).

The juxtaposition of Shechinah, law, and the mercy seat was no accident. God demanded perfect obedience to His law from eternity. But after the great disobedience, He knew that Israel was not capable of that perfect obedience, and therefore His mercy must be there as well. Israel would not survive without the mercy seat. The fact that the Pentateuch laid down so many specific punishments for specific sins was because the breakage of the law by the Israelites was anticipated. A fourth ingredient was then introduced into the Most Holy Place, once a year: the blood of the sacrificial animal without blemish. It was splashed by the High Priest on the ark and the mercy seat on the Day of Atonement. Here was the symbolic Ha-Mashiach blood by which God activated His mercy. The blood cleansed *all* the sins of *all* the people. Shechinah, law, mercy, and blood constituted the composite substance and complete essence of the almighty God's plan to restore humanity to perfection and immortality. This combination guaranteed the individual to pass the Judgment. It is the cataclysmic power that will effect the resurrection to immortality. (See Exodus 30 and Leviticus 16 and 17.)

What other explanation for these emblems can make such perfect sense? I challenge any Jew to provide an alternative to this explanation. I decry the calling of Israel's temple sacrificial service of expiation by the blood "cultic." But the accusation of primitive Judaism as a cult would be correct if Messiah was absent from this explanation.

The ark of the covenant coupled with the mercy seat, which was stained with the blood of the Day of Atonement, became the great symbol of power in the camp of Israel. Joshua used it to part the River Jordan so they could walk across and possess the Promised Land. (See Joshua 3 and Psalm 114.) Joshua also used it in the capture of the city of Jericho. (See Joshua 6.) On Israel's arrival in the Promised Land, the tent tabernacle had been camped at Shiloh, a landmark established by Jacob in his travels to and from Padan-Aram. He had built an altar there. (See Joshua 18:9; Judges 21:19; 1 Samuel 1:3.)

Israel had slidden into idolatry at the time of Eli's high priestly tenure. In a lost battle with the Philistines, four thousand Israeli warriors were slain. So, instead of putting away idolatry, they (Eli's sons Hophni and Phineas appear to have been the perpetrators) tried to use the ark of the covenant as a voodoo weapon of destruction to overcome the enemy. But God was not with them, and in the battle that followed, the Philistines captured the ark and killed another thirty thousand Israeli soldiers. Eli fainted at the shock of the news, breaking his neck and dying in the fall. The pregnant wife of Phineas went into premature labor with the shock and gave birth. As she was dying of blood loss in the abrupt delivery, she named the infant Ichabod, which means "The glory is departed from Israel," meaning the ark had been taken. (See 1 Samuel 4.)

The Philistines were troubled with the presence of the ark in their midst. After seven months they returned the ark to Bethshemesh, where Levites took charge of it. But the Bethshemites did not reverence the ark, and fifty thousand and seventy men died in Bethshemesh. They therefore sent it on to Kiriathjearim, to the house of Abinadab, where it stayed for twenty years. This story tells you how decrepit Israel's spirituality had become. The ark and mercy seat were neglected for twenty years, like junk in an attic, while Israel wallowed in idolatry!

> ... And all the House of Israel lamented after the Lord.
> And Samuel spoke ... saying, if ye do return unto the Lord
> with all your hearts, then put away the foreign gods ... and
> He will deliver you out of the hand of the Philistines. Then
> the Children of Israel did put away Baalim and Ashtaroth,
> and served the Lord only. (1 Sam. 7:2–4 KJV)

Israel subsequently defeated the Philistines and regained the territory they had lost. But the ark of the covenant stayed with Abinadab at Kiriathjearim until after David was proclaimed king. The Most Holy Place in the tent tabernacle at Shiloh remained empty, a sad and tragic vacuum, for all those twenty years. No Day of Atonement was celebrated for twenty years!

After David became king, he repeatedly smote the Philistines in an effort to destroy idolatry. In a massive rout, he gathered all their idols in the Valley of Rephaim and burned them. (See 2 Samuel 5.) Despite all his later lasciviousness, David was an absolute monotheist like Abraham and never wavered into Canaanite idolatry. How could anyone who was conversing with God on a daily basis waver into idolatry? David turned his attention to the empty Most Holy Place in the tent tabernacle at Shiloh and vowed to bring back the ark of the covenant. He first relocated the tent tabernacle to the City of David. He gathered an army of thirty thousand soldiers to emphasize the power of Israel. He formed an orchestra composed of all manner of instruments. These are listed as woodwinds, harps, lyres, psalteries, timbrels, cornets, and cymbals. As an accomplished musician he created glorious and victorious music in the worship of God. David danced to the music. (See 2 Samuel 6:3–6.) He placed the ark on a new cart and proceeded toward the city of David in Jerusalem. At Nachon's threshing floor, the oxen drawing the cart stumbled, and Uzzah the son of Abinadab, who was not a priest, reached to steady the ark. He died instantly on touching it. The music and the procession stopped abruptly, and there was a great silence. The fear of God was palpable in the throng. The ark was hurriedly and silently sequestered in the house of Obededom the Gittite. It was there for three months. (See 2 Samuel 6:9–11.)

David was highly displeased and upset with God for smiting Uzzah, the son of Abinadab. (See 2 Samuel 6:8.) After all, Uzzah was well intentioned, and his father, Abinadab, had cared for the ark for twenty years. Uzzah, he figured, had innocently reacted to prevent the ark from crashing to the ground. David became greatly fearful of God. He cancelled the transfer and sent everybody home.

After three months, on hearing of the prosperity of Obededom, he determined again with gladness to reunite the tent tabernacle and the ark in the City of David:

> Thereupon David went and brought up the Ark of God ... with great rejoicing. When the bearers of the Ark moved forward six paces, he sacrificed an ox and a fatling. David whirled with all his might before the Lord; David was girt with a linen Ephod. Thus David and all the House of Israel brought up the Ark of the Lord with shouts and blasts of the horn. As the Ark of the Lord entered the City of David, Michal [the queen], daughter of Saul looked out of the window and saw King David leaping and whirling before the Lord and she despised him for it ... When David finished sacrificing the burnt offerings and the offerings of well-being, he blessed the people in the name of the Lord of Hosts. And he distributed among all the people – the entire multitude of Israel, man and woman alike – to each

a loaf of bread, a cake made in a pan, and a raisin cake. Then all the people left for their homes. David went home to greet his household. And Michal [the queen], daughter of Saul, came out to meet David and said, "Didn't the King of Israel do himself honour today – exposing himself today in the sight of the slave girls of his subjects; as one of the riff-raff might expose himself?" David answered Michal, "It was before the Lord who chose me instead of your father and all his family and appointed me ruler over the Lord's people Israel. I will dance before the Lord and *dishonor myself* even more, and be low in my own esteem; but among the slave girls that you speak of I will be honoured. So to her dying day Michal daughter of Saul had no children." (2 Sam. 6, emphasis added)

It was clearly a party atmosphere that pervaded the transfer of the ark of the covenant, although at every six paces a sacrifice was made. Only the king comprehended the deep spirituality of the event. The Shechinah was being restored to the Most Holy Place with the ark of the covenant and the mercy seat and the bloodstains. God came back to His earthly abode in all His fiery glory after having been evicted for over twenty years. This event was of cosmic significance. David must have been initially in fear and trembling, given the previous experience. But David's behaviour conformed to God's will (otherwise he would have been dispatched instantly, as was Uzzah). Although his behaviour catered to a great party atmosphere, with the music, the dancing, and the goodies to eat, David realized fully the messianic scene he was acting out. When the guests went home, he went home also, to face the great disapproval of his queen, Michal, daughter of King Saul and sister of his beloved best friend Jonathan. Saul and Jonathan were both now dead.

It was at home in the palace, facing his wife's searing criticism, that the cosmic significance of the naked dancing became apparent. Michal's criticism must be considered sensible and of great behavioural value. But it was a superficial assessment that cost her, her fertility. God would not overlook her lack or rejection of spiritual insight. David had exposed himself in public. She felt that his nakedness belonged solely to her. She closed her mind to the spiritual explanation. That is why she was smitten with being barren all her life.

And what was this great spiritual truth that was demonstrated by King David's naked dance?

David was not totally nude when he danced. He wore the high priest's ephod. The ephod was a special part of the dress of the high priest. (See Exodus 28.) Its description surpasses the richness and extravagance of royalty. The most luxurious and opulent parts were the two large onyx stones, one mounted on each shoulder of the ephod. Each onyx stone was engraved in gold with six of the names of the tribes of Israel, the sons of Jacob. They signified that the high priest carried the full responsibility for the twelve tribes of Israel on his shoulders when he wore the Ephod. Zechariah called the ephod "filthy garments" because the high priest on the Day of Atonement symbolically carried all Israel's sins. (See Zechariah 3:1–5.) The high priest was dressed in his full regalia, including the ephod, only on very important occasions, such as the crowning of a monarch. But the one great yearly event for which the ephod was made and donned was the Day of Atonement. On that day he entered the Most Holy Place to splash the blood of the animal without blemish on the ark and the mercy seat. *All* the sins of *all* the people would be forgiven on that day. It was the holiest day of the year. Law, mercy, and blood mingled in the presence of the Shechinah on that one most holy day of the year, when repentance, forgiveness, and expiation by the symbolic blood would render Israel of perfect standing before God, worthy of the promised return to immortality. And the high priest also represented the responsibility God was taking through His Ha-Mashiach power and functionality to effect the return to perfection and immortality.

So King David stripped to his nakedness and donned the ephod. He was not the high priest; nor was he even a Levite. For wearing the high priest's ephod he should have been struck dead, as had happened to Uzzah on touching the ark. If David was doing this as an ordinary man or an ordinary king, he was being extremely presumptuous, and God should have struck him dead instantly, as He did to Uzzah. Why did God not liquidate him instantly? It was because David was of the tribe of Judah.

So What?

Because David was no ordinary king but was there by God's own anointing, he was a type of the Messiah. And through his loins the Messiah, King of Kings, was destined to come.

Stupendously, David was recalling the three greatest messianic redemptive ancestral events in Jewish history. And what were they? From the record in the Tanak, we have the knowledge that Jacob had the greatest understanding of the messianic event, perhaps even greater than the comprehension of Moses. Jacob figured in all three events:

1. **Jacob's dream at Bethel:** Here the Abrahamic covenant was entrusted to him:

    And he dreamed, and behold a ladder set up on the earth and the top of it reached to heaven; and behold the angels of God ascending and descending on it. And, behold the Lord stood above it, and said, I am the Lord God of Abraham, thy father, and the God of Isaac: the land whereon thou liest, to thee will I give it, and to thy seed ... and IN THY SEED shall all families of the earth be blessed. (Gen. 28 KJV)

    David was as yet in the loins of his forefather Jacob when Jacob had that dream. Looking back to Jacob, King David knew that he was to be the ancestor of the Messiah, for Messiah will appear through the royal line of Judah. He saw that he typified the Messiah, and he wanted to act the part. And God was delighted to let him.

2. **Jacob's wrestle with God at Jabbok (Peniel):** Here was the assurance that God would save him from death at the hands of Esau. He had no army at his back to protect him. But he had to be disabled further to rely completely on the redemptive power of the Ha-Mashiach, who would save him from eternal death. He trembled in the gully until he appropriated faith in the Mashiach as he limped up the bank relying fully on messianic salvation:

And Jacob called the name of that place Peniel; for I have seen God face-to-face, and my life is preserved … The sun rose upon him, and he limped upon his thigh. (Gen. 32 KJV)

When he did not rely on his own self-accomplishments for salvation from his brother's sword, then Messiah stepped in and delivered him from eternal death. David would later recall Jacob's limp and his own naked dance when he would carry the paraplegic Mephibosheth, his beloved friend Jonathan's son. These were all manifestations of the sinful, mutilated, and helpless state of humanity, totally without merit, lame, paraplegic, and naked before God. The Messiah would bear this shame for all humanity. Messiah would be "crushed" in a state of lameness, paraplegia, nakedness, and helplessness in this, His messianic condescension. This topic will be discussed further when Isaiah's writings are explored.

3. **Jacob's prophecy on his deathbed:** Jacob had the most outstanding blessing for his son Judah:

…The Sceptre shall not depart from Judah, nor a Lawgiver from between his feet, until Shiloh come, and unto him shall the gathering of the people be. (See Genesis 49 KJV.)

King David understood that he was not only the ancestor of the Messiah but also a type of the Messiah. He therefore presumed greatly and dared God to let him act the part in this great event of relocating the ark of the covenant. David celebrated this event and immortalized his thankfulness to God in Psalm 18. The Talmud endorses this idea.

Great deliverance giveth He to His king and showeth loving-kindness to His anointed [Heb. Messiah], to David and to his seed forevermore. (Ps.18:50, Lam. R. 1.51)

Rabbinic literature calls the Messiah the Son of David. Years after David, Isaiah would describe the Messiah as the "Leprous One," endorsed by the very perceptive Rabbi Judah the Prince, redactor of the Mishnah.

King David said to his wife, "I will dance before the Lord and dishonour Myself even more, and be low in my own esteem." He was describing the sin-bearer, the sacrificial lamb without blemish, who would be crushed by the load of the sins of all humanity. (See Isaiah 52; 53). Here is the Messiah snuffing out his life, redeeming humanity, and restoring them to immortality. And David felt he could bravely don the ephod without risking instant death. As a type of the Messiah he took upon his shoulders the responsibility in bearing the two onyx stones engraved with the names of Jacob's sons, representative of Israel and all humanity. David saw down the corridors of time, when the responsibility for Israel and all humanity would be heavy on the Messiah's shoulders. He danced furiously, not caring that the exposure of his nakedness lowered him to the basest and vilest in existence as he impersonated the sin-bearer. He intended to display his nakedness as he enacted the shame the Ha-Mashiach would bear. He became the "riff-raff" for all humanity in its degraded sinful condition. But the slave girls would honour him. Figuratively, the slaves to sin would honour the Messiah for their deliverance, because their sins were forgiven and they stood perfect before God because of the power and magnitude of the messianic redemption. The Jews enact the messianic sacrifice on every Day of Atonement. Do most of them do it unwittingly?

Imagine! The ephod, structurally in two parts, like aprons fore and aft, joined on the shoulders and loosely at the waist, but barely reaching the hips, could not conceal his nakedness. The flaps of the ephod were waving in the breeze of the energetic and furious dance of the magnificent royal physique. In his "leaping and whirling" before the Lord, his nakedness was certainly visible. The queen saw him from the palace window and was embarrassed at the display of his nakedness. The king cared not, however, as he was lost in the ecstasy that the Messiah would come through his loins. The words spoken by Jacob—"The Sceptre shall not depart from Judah, nor a Lawgiver from between his feet, until Shiloh come"—were ringing loudly in excessive decibels in his ears as he jumped and whirled in the air. The *entire multiverse* watched in silence at the great depiction by the naked king of the messianic condescension in the redemption of all humanity. They could not understand the mixture of David's mirth and the depiction of the messianic "crushing" in his human nakedness, shame, and punishment. It was a strange spectacle of God's great love for the human race. The angels folded their wings in awful incomprehension. And all around David the people viewed his nakedness. Did any of them understand the significance of David's shameful exposure? He sank to the depths as the "Leprous One" in condescension. He was the riff-raff of humanity. This is the picture of the Messiah not many Hebrews have recognized. Rabbi Judah the Prince saw it and embraced it:

> The Rabbis maintain that his name is "the leprous one of the School of R. Judah the Prince", as it is said, "Surely He hath borne our griefs and carried our sorrows, yet we did esteem Him stricken, Smitten of God, and afflicted." (Isa. 53:4, emphasis added)[104]

Many scholars believe that Psalm 22 is a view of the human Messiah being abandoned by Elohim, who allowed His humanity to suffer alone:

> The major Rabbinic passages addressing the subject [Psalm 22] of *a suffering Messiah* is found in Pesiqta Rabbati, a Rabbinic homiletic work that contains numerous Messianic passages, as well as four entire homilies that present apocalyptic Messianic visions, which mainly focus Messiah Ephraim. (Pesiqta Rabbati 34–37)[105]

It should be noted that Pesiqta Rabbati was written in the mid ninth century AD. But Daniel Boyarin is certain that a suffering Messiah is a hallmark of Judaism, ancient and rabbinic, and Psalm 22 and Isaiah 53 depict it. The confusion of the two messiahs of the rabbinic sages will be discussed later. Messiah ben Ephraim, as per rabbinic commentary, is a figure that dies in military battle and is considered a sort of pre-Messiah to the real Messiah, Messiah ben David.[106]

The nature of King David's messianic depiction here is worth defining. The sacrificial role was well understood by David. Incarnation, humiliation, blame, and crushing are all implicit in this condescension of deity. Read the words from Isaiah 53 used by the translators of *the Jewish Study Bible*: "despised," "shunned," "plagued," "diseased," "smitten," "afflicted," "bruised," "crushed," "maltreated." Isaiah expressed it thus: "And the Lord visited on Him the guilt of all of us ... He was cut off from the land of the living. Through the sin of My people, who deserved the punishment... Out of his anguish he shall see it. He shall enjoy it to the full through his devotion. My righteous servant makes the many righteous. It is their punishment that he bears." (Isa. 53:6b, 8b, 11). Messianic indeed, redeeming the world!

King David saw himself as he danced joyously, naked in his sinfulness, outside the gates of Eden, in the forlorn and doleful dying derelict bodies of his first ancestors, Adam and Eve. But he also danced joyously outside those gates in the wonderful realization that he was bringing together again the Shechinah, law, mercy, and the blood of the Messiah, the Son of David, who would restore perfection and immortality to all humanity, and with it, restoration to Gan Eden. The king comprehended messianic redemption and rejoiced in it. God loved David for it, as the almighty Elohim wept tears of joy at this expression of His immortal love for Israel and all humanity. His divinity would penetrate humanity and suffer their shame.

David was relocating the ark of the covenant and the mercy seat to the tent tabernacle, reuniting them with the Shechinah and the blood. What a thrilling and joyously salvific redemptive religion is here defined as primitive Judaism! What a shame that Israel has forgotten this redemptive religion and the most glorious freedom it affords. It is the balm in Gilead.

One wonders what David sang in his nakedness. Perhaps he sang these psalms:

> Why do the nations rage so furiously together,
> Why do the people imagine a vain thing?
> The kings of the earth rise up and the people take council
> together

Against the Lord and against ***His Anointed.***
Let us break their bands asunder, and cast away their yokes
from us.
He that dwelleth in heaven shall laugh them to scorn;
The Lord shall have them in derision.
(Ps. 2:1–4 KJV)

But Thou didst not leave His soul in hell;
Nor didst Thou suffer ***Thy Holy One*** to see corruption.
(Ps. 16:10 KJV, emphasis added)

All they that see Him shall laugh him to scorn,
They shoot out their lips, and shake their heads, saying:
He trusted in God that He would deliver Him;
Let Him deliver Him if He delight in Him.
(Ps. 22:7–8 KJV, emphasis added)

Thy rebuke hath broken His heart; He is full of heaviness.
He looked for some to have pity on Him, but there was
no man,
Neither found He any to comfort Him.
(Ps. 69:21 KJV, emphasis added)

The great rabbinic sages over the ages have agreed that these tanakian passages, all songs of David, are references to the Mashiach. The greatest sinner in Israel had the greatest comprehension of messianic salvation. His Mashiach would bear his sins and those of the entire world.

There is a mixture of charismatic and mystical flavors in the symbolism of David's naked dance, but it clearly is a depiction of messianic condescension. The Tanak views nakedness as both shame and purity. Both shame and purity are messianic pictures. Their solid combination belongs *only* to the Messiah. Adam and Eve were naked in the garden of Eden but did not know it because the purity of the glory of their perfection, immortality, and face-to-face communion with God enveloped them. But as soon as disobedience overtook them, they found themselves naked

with shame. After the fig leaves fell off, was their first apparel
made from the animal skins that resulted from their sacrificial sin
offerings—the animals without blemish that signified messianic
Redemption?

The prophets used nakedness when bearing messianic messages.
The nakedness of prophets is mentioned as a part of prophesying.
There is no erotic component in the following depictions.

Samuel recorded that King Saul was filled with the Holy Spirit
and prophesied:

> ... the Spirit of God came upon him [Saul] too, and he
> walked on speaking in ecstasy, until he reached Naioth
> in Ramah. Then he too stripped off his clothes and he
> too spoke in ecstasy before Samuel; and he laid naked all
> that day and all night. That is why people say, Is Saul too
> among the prophets? (1 Sam. 19:23, 24)

Micah prophesied about the idolatry of Samaria and Jerusalem:

> Because of this I will lament and wail;
> I will go stripped and naked.
> (Mic. 1:8)

Isaiah records the following:

> It was the year that Tartan came to Ashdod – being sent
> by King Sargon of Assyria – and attacked Ashdod and
> took it. Previously, the Lord had spoken to Isaiah son of
> Amoz, saying, Go untie the sackcloth from your loins
> and take your sandals off your feet, which he had done,
> going naked and barefoot. And now the Lord said, It
> is a sign and portent for Egypt and Nubia. Just as My
> servant Isaiah has gone naked and barefoot for three
> years, so shall the King of Assyria drive off the captives
> of Egypt and the exiles of Nubia, young and old, naked
> and barefoot and with bared buttocks – to the shame of
> Egypt. (Isa. 20:1–4)

Jeremiah records messianic condescension thus:

> Behold and see if there be any sorrow like unto My sorrow,
> which is done unto Me, with which the Lord hath afflicted
> Me in the day of His fierce anger. (Lam. 1:12 KJV)

The subject here is the desolation of Jerusalem. This verse is better translated by *The Jewish Study Bible*:

> Look about and see: Is there any agony like Mine, which
> was dealt out to Me when the Lord inflicted Me on His
> ***Day of Wrath?*** (emphasis added)

The Jewish Virtual Library has an excellent discussion on the book of Lamentations. Its author has not been definitely proven to be Jeremiah, though it has language in common with the book of Jeremiah, and many scholars believe Jeremiah is the author. In Lamentations, Jerusalem's sins against God are alleged but not specifically named. Idolatry is not mentioned. The key to the lamentations is that there is punishment for "generic" sin, which is being inflicted. The implied connection with Psalm 23 qualifies it to be messianic, and verse 1:12 could be interpreted as referring to the Day of the Lord (Day of Wrath), which is messianic. The agony borne here bears a close relation to the "Suffering Servant" of Isaiah 53, which is undoubtedly about messianic suffering for the sins of the human race.[107]

King David's "Naked Dance" depicts the messianic condescension for all humanity, steeped in sin. Modern Rabbinic Judaism has lost the recognition of primitive messianic redemptive Judaism since the destruction of the second temple. There is no longer any blood in the Day of Atonement as currently practiced.

Ah, David, will you dance naked again before your people?

King David had seized the throne of Israel after Saul and Jonathan were killed in battle. God had willed it. King Saul was the son of Kish, of the tribe of Benjamin. But Jacob had blessed and named Judah as the ancestor of the Messiah. Saul had been the people's choice, but David was God's choice, and He had sent Samuel to

Hebron to anoint David. David was of the tribe of Judah, and God had determined that David's royal line of the tribe of Judah would beget the promised Messiah.

When David seized the throne, the remnant of Saul's family took flight into hiding to save their lives. The nurse who cared for Jonathan's young child dropped him as she fled. She gathered him up and ran with him. When they got to Lodebar, east of the Jordan, it was discovered that Mephibosheth had been badly injured in the fall and was paraplegic. His spinal cord had been severed in the fracture that had occurred.

After David secured the kingdom, he searched for survivors of his beloved friend Jonathan's family. He found Mephibosheth, the paraplegic. He invited him to a royal feast at the palace. Mephibosheth was afraid that this was a plan to kill him so he could never challenge King David for the throne. The chariot bearing him, now a young man, arrived at the palace gates, and he shuddered in fear of death. As he was helped out of the chariot, David saw his disability immediately. He rushed out to the road and carried Mephibosheth in his arms to the royal table. David, a messianic figure, was dramatizing the function of the Ha-Mashiach in carrying decrepit and paraplegic humanity into immortality!

Here is the witness of a sixteen-year-old rock singer from Texas, USA, totally imbued with the redemptive concept as he pours out his soul in grateful adoration. He has immortalized the event in lyrical rock music. He has captured the broken state of humanity being carried in the Messiah's arms:

CARRIED TO THE TABLE
(Mephibosheth's Song)
Wounded and forsaken I was shattered by the fall,
Broken and forgotten, Feeling lost and all alone.
Summoned by the King, Into the Master's courts,
Lifted by the Saviour and carried in His arms
...

"CARRY ME!"

Leeland Dayton Mooring (Leeland *Sound of Melodies* album)

163

Would to God that Israel and all humanity will dance with David, exposing the nakedness of our shame and honesty. The admission of our breaking the law requires the mingling of the law with mercy and the blood in the presence of the Shechinah. That is the gist of primitive redemptive Judaism. That is the functionality of the almighty Elohim in the Ha-Mashiach, His power to redeem.

David wrote and sang much about the Ha-Mashiach. But the starkest experience was his own personal sin. The enormity of his quintuple sin should be understood. He faced the judgment bar of God. He coveted another man's wife, committed adultery with her, and then connived to hide her pregnancy. When he was cornered, he had her husband murdered. He broke five commandments as *coveter, thief, adulterer, liar, and murderer.* For a moment he thought he could get away with it. But there was a knock at his covetous, adulterous, lying, murderous bedroom door, where he had sequestered Bathsheba. It was Nathan the prophet, with the accusation "Thou art the man [who has stolen the sheep of the poor man and feasted on its flesh]." In his lust, he had been feasting in this bedroom on stolen flesh, breaking a fifth commandment. Nathan now stood there at the door, speaking for God:

> And Nathan said to David, That man is you! Thus said the Lord, the God of Israel "It was I who anointed you king over Israel and it was I who rescued you from the hand of Saul ... And I gave you the House of Israel and Judah; and if that were not enough, I would give you twice as much more. Why have you flouted the command of the Lord, and done what displeases Him? You have put Uriah the Hittite to the sword; you took his wife ..." David said to Nathan: *"I stand guilty before the Lord."*
> (2 Sam.12:7–13 emphasis added)

David stood there at his adulterous bedroom door, now hiding his guilty nakedness with a towel, with Bathsheba tremblingly cowering behind him, hiding her nakedness with a bedsheet. They stood in their shameful nakedness before God, the great Judge of all the earth, *accused, convicted, and sentenced to eternal death. So stands*

every human born on the planet, all guilty before the law of God.
Psalm 51 records how the Ruach Hakodesh found David and gifted
him with repentance, which he grasped with all his heart. Messianic
redemption was his only hope:

> Have mercy upon me, O God,
> Wash me thoroughly of my iniquity
> And purify me of my sin …
> Do not cast me out of your presence
> Or take your Holy Spirit from me …
> Save me from bloodguilt,
> O God, God my deliverer
> You do not want me to bring sacrifices …
> True sacrifice to God is a contrite spirit
> God, You will not despise
> A contrite and crushed heart
> Then you will want sacrifices offered in Righteousness
> Burnt and whole offerings.
> (Ps. 51: selected verses)

It is all there: the scene of the crime; the criminals who had
disobeyed Torah; the judgment bar with the Judge of all the earth
on His throne; the repentance gifted by the Holy Spirit in David's
contrite but frightened, fallen, frail, and quivering human heart;
the confession and punishment; and, finally, the sacrificial animal
without blemish, which provided the Ha-Mashiach's absolution. It
was a private Day of Atonement for King David, one of the most
heinous sinners of all time, because he knew better. But he stood
perfect before God because God now saw only His Ha-Mashiach
power, bleeding and dying on the altar, mightily protecting David,
who is now perfect in Messiah's blamelessness. The blood has been
splashed on the ark of the covenant and the mercy seat. Mercy has
triumphed over Justice. This is sheer *grace.* This is the marvelous
messianic miracle available to everyone born on the planet. Primitive
redemptive Judaism is the most exciting and saving religion. *Where
has it gone?*

The Coming King of the Messianic Age

At the core of David's vision in his role as king, a model of the Messiah ben David, King of Kings, we look again at Psalm 2.

> Ask it of Me, and I will make the nations your domain;
> Your estate, the limits of the earth.
> You can smash them with an iron mace,
> Shatter them like potter's ware.
> So now O kings, be prudent;
> Accept discipline, you rulers of the earth!
> Serve the Lord in awe, tremble with fright,
> Pay homage in good faith, lest He be angered,
> And your way be doomed in the mere flash of His anger.
> ***Happy are all who take refuge in Him.***
> (Ps. 2:8–12, emphasis added)

There is no doubt that David is making a messianic utterance here. It is reminiscent of the kingdom given to the Son of Man by the Ancient of Days in the book of Daniel, chapter 7. There is an exact parallel, which emphasizes the congruency of David and Daniel:

> As I looked on, in the night vision,
> One like a human being
> Came with the clouds of heaven;
> He reached the Ancient of Days
> And was presented to Him.
> Dominion, glory, and kingship were given to Him;
> All peoples and nations of every language must serve Him.
> His dominion is an everlasting dominion that shall not pass away.
> And His kingship one that shall not be destroyed.
> (Dan. 7:13, 14)

Both these scriptures are fully supported by rabbinic sages as messianic utterances. Both involve the humanity and divinity of this messianic person. David ends the Second Psalm on the same positive note that he began the First Psalm—that of happiness in his Messiah's accomplishment as Redeemer. (The messianic recognition of Psalm 2 and Psalm 89 in the Babylonian Talmud is noted in b.Suk. 52a.)[108]

Psalm 89 is attributed to Ethan the Ezrahite. But its subject is David in interaction with his Messiah:

> I have made a covenant with My chosen one,
> I have sworn to My servant David.
> I will establish *your offspring* forever,
> I will confirm *your throne* for all generations.
> Your wonders O Lord, are praised by the heavens,
> Your faithfulness, too, in the assembly of holy beings.
> For who in the skies can equal the Lord,
> Can compare with the Lord among the divine beings.
>   …
> Righteousness and justice are the base of Your throne,
> Steadfast love and faithfulness stand before You
>   …
> I have found David My servant.
> Anointed him with My sacred oil
> My hand shall be constantly with him,
> And My arm shall strengthen him.
>   …
> He shall say to Me,
> You are My Father, my God, the rock of my deliverance.
> (Ps. 89: selected verses, emphasis added)

The crowning Psalm may well be Psalm 110:

> The Lord said to my Lord,
> Sit at My right hand
> While I make your enemies your footstool.
> The Lord will stretch forth from Zion
> Your mighty scepter; hold sway over your enemies.
> (Ps. 110:1, 2)

Paul Sumner, in his *Hebrew Streams*,[109] has titled a study "David the Messiah." Here he lists the many fulfillments of the Messiah, for which God chose David as a type. It makes a wonderful study. Space does not permit a discussion of it here, but I will list Sumner's thoughts briefly. David was

- God's Anointed (1 Sam. 16:13; 2 Sam. 23:1; Ps. 89:36–37),
- God's Son (2 Sam. 7:14; Ps. 2:7–12; Ps. 22:10–11; Ps. 89:27–28; Ps. 110:3),
- God's Angel (1 Sam. 29:9; 2 Sam. 14:17, 20; 2 Sam. 19:27–28; Zech. 12:8),
- God's Throne (1 Chron. 28:5; 1 Chron. 29:23; Hos. 3:5),
- God's King (Ps. 72:17–19; Ps. 89:36–37),
- God's Priest (2 Sam. 6:12–19; Gen. 14:18–20; Ps. 110:4),
- God's Prophet (2 Sam. 23:2, Isa. 61:1–2), and
- God's Shepherd (2 Sam. 5:2; Ps. 78:70–71; Ps. 89:21; Ps. 102:10).

King David, now in the dust, understood every nuance of his being a type of the Messiah. He reveled in it. But he knew without a doubt that his Mashiach had forgiven and absolved him, and that he stood before God's judgment throne blameless.

At this point I draw further attention to David's position as God's son, a type of the Messiah. In the Babylonian Talmud (b. Sanh 38b; b Hag 14a; BerR 12:15), David is connected with Daniel's description of the Ancient of Days (*'atiq yomin*) and the Son of Man, in the provision of "thrones." (See Daniel 7.) Rabbi Yohanan is credited as saying that one throne was for God and the other for David.

Peter Schafer provides us with a most erudite discussion of this subject. (See his book *The Jewish Jesus*, pp. 68–102.) It describes a controversy between three early second-generation *tannaim*: Rabbis Aqiva, Yose (the Galilean), and Eliezer b. Azariah. Rabbi Yose disagreed with Rabbi Yohanan, who proposed in the Bavli the assignment of the two thrones to God and David. He believed the thrones were for God's attributes of justice and mercy. Rabbi Aqiva disagreed and insisted on Rabbi Yohanan's original idea: the thrones were for God and David. Rabbi Eliezer b. Azariah stated that the two thrones were the one God sat on and the other was God's footstool. But Rabbi Aqiva firmly insisted that the thrones were for God and David and, by inference, Messiah ben David, thus interpreting Daniel's vision as providing a throne for God and a throne for Messiah ben David, who was none other than the Son of Man of Daniel's vision. Schafer points out that Rabbi Yohanan's proposal and Rabbi Aqiva's seconding is a powerful solution to the problem raised by the plural of "thrones" in Daniel's vision. Schafer develops the Son of Man personality with the aid of the Similitudes of the first (Ethiopic) book of Enoch and the fourth book of Ezra, which I do not regard as canonical.

The major conclusion I draw here is that Rabbi Yohanan and Rabbi Aqiva saw David's type of the Messiah ben David depicted as the Son of Man, who is commissioned to establish the everlasting kingdom. Daniel Boyarin adds his powerful affirmation that the Son of Man of Daniel's vision is indeed the Messiah ben David, the messianic Son of God. (See Daniel Boyarin's book The Jewish Gospels, pp. 25–101.)

To close this story of David's Mashiach, I draw attention to the psalm that is beloved throughout the whole world. Composed by David the shepherd boy out on the green hills of Judaea while tending his father's sheep, it is the private adoration by a boy of his Mashiach. He had his harp and his sling with him. As the sun poured down on the hills and the sheep lazily grazed, he lay down and looked up beyond the sparse and fleecy clouds and beheld his Mashiach in the heavenly temple. He was hardly sixteen years old, but his manhood was upon him as he contemplated the roles his Mashiach would play in the redemption of the world.

The Ruach Hakodesh hovered over him and lovingly embraced this masculine masterpiece of God's marvelous creation, whose sinews would tear to pieces a lion and a bear that would hurt his flock. God saw a type of His Ha-Mashiach power who would tear to pieces the forces of sin and death. And the shepherd boy felt the arms of the Almighty about him as he breathed the rarified air on the lofted hilltop and beheld the Ha-Mashiach's power and glory in the heavenly temple. It was like a transfiguration as the shepherd boy's arms reached out and embraced his Creator's intangible form, enveloping the Divine Redeemer in his own vulnerable humanity. He was ecstatic in that moment of devekut, which would last his lifetime, spent looking over yonder into triumphant immortality. In glorious comprehension, he saw his Creator was also his Redeemer. When the event was over, a calm serenity overtook him as he basked in the sunshine of his Father's love for him. He thrilled with the idea that he was a type of his Lord. He saw his eternity in the Holy of Holies, where law, mercy, and blood would be exercised in the Judgment; where Messiah would be his Redeemer. He reached for his harp and sang:

> The Lord is my Shepherd, I shall not want.
> He maketh me to lie down in green pastures;
> He leadeth me beside the still waters.
> He restoreth my soul;
> He leadeth me in the paths of righteousness for His name's sake.
> Yea though I walk through the valley of the shadow of death,
> I will fear no evil; For Thou art with me;
> Thy rod and Thy staff they comfort me.
> Thou preparest a table before me in the presence of my enemies;
> Thou anointest my head with oil;
> My cup runneth over.
> Surely goodness and mercy shall follow me all the days of my life;
> And I will dwell in the ***House of the Lord*** forever.
> (Psalm 23 KJV, emphasis added)

The young lad saw his forever, his eternity, in the Most Holy Place of the temple, the house of his Lord, where dwelled the Shechinah.

There was a sudden noise and the sound of running feet in the valley below. He stood up and grabbed his sling in readiness to protect his flock. It was a breathless runner who yelled to him: "Go to the house, your father Jesse wants you now!" He ran down the hill in haste, into his father's presence. Samuel was there assembled with all his brothers. Samuel said, ***"This is he!"*** and he poured out a horn of oil on his head. He would be Israel's greatest earthly king. His body shuddered with the drips of warm oil running down his face and neck. He suddenly realized the awesome task that had been laid on him upon that lofty hilltop. The record says,

> And Samuel said to Jesse, Send and get him, for we will not sit down till he comes here. And he sent and brought him in. Now he was ruddy and had beautiful eyes and was handsome. And the Lord said, Arise, anoint him, for this is he. Then Samuel took the horn of oil and anointed him in the midst of his brothers. And the Spirit of the Lord *rushed* upon David from that day forward.
> (1 Sam. 16:11b–13a English Standard Version, emphasis added).

The youthful David did not ever forget that he was the standard-bearer for the coming King. Before Samuel's oil was poured on his head, God had anointed him with His divine embrace on the hilltop. David indulged in every opportunity to enact the Messiah. And God loved him for it, as tears rolled down the Almighty's divine cheeks. God *rushed to possess him,* He loved him so much and wanted to own him. He was a type of God's Ha-Mashiach functionality. The Almighty has some pleasures to ameliorate the sorrow He feels for our earthly lot. He will bring perfection and immortality soon. But God, it's a long time since you promised David that he would dwell in the *house of the Lord* forever. We don't want any more thousands of years, which to You are but as yesterday. Your beloved David is waiting in the dust. Hurry up, please! Rush again to possess him, and all of us who wait with him.

CHAPTER 13

Messiah in the Wisdom Literature

The Jewish Study Bible classifies the tanakian books of Job, Proverbs (Mishlei), and Ecclesiastes (Koheleth) as the Wisdom Literature. I prefer to exclude the book of Job rather arbitrarily, as I am compelled on present evidence to believe that it was written by Moses, and as I have discussed it within the chapter on Moses.

Tradition attributes Proverbs and Ecclesiates to the authorship of Solomon. Michael V. Fox and Peter Machinist have written the very erudite preamble commentaries to Proverbs and Ecclesiastes respectively in *The Jewish Study Bible* (pp. 1447–1449, 1603–1606). Most scholars agree that Solomon had something to do with these books, which reflect God's granting him wisdom when he came to the throne. His priority request of God was for wisdom. But the evidence is that these books are collections from various unknown authors and were a long period of time in the making. Fox's research reveals some sayings have been culled from Mesopotamia, and some from Egypt. (See *Instruction of Amenemope*: Proverbs 22:17 to 23:11.) He draws attention to Miriam Lichtheim's work titled *Ancient Egyptian Literature*, volumes 1–3. Solomon could well have had access to all foreign literary documents of value. He could have polished them into the gems they are.

Both books have been the subject of much talmudic and other discussion of the sages. Machinist points out that rabbinic tradition is quite ambivalent to Ecclesiastes (Koheleth) despite it being firmly ensconced in the Biblical canon. Some rabbinic sages argued—and others disagreed—"that Koheleth and these other books [Ezekiel and Song of Songs] did not reflect divine inspiration" and deserved to "be removed and stored away" (e.g., *b. Shab. 30b*; *m. 'Ed. 5.3*; *b. Meg. 7a*)."

A modern study of the evolution of "Wisdom" as a Jewish idea has been made by B. L. Mack in the book *The Messiah*. He traces it from Jewish sociological, cultural, and literary sources. His study is somewhat contrived and he does not adequately involve Philo's ideas which should have been included. He defines Wisdom as residing "in God" and gives Wisdom a feminine gender. He made no equivalence between 'Logos' and 'Word' and no involvement with creation and redemption.

Proverbs and Ecclesiastes would take volumes to discuss adequately. My discussion is limited to their messianic essences, which are very descriptive of *"Wisdom."* In his book *Star of Redemption*, Franz Rosenzweig makes two references to Ecclesiastes and one to Proverbs, but none of the verses he references is a messianic utterance. Abraham Cohen cites Ecclesiastes once and Proverbs twenty times in his book *Everyman's Talmud*, but none of these are messianic discussions. Joseph Klausner refers to each once in his book *The Messianic Idea in Israel*, but with no messianic intent. Gershom Scholem's book *The Messianic Idea in Judaism* makes no mention of Messianism in these two books.

Fox divides Proverbs into six major units, but I do not feel his division embodies the message of the book. He states, however, that Proverbs guides individuals (not the nation) in how to do what is wise in their day-to-day lives. It teaches the attitudes and courses of action that are right, just, and pious (p. 1447). But I assert that in guiding the individual, it also guides the nation.

Machinist sees a collective motivation for the books of Wisdom Literature and makes a masterful summary that Wisdom texts reflect on the nature of the world and the God who created and controls it, and on the place of humans in this divine creation (p. 1603). I wholeheartedly agree.

The *MacArthur Study Bible* (NKJV edition) commentary divides Proverbs into three segments. This is an amplification of Machinist:

1. Man's relationship to God
2. Man's relationship to himself
3. Man's relationship to others

The *MacArthur Study Bible* commentary summarizes Ecclesiastes in one word—the Hebrew word translated as "vanity," "vanities," and "vain life." It is expressed as the futile attempt to be satisfied in a life apart from God (pp. 924, 925).

These descriptive brevities I have culled clearly declare that the inclusion of these books in the canon was guided by inspiration, and I place them in a cosmic dimension. Proverbs extols "**wisdom**" as an entity and repeatedly draws attention to the connection of "wisdom" with God:

> The fear of the Lord is the beginning of knowledge.
> Fools despise wisdom and discipline.
> (Prov. 1:7)

The *omniscience* of Elohim shines forth in this statement. The statement "fear of the Lord is the beginning of knowledge" denotes the marvelous, awesome grandeur of Elohim and the mathematical precision of the Torah in describing redemption, which governs the multiverse. According to this verse, it behooves us to discipline our lives with the acknowledgment of the wonder, omnipresence, and omniscience of our God. He demands perfect obedience to this law but thankfully has provided mercy and pardon when we fail.

In the first nine verses of Proverbs, Fox sees the introduction to its poetic formulation that follows: "Ten Lectures" and "Five Interludes" beautifully delivered in a "Father-Son" disciplinary mode. Fox declares that this book personifies wisdom "as a nearly divine woman who represents a power transcending the individual teaching" (p. 1449). The outcome of being wise and disciplined in living has a repetitive messianic motivation. Redemption by Him guarantees survival and eternal life:

> So follow the way of the good
> And keep to the paths of the just.
> For the upright will inhabit the earth,
> *The blameless will remain in it.*
> While the wicked will vanish from the land
> And the treacherous will be rooted out of it.
> (Prov. 2:20–22 emphasis added)

Perfect uprightness and blamelessness are qualities seen only in *the redeemed state*. There is no doubt that such a state will be achieved in the eternal Messiah ben David's kingdom only after He has cleansed the multiverse of sin and death. The unredeemed (the "wicked" and the "treacherous") will be rooted out by the Messiah.

The exercise of wisdom and discipline in living begins here and now as a sanctification for that kingdom. But only redemption qualifies us for that kingdom, and the Day of Atonement mightily celebrates that redemption by the transforming messianic blood.

And so we may go on analyzing Proverbs (Mishlei) in detail and learning its motivation for disciplined practical living. *But the declaration of messianic personification reaches a dramatic climax stated in a mystical recognition of the event of messianic provision in bygone eternity.*

Listen to it:

> The Lord created me in the beginning of His course
> As the first of His works of old
> In the distant past I was fashioned,
> At the beginning, at the origin of the earth.
> There was still no deep when I was brought forth,
> No springs rich in water;
> Before [the foundation of] the mountains were sunk,
> Before the hills I was born.
> He had not yet made earth and fields,
> Or the world's first clumps of clay.
> *I was there* when He set the heavens into place;
> When He fixed the horizon upon the deep;
> When He made the heavens above firm,
> And the fountains of the deep gushed forth; ...
> *I was with Him as a confidant,*
> A source of delight every day,
> Rejoicing before Him at all times,
> ***Rejoicing in His inhabited world,***
> ***Finding delight with mankind.***
> (Prov. 8:22–30, emphasis added)

The Hebrew Messiah

This beautiful summary couched in terms of cosmic earthiness is so Davidic in conception that I am convinced Solomon composed it using his father David's messianic concepts. In this capsule we see that God planned redemption before He created our universe. It was not an afterthought. This is a most intriguing reality. "*Finding delight with mankind*" is such a mystical expression of pure devekut. It is so expressive of God's enjoyment of His creation, like a child's bliss with a desired and cherished toy, or a lover's ecstasy with a ravishing spouse.

Fox comments on this passage using a feminine gender in what he perceives as wisdom's personification as follows:

> Wisdom recounts her creation and her presence during the creation of the world. She was the very first of God's creations. An important Jewish interpretation starting with *Gen. Rab. 1.2, 5* and found in the Rashi to Gen. 1:1, uses Proverbs chapter 8 to argue that the Torah (identified with Wisdom) was created before the world and was used by God in creating it [commenting on verse], 22: '*created me*'. Since ancient times, interpreters have disputed whether the verb "kanah" means "created" or "*acquired.*" The latter allows for the possibility that *Wisdom existed from eternity and was coeval with God.*
> (p. 1463 *The Jewish Study Bible*)

That the redemptive force existed from eternity and was coeval with God and a part of God is much more consistent with monotheism than the alternative. Fox then discusses the messianic implication of this passage, but he prefers to interpret that Wisdom is a created being. Jewish commentators argue that wisdom is synonymous with Torah and that Torah coexists with God from eternity.

Peter Schafer, in his book *The Jewish Jesus*, very extensively discusses the dialogue in the Talmud about the "Hypostases of God." He sees this as a concept originating in Judaism in the Babylonian exile, and explicit in the Bavli. (See *The Jewish Jesus*, introduction, pp. 1–20.) He deciphers its discussion in the noncanonical books designated 1, 2, and 3 Enoch, the David Apocalypse, and the Hekhalot

Literature. Schafer's whole book is concentrated on this idea, which is well delineated in the Bavli. He clearly draws out the discussion in the Talmud and the continuing conversation by the Tannaim and Amoraim, some of whom proposed and some of whom strongly refuted it. Despite the idea having originated within Judaism (Enoch and Metatron), these rabbis argued within the context of achieving refutation of the minim—the heretical factions—who believed in the multiple divisions of the personhood of God defined as "*Hypostases.*" The minim (heretics) believed *El, Elohim, and YHWH* coexisted and were more or less independent of each other. It appears that some rabbinic sages were willing to elevate a human (Enoch) to Metatron status but were not willing to tolerate hypostases. Schafer deftly elaborates the Bavli account of the "semi-divine" status of Metatron, David, Messiah ben David, Akatriel YH, the Prince of the World, and the Celestial High Priest, as hypostases. He describes an antagonism existing between developing Rabbinic Judaism and primitive Christianity in the aftermath of the destruction of the second temple period.

Modern scholar Bart D. Ehrman, a rebel who left the Christological camp, rightly draws attention to the idea long existing in rabbinic discussion of *divine hypostases.* Divine hypostases are postulated divine beings, qualified as deity, coexistent with God, and more or less equal with God. Ehrman states that since this is a challenge to the sacredly held dominance of monotheism in Judaism, "divine hypostases" cannot be allowed and in fact have been argued against and suppressed in Judaism by many rabbinic sages. As evidence for divine hypostases, Ehrman points out the plurality of Elohim's name, and the Jewish discussion of Son of Man in the apochryphal book 1 Enoch. This book discusses the Son of Man in chapters 37–71, called the Similitudes. Here is an excerpt:

> Many great and glorious things are said in the Similitudes
> about this person – who now is thought of as *a divine*
> *being*, rather than, say, the nation of Israel. We are told
> that he was given a name "even before the creation of
> the sun and the moon, before the creation of the stars."
> (1 Enoch 48.2–3)

Ehrman goes on to say,

> We are told that all the earth will fall down and worship him. ***Before the Creation He was concealed in the presence of God Himself;*** but he was always God's chosen one, and it is he who has revealed God's wisdom to the righteous and holy, who will be "saved in his name," since, "it is his good pleasure that they have life" (*1 Enoch 48. 2-7).*[110]

Ehrman goes on to describe this "Son of Man" spoken of in the book 1 Enoch (1 Enoch 46.2–6; 51.3; 61.8; 69.79) being named as the "Elect One" sitting on God's "throne of glory" who "will judge the world" as the "Messiah" after the resurrection. Ehrman cites Alan F. Segal's book *Two Powers in Heaven: Early Rabbinic Reports About Christianity and Gnosticism,*[111] which presents a discussion of this notion in parts of Judaism, named as "two powers in heaven": God and the other (See also "Righteous One, Messiah, Chosen One, and Son of Man" in 1 Enoch 37-71 by J. C. Vanderkam, in the book *The Messiah* pp. 169-191).

In defence of monotheism in Judaism, *I totally reject* any creation of a "divine being" or "almost divine feminine figure in heaven called Wisdom" or any such things as *divine hypostases.* There is only one God, and we have no evidence that He undergoes genetic duplication like a reproductive cell. But I do embrace the tanakian reality that Elohim is expressed as a plural name. That plural name denotes the mighty facets of the power of Elohim to effect Creation and Redemption, which I carefully and emphatically insist on in my book as being His total priorities and functions for humanity. The Ruach Hakodesh and the Ha-Mashiach, the *functionalities* of Elohim, created humanity and, as eternally planned, have been gifted to the reclamation of humanity to restore Edenic devekut with God. It is our homegrown anthropomorphism that perceives these functionalities as forceful identities, as persons, and in Christianity as the Trinity. I do not recognize the apochryphal books as sacred, but I can appreciate the recognition of God's messianic functionality of Ha-Mashiach in the apochryphal books. There is only one God up in heaven and in the multiverse. Traditional Judaism embraces the Ruach Hakodesh as very God without compromising monotheism. Since God is the Redeemer, Ha-Mashiach must similarly be embraced as very God Himself. The work performed by both of Elohim's functionalities, as carried out by Ruach Hakodesh and Mashiach, provides repentance and expiation respectively. This is the redemptive message of the tanakian priests and the prophets, encompassing the great concepts of Creation and Redemption. *These functionalities stem from Sinai and were declared by Moses as Elohim's "Us."*

The book of Proverbs makes a mighty declaration of the power of God to effect redemption through the Ha-Mashiach:

> Happy is the man who listens to me,
> Coming early to my gates each day,
> Waiting outside my doors.
> *For he who finds Me finds life*
> And obtains favour from the Lord.
> But he who misses Me destroys himself;
> *All who hate Me love death.*
> (Prov. 8:34–36, emphasis added)

King David, that heinous sinner who received repentance as a gift from the Ruach Hakodesh, found absolution through the atonement by the blood of the animal without blemish, the symbol of the messianic expiation. David declared the following about the creation of the world:

> By the *Word* of the Lord the heavens were made,
> By the breath of His mouth, all their host ...
> For He spoke, and it was;
> He commanded and it endured
> (Ps. 33:6, 9, emphasis added)

The creating function of God is stated here as integral with Him as "the breath of His mouth." God created. And God's redemptive function is equally integral and powerful. He does not share these functions with anybody. Even when named as "Word" and "Holy Spirit," it is God Himself who creates and redeems.

But is this proverb and is this psalm a play on the Logos? Many Jewish rabbis endorsed the apochryphal books. Joseph Klausner leant very heavily on them and spent more than 170 pages discussing the Messiah in the Apochrypha and Pseudepigrapha in his book *The Messianic Idea in Israel.* Klausner makes six important references to Philo of Alexandria, an erudite and historic Jewish philosopher who thought and wrote in Greek. This eminent Jewish sage was steeped in Greek philosophy. In discussing Philo's ideas of the Messiah, Klausner quotes him thus:

> For "there shall come forth a man" says the oracle (Num. 24:7, LXX), and leading his host to war; he will subdue great and populous nations, because God has sent to his aid the reinforcement which befits the godly. (Philo, *On Rewards and Punishments,* chapter 16, sect. 95–97)

Klausner extols Philo before and after he quotes him:

> ... the Jewish Messiah was never thought of as exclusively spiritual ... he would never have been satisfied with a purely spiritual dominion. Even a person so deeply ethical as Philo of Alexandria cannot imagine a purely spiritual Messiah ... Thus throughout the earlier periods of the Messianic idea, Israel's best minds thought of Messiah as a king and warrior ... The Messiah must, therefore, be a military hero in the fullest sense of the term.[112]

Despite giving the Messiah stupendous cosmic tasks to accomplish Klausner insists that the Messiah will be purely human, albeit a very talented one:

> For redemption comes from God and through God. The Messiah is only an instrument in the hands of God. He is a human being, flesh and blood, like all mortals. He is but the finest of the human race and chosen of his nation ... [Here comes Klausner's heavy reliance on Philo:] Even such an extremely spiritual and ethical person as Philo of

Alexandria sees in the Messiah not only the spiritual and ethical side, but also finds in him "all-powerful strength of body" and "might"; for "leading his host to war he will subdue great and populous nations." At the same time Philo finds in the Messiah "holiness and beneficience."[113]

> Both with respect to holiness, righteousness, truth, and goodness, and with respect to might and authority, the Messiah is the "supreme man" of Judaism ... But with all his superior qualities, the Messiah remains a human being.[114]

Klausner fights hard to keep the Messiah totally human. But Philo has other ideas about the Messiah, which Klausner appears to ignore. The word "Logos" is Greek. Bart Ehrman explains Philo's ideas of the Logos quite succinctly. Ehrman says that thinkers who saw themselves standing directly in the line of the great fifth-century BCE Plato took the idea of the Logos in a different direction. Ehrman emphasizes that in the Hebrew Bible, God creates all things by speaking a "*Word*." In other words, Creation happened by means of God uttering his *Logos*.

> In the hands of Philo of Alexandria ... the *Logos* became a key factor in understanding both God and the world. ***Philo maintained that the Logos was the highest of all beings, the Image of God*** according to which and by which the universe is ordered ... Wisdom gives birth to Logos, which is, in fact, what Philo himself believed ... Thus Philo called Logos the "Image of God" and the "Name of God" and the "firstborn son" (e.g., *Agriculture 51)*. ... God "gives the title of 'God' to his chief Logos" (*Dreams* 1.230). Because the Logos is God, and God is God, Philo sometimes speaks of "two gods" ... Logos as "the second God" (*Questions on Genesis 2, 62)* ... [To] Philo Logos was indeed this Angel of the Lord (e.g., *Changing of Names 87, Dreams 239)*. In sum, for Philo the Logos is an incorporeal being that exists outside God but is his faculty of thinking; on

occasion it becomes the actual figure of God who appears *"like a man"* so that people can know, and interact with its presence. It is another divine being that is distinct from God in one sense, yet is God in another.[115]

Geza Vermes agrees with this endorsement of Philo's ideas. He stated that in the Platonic philosophical language, the Logos is the demiurge, the Craftsman responsible for the creation of the world. Although Vermes appreciates this rich Hellenistic meaning of Logos, he states unequivocally that *it possesses an important Hebrew and Aramaic background too.* Some scholars allege that Plato was "Moses speaking Greek." As described above, the Logos concept is pivotal with Philo of Alexandria. Vermes gives the Logos a very Jewish past reflected and recorded in the Palestinian Targums or Aramaic paraphrases of Genesis, which present a twofold understanding of *"be-reshit"* ("in the beginning"). Vermes sees it in the Dead Sea Qumran manuscripts as "sons of light," and the rabbis often referred to God as light. Vermes connects it to Proverbs 3:19: "The Lord with 'Wisdom' (be-hokhmeta) or with 'Word' (be-Memra) founded the earth; by understanding he established the heavens" (See *Christian Beginnings*, by Geza Vermes, pp. 126–130.)

So Logos is *not originally a Greek idea*, but antecedently a *very Hebrew idea* synonymous with Word. Moses clearly stated God created the universe by speaking the Word. The Hebrews owned the idea long before the Greeks got hold of it. Vermes emphasizes that in the antecedent Hebrew thinking that the Word (Logos) created the universe. David also said, "By the *Word* of the Lord were the heavens made ... He spake and it was done, He commanded and it stood fast" (Ps. 33:6.9 KJV). David's theological understanding was very deep. He knew his Messiah. The implication here is that the *Word (Logos)* is responsible for Creation, and now is, as enunciated in Proverbs, the messianic Redeemer, and is responsible for Redemption: "He who finds Me finds Life." This offered "life" to someone already alive is eternal life.

As previously discussed, the appearance of God in human form as a man has many instances in the Tanak. This medium famously appears to Abraham and Sarah under the terebinths, and to Jacob at the brook Jabbock. He is instrumental in the removal of Lot and his family from Sodom. He is seen in the fiery furnace of Nebuchanezzar. He is seen in heaven as the Son of Man "coming with the clouds" in Daniel's visions. The Israelites could not tolerate God's fiery majesty at Sinai, so God told Moses He would send a prophet "from your own people," referring to the Messiah who would be His presence with them.

Thus, in considering the books of Proverbs and Ecclesiastes, Jewish scholars theorize an involvement of wisdom, reason, hypostasis, Angel of the Lord, Word, and Logos. The *Jewish Study Bible* commentator employs a clumsy description of a contrived divine feminine figure in heaven, giving birth to the Logos, the firstborn of God. He is classified as a possible "duplicate" of God Himself and is involved with the Creation and Redemption of humanity. This is all figmental and unnecessary. There is no "divine feminine figure" giving birth in heaven. It is God Himself in the functionality of Word or Logos in Creation and now Messiah in Redemption. And as in Creation the Holy Spirit and the Word worked together, they now work again together to effect the Redemption. The use of the term "they" should not imply two "powers," but rather the plurality of Elohim, God Himself, eternally preexistent. He once said "Let *Us* make man." Now He says, "Let *Us* redeem man." This was all planned in eternity.

In defense of monotheism, it is so much simpler and the very axiom that God Himself is the Creator and Redeemer. These suggested mechanisms of the Hebrew rabbis, the Stoics, the Greek philosophers, Philo, and others are in fact attempts to explain the mechanism of messianic function within God. These are attempts to explain Creation and Redemption in terms of human concepts and relationships. In one sense we push the human description a little too far; we try to confine God to one sealed-off entity and the Logos to another separate entity. They are one and the same but seen in different functions. This is especially poignant in the concept of the messianic incarnation. God penetrates humanity for the purpose of redemption, but He does not come entirely as a human. Messiah is deity. In the redemptive act He does not renounce deity. Ruach Hakodesh and

Ha-Mashiach are simply (complexly) functionalities of God, with explanations of heavenly realities in terms of the confining idiomatic expressions of earthly relationships, conceived in the limited or confining human experience. The presence of Messiah ben David as eternal King of Kings is none other than God in the messianic functionality. The Father–Son relationship must be understood only in this functional manner. God does not possess a genetic son, in the sense of our genetic makeup. Messiah is not a separate person or separate deity. He is God Himself. Elohim, who describes Himself as "Us," is Creator and Redeemer. By the incarnation of Isaiah 9:6, God got very much closer to sinful humans. But in this closeness we are not to imagine that God has incorporated humanity into His eternal divinity or deity. Neither has He donated any divinity or deity to the human race. The Mashiach cannot be purely human but will use the fleshly human medium to bear the punishment of disobedience to the Torah, which results in death. Franz Rosenzweig felt that God donated a portion of Himself when He dwelled with Israel in the Most Holy Place of the temple as the Shechinah: "The Shekhina which He expropriated from Himself to the remnant of Israel." "Expropriated" refers to a taking over of ownership. If this was so, then God has taken it back, since the temple and Shechinah are no longer terrestrial. If this implies humanity's incorporation of divinity into itself, Rosenzweig is mistaken.

We may not understand this fully, but in coming as a human God is doing whatever He wants to redeem us. It is important that we do not confine Him within our earthly boundaries of expression. Divinity does not become a property of humanity in the redemption. We do not know and are not to assume that the Messiah ben David retains His human nature forever after the redemption is accomplished. Some have mistakenly assumed that Messiah ben David will forever retain His human nature. But He has assured us that He will eternally dwell with us in the earth made new. His "Us" capacity enables this.

It is my firm conviction that Ruach Hakodesh and Ha-Mashiach are not beings of a separate and individual trinity (three Gods) in heaven, comparable to or defined as "hypostases," but as functionalities of God Himself (One God). The eternal cosmic complexity of the Holy Spirit (Comforter providing repentance) and the Ha-Mashiach (the

Son, the Wisdom, the Word, the Logos, the penetrator of humanity as a birth to expiate, to atone) as functionalities within God (the Father) is beyond our understanding. But this is the machinery of redemption. An authentic Messiah coming to the earth in a penetrance of humanity by deity, therefore, must identify Himself and be defined as God, one substance with God. Therefore Messiah cannot be totally a human being, although He is partaking of humanity for the redemption. Adam came from the hand of God, pure, sinless, and immortal. The human Mashiach comes to earth as very God Himself, born from a surrogate womb to accomplish the expiation. He does not partake of any fallen human genes, received from a woman and her consort as is often proposed. There is a big difference. Adam was not endowed with deity, but the Mashiach is God indeed. Isaiah vehemently declared,

> For unto us a Child is born
> Unto us a Son is given,
> And the government shall be upon His shoulders,
> And His name shall be called
> Wonderful, Counsellor,
> ***The Mighty God, The Everlasting Father,***
> The Prince of Peace. (Isa. 9:6 KJV)

The Father–Son relationship, to which humans can relate and understand, has a persistent place in Holy Writ. It was first used by Moses in the Creation of the World, the Word, which the plural ("Us") Elohim spoke, and repeated in the promise to Eve as the "Seed." It was dramatized to Abraham as the son of promise, the son of his old age, and by the sacrifice of that son, Isaac. It was famously used by David to explain the penetrance of humanity by divinity (deity) as "Thou art my Son, this day have I begotten thee." Now here, in Proverbs, the writer uses "Wisdom," "Reason," the "Word," and the "Logos" and places Messiah in a heavenly setting. And the prophets all run with it as Messiah ben David, the "Stem" and "Root" of Jesse. Isaiah uses it most forcefully as the "Child," who is "the Mighty God, the Everlasting Father" who penetrates humanity in order to effect the redemption. The announcement of the arrival of this "Child" is dramatically linked to the "Light," which replaced the darkness at the Creation, *but here as the "Light of Redemption," replacing the darkness of an unredeemed world* (Isa. 9:2). Daniel sees the Messiah as "the Son of Man," first in the fiery furnace and then in heaven, being commissioned by the Ancient of Days and "coming with the clouds."

This powerful motif, this "Father–Son" earthly relationship, is fully exploited by the Scriptures to explain how Messiah enters to effect redemption. The *woman's womb* is persistently identified as the terrestrial vehicle of the divine penetrance. This is in a terrestrial setting and not up in heaven. The great importance of the woman in the scriptural context has never been discussed properly or adequately by the chauvinist rabbinic sages. Instead they made a welter of the male foreskin, creating a ritual that outshone the messianic mission in the Abrahamic covenant, of which it was only a sign. The Creator's masterpiece for the propagation of the race, that select wonder of the female reproductive miracle that cradles genetic protoplasm bursting with life in the womb, climaxing in the birth of a baby, a new individual, God's marvelous creation, has never been fully respected by those rabbinic sages. The Hebrew decision to limit the proof of the passage of Jewishness to the mother was a halfhearted method of admitting that paternity could not be pinned down. They did not have the proof of DNA. The rabbis' wisdom was blinkered by the magnification of circumcision as they gazed at their genitals in wonderment. A miracle doth the male genitals constitute, a solid part of genetic reproduction, but the sages were neglectful of the female womb. Scripture famously lists very important women in Hebrew history, *a matriarchal lineage*, more important in this context than the patriarchs: *Eve, Sarah, Rebekkah, Leah, Jochebed, the Princess of Egypt, Shifra and Pua, Deborah, Huldah, Jael, Hannah, Naomi, Ruth, Esther, the unnamed mother of King David, Bathsheba, and Isaiah's "young woman,"* the latter of whom conceives and bears a son to be called *"Immanuel, God with us."* Her surrogate womb was the vehicle for God to be with and redeem us. No human DNA or genes are involved, but *coming as a perfect second Adam*, He will be the royal Divine Implant, Messiah ben David, God Himself. If this mechanism of Redemption is unbelievable, *so is Creation*.

The feminine form, beauteous and magnificent to behold as presented so gloriously in Eve, is perhaps God's greatest masterpiece in all His creation in the multiverse. The world's greatest artists and sculptors have worshipped the female body. And the propagation of the human race proceeds only by the craving of men for unity with that female form in an ecstatic, throbbing reality of sexual cohesion. The Messiah would come to earth in the miracle vehicle of the woman's womb couching the force of the Almighty God, acting Himself as redeemer to save the human race, but remaining very God Himself. The rabbinic sages were indeed neglectful of the womb in their erudite discussions. But they did perceive the Shechinah as God's companionship and protection of Israel—as His dwelling with them, "With the Father" as Rosenzweig tried so delicately to phrase it. The Shechinah did not partake of the human medium, but Mashiach does. This is a great perception, perhaps the greatest contribution of the Jews to the understanding of communion with God in the act of redemption. We cannot assume that humanity now has been given any iota of deity. But humanity is restored to that primal devekut with God by the perfection and immortality provided by the divne-human Messiah.

Here I will belabor the point: in an explanation of the Wisdom Literature, the sages and scholars postulate a procreation of a "divine hypostasis" in eternity. Here, interpreting the Wisdom Literature, sages and scholars clumsily suggest that Wisdom is a feminine figure giving birth to the Logos up in heaven. The concept of Logos is indeed allowable as *an act of God planned in the eternity of heaven.* But as a sexual reproduction by God, as a hypostasis in actual fact, up in heaven, it is a fanciful flimsy flight of imagination and is totally unscriptural. The use of the Father–Son begettment on earth is a human conceptual vehicle to explain and introduce Messiah for the redemption of the fallen race. It must not be thought of as either a heavenly or earthly sexuality of deity. The eternal Messiah concept portrays God's miraculous functionality as Redeemer—coming to earth as a reproductive article—to be understood *only* in the human setting. It is not a sexual begetting but a miracle of incarnation. It must stay terrestrial, but it must couch deity. It must be understood as *the great condescension.* Isaiah's "young woman's" womb was indeed *a surrogate human womb.*

The human penetrance of Messiah to redeem must remain God's greatest miracle and is beyond our understanding at present. We name it in the Father–Son motif for our own understanding. It is God's way of saying that Creation and Redemption are His prerogatives that He will not share. It is the way He does it. It is His creative Sabbath and also His redemptive Sabbath. His functional power demands the sole ownership of worship as our Creator and Redeemer. Monotheism is triumphant. There is only One God, blessed be He. God comes as a human, bursting forth into and from the female womb, born on earth as the mighty God, the everlasting Father. He is planning Grace. His birth is aptly named Immanuel, God with us. And God will stay with us in the new earth eternally as Messiah ben David, King of Kings and Lord of Lords, forever and ever. That He will forever retain His human nature is a presumption.

The Wisdom Literature is a solid part of the Hebrew canon and is vital in the understanding of God's acts of Creation and Redemption. The conversations of the sages concerning the suffering of the Messiah that are said to have taken place in the celestial setting in the Midrash Pesiqta Rabbati will be discussed later in this book.

CHAPTER 14

The Supreme Messianic Lover

"Song of Songs" appears to be among scholars the preferred title of the first book of the Ketuvim to be read in synagogues on Passover. But some very decisive scholars label this book as "Song of Solomon" and insist that it was written by the young Solomon when he was in love with Abishag, his first wife. Solomon is mentioned in the song numerous times. Was it his experience? Some feel that it is too erotic and earthy a poem to have been included in the Tanak. Perhaps it embarrases them to read it. When I was a lad, my mother advised me to skip it when reading the Bible. I read it nonetheless!

Elsie Stern wrote the short but very insightful commentary on Song of Songs in the *The Jewish Study Bible.* I agree with her that the book has perhaps gleaned from the erotic imagery of Mesopotamia and Egypt. Nevertheless it uses the geography and beautiful scenery of Lebanon and the Holy Land. She dates it to approximately the third and second centuries BC. But some scholars attach the book very strongly to the authorship of Solomon, in 950 BC, perhaps because he has the reputation of being a romantic with multiple wives and concubines. There is no doubt he spent a lot of time in sexual activity. God was very peeved with Solomon's laxity and idolatry in the latter part of his life. As a punishment, God allowed the nation to be split into two.

Elsie Stern makes a very significant suggestion that at least one of the contributing authors must have been a female in order to capture the very tender and passionate feminine nuances of this romance. Women generally do not speak loudly about their lovemaking, in contrast to men, who are often strident about their prowess. The book is clearly an intertwining of the powerful erotic forces between a man and a woman, alternating in a fantastic throbbing reality both when together and when apart.

In our current concept of God, He is a Spirit, the Great Spirit, incorporeal in His eternity. He can, however, disguise Himself as a human in contact with humanity. We do not consider Him as a sexual being. But sexuality was invented by God for a terrestrial purpose. God performed the first marriage union after thinking up sexuality and the home. He values marriage and made sexual activity for procreation and enjoyment. In Malachi He values the marriage contract and takes a strong stand against divorce. He deplores the marriage of Israel with idolators:

> So be careful of your life-breath, and let no one break faith
> with the wife of his youth. ***For I detest divorce …*** do not
> act treacherously. (Mal. 2:15–16, emphasis added)

Song of Songs is a very Jewish book with very wide Jewish acceptance. The Sanhedrin overruled objections by a few rabbis to its inclusion in the Tanak. It is a vital, sacred recitation at Passover, and Jews call it the "Holy of Holies." Since this is where the essence of Judaism resides, it speaks of mercy and atonement by the messianic blood. It is indeed the manifest redemption.

The poem is also very widely "sung as part of the *kabbalat Shabbat* (welcoming the Sabbath) service on Friday night." These celebratory readings are to emphasize God's supreme love for Israel. The Talmud does not approve of the use of this scripture at secular settings and drinking halls (*b. Sanh. 101a*). I find it deeply satisfying that this poem is a love affair between God and Israel, and indeed all humanity. Stern states that the statements of desire and love are read as expressions of love and intimacy between God and Israel. Stern declares that the Targum to Song of Songs employs a similar strategy of expounding Song of Songs as a historical allegory; that it interprets Song of Songs as *a description of Israel's ongoing history of redemption by God.* (See *The Jewish Study Bible*, p.1565.)

Redemption by God was found in the symbolic activity in the temple. God's approach to erotic love needs to be understood here. He is the Creator of sexuality in humans. But our use of the erotic relationship as a model of God's love for us is a purely human way of expressing God's love. Since we do not know too much about God, we cannot exceed the bounds of our knowledge to ascribe sexuality to Him. Human love exceeds sexual love, and God's love for humans as expressed in the Scriptures far exceeds sexual love. And this is why Song of Songs is so vital to our relationship with God, as it equates to sexual love but also exceeds the erotic basis of human sexual love. When sexuality has physiologically burned out between a couple dedicated to each other, the love of pure companionship endures.

One wants to ask the question, is God a wife-beater or cruel neglectful husband when we see the miserable episodes of Israel's history? Hosea more than adequately answers that question. (See chapter 17, "The Sad Ha-Mashiach of Hosea.") The Tanak strongly testifies that God so greatly loves humanity that His messianic functionality is crushed and dies to redeem His wayward unfaithful lover. Repeatedly we have the assurance that humanity is God's most prized and loved possession in the multiverse. He is starved for the closeness He enjoyed with humanity in that primal Edenic devekut. He wants it back. God wants us back in His bosom. And here the inspired author(s) of Song of Songs use(s) the very erotic love between a man and a woman, that most physical and sensual maximally extravagant blending of two humans in flesh and spirit, to describe God's love for us. God expresses His own longing. We can therefore understand Him a lot better. Isaiah strongly expresses that God lays down His life for us:

> Out of His anguish He shall see it:
> He shall enjoy it to the full through His devotion.
> My righteous Servant makes the many righteous,
> It is their punishment that He bears;
> Assuredly, I will give Him the many as His portion,
> He shall receive the multitude as His spoil.
> For He exposed Himself unto death
> And was numbered among the sinners,
> Whereas He bore the guilt of the many
> And made intercession for sinners.
> (Isa. 53:11–12)

It is declared that when someone purposefully dies for someone he or she loves, in order that that person may live, that love is greater than an erotic love. But we are at liberty to use every way we love to compare our love for God and His love for us. However, remember we are strongly advised that we cannot express our love for God if we do not love our neighbour as ourselves. The Torah means nothing to us if we do not caringly and benevolently love our fellow humans.

Sexual intimacy brings that tangible human blending in a love that is heightened by all the senses. It employs every nerve-ending in a rich, entwining, ecstatic passion of two fleshly beings. Propelled by the enzymal and hormonal accelerants and the energy of the lifeblood in its expression, it achieves a condition that elevates the partners into a oneness of being and sensibility, almost out of this world! Song of Songs certainly describes it well. Its imagery is *subtle* in its propulsion, *perfuse* in its capture of the *entire* mind and body, and *intense* as it reaches into the sublime level like *lightning,* responding in a marvelous *thunderous* state of *climax.* This electric intimacy has no rival. This pure eroticism was gifted to humans by their Creator and Redeemer. We must not soil it. The Lord our God is one; blessed be He. His redemptive love for us will triumph.

Here are a few selected lines from Song of Songs:

> The king has brought me to his chambers.
> Oh, give me the kisses of your mouth
> O thou whom my soul loveth.
> I am the rose of Sharon, and the lily of the valleys.
> He brought me to the banquet room, his banner of love
> was over me.
> His legs are like marble pillars, set in sockets of fine gold.
> He is majestic as Lebanon, stately as the cedars.
> My beloved is mine, and I am his.
>
> Every part of you is fair, my darling. There is no blemish
> in you.
> O Love, with all its rapture! Your stately form is like the palm,
>   Your breasts are like clusters.

I am my beloved's, and my beloved is mine.
Let me be a seal upon you, like the seal upon your hand
and heart, as a seal upon your arm:
For love is fierce as death; passion is mighty as Sheol.
Vast floods cannot quench love, nor rivers drown it.
Hurry, my beloved, swift as a gazelle or a young stag,
To the hills of spices. (*Song of Songs* 1:2,4; 2:1,4,16a; 4:7;
5:15; 6:3; 7:7b,8,11; 8:6,7.

For the most tender, passionate, and sexually beautiful rendition of this song I have ever read, see *The Song of Songs: The World's First Great Love Poem*, translated by Ariel Bloch and Chana Bloch.[116] I quote three lines:

My love reached in for the latch and my heart beat wild.
I rose to open to my love, my fingers wet with myrrh,
Sweet flowing myrrh on the doorbolt.

God's love for humanity far surpasses any expression of marital love that occurs on earth.

CHAPTER 15

Jonah's Messianic Mission

Looking at Jonah's book from a Jewish point of view, we can see that his mission was one to the Gentiles. This should silence those rabbinic sages who felt that only the Jews would be in paradise.

Nineveh was the capital city of Assyria. Its population was mostly idolatrous and wicked, although more than 120,000 people there were not sinning willfully (Jonah 4:11). One wonders whether these were Jews fulfilling the function of the "salt of the earth." God finds it very difficult to tolerate willful sinning. When God finds such to be occurring, He becomes deeply distressed. He asked Jonah to convert the people of Nineveh to redemptive Judaism. Jonah was reluctant to do the job, as he felt they would not repent and his mission would be wasted. Furthermore, he 'accused' God of wasting his time, as God intended to save the city anyway, and if they did not repent, He would destroy them. So, either way, he felt his efforts would be wasted! Was Jonah attempting to force God's hand by sailing off to Tarshish instead? God sent a great storm, and the ship was about to break into fragments (Jonah 1:4). The superstitious sailors cast lots to find out who was responsible for the life-threatening storm. The lot fell on Jonah, who had to be wakened from sleep to be accused and questioned. Despite Jonah's challenge to God about the mission, by falling fast asleep in the storm, he demonstrated great confidence in his infinite God by his calm and placid demeanor. God loved him for it:

> They said to him, Tell us, you who have brought this misfortune upon us, what is your business? ... I am a Hebrew, he replied. I worship the Lord, the God of heaven ... The men were greatly terrified, and they asked him, What have you done? And when the men learned that he was fleeing from the service of the Lord ... they said to

him, What must we do to make the sea calm around us? ...
He answered, ***Heave me overboard!*** ... And they heaved
him overboard.
(Jonah 1:8–15, emphasis added)

A dramatic and drastic decision to drown Jonah. Can you imagine
it? The drama heightened further! Jonah was swallowed by a huge
fish, and he prayed in the belly of the fish. He accused God of
exposing him to the gastric juices in the fish that now threatened to
digest him. For salvation he now went straight to the symbolic source
of messianic redemption, the holy temple:

From the belly of ***Sheol*** I cried out, and You heard my
voice. You cast me into the depths ... Out of Your sight:
Would I ever gaze again on Your Holy Temple? ... And
my prayer came before ***You into Your Holy Temple*** ...
But I, with loud thanksgiving, Will ***sacrifice*** to You;
Deliverance is the Lord's! The Lord commanded the fish,
and it spewed Jonah out upon dry land ... [Jonah went] at
once to Nineveh ... and proclaimed: Forty days more and
Nineveh shall be overthrown!
(Jonah 2:1–11; 3:1–3, selected verses, emphasis added)

And the people of Nineveh repented. "***And God renounced the
punishment***. The forty days elapsed, and Nineveh was saved:

This displeased Jonah greatly, and he was grieved. He
prayed to the Lord, saying, O Lord isn't this just what I
said ... [and] that is why I fled beforehand to Tarshish.
For I know that You are a compassionate and ***gracious***
God, slow to anger, abounding in kindness, renouncing
punishment.
(Jonah 4:1–2, emphasis added)

Sadly, Joseph Klausner saw no messianic content in the book
of Jonah. Even more sadly, he made the statement "... since the
repentance [Nineveh's] was sufficient, and where there is no

punishment there is no redemption in the Messianic sense." Moses taught that repentance is insufficient and must be followed by expiation by the blood. Klausner forgot that mercy had triumphed over justice because the blood had been sprinkled on the ark of the covenant and the mercy seat. He should have looked at the Most Holy Place in the temple, just as Jonah did; there he would have seen it.[117] Jonah had gone to the source of redemption, the messianic blood splashed in the Most Holy Place.

The book of Jonah is rich in the primitive redemptive messianic Judaism of the Tanak. The emphasis the book places on repentance and expiation is enormous. God prefers mercy to justice. That is why in the Most Holy Place of the temple He placed the mercy seat on top of the ark of the covenant containing the law. That is where the Shechinah dwelled, on the mercy seat, between the cherubim. In His redemptive plan, the law will not be exacted without mercy. He doused it with His blood. Shout it from the lofty hilltop! Shout it from the whale's belly! Shout it from the Most Holy Place of the earthly temple! It is God's place of refuge and atonement in the heavenly temple! The "skirts of His robe fill the Temple" where "your guilt shall depart and your sin purged away." (See Isaiah 6.)

The Ruach Hakodesh gifted the people of Nineveh with repentance. Jonah saw the messianic redemption in the belly of the fish. We need not decry the idea of Jonah being in the belly of the fish for three days and nights, because he himself labeled the experience as being in Sheol. The Torah was disobeyed in Eden. Death passed upon humanity. But the Lord ordained a sacrifice outside the gates of Gan Eden. His mercy triumphed over justice in that sacrifice by Abel. Jonah saw the most wondrous vision in the belly of the fish, in Sheol, in the death that comes when the law of God is disobeyed. *That vision was of God in His holy temple. Ah! Humanity needs to live in that vision of the temple.* Habakkuk declares the significance of what happens in heaven when God implements the triumph of His mercy over justice. It happens in the heavenly temple's Holy of Holies. When the *Lord is in His holy temple, Let all the earth keep silence.* (See Habakkuk 2:20; see also my chapter 25, "The Ha-Mashiach of Habakkuk" ca 600 BC) The same happens in the earthly temple. *In the presence of the Shechinah, messianic blood is sprinkled on the ark of the covenant and the mercy seat by the High Priest, in silence.* Indeed! His mercy triumphs over justice, and He delivers us from eternal death. When that great Day of Atonement happens in the heavenly temple, the multiverse becomes clean again and humanity is restored to immortality. It will be implemented as the stepping stone to the messianic kingdom. Eternal death will spew humanity out on the dry land of an earth made new because of messianic blood. We will march back through the gates into Gan Eden triumphant because God's mercy triumphed over justice!

All this has not been lost on the sensibilities of God's chosen people, Israel:

> The Book of Jonah is read in the afternoon service of Yom Kippur, the Day of Atonement (see b. Meg. 31a) because of the theme of repentance. On that day Jews are supposed to identify with the Ninevites and their plea ... see *m. Ta'an. 2:1;* see also, for instance, *b. Ta'an.* 16a, cf. Rambam, *Mishneh Torah, b. Ta'an. 4:2.*[118]

Moses Maimonides, citing Jonah and Nineveh, said, "Israel is redeemed only by Teshuah [repentance]" (Mishneh Torah: Laws of Repentance 7:5). Maimonides's *teshuah* no doubt included the atonement. Clearly, Jonah links repentance and redemption to God in the Most Holy Place of His heavenly temple, where the divine Day of Atonement takes place, and the entire multiverse stays silent. Just as there was blood in the earthly temple, messianic blood must be splashed in the heavenly temple, of which the earthly temple was only a type:

> For the life of the flesh is in the blood, and I have assigned it to you for making expiation for your lives upon the altar; *it is the blood, as life, that effects expiation*. (Lev. 17:11, emphasis added)

This statement was beamed from Sinai and cannot be set aside. How dare anyone wipe out blood from primitive redemptive Judaism?

How dare anyone call it cultic? It is messianic. How dare anyone try to hose down the bloodstains on the temple mount? Where is the Jew who will challenge Moses, the prince of Egypt who beamed this from Sinai?

Jonah was upset with God's free gift of grace to the Ninevites. There are those like Jonah who are still upset that God's gift of grace is free and unfettered. They want to earn it with benevolent acts and other substitutes. All Israel stood perfect before God on the Day of Atonement. The blood of the bullock without blemish was carried by the High Priest in silence into the Most Holy Place. It was sprinkled on the ark of the covenant and mercy seat, and dripped on the temple mount where Abraham sacrificed Isaac. All Israel did was repent, and that was also a gift. The entire multiverse keeps silence because *the Lord is in His holy temple in heaven,* accepting the messianic propitiation. It is His own devising, and it is His act of self-sacrifice.

Stop grumbling, Jonah; be quiet! You should realize that you are greatly honoured as a messianic figure. You were heaved overboard into Sheol. After the sailors heaved you overboard, they made a sacrifice on the ship and the storm was silenced. And you did not have to stay in Sheol, because the infinite God, who lives in eternity, had positioned Himself in His temple. You faced eternal death when you saw Him there from the belly of the fish, but now you will live forevermore because the blood has been splashed on the law and the mercy seat in the presence of the Shechinah. Mercy has triumphed over justice: pure grace, unmerited favor. The Messiah is heaved overboard and is swallowed by Sheol. But He does not stay there. He is triumphant over death! Eternal death is vanquished! The multiverse is clean again. The belly of the fish is empty. Sheol has no hold on the Messiah, the antitype of whom Jonah was a type.

CHAPTER 16

The Messianic Utterances of Amos

As he states in the beginning of his book, Amos ministered during the reigns of Uzziah, king of Judah, and Jeroboam II, king of Israel. There is some disagreement among scholars about its dating and its interpolations.[119] The writing focuses on a period in the eighth century BC. Amos was a sheep breeder from Tekoa, but he was deeply conscious about the decrepit spiritual state of the Hebrews in his lifetime.

His messages focus on the dire spiritual state of the Jews and God's punishments for them. He predicted invasions from Syria and Assyria. The destruction of Solomon's temple was not far away. He sandwiched "the Day of the Lord" in the middle of the book, between the listings of the sins and the coming punishments. This citation was a rebuke to them. Then, at the end of the book, he salvaged the situation by the promise "I will set up again the fallen booth of David."

Both utterances—"*The Day of the Lord*" and "*I will set up again the fallen booth of David*"—are considered messianic arrival proclamations.[120] Both these cited sources, *The Jewish Study Bible* and Joseph Klausner, claim talmudic approval for this recognition.

The Day of the Lord: The wish for "The Day of the Lord" is cited as a misguided desire, and therefore an offence:

> Ah, you who wish for The Day of the Lord!
> Why should you want The Day of the Lord?
> It shall be darkness, not light! – As if a man should run
> from a lion
> And be attacked by a bear, Or if he got indoors,
> Should lean his hand on the wall, and be bitten by a snake!
> Surely The Day of the Lord shall be not light but darkness
> Blackest night without a glimmer.
> (Amos 5:18–20)

Here is classic, dramatic, and mocking imagery. If you are not prepared for the Day of the Lord, it is your worst nightmare and unwanted wish. It will be eternal death, the blackest night without a glimmer.

Amos accuses and pronounces punishments on Syria, Gaza, Tyre, Ammon, and Moab.

Amos enumerates Judah's and Israel's sins:

1. Oppression of the poor (2:6, 7; 4:1; 5:11; 8:4–6)
2. Sexual perversion and immorality (2:7, 8)
3. Acceptance of lying prophets and disregard of the true prophets (7:10–16)
4. Humbug sacrifices in the temple being used as indulgences instead of the penitent uplifting of justice and righteousness (4:4, 5; 5:21–25; 6:12b)
5. Indulging in degrading parties and revelry (4:1; 6:7b)
6. Insincere hoping for "The Day of the Lord" (5:18–20)
7. Idolatry (5:26, 27)

Amos calls for repentance. There is interaction with Amaziah, who reports him to King Jeroboam of Israel. They ask him to leave and "earn [his] living" in Judah. His vision of the "basket of figs" occurs, where there is a play on words: Instead of *kayitz*, a basket of summer fruit, Israel will be given *ketz*, punishment by death / the end.[121] There will be a dearth of sincerity and honesty. God will seek them out for punishment wherever they may be: Sheol, heaven, the top of Mt. Carmel, or the bottom of the sea.

But God loves His children, even in their perversity and abject sinfulness. He is their eternal Father. His Mashiach is coming for people just like them. But they must repent and claim their Redeemer.

The Fallen Booth of David: This second messianic mention is the final solution to Israel's and all humanity's sin problem. The coming Messianic Age is ill understood and in a "fallen" state in their minds and longing. They just wanted a political Messiah and an exalted national status in a sinful world. God had already let them try that at their request. They had achieved a grand political and exalted national status in the reign of King David. They could not hold it because of their wretched idolatry and misunderstanding of His redemptive mission. Their temple worship was a sham. Their animals of sacrifice were blemished hypocritical indulgences, devoid of repentance. Their temple loaves, the showbread, were tainted with leaven. Their tithes were dishonest. Their hearts were rotten to the core because there was no justice and no earnest attempts to seek righteousness. God was offering an immensely better and wondrous state. Mashiach brings perfection and immortality. But it was not the Mashiach for whom they were longing. God's longing was for them to be back in His bosom. His love was enormous, and He planned to redeem them Himself. He Himself would come in His messianic functionality:

> In that day I will set up again *the fallen booth of David:*
> I will mend its breaches and set up its ruins anew.
> I will build it firm as in the days of old,
> So that they shall possess the rest of Edom
> And all the nations once attached to My name –
> Declares the Lord who will bring this to pass …
> I will restore My people Israel …
> I will plant them upon their soil,
> *Nevermore to be uprooted*
> From the soil I have given them – saith the Lord
> (Amos 9:11–15, emphasis added)

There is an extensive study of the festival of Sukkot on the Rabbi Eliezer ben Yehuda page on the Internet (www.benyehuda. us/). Rabbi Eliezer ben Yehuda (AD 1858–1920) was a Lithuanian Jew who migrated to Israel and pioneered the return of Hebrew as Israel's dominant and official language. His study links this scripture in Amos with Leviticus 23:34–43. A Sukkah is a canopy that provides shelter. The rabbi links it to several aspects of Judaism. The mercy seat covered the ark of the covenant and was the Sukkah of forgiveness and protection for the sinner. The Sukkah signified God's protection of Israel during the forty years in the desert after they left Egypt. The Sukkah was their protection when the temples were destroyed. Following the loss of nationhood after the zenith of the splendor of the Davidic reign, the Sukkah was described as the fallen booth of David. And here in Amos is the declaration that the fallen booth of David will be raised by the Messiah ben David. His kingdom lasts forever.

This scripture declares salvation and is a definite application to the Messianic Age. David Castelli saw in this scripture a great ingathering of the exiles. (See *Il Messia*, by David Castelli, p. 87.)[122] It is deeply manifest of the great love of Elohim, blessed be He; the Lord is One. It has all the hallmarks of being eternal. Israel must realize that whatever they achieve in terms of land and Torah must be only stepping stones to bring about that messianic kingdom, the raising up of the fallen booth of David. That was the message of Amos and all the prophets. They prophesied for the Mashiach.

Insincere hope for the Day of the Lord is the mighty rebuke of Amos. What does this mean? It portrays the misguided desire for politiconational need alone. And it portrays the lack of insight into their real need for spiritual cleansing; the need for a longing for perfection and immortality. Perhaps there is a parallel today. Does Israel want world domination in the status quo, as Joseph Klausner hoped? Or is there a destined relief to be desired in the eternal kingdom of Messiah ben David, where they will *nevermore be uprooted?* Ah! The Abrahamic covenant, where Messiah must bring happiness to all nations. Is Messiah being preached in the synagogues across the planet? Will Israel magnify the fallen booth of David as Rabbi Eleazer ben Yehuda declared, the Sukkah of the mercy seat covering the law of God, on which the messianic blood has been sprinkled? The Lord our God is one, and He has taken refuge in His Sukkah, the Holy of Holies in His heavenly temple.

CHAPTER 17

The Sad Ha-Mashiach of Hosea

Hosea's theme is Israel's abandonment of God, their punishment, and God's call for repentance and reconciliation.[123] This is the "same old, same old" stale and repetitive story of their Biblical history. Hosea lists Israel's offences under the categories of cultic, religious, social, sexual, and political. It represents God's great patience, longsuffering, and tenacity. The Jews often stress their resilience, suffering, and tenacity in the diaspora. And so they are exemplary. But Hosea puts them to shame with the demonstration that God's tenacity and patience with them and all humanity is infinitely greater.

The book of Hosea was written about the middle of the eighth century BC, and it focuses on the time just before Israel was carried away in the Assyrian captivity. As he states, he ministered in the reigns of Kings Uzziah, Jotham, Ahaz, and Hezekiah of Judah, and in the reign of King Jeroboam II, son of Joash of Israel. The spiritual state of the Hebrews was dreadful, except for the reign of Hezekiah.

Hosea is considered one of the great proponents of Messiah. Joseph Klausner ranks him second only to Isaiah:

> Not for nothing was Hosea the older contemporary of
> Isaiah. Hosea is the spiritual father of the greatest prophet
> of the Messianic idea.[124]

Hosea recounts all Israel's sins, as categorized above. But he tells it as a beautiful but gruesome love story in the context of the marriage relationship. It recalls the Song of Songs, where the beauty of the feminine form is cravingly desired for sexual union by an ultramasculine, hormonally propelled husband. This background or motivation is therefore being used by God to analyze His own desire for Israel—and through Israel, all humanity. The Divine craving is infinitely greater. It bases the relationship in the reason for the Creation and in the devekut that was present in Gan Eden. And since the primal couple jilted God, and the marriage relationship broke when they were expelled from the garden, He has been heartbroken and devastated. Like a heartsick lover, He has pursued humanity ever since for reunion. There is no humanly closer relationship than the marriage relationship. It harvests all the fleshly and spiritual factors of union possible between two beings, so close is God to us. And he Himself devised a reconciliation/redemption in His messianic functionality to get us back into His embrace.

Hosea is indeed gruesome in his imagery of the broken love relationship with the adultery, fornication, prostitution, and double-crossing he describes. The imagery includes the worst ill treatment of women it is possible to devise. Perhaps an apology is owed to the most beautiful of God's creatures. God's great love for humanity is at stake in the experience that we encounter in this book of Hosea.

Hosea marries Gomer. Unfortunately she had a prostitute background, and that spoils the allegory because the primal couple did not have that background. But they did have free will, which the prostitute also has. And they did prostitute themselves underneath that fateful venomous tree, after the fact. Gomer played the harlot five times, but Hosea kept taking her back. Divorce was never on Hosea's mind. Gomer bore him two sons, whose names God used to define His relationship with Israel and Judah.

The rabbinic sages over the centuries saw God's righteousness as being in great contrast with Gomer's prostitution, the latter of which they were clearly instructed by Hosea to interpret as Israel's own disobedience and idolatry. God soundly rejected their behavior, but as usual He weakened. Yes, the Almighty weakened. He forgave them and took them back. But that was not easy, and He had to use His Ha-Mashiach functionality to do that. That is why Hosea's message is so powerfully messianic.

Great poetry flows from Hosea's pen; here are selected messianic passages:

The people of Judah and the people of Israel
Shall assemble together
And appoint one head over them;
And they shall rise from the ground –
For marvelous shall be the Day of Jezreel. (Hosea 2:2b)

Therefore, behold I will allure her,
And bring her into the wilderness,
And speak tenderly unto her.
And I will give her, her vineyards from thence,
And the Valley of Achor for a door of hope;
And she shall respond there as in the days of her youth
As in the day she came up out of the land of Egypt. (Hosea
2:16, 17 RSV)

And I will betroth thee unto Me forever
Yea, I will betroth thee unto Me in righteousness and in justice,
And in loving kindness, and in compassion.
And I will betroth thee unto Me in faithfulness;
And thou shalt know the Lord. (Hosea 2:19–20 RSV)

For the Israelites shall go a long time
Without king, and without officials, without sacrifice
And without ephod and teraphim.
Afterward, the Israelites will turn back
And will seek the Lord their God, and *David their king* - --
And *they will thrill over the Lord*
And over His bounty in the *days to come*. (Hosea 3:4, 5,
emphasis added)

Come, and let us return to the Lord;
For He hath torn, and He will heal us,
He hath smitten, and He will bind us up.
After two days will He revive us,
On the third day He will raise us up,
That we may live in His presence. (Hosea 6:1, 2)

> I will heal their backsliding
> I will love them freely;
> For Mine anger is turned away from him. (Hosea 14:4 RSV)

One wonders whether Hosea really had so much trouble with his wife, and whether there was a time that he had come to the end of his tether. But the descriptions of Israel's shenanigans must have brought God very often to the point of exhaustion. How much can a mortal man love a woman who does not motivate and reciprocate that love? How much can a fleshly love be expended to exhaust the expression of ecstasy in a dual pleasure? Does not that sublime state soil and shrivel, nauseate, collapse, and wither in the evidence of unfaithfulness? How did Hosea endure it? Was he not human? Was the story beyond reality and concocted to impress? Did Israel bring God to the brink of depression and suicide?

Ah! Mashiach! Where is Your husbandly pride and sensibility? Is there no limit to the depth of Your condescension? Does Your tenderness and desire born of the innate urge and propelled by the heavenly hormonal fire know no bounds, that You will love an object showing no sign of the decency of reciprocity? While Your love wants to triumph, does she not lie cold? How does love that does not beget love expand and last? Does not the Almighty have a sense of shame, spending the omnipotent energy of His Holy Being in the absence of the reciprocity sought? *So great is the love of God!* So stupendous is the Mashiach condescension! So craved by the Almighty is that devekut He enjoyed in Eden! He will be the triumphant lover! He will be satisfied with the climax of His redemption! He will enjoy that moment of cosmic silence as He bows His head in the heavenly temple. He will be ecstatic with the travail of His soul. The redeemed of humanity "will thrill over the Lord" in His bridal chamber. He will be satiated in the Sabbath of His Redemption as He entwines His arms about us. He will say with redemption as He did with Creation, "It feels very good." That is the message of Hosea. That was the anthropomorphic understanding Hosea had of the great redemption. Perhaps he had been inspired by the Song of Songs, where God is depicted as the great physical masculine lover of His beautiful bride; where He indulges His desire in the purity of the luscious fecund female form. He begets a multitude of children; He will be satisfied with the travail of His soul! Adam and Eve must have been absolutely beautiful, as they came from the creative hand of the Almighty. Humanity will again be spotlessly beautiful as they come from the redemptive hand of the Almighty. *Who can search the depth of the riches of His grace!* He is the great lover. It is past human comprehension. Isaiah grabbed it and ran with it in the sorrowful exultation of the Suffering Redeemer: "***He shall enjoy it to the full through His devotion***" (Isa. 53). Isaiah discovered the Redeemer was very God. He had learned from Hosea that humanity's jilted husband was none other than the Creator. Ah, how He loves! The Lord our God is one; blessed be He.

Jerusalem from the Mount of Olives (in Biblical Times)

CHAPTER 18

The God-Messiah of Isaiah

Interpretation of the Tanak is controversial among scholars. This is particularly so in consideration of the books of Isaiah and Daniel. The "literal," "spiritual," "allegorical," "metaphorical," "historical," "historical-critical," "conditional," "prophetic," "apocalyptic," etc., camps present formidable arguments among Jewish scholars, as among Christian scholars and also between Jewish and Christian scholars. Since the Tanak is the foundation of both Judaism and Christianity, the Tanak sometimes gets torn apart by the arguments of the scholars in these camps.

As an example of the stances some scholars take, I cite how Geza Vermes fell into a trap. He prizes himself as a historical scholar. He sums up the consideration of the messianic title "Son of God" as an idiom understood only metaphorically by Jews. (See *Christian Beginnings*, by Geza Vermes, pp. 237–238.) Does he speak for all Jews? Does he speak for Moses, David, and Isaiah? Has he clearly defined "Jewish Theology"? Does he consign the mighty redemptive function of primitive Judaism outlined by Moses to a metaphoric status? Moses and most religious Jews would not agree with him in a discussion of the expiation implicit in the Day of Atonement. Moses recorded clearly that the messianic symbol was inaugurated at the gates of Eden and mightily reaffirmed at Sinai. The blood of the animal without blemish symbolized messianic expiation. In Leviticus 17:11 Moses has God speaking: "For the life of the flesh is in the blood, and I have assigned it to you *for making expiation for your lives upon the altar; it is the blood, as life, that effects expiation.*" *God is the source of all life.* The messianic "Son of God" clearly defines the great redemptive functionality of the Almighty. Vermes should reconsider. Messiah is not a mere metaphor in Judaism. It is their solid, inexorable future, more solid than Vermes' physical existence! Or is Vermes some ghostly apparition that is a vapour, not actually there?

Without the background of formal scholarly theological training, I could be considered an inexperienced neophyte. But as a believer in the sacredness of the Tanak and its messianic redemption offered, I have been confronted with choices, which I have made. These choices guide my dedication and devotion to the scriptures.

Whether certain tanakian passages are "literal," "metaphorical," or "spiritual," etc., they all must be congruent with the great foundational concepts of Judaism. The great concepts of the Tanak, defined by Moses, were interpreted by him and the prophets who followed as *realities to come.* The great rabbinic sages also treated these concepts as realities to come. The concepts of Creation and Redemption in the Almighty's eternal plans are real and are the *most significant concepts of the Tanak.* They do not remain in an esoteric, ethereal metaphoric ideation. They were beamed from Sinai. They cannot be superseded or set aside, and they are the solid absolutes in primitive Judaism, absolutes that are present in our very existence. Therefore all interpretations, to hold their worth, must treat these great plans of God as realities: Creation at the dawn of time and Redemption to come at the end of time.

It was from Mt. Sinai that primitive redemptive Judaism was beamed to the World. Basic to that message was an explanation of what God was all about and what was His relationship to humanity. The law, mercy, and messianic blood were the principal ingredients in the solution that God was seeking to the enigma that this planet has presented to Him. No part of God's plan is an end in itself; nor is any part of His plan to go in a direction of its own. law, mercy, and messianic blood, the vital ingredients in the Most Holy Place, where the Shechinah dwelled, must always stand linked tightly together in the reclamation of humanity. We are indeed in an unhappy and unredeemed state. Their comingling is the *chemistry and perfume of redemption.* This is the essence and satisfaction of the saving religion that is primitive redemptive Judaism. Humanity is in great need of redemption. The Son of God redeems, He is no metaphor.

The story of Gan Eden and God's choice of the "Chosen People" in His covenant with Abraham form the literal and real blueprint on which primitive Judaism is built. They are the predictors of the Messianic Age and the new heaven and new earth. Redemption, planned from Elohim's eternity, was placed in position at Gan Eden's Gate as "the enmity" between Eve's Seed and the Serpent. It was a legal agreement with Abraham, signed as a covenant in Ur of the Chaldees. It was mightily reconfirmed with Jacob at Bethel. In a powerful earthquake it was beamed from Sinai, the fiery mountain, by Moses. It was David the shepherd boy's anointed mission on that lofted hilltop in Hebron. It was his inaugural anointing by Samuel in Bethlehem as king. It is the eternal kingdom of the Messiah ben David. *It is God's eternal plan.* As real as are all these events named, the future is very literal indeed.

The Ruach Hakodesh and Ha-Mashiach constitute the functionalities of Elohim in all these situations and must stay central in primitive Judaism. These functionalities get the work done. Nothing can go off on a tangent and detract from them. There is no future for the planet apart from the apocalyptic catastrophe that the Messianic Age will bring. Israel as a nation, and the modern world, cannot seek other solutions apart from this plan. Whether one is committed to primitive Judaism or primitive Christianity, the common goal of redemption is to be achieved. Israel's history illustrates that her choices that have not taken Ruach Hakodesh and Ha-Mashiach into central account have caused pain and devastation. Israel's abandonments of Edenic redemption, the Abrahamic covenant, and Sinai have resulted in the past in utter and dismal national failure.

The book of Isaiah is the central writing of the Tanak for an understanding of the Mashiach, the Messianic Age, and the new heaven and new earth. Isaiah's theology was inspired by that of King David.

The apocalyptics of Daniel and the other prophets are supplements. Isaiah's apocalyptic is indispensable to primitive Judaism. Prophecy and apocalyptic are also solid beliefs in the doctrines of Rabbinic Judaism, which have evolved since the second temple destruction in AD 70. But these have been ignored by the Jews. The Talmud does not contain the unanimity that the Tanak does with respect to apocalyptic.

The book of Isaiah has as its historical scope the reigns of four kings of Judah, namely Uzziah (Azariah), Jotham, Ahaz, and Hezekiah. Isaiah was more or less a contemporary of Hosea,

Amos, and Micah. What a powerful tour de force the Almighty was conducting through this rich array of contemporary prophets! Was Israel deaf, dumb, and blind to God's efforts in this tour de force?[125]

In his excellent preview of the book of Isaiah in *The Jewish Study Bible*, Benjamin D. Sommer feels, in agreement with many other scholars, that this book has two authors separated by about two hundred years. The author Isaiah, son of Amos, wrote the first thirty-nine chapters (dating from 800 BC) and chapters forty through sixty-six were written by "Deutero-Isaiah" in a historical setting two hundred years later. This opinion has merit, since the great rabbinic commentator Abraham Ibn Ezra of the Middle Ages rightly identified the Babylonian exile of the sixth century BC in Deutero-Isaiah's writing[126].

Some scholars envision Trito-Isaiah, to whom they credit chapters fifty-six through sixty-six. This third author is thought to have lived in the time of the rebuilding of the temple in 515 BC. This segment of Isaiah is written in a mixture of prose and poetry, in contrast to Deutero-Isaiah which is judged to be pure poetry. Max Weber writes, in his book *Ancient Judaism*, with an authoritative tone, that Trito-Isaiah is indeed a third prophet participating in this book.

But the finding of the book of Isaiah as one word-for-word document in the Dead Sea Scrolls that does not acknowledge two or three authors presents some consternation. Nonetheless, the book of Isaiah has the Mashiach as its central theme. A triple authorship does not detract from or present any challenge to its message. Sommer himself sees its unity. He notes that Isaiah is cited in rabbinic literature more than any other prophetic text, and more haftarot are taken from Isaiah than from any other prophetic book. (Haftarot are the prophetic readings chanted in synagogues on the Sabbath, holidays, and fast days.)[127]

It is also significant that the *MacArthur Study Bible* (NKJV edition) also notes that Isaiah is quoted directly in the NT [B'rit Hadashah] over sixty-five times, far more than any other OT [tanakian] prophet, and mentioned by name over twenty times[128].

The problems of the kingdom of Judah and the northern kingdom of Israel occupy a large portion of the first thirty-nine chapters of Isaiah. The destruction of the northern kingdom of Israel by the Assyrians and the threat to Judah necessitating alliances with Egypt were his concerns. He advocates reliance on God. He recognizes the continuance of the Hebrews in enormous idolatrous sinfulness. The book of Isaiah is arranged in alternating portrayals of the *sinfulness of the Hebrews* with portrayals of *messianic redemption*. Isaiah intersperses the horrible religiosociopolitical condition of the Hebrews with beautiful messianic pictures, thus encouraging the Hebrews.

The sequence of portrayals is as follows:

1. Messiah as the Antidote to sinfulness (chapters 1–2)

Chapter one is a huge indictment of Judah:

> Alas sinful nation, a people laden with iniquity,
> A brood of evildoers,
> Children who are corrupters …
> The whole head is sick,
> And the whole heart faints,
> From the sole of the foot even to the head,
> There is no soundness in it,
> But wounds and bruises and putrefying sores.
> (Isa. 1:1–6 selected verses, NKJV)

This description could not be worse. But he saw a "remnant" being the object of God's protection from meeting the fate of Sodom and Gomorrah (Isa. 1: 9–11).

Immediately following this indictment, Isaiah looks down the corridors of time. This scripture primarily applies to the post-reconstruction era of Solomon's temple. But he also views the Messianic Age farther along down the line. Having condemned the Hebrew people, he seeks to encourage them. That this scripture (Isa. 2:1–5) points to the Messianic Age and inaugurates the catastrophic end to history cannot be denied:

In the days to come,
The Mount of the Lord's House
Shall stand firm above the mountains
And tower above the hills;
And all nations can gaze on it with joy.
And many people shall go and say:
"Come, Let us go up to the Mount of the Lord,
To the House of the God of Jacob.
That He may instruct us in His ways
And that we may walk in His paths."
(Isa. 2:1–3a)

2. Messianic Sacrifice, Atonement, and Mediation in the Heavenly Temple (chapters 3–6)

The dreadful gloom of the situation in Judah and Israel is uttered in his discouraging, condemnatory language that now follows in chapters 3–5. Isaiah dispenses it in large and bitter doses in these chapters. This gloom of the Hebrews is matched with the assurance that God is still in control in the heavens. In fact, He is in the heavenly temple with messianic mediation taking place. Whenever God is depicted in the heavenly temple, it is for messianic sacrifice and mediation on behalf of humanity, for redemptive purpose. Listen to it:

In the year that King Uzziah died,
I beheld my Lord seated on a high and lofty throne,
and **the skirts of His Robe filled the Temple**.
Seraphs stood in attendance on Him.
Each of them had six wings: with two he covered his face,
With two he covered his legs, and with two he would fly
And one would call to the other,
Holy, holy, holy! The Lord of Hosts!
His presence fills all the earth ... I cried,
Woe is me; I am lost!
For I am a man of unclean lips
And I live among a people of unclean lips;

> ***Yet my own eyes have beheld***
> ***The King Lord of Hosts.***
> (Isa. 6:1–5, emphasis added)

The translators of *The Jewish Study Bible* are averse to allowing humans to see God's face, since Moses was not allowed to see God's face. Isaiah does not specifically say in this instance that he sees God's face; therefore, the encounter does not violate that rule. The other interpretive possibility is that God in the temple is in His divine-human form following the divine penetrance of humanity. Close encounters with this divine-human manifestation of God are allowed, as occurred with Abraham under the terebinths and with Jacob at Brook Jabbok, and now with Isaiah viewing the divine-human Messiah ben David, King Lord of Hosts in His temple.

The Talmud has Michael, the great heavenly prince, officiating in the temple:

> Zebul is that where the celestial Jerusalem is and the Temple in which the altar is erected, and ***Michael, the great Prince, stands and offers a sacrifice upon it ...*** (See Chag. 12a, 12b re: heaven, emphasis added) [129]

Isaiah beholds the "unclean" state of humanity. And the atonement follows:

> Then one of the seraphs flew over to me with a live coal, which he had taken from the altar with a pair of tongs. He touched it to my lips and declared,
>   "Now this has touched your lips,
>   Your guilt shall depart
>   And your sin be purged away."

Here is a picture of the final cosmic Day of Atonement where messianic blood is offered on the altar. The messianic sacrifice as in Isaiah chapter 53, where the suffering Servant atones and mediates, will be discussed later.

3. Messiah Atoning with the Divine Penetration of Humanity (chapters 7–8)

Here is the prediction of the birth of Immanuel, born of a woman. The KJV translates Isa. 7:12–14 thus:

> And he said, Hear ye now O house of David:
> Is it a small thing for you to weary men,
> But will ye weary my God also?
> Therefore the Lord Himself shall give you a sign;
> Behold, the virgin shall conceive, and bear a Son,
> And shall call His name ***Immanuel.***
> Butter and honey shall He eat,
> That He may know to refuse the evil and choose the good
> For before the child shall know to refuse the evil, and choose the good,
> The land that thou abhorrest shall be forsaken by both her kings.
> The Lord shall bring upon thy father's house,
> ***Days that have not come ...*** (emphasis added)

The Jewish Study Bible translates this as follows:

> Listen, House of David, [Isaiah] retorted
> Is it not enough for you to treat men as helpless
> That you also treat my God as helpless?
> Assuredly, my Lord will give you a sign of His own accord!
> Look, the young woman is with Child
> And about to give birth to a Son.
> Let her name Him ***Immanuel.***
> (By the time He learns to reject the bad and choose the good,
> People will be feeding on curds and honey.)
> For before the Lad knows to reject the bad and choose the good,
> The ground whose two kings you dread shall be abandoned.
> The Lord will cause to come upon you and your people

> And your Ancestral House such ***Days as never have come
> since ...***
> (Isa. 7:12–14, emphasis added)

There is much disagreement among scholars whether the woman is a virgin or not.[130] The Hebrew word used here, "*almah*," is rightly translated as "young woman," not "virgin." The Hebrew word for "virgin" is "*betulah*," which is not the word used here. But few will deny that these verses, which deal with a context involving King Ahaz and the king of Assyria, are indeed a messianic utterance. This is vehemently applied to the fact that the Child is messianic and is of the Ancestral (father's) House, and is invoked with days of Messiah that are to come. The Child is thus designated as Messiah ben David. This is absolutely authenticated with the Child being named Immanuel, which means "With us is God."[131] Isaiah will reinforce this in chapter 9:6, as will be discussed later.

Isaiah learned a lot from David's theology. Unmistakably, there is utterance here of the same penetrance of humanity by deity consistent with Psalm 2, where David insists on the Messiah as God's Son:

> Let me tell of the decree:
> The Lord said to Me,
> You are My Son,
> I have ***fathered*** You this day.
> (Ps. 2:7, emphasis added)

It should be noted in passing that the word "son" is a human word describing a human relationship. Its use to describe a functionality of God effecting redemption is at best confined to the human understanding of it. But David, Isaiah, and Daniel all use it. This may be perceived as a threat to monotheism, the existence of two divine persons, but it need not be deduced as such, despite its restrictive connotation—that is, human terminology.

Several scholars (Klausner, Castelli, Welhausen)[132] connect these messianic utterances with the prophecy of Balaam recorded by Moses:

What I see for them is not yet,
What I behold will not be soon:
A Star rises from Jacob,
A Sceptre comes forth from Israel ...
A Victor issues from Jacob.
(Num. 24:17–18, emphasis added)

Moses also quotes Jacob as blessing his son Judah thus:

The Sceptre shall not depart from Judah,
Nor the ruler's staff from between His feet,
Until Shiloh come;
And unto Him shall the obedience of the people be.
(Gen. 49:10 KJV)[133]

In these lucent and consistent pronouncements, Isaiah's words are the unmistakable waymarks of the Ha-Mashiach penetration of humanity. Some rabbinic sages authenticated this birth, cited previously, as grandly messianic:

Blessed is the *womb* from whence he came,
Blessed is the generation whose eyes behold him.
(PesR 36, S 2, emphasis added)

This rabbinic saying acknowledges the human birth of the Mashiach.

Threatening political situations next seem to overwhelm Judah again. These are painfully recited in chapters 7–8, but Isaiah sees the remnant as being preserved. Again Messiah is intoned.

Some repetition is needed here. Elohim clearly penetrates humanity in His function as Ha-Mashiach. Two definite pictures of the Messiah are present in Isaiah. The Tanak and the Talmud are clear about His coming as a human. The Tanak is clear about who He is, but the Talmud is not convincingly clear about His origin and His longevity in eternity. The Talmud, in its many utterances on Messiah, is not coherent. Several seventh-century AD rabbis dabbled with a "hypostasis" in heaven representing a second God. Isaiah is absolutely clear in defining the Messiah and is the authoritative source. All the other prophets who spoke about Messiah spoke in unison with Isaiah. King David, who lived long before them, pioneered their thoughts.

In Abel's sacrifice for his sins, the animal without blemish was the symbol of the messianic atonement. In defining "atonement," the Jewish Virtual Library quotes Moses:

> For on this day shall atonement be made for you, to cleanse
> you; from all your sins shall ye be clean before the Lord.
> (Lev. 16:30)

This was accomplished by the sacrifice of an animal without blemish. Its blood was taken into the Most Holy Compartment of the temple, where it was splashed on the ark of the covenant and the mercy seat. Judgment, mercy, and atonement occurred in the presence of the Shechinah, by this highly symbolic event, the splashing of the blood by the high priest on the Day of Atonement.

Adam, Abel, Noah, Abraham, and Jacob offered similar animals without blemish as sacrifices for sin, symbolizing the messianic expiation and cleansing. And Moses at Sinai emphasized the Passover Festival, the Aaronic priesthood, and the Day of Atonement, which all signified messianic atonement for sin. Only God, who ordained the Torah to keep order in the multiverse, can forgive the disobedience to the Torah. Not only is this logical in primitive Judaism, but it was in the mind of God from eternity. So it is logical and in accordance with the Tanak that Ha-Mashiach emanates from the fabric that is God, and His blood expiates for sin. The Messiah is the functionality of Elohim to redeem humanity. Messiah is deity. When Isaiah introduces the Messiah, he utters the penetrance of humanity by divinity. It is expressed in "Father-Son" terms. How this is possible in God terms, or how it happens, is God's business. We will ask Him to explain it when we see Him.

4. Messiah as the Dawn of a New Creation (chapter 9)

He comes as the new creation, penetrating humanity in the flesh of unfallen Adam. As an aside, this idea has attracted much mileage because of the two different accounts of Creation given at the beginning of Genesis. The first has Adam being made earlier in Creation week, with a controversial significance. (See *The Jewish Jesus*, by Peter Schafer, pp. 197–213.) The rabbis had much to say about this. (See m Sanh 4:5; t Sanh 8:7; b Sanh 38a, b, a Baraitha; b Hag 12a; BerR 8:1, 10; 12:6; WaR 18:2.) Some of the midrashim gave unfallen Adam almost a semidivine status, alleging the angel Michael instructed other angels to worship Adam because he was "the image of the Lord God." The socalled semidivinity of Adam has no basis in the Tanak. There is evidence in the discussion, including what Philo had said about unfallen Adam, which makes Adam a symbol of the Messiah. Later, other rabbis attacked the so-called elevation of the unfallen Adam. A possible conclusion from all this is that the messianic birth was similar to that of—that is, in the same flesh as—the unfallen Adam, the second Adam. Franz Rosenzweig believed that as an absolute.

God's taking on of humanity is His own action, but we look at it from the human viewpoint. David broaches the subject in Psalm 40 when discussing the symbol of expiation. There is no doubt that this is a messianic psalm, despite some controversy about it. On many occasions throughout Jewish history, the symbol of atonement, the animal without blemish, became an end in itself, and the messianic reality for which it stood was lost or ignored in Jewish scholarly comprehension. David takes this up:

> I put my hope in the Lord ...
> He lifted me out of the miry pit, the slimy clay,
> And set my feet upon a rock ...
> You, O Lord my God, have done many things; the wonders
> You have devised for us cannot be set out before You ...
> You gave me to understand that
> You do not desire sacrifice and meal offering,
> Then I said, See, I will bring a scroll
> Recounting what befell me to do
> What pleases You my God, is my desire;
> Your teaching is in my inward parts
> I proclaimed [Your] ***righteousness*** ...
> (Ps. 40:1–10, emphasis added)
> (cf. Jer. 23:5, 6 "sid-qe-nu")

Jewish commentators note that this is a difficult psalm to interpret.[134] The identity of the scroll being referred to is not clear, but most likely it is the Torah of Moses, the Pentateuch. The reason to "nullify" the symbolic sacrifice is that it is an "indulgence" if repentance and messianic sacrificial atonement are not present with it. It is very clear that God's messianic atonement is the reality that effects salvation. This is further termed by David in this psalm as "Your *beneficence* … Your faithful *deliverance* … Your steadfast *love*… Your *compassion*." (See Psalm 40:9–12). The perfect messianic body has to be the real sacrifice being offered, for which the animal without blemish is only the symbol.

Isaiah is adamant on both counts: Messiah is deity and Messiah makes the penetrance of humanity. This is clearly enunciated in Isaiah chapter 9. He starts the chapter with the defining of the most auspicious of earthly events, portrayed as darkness being dispelled by light. This is reminiscent of Genesis 1, the Creation of the world, prior to which darkness prevailed. But lo and behold, the new creation wrought by redemption is the arrival of the Messiah in a human body (the "second Adam"). The darkness of iniquity pervading the world, a parallel to the darkness that prevailed before creation, is now dispelled by the messianic light of redemption. (See Isaiah 60:2.)

> The people that walked in darkness
> Have seen a brilliant light;
> On those who dwelt in a land of gloom
> Light has dawned …
> *For a Child has been born to us,*
> A son has been given us.
> And authority has settled on his shoulders.
> He has been named
> *"The Mighty God* is planning Grace;
> *The Eternal Father,* a peaceable ruler" –
> In token of abundant authority
> And of peace without limit
> Upon David's throne and kingdom,
> That it may be firmly established

In justice and in equity
Now and evermore."
(Isa. 9:1–6 emphasis added)

That this passage is messianic is accepted by the majority of the rabbinic sages down through the ages is undisputed. Some Jewish scholars strain at denying the "child" that is born here the titles here given, namely "The Mighty God" and "The Everlasting Father." David Castelli is forthright in agreeing that this child is the Messiah. (See *Il Messia*, by David Castelli, p. 98.)[135] The margin commentary in *The Jewish Study Bible* (page 802) attempts to link this verse up with Isaiah 39:1. Here the Babylonian king Merodach-baladan came to visit Hezekiah. The name Merodach-baladan means "the god Marduk has provided an heir." This interpretation is so farfetched and preposterous that it is not worthy of serious consideration. It intimates that Isaiah recognizes a heathen god attributing grace to it. It denies Isaiah the redemptive declaration of the messianic intent of this passage.

Isaiah clearly states in the introduction to this cosmic event at the commencement of the chapter, "The people who walked in darkness have seen a brilliant Light." Just as the darkness of space preceeded the Creation, the darkness of sin and death preceeds the Redemption. The god Marduk has absolutely nothing to do with this messianic passage. Clearly Isaiah is talking about redemptive light replacing the darkness of iniquity. In the context of this passage this key verse is announcing that deity is penetrating humanity in this the arrival of the messianic Child to rule on the throne of David. The Hebrew words are quite straightforward: "And his name is called Pele-joez-el-gibbor-Abi-ad-sar-shalom."

Just as the Creation produced the perfect Adam, the Redemption produces the Second Adam, the Messiah who restores the first Adam and his progeny to perfection and immortality by His provision of redemption. The penetration of humanity by divinity is not to be construed in the human terms, as is usually done, that God has procreated an offspring. This must only be construed as the messianic functionality of Elohim coming to earth as a human. He Himself, by His almighty power, will arrive as a human to redeem humanity.

But He remains very God in His infinity. The sexual connotation of making an offspring cannot have any meaning here, although we use the father–son relationship to explain matters, as in the use of the word "begotten." The humanity of Messiah who is very God is a miracle that cannot be understood. The Messiah is very God, and very eternal, as Isaiah qualifies His kingdom as being "from henceforth even forever." Isaiah says in capping the event, "The zeal of the Lord of hosts shall bring this to pass" (Isa. 9:6). Without the shadow of a doubt, Isaiah is saying that God's zeal accomplishes this penetrance of humanity. Messiah's eternal throne that will last forever is indeed Davidic. If Messiah arrives only as an ordinary finite, though exceptional, human, he cannot last forever. The Messiah will then be a transient. If He is not immortal, how can he impart immortality to humanity? We have to get back into Gan Eden. Messianic atonement must solve the sin problem before the eternal kingdom is realized, or He will not have any subjects to serve him forever and ever.

Again it must be insisted: *God alone can create, and God alone can redeem.* Blessed be He; the Lord our God is one.

David elaborated this cosmic event in everyday language. He was emphatic about the penetrance of humanity by divinity in the coming of the Messiah:

> Why do the nations assemble, and people plot vain things,
> > Kings of the earth take their stand
> Against the Lord and against His Anointed?
> … He who is enthroned in the heaven laughs;
> The Lord mocks at them …
> But I have installed My King on Zion, My holy mountain!
> Let Me tell of the decree: The Lord said to me,
> ***You are My Son, I have fathered You this day.***
> (See Psalm 2:1–7, emphasis added)

In his naked dance King David understood this perfectly. The penetrance of humanity by divinity was *a massive condescension* that he was privileged to enact in that naked dance. We have absolutely no knowledge of God as a sexual being capable of begetting children. We have described God over and over again in the masculine gender as our Father in a human context. But we have no proof of God's masculinity. So we dare not and cannot decry or prove the father-son relationship. We couch God's love for us as a father loves his child. We understand it in the human context. The Tanak presents God as our Father and us as His children. David describes the Ha-Mashiach functionality of God in human terms, and His penetrance of humanity as a "begotten son." That is the best way our restricted and inadequate knowledge and language can describe this miracle. We do understand our own earthly relationships, and that is as far as we can take our understanding of this great reality.

5. Messianic Restoration of the Davidic Kingdom (chapters 10–11)

In these chapters God is seen to best His foes.

> The *Light* of Israel will be fire, And its *Holy One* flame.
> (Isa. 10:17)

The concept descends to an earthly setting but its vista is cosmic:

> But a shoot shall grow out of the stump of Jesse,
> A twig shall sprout from his stock.
> The spirit of the Lord shall alight upon him:
> A spirit of wisdom and insight,
> A spirit of counsel and valour,
> A spirit of devotion and reverence for the Lord.
> He shall sense the truth by his reverence for the Lord:
> He shall not judge by what his eyes behold,
> Nor decide by what his ears perceive.
> Thus shall he judge the poor with equity
> And decide with justice for the lowly of the land ...
> Justice shall be the girdle of his loins
> And faithfulness the girdle of his waist.
> The wolf shall dwell with the lamb,
> The leopard lie down with the kid.
> (Isa. 11:1–6a)

Here is a mixture of the human manifestation of Ha-Mashiach, who acts on behalf of the poor and oppressed of the land. The Lord of Glory longs to bestow His riches on the deprived poor of the earth. This will be achieved in the messianic kingdom. There will be no poor or oppressed in the messianic kingdom. The end in the prophetic utterance here sees the catastrophic installation of the messianic kingdom, with its marvelous serenity.

The commentators of *The Jewish Study Bible* interpret this passage to show that this is a picture of an ideal king in the peaceful future. They see here a messianic and eschatological prophecy comparable to that of Isaiah 2:1–4 and 9:1–6. They see that a perfect Davidic king will reign in Jerusalem.[136]

This is the Messianic Age, which culminates in King Messiah's eternal kingdom. The perfect and immortal kingdom comes after the Judgment and the Resurrection: "They shall never again know war" (Isa. 2:4c).

6. The Messiah Championing the Weak (chapters 12–32).

These chapters contain language that is a poetic mixture of diatribe, condemnation, and a repetition of promises of deliverance to the poor and despised. The "Pronouncements" are herein contained. The histories of the kings of Judah and Israel, and Assyria and Babylon, are referenced.

In chapter 32 there is a repetition of the prediction of a Messiah who provides good governance for the weak, the disabled, and the downtrodden.

> Behold a king shall reign in righteousness,
> And ministers shall govern with justice;
> Every one of them shall be
> Like a refuge from gales,
> A shelter from rainstorms;
> Like brooks of water in a desert,
> Like the shade of a massive rock
> In a languishing land ...

No more shall a villain be called noble,
Nor shall "gentleman" be said of a knave.
(Isa. 32:1–5)

7. The Messiah Healing and Ingathering Scattered Israel (chapters 33–39)

Isaiah 33 unmistakedly defines who the Messiah is:

For the Lord shall be our ruler,
The Lord shall be our prince,
The Lord shall be our king,
He shall deliver us.
(Isa. 33:22)

In chapter 35 messianic language is again intoned. A great ingathering of diasporic Israel is predicted:

Strengthen the hands that are slack;
Make firm the tottering knees!
Say to the anxious of heart,
Be strong, fear not;
Behold your God!
Requital is coming,
The recompense of God---
He Himself is coming to give you triumph.
Then the eyes of the blind shall be opened,
And the ears of the deaf shall be unstopped.
Then the lame shall leap like a deer,
And the tongue of the dumb shall shout aloud ...
And the ransomed of the Lord shall return,
And come with shouting to Zion,
Crowned with joy everlasting.
They shall attain joy and gladness,
While sorrow and sighing flee.
(Isa. 35:3–6a, 10, emphasis added)

Isaiah chapters 36–39 are occupied by Hezekiah's encounter with Sennacherib of Assyria, the latter's attack on Judah (see 2 Chronicles 32), Hezekiah's illness and healing, and his boastful imprudence of letting spies in. Isaiah is upset and rebukes Hezekiah for boasting of his riches:

> Behold the days come, that all that is in thy house ... shall
> be carried to Babylon, nothing shall be left, saith the Lord.
> And of thy sons ... shall be eunuchs in the palace of the
> king of Babylon (Isa. 39:6, 7 KJV)

This is a very discouraging future, which Hezekiah meekly accepts. He had forgotten that he was reigning by the providence of God, and not by his own power.

Now occurs *the transition* between Isaiah and the disputed second author, Deutero-Isaiah, who is said to have lived some two hundred years later. It is a very smooth transition because the plan already in the structure of the book continues. Gloom and doom is followed by the corrective messianic declaration. Messiah dramatically reappears in chapter 40.

8. The Messiah Arriving with His Forerunner (chapters 40–41)

There is a link here with the last of the prophets, Malachi. Isaiah predicts the arrival of Elijah, the forerunner, followed by the Messiah.

> Comfort, O Comfort My people,
> Says your God.
> Speak tenderly to Jerusalem,
> And declare to her
> That her term of service is over,
> That her iniquity is expiated;
> For she has received *at the hand of the Lord*
> Double for all her sins.
> A voice rings out:
> Clear in the desert

A road for the Lord!
Level in the wilderness
A highway for *our God!*
Let every valley be raised,
Every hill and mount made low.
Let the rugged ground become level
And the ridges become a plain.
The Presence of the Lord shall appear,
And all flesh, as one, shall behold ---
For the Lord Himself has spoken.
(Isa. 40:1–5, emphasis added)

Again, here is proof of the Messiah's deity. The rest of chapter 40 talks of the greatness of God and the insignificance of man. God goes on to taunt idolatry. (See Isaiah 40:19–20.)

In chapter 41 God emphasizes the covenant work after encouraging Israel, again asserting the divinity of the Mashiach:

But you Israel, My servant,
Jacob, whom I have chosen,
Seed of Abraham My friend –
You whom I drew from the ends of the earth …
Fear not, for I am with you,
Be not frightened for I am your God …
Fear not, O worm Jacob, O men of Israel:
I will help you – declares the Lord –
I your Redeemer, The Holy One of Israel.
(Selected from Isa. 41, emphasis added)

9. Messiah as a Servant, to Underpin Implementation of the Abrahamic Covenant (chapters 42–48)

This is *My Servant,* whom I uphold,
My Chosen One, in whom I delight.
I have put *My Spirit* upon Him,
He shall teach the true way to the nations …
Thus said God the Lord …

> *I the Lord,* in *My Grace,* have summoned you,
> I created you, and appointed you
> *A covenant People, a Light of Nations* –
> Opening eyes deprived of light,
> Rescuing prisoners from confinement,
> From the dungeon those who sit in darkness.
> (Isa. 42:1–7, emphasis added)

The Redeemer is God, the Lord. The Abrahamic covenant is reinforced with the naming of Israel as a covenant people, a light of the nations, and rescuers of prisoners and those who sit in darkness. Israel cannot evade this responsibility. Messiah is the medium to perform the messianic redemption. Israel must proclaim messianic redemption to the world.

Chapters 43 to 48 criticize Israel for idolatry and call for a return to the worship of the true God.

10. Messiah the Suffering Servant (chapters 49–53)

There are three fulfillments of servanthood here. Isaiah (Deutero-Isaiah), as the prophet, is serving his God. Israel, collectively indentured to the Abrahamic covenant, is to be a light to the nations (Gentiles). But the messianic fulfillment is that of the *atonement,* as both preceeding stated fulfillments are enabled by it. The messianic role here is absolutely clear:

> And now *the Lord* has resolved –
> *He who formed Me in the womb to be His Servant* -
> To bring back Jacob to Himself,
> That Israel may be restored to Him ...
> *I* will also make you a light of nations,
> *That My salvation may reach the ends of the earth.*
> Thus said *the Lord,*
> *The Redeemer* of Israel, *His Holy One.* ...
> (Isa. 49:5–7, emphasis added)

The Messiah here originates on terrestrial soil *as a human from the womb.* But He accomplishes the atonement and salvation of Israel, planned from eternity. The human penetrance by divinity to embody Messiah is obvious.

The messianic intonation of this passage is unmistakable. The Lord resolved to penetrate humanity to "bring back Jacob to Himself." Again the penetration of humanity by Divinity is accomplished, and the scope of the messianic mission of atonement announced, to "Bring back Jacob to Himself," "Restore the survivors of Israel," "Make you a light of the nations," "That My salvation may reach the ends of the earth." This would be the fulfillment of the Abrahamic covenant. In verse 8b God states, "I created you and appointed you a Covenant People." This idea absolutely captivated Gershom Scholem. He was thrilled by it, that he should be part of a people chosen by God:

> ... we are first and foremost Jews, and we are Israelis as a manifestation of our Judaism. I was one of those people who took the Biblical passage "And you shall be unto Me a kingdom of priests, and a holy nation" [Exodus 19:6] *as the definition of Zionism.*
> (*On Jews and Judaism in Crisis*, by Gershom Scholem, p. 36, emphasis added)

So Messiah arrives as a human. Did He leave His divinity behind? That is a big question, but the Tanak has already answered it. Isaiah addresses the "Child" as "The Mighty God" and "The Everlasting Father." So God is down on earth as the Messiah, who now behaves as a human. He has not given up anything. At no time does He not retain His divinity, and He can use it when He wills it. Does that answer trouble anyone? What human can lay down his life and take it up again? Only God can do that.

This leads us to the "Suffering Servant," where the atonement is made.

The Messiah's state of condescension flows from Isaiah's pen. The humiliation of the Messiah knows no depths. King David had danced naked to emphasize messianic condescension. Isaiah borrows Psalm 22 as a template for the suffering Messiah. Hosea had emphasized the emotional depths of God's love in a husband's love for his erring wife. Isaiah now outlines the suffering that the Messiah undergoes:

> I did not run away.
> I offered My back to the floggers,
> And My cheeks to those who tore out My hair.
> I did not hide My face
> From insult and spittle.
> But the Lord will help Me –
> Therefore I feel no disgrace;
> Therefore I have set My face like flint,
> And I know I shall not be ashamed.
> My Vindicator is at hand –
> (Isa. 50:5b–8a)

> His visage was so marred more than any man
> And His form more than the sons of men.
> (Isa. 52:14b KJV)

> He was despised, shunned by men,
> A man of suffering, familiar with disease.
> As one who hid His face from us,
> He was despised, we held Him of no account.
> Yet it was our sickness that He was bearing,
> Our suffering that He endured.
> We accounted Him plagued,
> Smitten and afflicted by God;
> *But He was wounded for our sins,*
> *Crushed because of our iniquities.*
> *He bore the chastisement that made us whole,*
> *And by His bruises we are healed.*
> We all went astray like sheep,
> Each going his own way;
> *And the Lord visited upon Him*
> *The guilt of all of us.*
> He was maltreated, yet He was submissive,

He did not open His mouth;
Like a sheep being led to slaughter,
Like a ewe, dumb before those who shear her,
He did not open His mouth.
By oppressive judgment He was taken away,
Who could describe His abode?
(Isa. 53:3–8a, emphasis added)

11. The Death of the Messiah (chapter 53)

Because Messiah is divine, as Deity He has power to lay down His life as a sacrifice. He has the Logos power to be human, live as a human, and die as a human. The angel brandishing the sword at the gates of Eden symbolized messianic death, which kept those gates open wide for the redeemed. His death will be special as His blood being shed is the cosmic event that restores immortality to humanity. It is His blood that is taken into and splashed in the Most Holy Place in the heavenly temple, and God exercises His mercy in that heavenly Day of Atonement for all humanity. The whole world then stands guiltless before God. In Israel's history, the Passover Lamb symbolized release from slavery, from sin, and from death. Messianic blood was splashed on the doorposts and lintels of their dwellings. Death could not claim them: "I will pass over you *when I see the blood.*" Israel! Do not belittle the blood! Magnify it! The blood is not cultic. It is the expiation, the redemption! Our good works are filthy rags!

David, the Psalmist, saw that picture of the humiliation of the Messiah as he danced his naked dance wearing only the high priest's ephod. He saw the throes of death engulfing his Messiah when he sang,

Thy rebuke hath broken His heart, He is full of heaviness.
He looked for some to have pity on Him, but there was no
man, neither found He any to comfort Him. (Ps.69:21 KJV)

David looked down the corridors of time and saw God die as a human without blemish, the great messianic sacrifice whose blood atoned for all his dreadful sins, his covetousness, robbery, adultery, lying, and murder. The blood, which the high priest took into the Most Holy Compartment and splashed on the ark and the mercy seat, was messianic blood. Some have felt that God is a relentless, vengeful, and exceedingly cruel God, exacting His vicious judgment in this scene of messianic demise. Ah! The picture here is that of a loving God in the functionality of the Ha-Mashiach, Himself suffering the anguish, despair, and shame, and laying down His life to pay the price of disobedience to Torah. *He is reclaiming His great love object, the human race, with His own condescension and death.* What a God! What stupendous love! He is Himself restoring immortality to them, keeping the gates of Gan Eden wide open to them. He created and He redeems. Israel! Your Mashiach must die and live again! What a cost for the redemption!

Isaiah described that death:

> For he was cut off from the land of the living Through the sin of my people who deserved the punishment And his grave was set among the wicked, And with the rich in his death – though he had done no injustice And had spoken no falsehood. (Isa. 53:8b, 9)

12. Messianic Resurrection (chapter 53)

His deity had power to lay down His life and taste of death. But His deity would also raise Himself from the grave. It is a miracle. Do you believe that God created? Then why do you not believe that God redeems? Israel! Do you believe in the resurrection? Messiah rises from the grave and makes it possible!

David recognized that special death and resurrection as he sang another psalm:

> But thou didst not leave His soul in Sheol; Nor didst Thou suffer Thy Holy One to see corruption. (Ps.16:10 KJV)

Isaiah is leaning heavily on David's theology. Psalm 22 records it all. Isaiah does not leave him in the grave either. They both see Him dying as a man, but achieving the redemption as God:

> But the Lord chose to crush him by disease
> That, if he made himself *an offering for guilt,*
> *He might see offspring and have long life,*
> And that through him the Lord's purposes might prosper.
> Out of his anguish he shall see it;
> He shall enjoy it to the full through his devotion ...
> He shall receive the multitude as his spoil
> *For He exposed Himself unto death.*
> (Isa. 53:10–12, emphasis added)

The Jewish Study Bible, in the margin comments, interprets this passage in Isaiah 53 to be the sufferings of Israel. Israel's history of suffering as a consequence for her idolatry and unfaithfulness to God is noted. Isaiah clearly portrays her sinfulness in the opening passage of his book. Israel has suffered for sin and also has suffered unjustly at the hands of her foes. But this is not the messianic suffering for the sins of the whole world so that eternal death could be vanquished. That can only be accomplished by the Mashiach. That is what the expiation outlined by Moses is. That is why primitive Judaism offered an animal without blemish, symbolic of the Mashiach. Israel has never been without blemish and can only be viewed blameless in the redeemed state, when messianic blood has been splahed in the Holy of Holies. The prophets always outlined Israel's sins and suffering as punishments from God. For the provision of perfection and immortality, Israel does not atone for herself or anyone. That is the messianic work of Redemption. Israel did not create herself, and she cannot redeem herself. Israel is the beneficiary of messianic forgiveness and expiation. The messianic tone and intent here have been recognized by rabbinic sages down through the ages. Rabbi Judah the Prince saw its messianic intent:

> The Rabbis maintain that his [Messiah's] name is the "leprous one of the School of Rabbi Judah the Prince", as it is said, "Surely he hath borne our griefs, and carried our sorrows; yet we did esteem him stricken, smitten of God, and afflicted". (Isa. 53:4)[137]

There is no doubt that Rabbi Judah the Prince held this chapter as messianic, and not as referring to Israel as a nation atoning for herself. Israel cannot be her own Messiah despite her suffering, which many will contend was brought upon herself by her own actions, as the prophets declared. There is nothing in the book of Isaiah that supports Israel being her own Messiah. Israel's woeful wickedness was "head to toe" putrefaction in Isaiah's language. (See chapters 1 and 2.)

Eve saw that future outcome, and that is why she longed to be the mother of the Messiah. Abraham was promised that same saving Messiah when he was on Mt. Moriah. God clutched His hand tightly, that hand that clutched the knife to slay his son Isaac. Jacob saw it as the Lord stood at the top of that ladder at Bethel, beckoning him home to paradise. Jacob wrestled with Him for salvation at the brook Jabbock. Enoch and Elijah saw it as the reason they could stay up in heaven. Messianic sacrifice saves the human race. Israel can help to save the human race by propagating her fantastic Mashiach redemption. Israel cannot offer her miserable record as the redemption of the world. God offers His own suffering as the mighty redemption that saves Israel. (See Daniel Boyarin's *The Jewish Gospels*, pp. 129–156.)

After announcing the penetration of humanity by divinity, Isaiah lapses first into a description of the state of Israel. The people of Israel are downtrodden and destitute of courage. But exaltation awaits God's chosen people, and his description starts to look like the beginning of the Messianic Age. Jerusalem is exalted:

> … All flesh shall know that *I, the Lord, am thy Saviour*
> *And thy Redeemer,* the Mighty One of Jacob.
> (Isa. 49:26b KJV)

> How welcome on the mountain are the footsteps of the herald
> Announcing happiness, heralding good fortune,
> Announcing victory, Telling Zion, "Your God is King!" Hark!
> Your watchmen raise their voices, as one they shout for joy;
> For every eye shall behold the Lord's return to Zion.
> Raise a shout together, O ruins of Jerusalem!

> *For the Lord will comfort His people, Will redeem Jerusalem.*
> The Lord will bare His holy arm in the sight of all the nations.
> And the very ends of the earth shall see the victory of our God.
> (Isa. 52:7–10 emphasis added)

Israel suffers for her own sins as a punishment. She sometimes is punished unjustly, as in the Nazi Holocaust. But she does not and cannot suffer for expiation and atonement, as she is not the Messiah. The book of Isaiah emphasizes a person, a divine being born as a Child who is the mighty God planning grace, the Redeemer, Immanuel, God with us. Max Weber, the relentless expositor of primitive redemptive Judaism, makes a very strong case for this:

> ... a single eschatological figure seems to be thought of as the vessel of significant suffering for salvation ... the figure receives again a plainly personal and soteriological turn ... It is no new thought for prophecy that the Servant of God (Isa. 53:11) pleads on behalf of the wicked. (Jer. 15:1; Ezek. 14:14). That he gives his life for "bearing the sins of many" ...[138]

There is absolutely no doubt that Israel is not her own Messiah. What a silly idea! Isaiah loudly declares above: *"For the Lord will comfort His people, will redeem Israel!"* The Lord of glory is their Mashiach.

Isaiah states exactly what the Messiah accomplishes:

> My righteous Servant makes the many righteous,
> It is their punishment that he bears;
> Assuredly, I will give him the many as his portion,
> He shall receive the multitude as his spoil.
> For he exposed himself to death
> And was numbered among the sinners,
> Whereas he bore the guilt of many
> And made intercession for sinners.
> (Isa. 53:11b–12)

It would require volumes to discuss Messianism in the book of Isaiah. It is not possible here to be exhaustive. The half has never yet been told!

13. The Solitary Nature of the Messianic Sacrifice (chapter 61)

Messiah conquered His enemies alone. And now He provides redemption through His own suffering alone. Now He allows His own blood to be shed in divine condescension. No one can contribute an iota to His own provision for the redemption of humanity. Fruits and vegetables, benevolent acts, a deep study of Torah, the righteousness of filthy rages, and the Enlightenment are not salvific; nor are they supplements. "He trod the winepress *alone.*" "So My *own* arm wrought the triumph."

The victory is quietly dispensed as a healing. The messianic mission to the dregs of humanity is triumphantly low-key. It is for the destitute, sad, and sinful dregs of humanity that He has come:

> The Spirit of the Lord God is upon Me
> Because the Lord has anointed Me
> He has sent Me as a herald of joy to the humble,
> To bind up the wounded of heart,
> To proclaim release to the captives,
> Liberation to the imprisoned;
> Proclaim the year of the Lord's favor
> And a *Day of Vindication* by our God;
> To comfort all who mourn.
> (Isa. 61:1, 2)

14. Messiah the Divine Warrior (chapter 63)

Isaiah chapter 63 recites messianic bloodshed:

> Who is this coming from Edom;
> In crimson garments from Bozrah –
> Who is this, majestic in attire,
> Pressing forward in His great might?

"It is I, who contend victoriously,
Powerful to give triumph."
Why is your clothing so red,
Your garments like his who treads grapes?
"I trod out a vintage alone;
Of the peoples no man was with Me.
I trod them down in My anger,
Trampled them in My rage;
Their life-blood bespattered My garments,
And all My clothing was stained.
For I had planned a *Day of Vengeance,*
And *My year of Redemption arrived.*
(Isa. 63:1–4, emphasis added)

This chapter of Isaiah is clearly messianic. *The Jewish Study Bible* commentary in the margin calls the Messiah here "***The Divine Warrior.***" Here is another recognition of the deity of the Mashiach. Abrogation of the Torah is enemy territory. Edom is enemy territory, and Bozrah its capital city. He walks out of Bozrah alone, having bloodied Himself with the blood of His enemies. Messiah clearly trumpets His victory over His enemies—sin and death. The lifeblood of His enemies has been spilled. The Serpent has been given the lethal head crushing.

In Jacob's blessing of Judah and proclamation of the Messiah, there was a similar scene:

He washed His garments in wine,
And His clothes in the blood of grapes.
His eyes shall be red with wine,
And His teeth white with milk.
(Gen. 49:11, 12, KJV).

Clearly here is depicted the messianic condescension and shame, but with a triumphant view. The "head wound" and the "heel wound" are both exceedingly bloody. Two sources of blood are noted: His enemies He vanquished and His own shed in the suffering of the atonement. But only Messiah triumphs. His day of vengeance over His enemies and the provision of redemption for humanity have been accomplished. *It was done solely by His deity in human flesh.* He is correctly called the Divine Warrior. Here is a frank admission that the messianic Redemption is accomplished by the suffering and death of the Mashiach. Here is the recognition that the messianic Redeemer is divine, God Himself. Listen to this:

> Then I looked but there was none to help.
> I stared, but there was none to aid –
> So *My own arm wrought the triumph,*
> And My own rage was My aid.
> I trampled peoples in My anger,
> I made them drunk with My rage,
> And I hurled their glory to the ground.
> (Isa. 63:5, 6, emphasis added)

15. Messiah the Coming King in His New Eternal Kingdom (chapters 65–66)

Isaiah's final vision is as follows:

> For, behold I create new heavens and a new earth, and the former shall not be remembered, nor come into mind … And I will rejoice in Jerusalem, and joy in My people; and the voice of weeping shall be no more heard in her, nor the voice of crying … And they shall build houses and inhabit them; and they shall plant vineyards and eat the fruit of them … And it shall come to pass that from one new moon to another, and from one Sabbath to another, shall all flesh come to worship before Me, saith the Lord.
> (Isa. 65:17, 19, 21; 66:23 KJV)

According to an early *Tannaitic Midrash (Sifre),* and also in several *Talmudic Baraitoth,* the Jewish Messiah must bestow upon his people the following benefits:

    i.   Material welfare
    ii. An end to foreign domination
    iii. His might in the Torah

In the support of these benefits, Isaiah is quoted:

> The shoot from the stock of Jesse,
> And a branch from his roots shall blossom …
> The spirit of wisdom and understanding,
> The spirit of council and might,
> The spirit of knowledge and the fear of the Lord.

This is understandable considering the downtrodden national and political plight of Israel. Judah had had no national prosperity since Hezekiah's reign. But the messianic intention was to provide much more abundant riches—namely perfection, immortality, and fulfillment in the everlasting kingdom of the Messiah ben David:

> For as the *New Heavens and the New Earth*, which I will make, shall remain before Me, saith the Lord, so shall your seed and your name remain. And it shall come to pass that, from one new moon to another, And from one Sabbath to another, shall all flesh come to worship before Me, saith the Lord. (Isa. 66:22, 23 KJV)

Those who think God has done away with the Sabbath will be observing it in the new earth. It will be the Sabbath of Creation and Redemption.

In conclusion, Isaiah is called the messianic prophet(s). The writings are steeped in Messianism as the dominant subject, and the Messiah described is God Himself. All Israel's sinfulness and woes will be solved by the Ha-Mashiach. He brings His messianic eternal kingdom. Hear, O Israel, the Lord our God is one. Blessed be He. *Elohim created the world. Elohim redeems the world. No one shares in these exclusive actions of Deity.*

The Messiah portrayed by Isaiah and in harmony with the Tanak is Davidic. As predicted by Jacob, the Messiah would come through the royal line of Judah. There is a competing Messiah named Ephraim with major rabbinic support who is descended from his other son, Joseph. I will deal with this in the chapter titled "The Messiah of the Talmud." Isaiah may have been three people, but they describe only one Messiah. He is Messiah ben David, who is God Himself. Hear it again:

> For unto us a Child is born
> Unto us a Son is given.
> And the government shall be upon His shoulder
> And His name shall be called
> Wonderful, Counsellor, The Mighty God, The Everlasting Father,
> The Prince of Peace. (Isa. 9:6 *KJV*)
> His name is Immanuel, *God with us.*

CHAPTER 19

Micah's Messiah from Bethlehem Ephrath

Micah lived in the days of Jotham, Ahaz, and Hezekiah, kings of Judah. His book dates to the late eighth and early seventh centuries BC. He was contemporary with Isaiah and Hosea. What a marvelous and divinely inspired trio! All three prophets are abundantly rich in messianic information. There is some controversy among scholars about the dating of Micah and his writing being disturbed by possible interpolations and editing. But his message is a perfect unity. He emphasizes Israel's transgression, the judgments of God, and the messianic redemption. His small book encompasses the denouement from Creation to the Messianic Age. With the influence of these three prophets being exerted in this time period, one wonders why the course of Israel's future did not get saved from exile. Hosea could have prevented the Assyrian captivity if Israel had listened to him. All three of them could have prevented the Babylonian conquest and exile. The Hebrews were indeed wayward and stubborn sinners, deaf and blind to their negative spiritual assets. They need not have been devastated.

For its small volume, it is my impression that no other book of the Tanak exudes as much concentrated messianic perfume as does Micah. Micah's Messiah is bold and mighty, robust and beautiful. His Messiah connects earth and heaven. Micah presents three major convincing beliefs about Messiah:

1. Messiah Is from Everlasting

And you, O Bethlehem of Ephrath,
Least among the clan of Judah,
From you One shall come forth

242

> To rule Israel for Me –
> *One whose origin is of old,*
> *From ancient times.*
> (Micah 5:1, emphasis added)

If this is a reference to Mashiach, as I most certainly believe, the Mashiach is deity. Daniel describes God as the Ancient of Days. Isaiah insists He is God. And He comes to be born in Bethlehem, and thus He is clearly linked to David. (See 1 Samuel 17:12.)[139] Micah cites Mashiach's arrival as a birth by a woman and tells of what He will accomplish:

> Truly He will leave them [helpless]
> Until *she who is to bear hath borne;*
> Then the rest of His countrymen
> Shall return to the children of Israel.
> He shall stand and shepherd
> By the might of the Lord,
> By the power of the name
> Of the Lord His God.
> And they shall dwell [secure].
> For lo, He shall wax great
> To the ends of the earth,
> And that shall afford safety.
> (Micah 5:2–4a)

Note that an ingathering of the exiles will occur: "The rest of His countrymen shall return." The last three lines above invoke a new heaven and a new earth, because that is the only guarantee of true safety. So here is further evidence that the Messiah, Deity in verity, comes as a penetration of humanity. That is the only explanation for a human birth being discussed here. The Messiah comes from the eternity of God, the Ancient of Days.

David Castelli and Joseph Klausner both agree that this scripture is a mighty proclamation of the "King-Messiah."[140]

Micah joins hands with Isaiah (see Isaiah 7:13–17; 9:1–7), Daniel (see Daniel 7:13), Habakkuk (see Habakkuk 1:12), and David (see

Psalms 2; 72; 118; 132). *The Jewish Study Bible's* rendition of Micah 5:2c is "One whose origin is from of old, from ancient times." The phrase "Ancient times" is interpreted by Rashi and other rabbis as "before the sun was," indicating "before Creation" (cf. Daniel's "Ancient of Days").[141] Isaiah's messianic prophecy stands with Micah's:

> For unto us a Child is born, Unto us a Son is given …
> And His name shall be called … The Mighty God,
> The Everlasting Father … (Isa. 9:6 KJV)

2. Messiah Will Be Born as a Human

He is born on the planet earth. (See Micah 5:2b.) Isaiah agrees (see Isaiah 9:6), and so does David (see Psalm 2:7). Joseph Klausner, a great expositor of the messianic idea in Israel, presents a contorted argument to deny messianic birth in Bethlehem:

> It is obvious that here is indicated only a king from the royal line of the house of David, which originated in Bethlehem, and there is no need to suppose that this king himself is to be born in Bethlehem. Likewise, the words "from of old, from ancient days" indicate only the antiquity of his origin since from the time of David to the time of Micah several centuries had passed, but nothing more.[142]

This is a weak statement to come from an eminent biblical scholar. Having recognized the messianic nature of this scripture, I find that this statement appears as a very anaemic attempt to deny Messiah's birth in Bethlehem and Messiah's existence from eternity, since God Himself is the Redeemer. Most rabbinic sages and many Jewish Biblical scholars equate "Ancient Times" and "Ancient of Days" with God. And David was born in Bethlehem, *and it is a given that Messiah ben David will also be born in Bethlehem*, as Micah asserts. The margin commentary on the line "Until she who is to bear has borne" in *The Jewish Study Bible*, p. 1213, says,

Traditional Jewish interpretations of this verse tend to focus on comparisons between the birth pangs of a woman and the hardship of Israel prior to the coming of the Messiah … Rab said: The son of David will not come until the [Roman] power enfolds Israel for nine months, as it is written, Therefore will he give them up, until the time that she, which travaileth, hath brought forth … (*b. Sanh. 98b*).

Rab makes no mistake that a woman was indeed going to give birth. What is startling is that he declares it to be in world domination by the Roman power, coinciding with Israel's travail brought upon them by the Romans. He is using this scripture as the nine-month gestational period in humans, trying to deny the actual birth of an infant. Rab's interpretation is contrary to David's, Daniel's, Isaiah's, and Micah's revelation here that a woman gives birth to none other than the Messiah in these dominantly messianic passages, recognized by the rabbinic sages down through the centuries. These birth pangs are painful indeed for the depicted Messiah's mother. Rashi's idea allows nine months of a woman's gestation to be full of pain, but after the birth pangs there is no baby! Israel's painful "birth pangs" inflicted by the Romans is a less likely alternate application, as the Messiah is born in the Hebrew milieu. But the intention in this messianic passage is that Messiah comes to earth borne by a woman. "Birth pangs" also has an application in the "Last Days" with the Messiah as the baby.

Sheer poetry with immortal portent flows from the prophet's brain, put there by Elohim. I repeat the beautiful words in the *KJV* translation:

> But thou, Bethlehem Ephrathah,
> Though thou be little among the thousands of Judah,
> Yet out of thee shall He come forth unto Me
> That is to be ruler in Israel,
> ***Whose goings forth have been***
> ***From of old, from everlasting.***
> (Micah 5:2 KJV)

There is no doubt that the Messiah is from everlasting and that He will be born on the earth.

It is sad that Klausner dwells in the status quo and sees no apocalyptic in the messianic arrival. Gershom Scholem certainly disagrees with him. Sad indeed is Klausner's description of the eternal messianic kingdom:

> But the real prophetic feeling in Micah comes to light in all those places in which he speaks about universal peace, about the cessation of war and the complete freedom which the peoples will have, ***each to walk IN THE NAME OF ITS OWN god, and at the same time to find instruction in Zion and the word of the Lord in Jerusalem.***[143]

There can be no complicity of Elohim with other gods, even if they are part-time or "on the side" at the same time. Klausner is adamant that the status quo of history lives on. Strangely, Klausner goes on to cite Isaiah, but Isaiah talked of a *new earth*, where "*from one Sabbath to another shall ALL FLESH come to worship before Me, saith the Lord*" (Isaiah 66:23). There will be no "other gods" in the eternal kingdom of Messiah ben David. Klausner is clearly mistaken. God does not tolerate "each to walk in the name of its own god," unmistakedly a continuation of idolatry, for which Israel suffered so much. Klausner errs massively in this proposed collusion of the worship of God with "its own god" clearly tantamount to idols.

3. Messiah Is One with God

Messiah is one in the atonement; He cleans up sin in Israel. (See Micah 7:14–20.) This scripture is vehemently asserted as messianic by the rabbinic sages. Again Micah unites with Isaiah (see Isaiah 9:6) and David (see Psalm 2:7–9). It is messianic blood that atones for sin, and Micah presents the redemption as being accomplished by God. The Tanak presents Messiah as one who cleans up the planet and ushers in the perfect messianic kingdom, where humanity again will posses immortality and in which King Messiah rules eternally, in a land "That shall afford safety."

Micah recites beautiful poetry of the messianic atonement and forgiveness:

> Who is a God like you,
> Forgiving iniquity
> And remitting transgression;
> Who has not maintained His wrath forever
> Against the remnant of His own people,
> Because He loves graciousness!
> He will take us back in love;
> He will cover up our iniquities,
> You will hurl all our sins
> Into the depths of the sea.
> You will keep faith with Jacob,
> Loyalty to Abraham,
> As you promised on oath to our fathers
> In days gone by.
> (Mic. 7:18–20)

How stupendous is His love and justice, His great mercy! He is sheer grace, hurling all our sins into the depths of the sea—not just throwing, but "hurling" our sins to the deepest spot in the ocean. "As far as the east is from the west, so far hath He removed our transgressions from us." Primitive redemptive Judaism portrayed in the Tanak is such sweet religion. It is totally reliant on Messiah to bring the triumphant kingdom. It is the saving "Balm in Gilead to heal the sin-sick soul."

Ah, Abraham! Your offering of Isaac on the temple mount was mighty.

Ah, Jacob! You did not hobble up the bank of the brook Jabbok for naught.

Ah, David! You danced naked to depict messianic condescension and nakedness in His suffering.

What glorious pictures of the messianic redemption! What immortal scenes of Israel's salvation! These are great enactments of messianic power. What a sweet and mighty religion indeed is primitive redemptive Judaism—vitalizing, rejuvenating, replenishing the fortitude found forever in devekut with Elohim. It makes the heart glad!

> Great is Thy faithfulness! O God my Father.
> There is no shadow of turning with Thee.
> Thou changest not, Thy compassions they fail not.
> As Thou hast been Thou forever wilt be.[144]
> (See also Lamentations 3:23, 24)

Blessed is He; the Lord our God is one, "One whose origin is of old, from Ancient Times," our Redeemer!

CHAPTER 20

The Comfort and Consolation of Nahum

The name "Nahum" means "comfort" or "consolation." The identity of Nahum is unclear, and the location of Elkosh, the city of his birth, is unknown. Based on allusions in its words, the book of Nahum is dated to the first half of the seventh century BC. The book is about Nineveh, the capital city of Assyria—specifically God's judgments and punishments of Assyria. Israel's plight is paramount. The northern kingdom of Israel was already destroyed and exiled in their Assyrian devastation about 722 BC. While Assyria had power, the kingdom of Judah lived in the fear of meeting the same fate as had befallen Israel. Biblical scholars are in disagreement about interpolations, but the message of the book is intact.

Joseph Klausner wrote authoritatively about the messianic idea in Israel. Steeped in Rabbinic Judaism, he had an eye for identifying messianic utterances, although I see him disregarding some. He sees a paucity of messianic declaration in Nahum.[145] I agree, but what is there is extremely vital. The one great messianic utterance in the book occurs as a big divide between God's fury and the punishment of Assyria. The lead-up to it occupies an enumeration of God's disturbed emotions. Having allowed the northern kingdom to be destroyed by Assyria for Israel's idolatry, God is angry, upset, and frustrated by the outcome. This is Nahum's description. Is it the preamble to God having a nervous breakdown?

Nahum's description of the whirlpool of God's enumerated emotions is turbulent and disturbing indeed. God is passionate, vengeful, fierce in wrath, raging, and does not remit all punishment. He travels in a whirlwind storm, producing dust clouds with his feet; dries up the sea with rebuke; and causes rivers to stop flowing. Bashan and Carmel are in drought, the flowers of Lebanon wither, the mountains quake in fear, and hills melt. The earth heaves with His fiery anger and fury; rocks shatter. He chases His enemies into darkness, wreaks utter destruction. Adversaries get only one chance at being destroyed by Him. He burns them up like dry straw. Is God having a temper tantrum? Is He at the end of His tether? It certainly sounds like it.

Nahum has never seen God so upset and disturbed. It is not certain who is included in His invective. God allowed the northern kingdom of Israel to suffer unmercifully, and now God is threatening Assyria, the instrument of Israel's punishment. I suspect God is upset with Himself as well, for having allowed Israel's cruel fate. Such is the havoc free will has caused since the great disobedience of Gan Eden.

How Nahum received the imagery of a disturbed and angry God through inspiration is difficult to decipher. He subjects God to massive anthropomorphism. It looks as if Nahum was trying to appease God while receiving the message. Perhaps he is exaggerating God's anger. God is never devoid of mercy. In the middle of the diatribe, thrice he tries to intervene to cool the Almighty, reminding Him of His "saving" and "forgiving" character:

> The Lord is slow to anger and of great forbearance … The Lord is good to [those who hope in Him], A haven on a day of distress; He is mindful of those who seek refuge in Him … I will afflict you no more. (Nahum 1:3, 7, 12)

But God is clearly at the end of His tether. He ends this diatribe with a very severe doom pronounced on Assyria. He has allowed an idolatrous nation to destroy His chosen people, who themselves had embraced idolatry. God curses Assyria:

> No posterity shall continue your name … I will make your grave accord with your worthlessness. (1:14)

Some scholars would like to place this pronouncement also on the northern kingdom. But the northern kingdom of Israel had already been destroyed by Assyria. In this moment of His deep sorrow and dissatisfaction, He longed for Abraham, Jacob, and David to bring Him some salve. He ends up applying the salve to His wounds

Himself. The salve is His accomplishment of redemption. It is Rosenzweig's idea, the Sabbath of His redemptive act.

Suddenly the Almighty releases His Ha-Mashiach functionality. There is an abrupt calm as Nahum has the great messianic vision. He looks at the great expanse of history and sees when the existing order will be destroyed:

> Behold on the hills, the footsteps of a Herald
> Announcing good fortune! Celebrate your festivals, O Judah,
> Fulfill your vows, Never again shall scoundrels invade you,
> They have totally vanished.
> A shatterer has come up against you.
> Man the guard posts, watch the road;
> Steady your loins, brace all your strength!
> For the Lord has restored the Pride of Jacob
> As well as the Pride of Israel.
> (Nahum 2:1–3a, emphasis added)

What are You saying, God? The pride of the kingdom of Israel is no more. You know that You will allow Judah to be devastated shortly by Babylon. Are you giving us false hope? Are you rubbing salt into our wounds? Are you totally betraying us?

See, God had given Israel free will, and they continued to make wrong choices and reap suffering. God would go into similar diatribes in the future. But now God Himself was looking down the corridors of time, to when His Ha-Mashiach power would atone for all sin and finally put an end to history. His Ha-Mashiach power would bring in perfection and immortality with the messianic kingdom. What alternative does God have? The Ha-Mashiach functionality of the Almighty has been in place since eternity. He is leaning heavily on that fulfillment. Great is Jehovah the Lord. The Lord our God is one; blessed be He.

Nahum had read Isaiah's writing and recognized the beauty of the coming Messiah bearing the gospel of peace. He had pictured His beautiful messianic feet walking over the hills and valleys of Judaea. Isaiah had seen Him ministering to the needs of humanity. The King James translation is such grand literary form, music to the ears. Its message from Isaiah would pour balm into the careworn lives and wounded hearts of Israel and all humanity:

> Awake, awake, put on thy strength, O Zion; put on thy beautiful garments, O Jerusalem, the Holy City; for henceforth there shall no more come unto thee the uncircumcised and the unclean ... ***How beautiful on the mountains are the feet*** of Him that bringeth good tidings, that publisheth peace; that bringeth good tidings of good, that publisheth salvation; that saith unto Zion, Thy God reigneth. Thy watchman shall lift up the voice; with the voice together shall they sing; for they shall see eye to eye, when the Lord shall bring again Zion. Break forth into joy, sing together, ye waste places of Jerusalem; For the Lord hath comforted His people, He hath redeemed Jerusalem The Lord hath made bare His holy arm in the eyes of all the nations, and all the ends of the earth shall see the salvation of our God.
> (Isa. 52:1, 7–10 KJV, emphasis added)

Nahum and Isaiah were watchmen seeing eye-to-eye, lifting up their voices in harmony, singing the praises of their Messiah, and looking for the time when perfection and immortality would be restored. The problem is that people with free will reap what they sow, and we blame God as if He is responsible for the outcome. God gets upset that He has allowed it. But now God has averted a nervous breakdown. He has recovered His composure as He envisages His mighty redemption.

CHAPTER 21

The Messiah of Zephaniah

Zephaniah was the son of Cushi and prophesied in the days of Amon, king of Judah.

There were two impending catastrophes that came to fruition: the destruction of the kingdom of Israel by Assyria, and the destruction of Judah by Babylon. Prophetic clusters warned both kingdoms of these impending catastrophes and tried to manage their spirituality:

1. Dealing with the Annihilation of the Northern Kingdom of Israel

Hosea, Micah and Isaiah faced the devastation of Israel by the Assyrians, and as characteristic, when the Hebrews were in national and political trouble, messianic expectation drew increased attention. There was nothing else to salvage in their lives after the mortal blow inflicted on Israel. What a great explanation this cluster of prophets gave, when deciphered in terms of the sin problem and the messianic kingdom: messianic atonement for sin, and the resultant restoration of perfection and immortality the Messiah ben David's kingdom would bring. Unfortunately God's chosen people mostly saw their political and national goals as being important. They could not see that the Abrahamic covenant was the only bolster they had for national exaltation. It was Abraham's and Jacob's vows to which they had put their signatures. In messianic expectation, Israel did not focus on the two desired results, as stated above. Sin cannot continue into the kingdom of Messiah ben David. That should feature today.

2. Dealing with the Destruction of the Kingdom of Judah

Nahum, Zephaniah, Jeremiah, Habakkuk, Daniel, and Ezekiel constituted a cluster of prophets who arose with the need to explain God's anger in connection with the Assyrians, and later the Babylonians. Zephaniah was a contemporary of Nahum. They both were obsessed with God's perceived anger. God's fury was their dominant theme. They had to explain whether the entire Jewish dispensation would be destroyed. There seemed to be nothing left of the Hebrew race. The diaspora was devastating. It is obvious that the Abrahamic covenant was long lost as a mission. How could they deal with God's anger? God was extremely peeved with all the inhabitants of the earth. This prophetic cluster had to explain the annihilation of the northern kingdom. And then, suddenly, they were confronted with the devastation of the kingdom of Judah. What was God up to? They saw it as Him destroying His people. They had paid no attention to Torah in their intense enjoyment of idolatry. They perceived a very angry God who had taken away their land. The prophetic cluster had no alternative but to try to define Messiah. As had happened with Isaiah, Hosea, and Micah, all they now had left in terms of hope was Messiah. Moses had brought them out of Egypt, and now they were looking for "[That] Prophet like unto me [Moses]" (Deut. 18:15) to rescue them from Assyrian and Babylonian slavery.

I refer again to Joseph Klausner. He saw a messianic universalism in the message of Zephaniah.[146] His idea is welcome, and I agree that this universalism that he describes is what is intended for the planet. But he is looking for it *within the milieu of history,* the status quo. Gershom Scholem[147] and I[148] disagree with Klausner. We believe in the opinions of all the tanakian prophets who wrote about it, that this universalism comes only *after the judgment and the resurrection when the Utopia is installed,* in the apocalyptic catastrophic destruction of history. Scholem railed against the projected achievement of any such universalism "within history" as we know it. Particularly, he castigated the Jewish movement—which saw the enlightenment that followed the French Revolution, associated with socialism—that they hoped would bring in a messianic universalism. He blamed Kabbalism for having been its expositor. The Kabbalists eclipsed the apocalyptic catastrophic event. They looked for a Messiah through a mystical devekut.

In my opinion, in the interpretation of Zephaniah this messianic universalism is indeed there as Klausner observes, but Zephaniah describes it within the context of an occurrence after the catastrophic destruction of history, as I shall now show.

The book of Zephaniah must be viewed in the context of God's wrath, a total wrath as the prophet portrayed it. God Himself vocalizes this as "***All My Blazing Anger***" (Zeph. 3:8b) against all perpetrators of disobedience to His law. The idolatry of Israel, and the idolatry and cruelty of Assyria, are not to be overlooked as causes for His anger. As I see it, the entire book is the vocalization of the Almighty. *The Jewish Study Bible* (p.1241) offers a very excellent outline, which fits God's "Blazing Anger." With modification for brevity, its components are as follows:

- (i)   Doom and its description (1:1–18)
- (ii)   Repentance is needed (2:1–4)
- (iii) Destruction of idolatrous nations, including Assyria, and their gods
- (iv)   The remnant of God's people will be restored (2:5–3:13)
- (v)   Joy will come to Jerusalem (the messianic kingdom) (3:14–20)

(i) Doom (1:1–18):

God "will sweep everything away from off the face of the earth." What could be clearer than that? That was duplicated in what happened in Noah's day: "I will destroy mankind from off the face of the earth."

Attention is turned to His people (Judah). In the section 1:4–6 and 8–13 God blasts His chosen people for their idolatry and crookedness.

In His great disapproval of His chosen people, there are two very significant pronouncements trumpeted. These are exceedingly important in ushering two hugely significant messianic events:

(a). **"For the Day of the Lord is Approaching:" Messianic Provision** (1:7-14)

God prepares a *sacrificial feast* in which His guests purify themselves in messianic redemption. This is none other than the atonement for sin, which is saving for some and death for those who do not claim atonement. The messianic sacrifice symbolized by the sacrifice of the animal without blemish purifies the world. It is akin to what the rabbinic sages understood would be the big question in the Judgment: "Did you hope for the salvation of the Messiah?" (Shab. 31a).[149]

(b). **A Very Bitter Day of Wrath Is Coming: Consequences of Neglect**

Trouble, distress, calamity, desolation, darkness, deep gloom, densest clouds, horn blasts, alarms, and bloodshed. This is otherwise described as "Pangs of Messiah." Daniel explained this "time of trouble" (Dan. 12:1) as happening just before the ushering in of the Messiah's kingdom.

Throughout the great diatribe of anger and litany of offences committed, there is a silver thread: the guests bidden to the feast are purified by messianic atonement. (See Zephaniah 1:7.)

(ii). Repentance (2:1–4):

Seek the Lord all you humble of the land, who have tried hard to fulfill His law, seek righteousness, seek humility. (See 2:3.) The remnant of My people (see 2:9b) are chosen by messianic redemption. Repentance, the gift of the Ruach Hakodesh, must be appropriated.

(iii) The Destruction of the Wicked (2:5–3:13)

Assyria and idolatry will be destroyed.

(iv) The Remnant: (2:5–3:13):

The remnant of Israel will be restored.

(1) For then I will make the people pure of speech so that they invoke the Lord by name and serve Him with one accord ... My suppliants shall bring offerings to Me in Fair Puzai (Zion). (3:9, 10)

(2) But I will leave within you a poor, humble folk, and they shall find refuge in the name of the Lord. The remnant of Israel will be spared ... the remnant of Israel ... only such as these shall ... lie down with none to trouble them. (3:12, 13)

This silver thread is the only motivation God has to appease His anger. It is a remnant that prevents Him from totally wiping out life on the planet. He has the messianic redemption in store for them. In bringing in the Messiah's kingdom, He brings in perfection and immortality.

(v) Joy (3:14–20):

Zephaniah's Messianic Age, emphasis added:

> Shout for joy, Fair Zion, Cry aloud, O Israel!
> Rejoice and be glad with all your hearts,
> Fair Jerusalem!
> ***The Lord has annulled the judgment against you,***
> He has swept away your foes.
> Israel's sovereign the Lord is within.
> You need fear misfortune no more. (Zeph. 3:14–20)

Guilt and punishment can only be annulled in the Most Holy Place of the temple, where mercy triumphs over justice when the messianic blood is sprinkled on the ark of the covenant and mercy seat in the presence of the Shechinah. The Lord our God is one. Blessed be He.

The last words in Zephaniah's brief book are as a cooing dove of love and embrace as Messiah rejoices with His spoils. Peace, perfection, and immortality are restored. The universalism comes with the apocalyptic fulfillment.

Zephaniah closes his book with the same conclusion as Amos. (See Amos 9:14, 15). The progression from "Doom" to "Joy" is made possible by the messianic deliverance.

CHAPTER 22

Messiah in the Oracles of Jeremiah

Jeremiah is identified as the son of Hilkiah, a priest. He himself became a priest and prophet. There are seven other Jeremiahs named in Biblical writing, but he is considered the author of the book, although there is evidence of two versions of it. He had a scribe named Baruch, who did much of the writing for him. His ministry is dated to 627–586 BC.[150] He lived in the terrifying period of the Babylonian annihilation of the kingdom of Judah, Solomon's temple, and Jerusalem. His prophetic ministry occupied the reigns of Judah's final five kings: Josiah, Jehoahaz, Jehoiakim, Jehoiachin, and Zedekiah. Idolatry had supplanted primitive redemptive Judaism. Josiah was assessed as a good king, but his reforms were superficial and transient. The *MacArthur Study Bible* commentary points out that *religious insincerity, dishonesty, adultery, injustice, tyranny against the helpless, and slander prevailed as the norm, not the exception* in those dynastic times.[151]

Judah's cup of iniquity was full and brimming over. For his call for reformation, he was persecuted both by his own people and by the invaders. He was imprisoned by Zedekiah for a time (see Jeremiah 32:2) and lived the last part of his life exiled in Egypt. He had to contend with false prophets in Israel. He castigated the entire rotten establishment of the religious structure in the Judaism of his day:

> As the thief is ashamed when he is found, so is the house
> of Israel ashamed; they, their kings, their princes, and their
> priests, and their prophets. (Jer. 2:26 KJV)

God was at His wit's end with Israel and called her a harlot. The book of Jeremiah describes a very angry God. Idolatrous Israel had killed her own prophets "Like a devouring lion" (Jer. 2:30 KJV). Adultery was the rule of the day. "They were like fed horses in

259

the morning; everyone neighed after his neighbour's wife" (Jer. 5:8 KJV). Israel had polluted the Holy Land with her harlotry and wickedness. (See Jeremiah 3:2.) Israel was making a pretense of serving God while majorly pursuing idolatry and adultery. "Your burnt offerings are not acceptable, nor your sacrifices sweet unto Me ... Trust not in lying words, saying, The Temple of the Lord, The Temple of the Lord, The Temple of the Lord, are these" (Jer. 6:20; 7:4 KJV). Israel had made sacrifice without repentance and confession, using the temple as a source of indulgences. They were given to "perpetual backsliding." God called them "an evil family" (Jer. 8:3, 5 KJV). God pleaded urgently for reformation:

> Circumcise yourselves to the Lord, and take away the foreskins of your heart, ye men of Judah and inhabitants of Jerusalem, lest My fury come forth like fire, and burn that none can quench it, because of the evil of your doings. (Jer. 4:4 KJV)

Their ritual circumcision was a mockery. Their hearts were insincere. Judah gave God a deaf ear. God swore at them, in effect telling them to "*Go to hell.*" And what a hell it was:

> The Lord said to me, "Even if Moses and Samuel were to intercede with Me, I would not be won over to that people. Dismiss them from My presence, and let them go forth! And if they ask you, 'To what shall we go forth?' answer them, 'Thus saith the Lord:
> Those destined for the plague, to the plague;
> Those destined for the sword, to the sword;
> Those destined for famine, to famine;
> Those destined for captivity, to captivity ...
> I will make them a horror to all the kingdoms of the earth ...
>
> But who will pity you, O Jerusalem,
> Who will console you?
> Who will turn aside to inquire
> About your welfare?

> You cast Me off
> You go ever backward
> So I have stretched out My hand to destroy you;
> I cannot relent ..."
> (Jer. 15:1–6)

But God takes pity on Judah. His name is Rachmana. He remembers the Abrahamic covenant. Some turn to Him and claim His redemption. But it is only a remnant of them:

> The Lord said:
> Surely, a mere remnant of you
> Will I spare for a better fate!
> (Jer. 15:11)

Jeremiah has difficulty delivering these dire messages from God. He is persecuted for it. He is derided. He is hated because he is a bearer of bad news. He complains to God. (See Jeremiah 20:1–11.) God encourages him, and he takes his dire warnings to the last four kings of Judah in succession. He blames these kings for not guiding the people and instead leading them into idolatry and adultery. (See Jeremiah 23:1, 2.) What a far cry from the zenith of King David's reign!

A lot of history ensues. Nebuchadnezzar II of Babylon destroys Jerusalem and the temple of Solomon. They stood for idolatry and adultery, and God could not tolerate His people anymore in that era. But He had not forgotten His covenant with Abraham:

> And I Myself will gather *the remnant* of My flock from all the lands to which I have banished them, and I will bring them back to their pasture, where they shall be fertile and increase ... (Jer. 23:3–4)

(But Israel has had no king since Zedekiah. The Hasmoneans were not from the royal line of Judah. And they were short-lived). Then pours forth God's messianic promise from Jeremiah's lips:

261

> See, a time is coming – declares the Lord – when I will
> raise up *a true branch of David's line.* He shall reign as
> king and shall prosper, and He shall do what is just and
> right in the land. In His days Judah shall be delivered and
> Israel shall dwell secure. And this is the name by which He
> shall be called: "The Lord is our Vindicator."
> (Jer. 23:5, 6)

The KJV renders this last clause *"**The Lord our Righteousness.**"*
This encompasses the entire messianic atonement and kingly domain,
the new order. As Gershom Scholem termed it, acute Messianism
prevailed in this prediction. This prophecy has not yet come to pass.

God's lips are still smarting from viewing the gross idolatry
and adultery that prevailed in the land, and He lashed out at it, even
though He had introduced Messiah as His final solution. Here is a
summary of the tornado of God's invective. It is particularly against
the evil priests, false prophets, and wicked kings who have been
leading His people astray. Israel has polluted her own temple:

> Lo, the storm of the Lord goes forth in fury,
> A whirling storm [a tornado],
> It shall whirl down upon the heads of the wicked.
> The anger of the Lord shall not turn back
> Till it has fulfilled and completed His purposes
> In the days to come
> You shall clearly perceive it.
> (Jer. 23:19, 20)

God clearly declares that the punishment will come because they
have purposefully chosen the wrong path. Israel cannot hide:

> If a man enters a hiding place,
> Do I not see him? – says the Lord.
> For I fill both heaven and earth – declares the Lord.
> (Jer. 23:14)

Was Malachi looking back when he declared that the Messiah is "A refining fire?" Israel is "broken in pieces as a potter's vessel."

The message of Jeremiah is being given before the actual event of the Babylonian devastation of Judah. It is amazing that Judah is being warned. They will not heed it. Then it happens—Israel gets carried away captive into Babylon. The punishment and suffering are massive. Jerusalem lies wasted, and Solomon's temple is razed to the ground. The Shechinah has departed from Israel. *The ark of the covenant, the mercy seat, the bloodstains and the Shechinah are gone! Ichabod! The glory is departed!* The Abrahamic covenant remains an unfulfilled task.

Jeremiah obtains some redress from God. He prophesies that the Babylonian captivity will be limited to seventy years and Babylon will be punished. (See Jeremiah 25.) God has allowed it and now has the audacity to punish Babylon for doing it. Does not that mean that Israel has brought this about on themselves by the exercise of free will? So God's interference is a salvage operation. But the leaders of the time—the priests, false prophets, and kings—do not accept Jeremiah's predictions of coming destruction, and they seek to kill him. Jeremiah makes the prognosis worse by predicting a *"Time of Jacob's trouble."* Looking back, we see that it is a brook Jabbok experience, when Jacob is wrestled by a person who is divine and human. Jacob is assured of messianic intervention. Messiah softens his brother Esau's heart, and he is saved from death. Jeremiah looks forward down the corridors of time and sees history repeating itself. There will be more apostasies and more punishments. But God reassures him of His salvage operation:

> I will bring again the captivity of Jacob's tents, and have mercy on his dwelling places ... And ye shall be My people, and I will be your God ...*For the Lord hath redeemed Jacob, and ransomed him ...*
> (Jer. 30:18, 22; 31:10 KJV, emphasis added)

God has not given up. But Jeremiah's prophecies are rejected by the powerful, and he is imprisoned by King Zedekiah.

The Ha-Mashiach bridges the great gulf between Israel's sin and rejection by an angry God. That is the gist of Jeremiah's witness and prophecy. Israel will suffer the results of her sin, and devastation by Babylon, but the time is coming when messianic salvation will take place. "***The Lord our Righteousness***" will be offered to the "remnant of His flock." They will triumph. Ha-Mashiach is the only answer and effects redemption. *The Ha-Mashiach is still the only and final answer to all Israel's woes—the true branch of David's vine.*

What is in modern Israel's future in the light of the Babylonian devastation? When will the true branch sprout? When will modern Israel wake up to messianic redemption?

CHAPTER 23

The Messianic Vision of Obadiah

Nothing is known about the personal history of Obadiah, who had a vision recorded in the shortest book of the Tanak. Its dating is hotly disputed in modern times, with suggestions that it was written even as late as 450 BC. Prior, it had been accepted by the rabbinic sages that he lived in the time of King Ahab of Israel and Jehoshaphat, king of Judah, about 850 BC.[152] The acceptance into the Tanak of Obadiah was decided by the Sanhedrin. Its importance, therefore, was elected by inspiration. Verses 1–7 of this one-chapter book are almost identical with scattered verses in Jeremiah 49:7–22. The conclusion is that one of them copied from the other, or they both copied from a third unknown source.[153] This does not detract from the message of the book. God was repeating His warnings.

The vision of Obadiah is fascinating not only because it contains a messianic prophecy. It is also concerned with an antimessianic history in its apotelesmatic anatomy.[154] In my opinion, this perspective in the interpretation of Obadiah is shared with Daniel's abomination of desolation. The subject of the vision is Edom, otherwise known as Esau's descendants. There is a conviction among some scholars that in this book, Edom is synonymous with all the nations that persecute God's chosen people.[155] I agree. I therefore regard this book as apotelesmatic.

Obadiah's "AntiMessianism" is important, providing a definition of the abomination. Pride is the dominant factor in the manifestations of all forms of the abomination. Edom's malfeasance is seen in verse 3: "Your arrogant heart has seduced you."

Lucifer's Pride: Pride was the cause of Lucifer's fall and the origin of evil in the multiverse (Obad. 3, 4). This is one application of

Obadiah. Lucifer's pride was the original abomination. He wanted to ascend above God. He took advantage of the vulnerability of Adam and Eve in Gan Eden. It was there that messianic promise was first given to humanity. Lucifer posed a rival system to God's law when he said, "Ye shall not surely die" (Gen. 3:4). God was quick to give Eve assurance of messianic deliverance when He outlined the enmity between her seed and the Serpent's seed. (See Genesis 3:15.) Was Lucifer guaranteeing messianic redemption when he alleged, "Ye shall not surely die?" Did he already know that God had planned redemption from eternity? But the primal couple did die, and he was proved to be a liar and the father of lies. Fortunately God provided redemption and they were assured of future restoration of Edenic devekut with God, because of messianic crushing, thus bearing their sins.

Cain's Pride: The next recorded rival system was seen when the original two brothers fell out. (See Genesis 4:3–7.) The younger Abel's sacrifice of the messianic substitutionary Lamb without blemish was accepted, and Cain's "fruits and vegetables," products of his pride, were rejected. Messianic promise was the lightning bolt of God that consumed Abel's sacrifice. This is an apotelesmatic application, which is easily deduced from the book of Obadiah.

Esau's Pride: In the present context, Esau's pride was the rejection of the Abrahamic covenant in his preference for illicit sex and idolatry. Again the older brother elected his own rejection by God. Esau felt that God was not that fussy about his practice on the side of idolatry to gain sexual satisfaction. The younger brother was then given the vision of "Jacob's Ladder" as the Messiah Himself stood at the top, opening the gates of heaven to humanity. Basically, the vision of Obadiah stresses that Edom, the idolatrous children of Esau, will not win in the end. The Idumeans or Edomites have slipped into oblivion, while the chosen people are still around. The Nabataeans from the eastern Arabian Desert finally utterly destroyed the Edomites. As the descendants of Esau, they have been obliterated.

Edom had refused Israel passage through their land when they journeyed from Egypt to the Promised Land. This was tantamount to obstructing the fulfillment of the Abrahamic covenant, the proclamation of the messianic *Day of the Lord.* Edom had attacked Israel opportunely whenever they were fighting other foes. Edom jeered at and mocked Israel's discomfitures and defeats. Edom attacked and cut down many Israelis as they fled in their defeats. God does not countenance anti-Semitism. Those persecuting Israel today should take note.

> How could you stand at the passes
> To cut down its fugitives!
> How could you betray those who fled
> On *that Day of Anguish!*
> As you did, so shall it be done to you;
> Your conduct shall be requited.
>
> Yea, against all nations
> The *Day of the Lord* is at hand.
> That same cup that you drank on My Holy Mount
> Shall all nations drink evermore.
> Drink till their speech grows thick
> And they become as though they had never been.
> (Obad. 14–17, emphasis added)

Here is a warning to all nations: The chosen of God have a mission. They must not be prevented in that mission. God will punish any nation that hurts them. The messianic promise is given as a dire warning to all nations: *The Day of the Lord is at hand.* (See Obadiah 15b.) The *messianic prophecy* then flows from Obadiah's pen:

> But on Zion's mount a remnant shall survive,
> And it shall be holy,
> The House of Jacob shall dispossess
> Those who dispossessed them.
> The House of Jacob shall be fire,
> And the House of Joseph flame,
> And the House of Esau shall be straw;
> They shall burn it and devour it,

> And no survivor shall be left of the House of Esau,
> For the Lord has spoken ...
> (Obadiah 17–21)

Let not the world treat Israel lightly. They have a mission to accomplish. Messiah must be unleashed on civilization. History must end. Anti-Messianism is the abomination of desolation and will not prevail.

CHAPTER 24

Daniel's Visions of Messiah, the Son of Man

Daniel is the prophet of the apocalyptic. Messiah is the dominant theme of his book. He saw the Messiah's kingdom approaching toward him like a bullet train, and this motivated his apocalyptic writing. He saw the Messiah at every earthly crisis. His book is an exegesis of the apocalyptic mind of God:

> *But there is a God in Heaven Who has made known what is to be at the End of Days.*
> (Dan. 2:28)

And the "End of Days" was consumed by messianic power. Dramatic events were to unfold with cataclysmic results. And what was in God's apocalyptic mind?

> *…until the measure of transgression is filled and that of sin complete, until iniquity is expiated, and eternal righteousness ushered in; and prophetic vision ratified, and the Holy of Holies anointed.*
> (Dan. 9:24)

After that:

> *At that time, the great Prince Michael will appear and your people will be rescued, all who are found inscribed in the book. Many of those that sleep in the dust of the earth will awake, some to eternal life.*
> (Dan. 12: selected verses)

Daniel commences with the description of the Messiah in chapter 2 as a "*Stone*" that grows into the whole world. The "*Son of Elohim*, the Messiah in the "Fiery Furnace," dazzled him in chapter 3. He saw the human penetrance of messianic deity as the "*Son of Man*" in chapter 7 (cf. Gen. 3; Deut. 18; Ps. 2; Isa. 7; 9; Mic. 5). He connects with the entire Tanak in naming the Messiah as the "*Anointed One*" in chapter 9. He saw the Messiah as Israel's patron and special protector in the person of "*Michael the Great Prince*" in chapter 12. These were all messianic milestones to the restoration of immortality in King Messiah ben David's eternal kingdom, which will be ushered in by Judgment, Resurrection, and the Utopia. He saw history being totally wiped away, utterly destroyed.

Four mighty miracles highlighted his life: The fiery furnace, the lion's den, the writing on the wall (all of which happened in real life), and the establishment of the Messiah's kingdom, the mightiest vision of the future.

Through all this history that rapidly approached and passed him by in vision, Daniel's writing is extremely conscious of the plight of his own personal life, that of his people, and that of his religion. His agonizing prayers encapsulate the travails he and his people were going through. The future solution God outlined to him was not simply a restoration to the Holy Land but went far beyond that in outlining the future of all humanity into the Messiah ben David's eternal kingdom. As a captive in Babylon, he longed for Jerusalem. The view offered included both a "human" Messiah in tandem with a dazzling, powerful, "divine," and kingly Messiah ben David, one who will rule the world eternally from the "New Jerusalem." In the near events the temple would be rebuilt. But the "helper," in the understanding of the vision, looked beyond the future destruction of the rebuilt temple to the eventual establishment of the everlasting messianic kingdom (Dan. 12). Thus he eminently qualifies to be the prophet of the apocalyptic.

There is controversy among scholars about the dating of Daniel's life and the writing of the book bearing the title of his name. Some scholars date it to about 605 BC.[156] Others feel it was written retroactively in its final version, about 164 BC.[157]. After careful study, I have concluded that it might be best to date the original writing to 605 BC and the editing to 164 BC.[158] I am of the opinion that Moses Stuart was correct when he said that the whole book of Daniel proceeded from one pen and one mind.[159] If one disagrees with this view, that disagreement may be allowed, since it is well known that editing and interpolations of various books of the Tanak took place. But a total retroactive writing of the whole book would deny inspiration and the veracity of the prophet. By that logic, a total denial of the inspiration of the entire Tanak would follow, and the sacredness of the canonical writings would not prevail. I am persuaded that the august Sanhedrin that decided to include the book of Daniel in the canon of Holy Scripture was inspired by Ruach Hakodesh to do so. Its triumphant proclamation of apocalyptic and catastrophic Messianism makes the Tanak complete.

The extreme and significant part of Daniel's apocalyptic message, the "Messianic Kingdom," is still in the future. For us, that is the most important part of his book. If we allow for Babylon, Medo-Persia, Greece, and Rome to have been positioned retroactively by an editor in 164 BC, we must still envision what happens after and still ahead of us, as *our eternal destiny.*

A. The Apocalyptic of Daniel

Following are the components of the apocalyptic of Daniel:

1. The penetrance of humanity by Divinity
2. The stone from the mountain cut without hands
3. The appearance of Michael the great prince
4. The Judgment
5. The Resurrection

1. The Penetrance of Humanity by Divinity

This is assumed by Daniel and described by him as "*Sonship.*" For evidence, I present the "Father/Son" relationship outlined in the whole Tanak between God and the Messiah. The Biblical story began at the gates of Eden in the enunciation to the woman (Eve) of the promised "*seed.*" David elaborated on this in Psalm 2 as "You

271

are My Son, I have fathered You this day." Isaiah spoke of it as "the conception of a woman" to be named Immanuel in Isaiah 7:14–16, and again as "a Child is born, a son is given … the Mighty God, the Everlasting Father" in Isaiah 9:6. Daniel takes this divinity of the Messiah very seriously:

Daniel 3:25 describes the fiery furnace: "… the fourth looks like a divine being." It is also translated as "the *Son of Elohim*."[160] The Hebrew word is "elahiyn" in the Masoretic text.[161] Some scholars have viewed the majestic plural word "Elohim" as an attempt to produce a certain "universalism of gods."[162] The tanakian concept is not so at all. "Elohim" richly binds together God's activities in Creation and the reclamation management of humanity, through His Ruach Hakodesh and Ha-Mashiach *functionalities*. It has nothing to do with a division of His person. He is adamant about this when He commands, "Thou shalt have no other gods." Elohim in Genesis 1:1 in Creation is the same in Daniel 3:25 in Redemption. Moses knew no "El" and "Ba'l" (Baal). His God was not conjured up from "Canaanite (Ugaritic) representations."[163] Messiah and the Holy Spirit are God's powerful outreaches, contained within the eternity of Elohim as the only God, the monotheist God of the Hebrews. I deny a "Young God" and an "Old God," a "Storm (War) God" and a "God of Peace," as different individuals. These ideas are manufactured by the terrestrial compartmentalization of our thinking. Some rabbinic sages thought in these terms, as do some modern scholars.

Daniel 7:13 occurs within the vision of the four beasts: "One like a human being." This is also translated as "One like the *Son of Man*" (NKJV). He collaborates with the "Ancient of Days." This scene in heaven is widely acclaimed by the rabbinic sages and Jewish scholars as messianic. The Ancient of Days confers on this "Son of Man" "an everlasting dominion" (Dan. 7:14). The messianic kingdom is about to be ushered in. The association of "divine" and "human" appearances in this supernatural being who will usher in the messianic kingdom is the messianic functionality, God Himself, and He must embody or comprise a oneness relationship with Elohim to qualify for this. This "divine-human" being appeared to Jacob at the brook Jabbok, and to Abraham under the terebinths. King David encounters Him as the "begotten" of the Father (Ps. 2:7). Isaiah hails him as "Immanuel born of a virgin [a young woman]" and states, "For unto us a Child is born, a son is given" *who is in actuality* "the Mighty God and Everlasting Father" (Isa. 7:14; 9:6). He is the Ha-Mashiach *functionality* of Elohim. We cannot give God "One Single Characteristic" and restrict Him to a "body" that is comparable to our physicality. When God functions as Messiah, He does not divide or split or breed a hypostasis, an entity outside of Himself. He is the Mashiach. Substantially and in eternity He is the Great Spirit.

He now appears "with the clouds of heaven." The rabbinic sages recognized this terminology and this passage of Scripture as describing the Messiah (b. Sanh. 98a; Num. Rab. 13:14; 'Aggadat Ber'esit 14:3, 23:1). With regard to "[He] comes with the clouds of heaven," some scholars have questioned direction of movement. Is He arriving for His audience with the Ancient of Days, or is He leaving the presence of the Ancient of Days?[164] Both directions are applicable if this is not to be taken as an Enochian tale, in which Enoch's translation is regarded as a deification. The Tanak knows no Enoch Metatron. The Talmud allows the Son of Man to sit on a throne. He is assumed to be on the downward journey to earth since He is about to claim an eternal kingdom entrusted to Him by the Ancient of Days. His catastrophic arrival as Messiah on earth is about to take place. With regard to the dispute in direction of travel, He can be assumed to be making at least three journeys directionally: (1) His corporeal penetrance of humanity, (2) His return to heaven to sacrifice in the Heavenly Temple, and (3) His return to earth with the eternal kingdom of Messiah ben David. These travels or journeys may stupendously record the sequence of redemptive events.

The messianic nature of these above references of *Son of Elohim* of Daniel 3:25 and *Son of Man* of Daniel 7:13 have long been held as messianic in Hebrew thought and in the Talmud as cited above. There has been no attempt of which I am aware to provide an explanation of *the conjugation* of the divinity and humanity of the messianic figure in Daniel. Jewish scholars, apart from Daniel Boyarin, to my knowledge either deny it without citing good reasons or avoid it. But strangely, great things are expected of the Messiah by these scholars, implying that He will be all-powerful and eternal. He is allowed by the Talmud to exist before the creation of the world. He is equated with Michael. The names "YHVH" and "Redeemer" are treated synonymously in the Tanak. In Geza Vermes's palpable anxiety to disconnect Yeshua of Nazareth of the Synoptic Gospels from Daniel's "Son of Elohim" and "Son of Man," he goes through linguistic contortions ("circumlocutional use") to try to disprove a connection. Unfortunately he avoids considering the divine penetration of humanity that is involved in the Messiah of the Tanak. However, in rare candor, Vermes admits the following:

> Sporadic though the evidence may be, it seems reasonable to deduce that mainstream Jewish interpretative tradition recognized Daniel 7:9-14 from the early second century AD at least, but *almost certainly even earlier,* as a Messianic text depicting the coming of the new, glorious, and exalted David.[165]

But again strangely, he denies that "Son of Man" is a messianic title and desperately tries to diminish its significance. He makes a bold attempt to diminish Messiah by the idea that every Jew is referred to in the Talmud as "a son of God." He does not delve into the idea that the Messiah up in heaven, as Daniel saw the Messiah, looks like a human. He makes no attempt to properly orient the human/divine/deity implications of two other accepted great messianic references in the Tanak—Psalm 2:7 and Isaiah 9:6, where the messianic functionality is expressed as a Father–Son relationship between Elohim and Messiah—although he mentions these texts in passing as being messianic. These texts have wide acceptance as messianic in the Talmud. The reason for the concept in the Tanak that the Messiah has both human and divine qualities escapes Vermes.[166]

Daniel Boyarin is quite the opposite of Geza Vermes in his understanding of Daniel 7. Boyarin is mighty in his declaration:

> The second-God Redeemer figure [Son of Man] thus comes, on my view, out of the earlier history of Israel's religion. Once the Messiah had been combined with the

> younger divine figure that we have found in Daniel 7,
> then it became natural to ascribe to him also the term
> "Son of God" ... What could be more natural, then, than
> to adopt the older usage "Son of God," already ascribed to
> the Messiah in his role as the Davidic king of Israel, and
> understanding it more literally as the sign of equal divinity
> of the Ancient of Days and the Son of Man. Thus the Son
> of Man became the Son of God ... -- and all without a
> break with ancient Jewish tradition. (See Daniel Boyarin,
> *The Jewish Gospels*, pp. 46, 47)

Now, in this context, Boyarin is in a discussion of early Christianity, which he classifies as a Jewish sect in his book, but there is no doubt that he totally believes that *the Messiah predicted in Daniel 7 is indeed divine and human.* He perceives this in a "binitarian" view, which he clearly sees is contrary to monotheism. He even attributes to the prophet Daniel a downplaying of the "two Gods" perceived in the vision—the Ancient of Days and the Son of Man—because of the prophet Daniel's own dedication to monotheism. But Boyarin insists that as a messianic synonym, "Son of Man" is valid indeed. Boyarin declares that He existed within God before the creation of the universe and will one apocalyptic day exercise judgment in that universe. Boyarin unnecessarily supplements the Son of Man description by citing the books of First Enoch and Fourth Ezra as evidence, both noncanonical Jewish books. These books cannot be used as proof.

My conclusion is that the prophet Daniel is told, and Boyarin sees, that God and Messiah can be expressed in human terms as a father–son relationship. ***But we can accept this ideation only in the oneness of the substance of God, in this Father-Son nomenclature.*** Messiah is God's functionality. Boyarin clearly states that this Son of Man who qualifies as the Son of God is indeed the Messiah ben David, who inaugurates the apocalyptic everlasting kingdom, where there will be perfection and eternal life. Unmistakably the prophet Daniel depicts it. This is totally compatible with David's and Isaiah's theology. Boyarin has made the clearest modern Jewish pronouncement here that Messiah ben David, Son of Man, is indeed the Son of God. Boyarin is adamant that it is an ancient Jewish doctrine, at least as ancient as the book of Daniel. I contend that Moses's concept named "Seed of the woman" and David's theology were built on this Father–Son relationship of Messiah and God in the redemption. Messiah is substantially deity, our monotheist God. Blessed is He; the Lord is one.

Joseph Klausner makes a very bold statement. After discussing the book of Daniel at great length, he summarizes:

> From what we have said, it follows as a matter of course that almost all of Daniel is Messianic in spirit; but chapters 2, 6-9, and 12 are Messianic in essence.[167]

But after admitting that this "Son of Man" is messianic,[168] he draws back and argues against it:

> But in a comparatively short time after the composition of the Book of Daniel it was thought among the Jews that *this 'son of man' was the Messiah.* This is not surprising: *a human being that could approach the throne of God and could be given "dominion and glory and a kingdom"* and whom all the peoples would serve and *whose dominion would be an everlasting dominion could not possibly be other than the King Messiah.* So thinks the author of the Ethiopic book of Enoch.

And now comes Klausner's incomprehensible substitute explanation:

> Actually there is no individual Messiah in Daniel: **the entire people of Israel is the Messiah** that will exercise everlasting dominion throughout the whole world.[169]

This last statement is illogical, preposterous, absurd, and confused. It cannot be sustained in his otherwise praiseworthy book. It is incongruent with the Tanak and all the yearning in Jewish hearts. Jews do not yearn for themselves and their own "messianic merit," if such is ever illogically assumed. An individual divine Messiah manifest on the planet is undeniable. As a people, Israel needs atonement and can never regain perfection and immortality on their own merit. Nor ever can any Jew atone for his own sins. It was and is blasphemy for Jews to forgive sins. Only God can forgive sins. It is good for Jews to yearn to be better people, but to assume a status as a people to be their own Messiah is concocting a mechanism of salvation similar to that of the enlightenment. It is an abomination. Daniel would turn in his grave. God conceived of Messiah long before Creation, and the Talmud identifies an individual glorious Messiah, although the qualifications the Talmud assigns Him are confused and controversial in the discussions of the rabbinic sages. There is absolutely no doubt that that Son of Man up in heaven in Daniel 7 is *the individual Messiah* receiving a kingdom. He is not the sinful, idolatrous "composite Israel" desperately needing redemption. Daniel's prayer in chapter 9 admits the great sinfulness of his people. Gershom Scholem would not agree that Israel is its own Messiah. He looks for cosmic intervention, a collapse of history, an *acute Messianism.* Boyarin undoubtedly agrees that the Son of Man in Daniel is a divine-human Messiah and not Israel as a whole. Franz Rosenzweig wanted the heavens to open and for that Messiah to descend. Klausner is deluded in this declaration that "the entire people of Israel is the Messiah ..."

The claim that Israel will be its own Messiah is tantamount to Cain's "fruits and vegetables," to the desecration by Antiochus IV Epiphanes, and the Romans in the temple—all abominations rejected by God. If Israel builds the third temple and installs Israel as its own Messiah, God will engineer its destruction. The Abrahamic covenant embodies a mission to proclaim the Messiah, not to be the Messiah. The Jews as a composite people can never bestow the eradication of death and the restoration of perfection and immortality to humanity. Their four-thousand-year history *screams out imperfection and mortality!* Every Jew who has broken the law is a sinner, but he is also a "son of God" only as viewed and contained within the redemption by the Mashiach.

2. The "Stone from the mountain cut without hands"

This stone is interpreted as the messianic king who finally rules an everlasting kingdom. He also is *"the God of Heaven [who] will establish a kingdom that shall never be destroyed"* (Dan. 2:44). He belongs to the earth as the Messiah. He is deity, born as a "child" and "son" on the planet (Ps. 2:7, Isa. 9:6), synonymous with the God of heaven. The Father–Son relationship between YHVH and Ha-Mashiach cannot be viewed in sexual earthly terms and meanings. Rather it is in messianic *functionality* encompassed within Elohim, bestowed on the earth, embodied in a human, but *in verity the visiting deity, Elohim.* Only deity can atone, vanquish death, and restore immortality. Again, the "Stone cut without hands" context precludes the Jews being a composite Messiah. Messiah forgives and atones. Jews who claimed to be able to forgive sins were accused of blasphemy and put to death. Any Jew who presumes that Israel is its own Messiah, must therefore by their own law be put to death. The Jews collectively as a sinful people, utter blasphemy and desecrate the Day of Atonement and the Most Holy Place of the temple if they present themselves as the Messiah.

3. The Appearance of Michael, the Great Prince

Michael "stands beside the sons of your people." Michael has been described, in the Talmud, as "standing up" in the heavenly temple, offering sacrifice on behalf of Israel. Michael's appearance was in the future of Daniel's time. (See my digression on the subject of Michael later in this chapter.) The time of trouble of which Daniel speaks, the "pangs of the Messiah" described by the rabbinic sages, may be about to take place right now. Israel is ripe for it. It happens before the Judgment and Resurrection, in the tanakian timetable.

4. The Judgment

Effected by the Messiah, Judgment cannot be avoided and will determine who goes to Gan Eden and who goes to Gehinnom. (See

Daniel 7:9; cf. Isaiah 3:14; 6:1.) This must happen in every person's life. The important criterion of judgment is in the talmudic words "Did you hope for the Salvation of the Messiah?" (Shab. 31a).[170] I point out that here indeed is a very personal redeeming Messiah, God Himself, who is repeatedly defined as the Redeemer of the world. Messiah is therefore the functionality of Elohim, a manifestation of the power of divinity.

5. The Resurrection of the Dead

This follows: "At that time your people will be rescued, all who are found inscribed in the book. Many of those that sleep in the dust of the earth will awake ..." (Dan. 12:2). The strength of the dictum "Your people will be rescued" cannot be contorted into a proclamation that Israel will rescue itself by some mysterious "messianic property" within themselves. The "rescue" comes from outside, or else the record should say, "Your people will rescue themselves." The vast majority of Jews are well-intentioned good people striving to keep the law. They strive to "love their neighbor as themselves" by their benevolent acts. But not one of them has kept the law *one hundred percent*. Just ask Isaiah for his opinion. Flavius Josephus's "inviolable piety" is a big humbug akin to "Thou shalt not surely die" spoken by the Serpent in Gan Eden. The resurrection of the dead occurs only by messianic power and merit. *Grace* has been proclaimed as the messianic salvation by the rabbinic sages. I repeat, the important question posed in the Judgment, according to the rabbinic sages, is "Did you hope for the salvation of the Messiah?"

All these events are predicted by Daniel and are bulwarks in Judaism. The "penetrance" of humanity by divinity, and the appearance of the "Anointed One," are elaborated specifically by Moses, David, Isaiah, Daniel, Micah, and other prophets. The editor(s) of the book of Daniel, who may have interpolated what is alleged as a retrospective view in 164 BC, obviously could not change the future event of the great drama of the resurrection of the dead. It was still in their future.

B. The Highlights of Daniel's Life in Babylon

In my treatment of Daniel and his visions, I will try to refrain from the studious language, "expertise," and repartee of Biblical scholars in the citations I use. I will address important concerns to the devotional orientation, as it is primarily for the devotional audience that I write. After all, I myself look for the messianic redemption from the sacredness of the Tanak.

1. Nebuchadnezzar's Dream of the Image

The interpretation by Daniel is well known. We are living in the feet of iron and clay and looking forward to the stupendous "stone" to strike the image on its feet and "grind it to powder." Gershom Scholem believed in acute Messianism, a catastrophic apocalyptic end to history as we know it.

2. Nebuchadnezzar's Great Image and the Fiery Furnace

What was most significant here is the fourth person in the furnace seen by the king: "But I see four men walking about unbound and unharmed in the fire and the fourth looks like a divine being" (Dan. 3:25). How was the king able to recognize a "divine being"? The original Hebrew words of the Masoretic text are "***Dameh l'var-elahiyn***," which should be translated "***Son of Elohim***" in English. So it is assumed that Nebuchadnezzar, or at least Daniel, understood the human penetrance by divinity in this "divine being" as a "son" relationship of the Messiah with Elohim. This can only be understood to be "within Elohim," if monotheism is to be preserved. If this was an "editorialized" insertion in the year 164 BC, the penetrance of humanity by divinity, and the Son-ship of the Messiah within Elohim was understood and believed by the editors. I do not infer anything into the "Son-ship" relationship other than that of a functionality of Elohim. It is an anthropomorphism because of the inadequacy of the human mind to conceive, understand, and express the divine concept. Monotheism must be preserved. There is no procreative or sexual connotation here by any stretch of the imagination. We cannot ascribe our human sexuality to God. Calling God our Father is the human way we get close to Him to love Him.

3. Nebuchadnezzar's Dream of the Tree

The interpretation by Daniel included the humiliation of the king. But it stimulated his recovery and his extolling of the God of heaven.

4. Belshazzar's Feast and the Writing on the Wall

The words "Mene," "Tekel," and "Upharsin" were interpreted by Daniel as judgments and punishments that took place almost immediately. "God has numbered [the days of] your kingdom and brought it to an end ... you have been weighed in the balances and found wanting ... your kingdom is divided and given to the Medes and the Persians" (Dan. 5:26–28). The Medo-Persians arrived and took the kingdom. Daniel continued in prominence.

5. The Lion's Den

A personal jealous plot was hatched against Daniel, who was one of three in charge of the empire appointed by the king. Daniel's miraculous deliverance from the lions' mouths was a reward for the faiths of both Daniel and King Darius.

Subsequently there was a widespread acknowledgment of the God of the Hebrews:

> Then King Darius wrote to all peoples and nations of every language that inhabit the earth ... I have hereby given an order that throughout my royal domain men must tremble in fear before the God of Daniel, for He is the living God who endures forever; His kingdom is indestructible, and His dominion is to the end of time; He delivers and saves ... (Dan. 6:26–28)

Darius's knowledge of Judaism included "the end of time." In these events Daniel's messianic belief and expectations are crystal-clear. Here is vindication. The God of Daniel delivers and saves. Again, Israel cannot deliver and save Israel. God is the Creator, and God is the Redeemer. The Lord our God is one; blessed be He.

C. Daniel's Visions

1. The Vision in His Bed, of the Four Beasts (Dan. Ch. 7)

They came from the sea after the 4 winds had stirred it up:

i.   A lion with eagle's wings, etc.
ii. A bear, raised up on one side, with three fangs, etc.
iii. A leopard with four wings and four heads
iv. A fourth beast, fearsome, dreadful, and powerful, with great iron teeth, and it had ten horns; three of the horns were uprooted to make room for a little horn, which had eyes of a man, and a mouth speaking arrogantly.
     (See Daniel 7:1–9)

While these four beasts were in the limelight, Daniel saw the "Ancient of Days":

> Thrones were set in place,
> And the Ancient of Days took His seat.
> His garment was like white snow,
> And the hair of His head was like lamb's wool.
> His throne was tongues of flame;
> Its wheels were blazing fire.
> A river of fire streamed before Him;
> Thousands upon thousands served Him
> Myriads upon myriads attended Him;
> The court sat and the books were opened.
> (Dan. 7:9, 10)

Here is a judgment scene. The scene viewed by Daniel has to be extremely expansive because of the myriads attending God. God is on the judgment throne. A messianic decision will be made, and sentence pronounced. Attention turns to the horrible fourth beast, whose little horn speaks arrogantly against God. He is killed and burned. The other three beasts were deprived of their dominion but were allowed to live for a time and a season.

Then Daniel sees the human in the heavens:

> **The Son of Man**
> One like a human being
> Came with the clouds of heaven;
> He reached the Ancient of Days
> And was presented to him.
> Dominion, glory, and kingship were given to him;
> All peoples and nations of every language must serve him.
> His dominion is an everlasting dominion that shall not pass away.
> And his kingship, one that shall not be destroyed.
> (Dan.7:13, 14)

Daniel was distressed that he did not understand what was going on, so he asked one of the "attendants," who told him:

> These great beasts, four in number [mean] four kingdoms
> will arise out of the earth; then holy ones of the Most High
> will receive the kingdom, and will possess the kingdom
> forever ...
> (Dan. 7:17, 18)

Thus far, this scenario in Daniel's first vision is a parallel to Nebuchadnezzar's first dream, the dream of the image, which is destroyed by the stone in the days of the kings of the feet. This explanation of the four kingdoms of Babylon, Medo-Persia, Greece, and Rome, and the mixture of weak and strong nations that follow, has been universally accepted among Biblical scholars.

But Daniel is still perturbed by the fourth beast, which was

> ... very fearsome, with teeth of iron, claws of bronze, that
> devoured and crushed, and stamped the remains; and of

> the ten horns on its head; and of the new one that sprouted, for which three fell – the horn that had eyes, and a mouth that spoke arrogantly ... that horn [that] made war with the holy ones and overcame them. (Dan. 7:19, 20)

The attendant tells Daniel that the fourth beast will break up into ten kingdoms, three of which will form the little horn, which

> ... will speak words against the Most High, and will harass the holy ones of the Most High. He will think of changing times and laws, and they will be delivered into his power for a time, times, and half a time. Then the court will sit and his dominion will be taken away ... And given to the people of the holy ones of the Most High. Their kingdom will be an everlasting kingdom. (Dan. 7:25–27)

Retrospectively from our viewpoint, Daniel's first vision is very clear. If it is accepted that the fourth kingdom of history was indeed Rome, then it is clear that God's "holy ones" (Israel) were devastated inhumanly by Rome. This is clearly borne out in the history of Israel in Roman times. There was a cruel and indescribably wicked period, which included the destruction of the second temple and Jerusalem. Imperial pagan Rome, papal Rome, and the Christian kingdoms that followed persecuted the Jews. Muslim and Crusader desecrations of the Holy Land occurred. The persecution of the Jews continued during the Middle Ages by so-called "Christian" powers in various countries and culminated in the Nazi holocaust. The interposed scene in heaven in the middle of this vision is highly significant. It is clearly messianic—the Ancient of Days, sitting in judgment, introducing the coming Messiah, the "One like a human being," and the Messianic Age.

Daniel sees the Messiah as the "Stone" in Nebuchadnezzar's dream, the fourth person in the fiery furnace ("the Son of Elohim"), and now in the scene in heaven in his own first vision, the "One like a human being" and "Son of Man," to whom the Ancient of Days awards

> Dominion, glory, and kingship … All peoples and nations
> of every language must serve him. His dominion is an
> everlasting dominion that shall not pass away, and his
> kingship, one that shall not pass away" (Dan.7:13, 14).

It is important to consider the implications of the Son of Man. Scholars see Dan. 7:13, Ps. 110, 1 Kings 22:19, Isa. 6 and 51:12, and Zech. 12 as describing the same scene in heaven with the Son of Man and the Ancient of Days. In the Daniel reference the presence of "Thrones" has caused consternation. I discuss this elsewhere. But it must be emphasized here that this Son of Man can be no other than the Messiah who receives the work of judgment and is to be the successor on David's throne.

The question must be asked: what is "one like a human being" doing up in heaven, to whom the Ancient of Days defers, and to whom is awarded the eternal future of the planet earth as an everlasting kingdom? It is an amazing answer that is found in the commentary of this passage in *The Jewish Study Bible*. The commentator, Lawrence M. Wills, states that for Daniel it most likely represented a heavenly figure who will exercise judgment, *perhaps Michael*. (See margin comments, pp. 1656, 1657.)

The commentator thus links this up with Daniel 10:13 and Daniel 12:1. I agree. This assumption about Michael by Lawrence M. Wills is tantamount to the acceptance of Michael as the Messiah in this explanation. I concur.

Michael the Great Prince

At this point it is vital to make a significant digression into a discussion of Michael, who figures prominently in the book of Daniel:

Michael is variously treated in the Talmud by rabbinic sages as follows:

i. He is called an "archangel." The Tanak does not define him as an "archangel," and I suspect this title was borrowed from the B'rit Hadashah's Jude (verse 9), or from the apocryphal and pseudepigraphic writings. The Talmud states he had no

285

part in Creation. (See Genesis R. 1. 3, cited by Cohen.)[171] It is also noted that the apostle Paul called Yeshua of Nazareth "the archangel" (1 Thessalonians 4:16).

ii. Michael is described in the heavenly temple: "Zebul is that where the celestial Jerusalem is and the temple in which the altar is erected, and Michael, the great Prince, stands and offers a sacrifice upon it …" (Chag. 12a cited by Cohen).[172]

iii. In Daniel 10:13 Michael is called a "Prince of the first rank," and in 12:1 Michael is called "the great Prince who standeth for the children of thy people." This is interpreted as Michael being the special guardian of Israel. Abraham Cohen calls Michael an "angel"—in this instance, one of four named special angels. Michael is cited as being superior to Gabriel, and the Talmud assigns various jobs to him. (See Ber. 4b.) Cohen, with the backing of the Talmud, is doing this on his own, as the Tanak does not label Michael as an "angel" or as an "archangel." According to the Talmud, one of the jobs performed by Michael is the visit to Abraham to announce the birth of Isaac. (See Numbers R. 11. 10.)[173] In the Tanak, that job was performed by God in human form. If this is the case, the Talmud is unwittingly labeling Michael as deity.

iv. The meaning of the name "Michael" in talmudic literature is "who is like El"[174] (i.e., "One like Elohim"). He is Israel's tutor, protector, mediator, and defender, "… and wherever he appears the glory of the Shekinah is bound to be found" (Ex. R. 11.5)."[175] The question this poses is, is he synonymous with the Shechinah? Is Michael God-like?

v. Michael is seen standing in the Most Holy Place in the heavenly temple, with God sitting on the throne. They are one in the work of redemption.

vi. Michael is clothed with the Shechinah. Myriad angels wait on him. He is not an angel, but he could be "in charge of angels." In this capacity I name Him as a functionality of Elohim.

It seems obvious that Michael is not an angel in the above circumstances. No "angel" gets around clothed with the Shechinah, which must be designated as deity alone, if Shechinah is defined as God's presence or aura. The conclusion is that Michael is a manifestation of deity, a functionality of Elohim, synonymous with Ha-Mashiach. Is he a Metatron "hypostasis" of God? There are only two functionalities of God known to us, namely Ruach Hakodesh and Ha-Mashiach. They are not separate from Elohim. The Tanak does not recognize the existence of a Metatron. The Lord our God is one. Blessed be He.

Again, "Zebul is that where the celestial Jerusalem is and the Temple in which the altar is erected, and Michael, the great Prince, stands and offers a sacrifice upon it [as an atonement in His redemptive and mediatorial roles]; as it is said, I have surely built thee an house of habitation, Zebul, a place for thee to dwell in forever (1 Kings viii. 13)."[176] Cohen is citing here the famous sugya in b Hagiga (12b) and Seder Rabba di-Bereshit (*Synopse zur Hekhalot Literature*, S 772; see Schafer below). As noted above, the Talmud denies Michael a part in the creation of the world. Michael is not called an archangel in the Tanak. But Cohen labels him an archangel. Cohen probably is again taking this cue from the B'rit Hadashah's Jude 9, or apocryphal writings, as already noted above, which do label Michael as an archangel. It is rather surprising here that the commentator in the margin of *The Jewish Study Bible* is assigning the Judgment to Michael. I have not seen this discussed in the Talmud, except concerning the judgment scene, where the Son of Man is allowed to sit on a throne with the Ancient of Days in Daniel 7. In the marginal comments on Daniel 12:1, which again mentions Michael, the commentator again links him to the powers of Judgment.[177] I make a great deal of this discussion of Michael because I firmly believe he is one and the same as the messianic functionality of Elohim.

Peter Schafer points out that Michael, as the great prince, is the most likely candidate to be the Celestial High Priest in the heavenly temple. He cites Gershom Scholem (*Jewish Gnosticism*, pp. 5, 44f, 46) and Ithamar Gruenwald ("*Re'uyot Yehezqel*," p. 101, *Hekhalot Literature*) besides several other talmudic sources in support. (See the chapter "God and Metatron" in *The Jewish Jesus*, by Peter Schafer, pp.116–173.) Scholem is emphatic that the prince in the passage in "*Re'uyot Yehezqel*" is indeed Michael, who offers the heavenly sacrifice.

Michael the Archangel: This title given to Michael I believe to be highly significant, although this is noted in the B'rit Hadashah (Jude verse 9). The Tanak and the Talmud accept the existence of good and bad angels. It is conceivable that since a functionality of Elohim was expressed as Ha-Mashiach for the redemption of disobedient humanity, God also had been obliged to express a functionality for the redemption of evil angels. Thus He expressed messianic functionality as an "Archangel" for the redemption of sinful angels. If God loves us so deeply, He must also love His other created beings who have fallen. He penetrated humanity for this purpose; why would it be surprising that He penetrated the angelic host as an archangel for their salvation? The necessity and presumed great effort by God to redeem fallen angels is an area left untouched and unexplored by scholars. Why should Elohim not want to save the fallen angelic host? It seems reasonable to assume that God has also redeemed a host of fallen angels by the Ha-Mashiach functionality, in this case titled as Michael the archangel. Blessed be He; the Lord our God is one. How stupendous is our God!

The implication of the penetrance of humanity by divinity that is mentioned must not be lost. Messiah is a functionality of Elohim who penetrates humanity for the purpose of atonement as the lamb without blemish, and He will be the one to rule the new earth forever and ever. He acts in two roles, and this matter will be brought into discussion again and again in the progress of this book. He is seen in heaven unmistakably wearing his *human role*, the messianic functionality of Elohim. He will be seen on the earth in His *divine role*. Messiah thus is unmistakably divine and human. Hear, O Israel; the Lord our God is one. Blessed be He.

We return to Daniel's first vision. Numerous scholars have provided further interpretations of the "little horn," the "ten horns," the "three uprooted horns," the arrogant words spoken by the little horn with a human mouth, and the timelines in this vision. The persecution of the "holy ones" has applications. The interpretations have historical value and are eminently discussed in scholarly works about Daniel. These are not my concerns in this book, and I will not elaborate here on these interpretations. For us the messianic kingdom is approaching and will fulfill the deepest longings of our hearts.

The Ancient of Days has released His messianic functionality upon the earth. The atonement, the Judgment, and the Resurrection are inevitable in God's timetable. These are about to happen and must concern us.

2. The Vision on the Banks of the Ulai River (Dan. Ch. 8)

Daniel saw a ram with two horns, the second one to come up reaching higher. The ram pushed north, south, and west and became great. Then along came a male goat at tremendous speed from the west, with one notable horn between his eyes. He crashed into the ram, broke the ram's two horns, cast him to the ground, and trampled on him. The goat then grew great and strong. In attacking the ram, the goat had broken his own horn, but now in its place grew four horns. Out of one of them came a little horn that grew toward the south and east and toward the Glorious Land. It grew upward and brought down some of the stars and trampled on them.

He exalted himself as high as the prince of the host, took the daily sacrifice away, and cast down the sanctuary.

> It vaunted itself against the very Chief of the Host ... the regular offering [the daily] was suspended, and His Holy Place was abandoned ... It hurled truth to the ground ...
> (Dan. 8:11, 12)

In the vision Daniel heard one "holy being" ask another "holy being" how long this situation would last. The answer came:

> For 2300 evenings and mornings, then the sanctuary shall be Cleansed. (Dan.8:14)

It should be noted here that the KJV has mistranslated the 2,300 evenings and mornings as 2,300 days. As well, *The Jewish Study Bible* uses the word "cleansed," which is also a mistranslation. The words "vindicated" and "made right" may be more appropriate. The outcome sought was the undoing of the power of the nasty little horn that discontinued the evening and morning burnt offerings.

Daniel had difficulty understanding the vision. Then an individual who "looked like a man" and had "a human voice" instructed the angel Gabriel to help Daniel "understand the vision" (Dan. 8:15–17). This person, who looked and spoke like a man, is of great interest, since he seemed to have authority over the angel Gabriel in the vision. Is this the Ha-Mashiach, the human penetrance by the divine? Is this a peek into the heavenly future? Gabriel helps Daniel:

> The two-horned ram that you saw [signifies] the kings of Media and Persia ... and the He-goat – the king of Greece, and the large horn on his forehead, that is the first king. One was broken and four came in its stead – that [means] four kingdoms will arise out of a nation ... When their kingdoms are at an end ... Then a king will arise, impudent and versed in intrigue ... But will be broken, not by [human] hands. (Dan. 8:20–25)

Even though Daniel was given the meaning of the vision, he was still disturbed because he did not understand the application of the 2,300 evenings and mornings. He was greatly upset because of the devastation of the temple service and the desecration of the worship of God. He still did not know who was the king who created havoc with the temple and the worship of God. He was told "to keep the vision a secret, for it pertains to far-off days" (Dan. 8:26). *The Jewish Study Bible* margin commentary cites this as a literary device to increase awe, secrecy, and mystery.[178] As discussed earlier, some scholars who date the book of Daniel to 164 BC see this as a retrospective naming of Media and Persia. Other scholars see it as written in 605 BC and quite prophetic. Still other scholars date Daniel to between 536 and 530 BC.[179]

Many commentators agree that the he-goat is Alexander the Great and that when he died his four generals divided up his kingdom among themselves: the Seleucid, Ptolemaic, Antigonid, and Attalid dynasties.[180] Jewish commentators rely heavily on 1 Maccabees, 2 Maccabees, and Josephus for the interpretation of this vision of Daniel, and they implicate Antiochus IV Epiphanes. He made two invasions of Egypt (dated 170/169 and 168 BC). He pillaged, massacred, and desecrated the temple and Jerusalem on the journey to Egypt.[181] There is a link to Daniel 11:28–32 in the description of the Antiochus IV Epiphanes attacks. Jewish literature sees Antiochus IV Epiphanes as an antimessianic figure. He set himself up as God and stopped the sacrificial system that was symbolic of the messianic atonement. He exerts himself "against the chief of chiefs" (Dan. 8:25b).

3. The Vision of the Seventy Weeks (Dan. Ch.9)

Daniel wanted to know the duration of the "desolation" of Jerusalem. He looked up the prophecy of Jeremiah (Jer. 25:11, 12) and discovered it was prophesied to be seventy years. The historical setting of the Jeremiah prophecy is the Babylonian captivity. Daniel was very sad. He realized this was a period of punishment of the chosen people. Daniel devoted himself to prayer, supplication, repentance, and confession. He fasted and dressed in sackcloth and ashes. He prayed thus:

> O Lord, great and awesome God, who stays faithful to His covenant with those who love Him and keep His commandments! We have sinned; we have gone astray; we have acted wickedly; we have been rebellious and have deviated from Your commandments and Your rules ... All Israel has violated Your teaching and gone astray disobeying You; so the curse and the oath written in the Teaching of Moses ... have been poured down upon us ... yet we did not supplicate the Lord our God ... O Lord, hear! O Lord, forgive! O Lord, listen and act without delay for Your own sake, O my God; for Your name is attached to Your city and Your people!
> (Dan. 9:4–19, selected verses)

This is a long confessional prayer. While he prayed, Gabriel interrupted him.

> Daniel, I have just come forth to give you understanding ... so mark the word and understand the vision. Seventy

weeks have been decreed for your people and your holy city until the measure of transgression is filled and that of sin complete, until iniquity is expiated, and eternal righteousness ushered in; and prophetic vision ratified, and the Holy of Holies anointed. You must know and understand. From the issuance of the word to restore and rebuild Jerusalem until the [time of the] Anointed Leader is seven weeks; and for sixty-two weeks it will be rebuilt, square and moat, but in a time of distress. And after those sixty-two weeks, the Anointed One will disappear and vanish. The army of a leader who is to come will destroy the city and the sanctuary, but its end will come through a flood. Desolation is decreed until the end of war. During one week he will make a firm covenant with many. For half a week he will put a stop to the sacrifice and the meal offering. At the corner [of the altar] will be an ***appalling abomination*** until the decreed destruction will be poured down upon the appalling thing.

(Dan. 9:22–27, emphasis added)

Several interpretive elements need to be evaluated or clarified here.

- "Seventy weeks

The Hebrew word here, "shav'uim," means "seventy weeks." The word "shiv'im" means "seventy." *The Jewish Study Bible* margin commentator notes that such close textual study and revocalization of texts for interpretive purposes would characterize later rabbinic interpretation. The commentator selects the time period in Daniel's vision to be seventy weeks of years (490 years).[182]

Two major interpretations are expounded for this vision or prophecy. The first is the 'Non-Christological' interpretation, which explains it in terms of Antiochus IV Epiphanes. The second is the 'Christological' interpretation, which categorizes a messianic interpretation[183] Many scholars favor the latter because it is held that this vision is messianic in intent and context. It suits the Christological interpretation.

- "Anointed One [Leader]"

The Hebrew word that has been translated as "Anointed Leader" and "Anointed One" is "Mashiach."[184] The explanation given is that this Anointed One could be Zerubbabel, Joshua the high priest, or the high priest Onias III. These alternatives should be regarded as incorrect and misleading, since the word is "Mashiach," which must be translated "Messiah," as the KJV has translated it. None of those named accomplished messianic atonement. Zerubbabel was considered but then faded as a candidate. The Hasmonean dynasty was not from the tribe of Judah and must be discounted.

- "Until iniquity is expiated and eternal righteousness ushered in"

This is clearly a messianic task, for the Messiah atones for sin and, as Redeemer, installs his eternal righteousness. (See Jeremiah 33:16.)

- "The Anointed One [Messiah] will disappear and vanish"

The KJV translates this as "cut off," indicating death. *The Jewish Study Bible* marginal comment states that this is likely the "death of Onias III, the high priest who was killed in 121 BC." This is again an incorrect interpretation, because it was never claimed that he was a messiah. The time element does not fit him either.

- "From the going forth of the commandment ... unto Messiah, the Prince, shall be seven weeks and threescore and two *weeks*" (KJV).

The vision of the "Seventy Weeks" is concerned primarily with the appearance of the Messiah and His atonement and subsequent destruction of the temple and Jerusalem. The NKJV is a clearer and a more literary translation of the critical verses, Dan. 9:22–27, and is clearly messianic in application.

This is as follows:

And he [Gabriel] informed me and talked with me, and said,
O Daniel, I have now come forth to give you skill to
understand ...
Therefore consider the matter and understand the vision:
Seventy weeks are determined
For your people and for your holy city,
To finish the transgression,
To make an end of sins,
To make reconciliation for iniquity,
To bring in everlasting righteousness,
To seal up the vision and prophecy,
And to anoint the Most Holy
Know therefore and understand,
That from the going forth of the command
To restore and build Jerusalem
Until Messiah the Prince,
There shall be seven weeks, and sixty-two weeks;
The street shall be built again, and the wall,
Even in troublesome times.
And after sixty-two weeks
Messiah shall be cut off, but not for Himself;
And the people of the prince who is to come
Shall destroy the city and the sanctuary.
The end of it shall be with a flood,
And till the end of the war desolations are determined.
Then He shall confirm the covenant with many for one week;
But in the middle of the week
He shall bring an end to sacrifice and offering.
And on the wing of **abominations** shall be one who makes
desolate,
Even until the consummation, which is determined,
Is poured out on the desolate.
(Dan. 9:25–27 NKJV, emphasis added)

- "The army of a leader who is to come will destroy the city
  and the sanctuary, but its end will come through a flood.
  Desolation is decreed until the end of war."

This last sentence is difficult: "Desolation is decreed until the end of war." Will the third temple never be rebuilt till the messianic eternal kingdom is established?

The application here could be postmessianic, since the destroyer comes in his wake. If the death or "cut off" of the Messiah is accepted, then this wicked leader is postmessianic in this instance. There is the distinct possibility of this messianic death or vanishing not being related to the messianic kingdom that follows the resurrection. Resurrection has not yet occurred, and history has not yet been catastrophically eradicated. The problem with interpretation is that the "Messianic Kingdom" is not transient but lasts forever and ever. Therefore, it should be concluded that this temporary messianic appearance resulting in death (see Isaiah 53) is neither coupled with nor is the same as the messianic kingdom, which lasts forever.[185]

- "At the corner [of the altar] will be an **appalling abomination** until the decreed destruction will be poured down upon the appalling thing." (emphasis added)

The Jewish Study Bible (margin p. 1660) commentary supposes this appalling abomination as probably new altar stones placed upon the altar in the temple, upon which pagan sacrifices were offered (1 Macc.1.54; 2 Macc. 6.5). This comment places the "seventy week" vision in the Antiochus IV Epiphanes setting. Some scholars feel that the abomination applies to the sacrifices to the Roman emperor, in a setting later than Antiochus IV Epiphanes. The Christological interpretation relates this as applying to Roman times. The case is also made for the apotelesmatic principle, which could relate it to both.[186] It should be noted that pollutions and stoppages of worship in the temple occurred significantly in both the time of Antiochus IV Epiphanes and also in the time of the pagan Roman emperors. Joseph Klausner excellently chronicles the latter.[187] I favor the dual, or apotelesmatic, application. Both Antiochus IV Epiphanes and the pagan Romans desecrated the temple, before the latter finally burned the holy house in AD 70.

Concluding Daniel's vision of the seventy weeks, it is quite likely that the messianic application predominates because it is a time period clearly pointing to the arrival of Messiah. This arrival does not proceed to the resurrection and the messianic kingdom, which are the more apocalyptic and catastrophic events for which there is much messianic expectation and longing. It appears anticlimactic because the Messiah dies and vanishes from view, likely as the "Suffering Servant" of Isaiah. Clearly the language of this messianic accomplishment is well outlined by Daniel in the words of Gabriel:

> ... until iniquity is expiated and eternal righteousness ushered in; and prophetic vision ratified, and the Holy of Holies is anointed
> (Dan. 9:24)

Since the wicked power is to destroy the second temple, the Holy of Holies referred to here as anointed must take place predestruction or alternatively be in the heavenly temple, where Michael stands and makes sacrifice.

Messianic Functions: Because the complex functions here outlined are exclusively messianic, they must be emphasized:

i.   **Iniquity is expiated:** "When thou shalt make his soul an offering for sin" (Isa. 53:10 *KJV*), or, "That, if he made himself an offering for sin.... (Isa. 53:10), and "And the Lord visited upon him the guilt of all of us" (Isa. 53:6). These scriptures epitomize the Day of Atonement.

ii. **Eternal righteousness is ushered in**: "My righteous servant makes the many righteous, it is their punishment that he bears" (Isa. 53:11; cf. Jer. 33:16, "The Lord our Righteousness").

iii. **The prophetic vision is ratified**: "So mark the word and understand the vision" (Dan. 9:23), "It pleased the Lord to bruise him" (Isa.53:10 *KJV*), or "But the Lord chose to crush him" (Isa. 53:10)

iv. **The Holy of Holies is anointed:** Clearly, this recalls the Day of Atonement; the blood of the animal without blemish was taken by the high priest into the Most Holy Place. It was splashed on the mercy seat and ark of the covenant in the presence of the Shechinah. This applies also in the heavenly temple, where God has a throne. Up in heaven the Messiah has the function of intercession: "Whereas he bore the guilt of many and made intercession for sinners" (Isa. 53:12). Note that it is for "sinners" that he pleads. Redemption is the Messiah's primary function. "I have no pleasure in the death of the wicked, (Ezek. 18:23 *KJV*), or, "Is it My desire that a wicked person shall die? says the Lord God. It is rather that he shall turn back from his ways and live" (Ezek. 18:23).

4. Daniel's Vision by the Tigris River (Dan. Ch. 10-12)

> ... I Daniel, kept three full weeks of mourning ... I was on the bank of the great river—the Tigris—that I looked and saw a man dressed in linen, his loins girt in fine gold. His body was like beryl, his face had the appearance of lightning, his eyes were like flaming torches, his arms and legs had the colour of burnished bronze, and the sound of his speech was like the noise of a multitude (Dan. 10:5, 6).

The man apologizes for being delayed by the Prince of the Persian Kingdom:

> [The] Prince of the Persian kingdom ... opposed me for twenty-one days; now Michael, a Prince of the first rank, has come to my aid, after I was detained ... So I have come to make you understand what is to befall your people in the days to come, for there is yet a vision for those days ... Now I must go back to fight the Prince of Persia. When I go off, the Prince of Greece will come in. No one is helping me against them except your Prince, Michael. However, I will tell you what is recorded in the book of truth ... Persia will have three more kings, and the fourth will be wealthier than them all; by the power he obtains through his wealth, he will stir everyone up against the kingdom of Greece. Then a warrior king will appear who

will have an extensive dominion and do as he pleases. But after his appearance, his kingdom will be broken up and scattered to the four winds of heaven, but not for any of his posterity, nor with dominion like that which he had: for his kingdom will be uprooted and belong to others beside these. (Excerpts from Dan. 10)

There follows an extensive account of the activities of the king of the south, the king of the north and his sons, and

a contemptible man, on whom royal majesty was not conferred ... [who] will seize the kingdom through trickery ... Having done his pleasure, he will then attend to those who forsake the holy covenant. Forces will be levied by him; they will desecrate the temple, the fortress; they will abolish the regular offering and set up the **appalling abomination** ... He will invade the beautiful land ... He will pitch his royal pavilion between the sea and the beautiful holy mountain, and he will meet his doom with no one to help him. At that time, the great prince, Michael, who stands besides the sons of your people, will appear. It will be *a time of trouble*, the like of which has never been since the nation came into being. At that time, your people will be rescued, all who are found inscribed in the book. Many of those who sleep in the dust of the earth will awake, some to eternal life, others to ... everlasting abhorrence ... But you Daniel, keep the words secret and seal the book until the time of the end.
(Dan. 11:21–12:4, emphasis added)

The vision continues on the banks of the Tigris as Daniel hears questions being asked and answered by heavenly beings:

Q: How long until the end of these awful things?
A: For a time, times, and half a time.

Daniel does not understand, so he asks a question:

Q: My Lord, what will be the outcome of these things?
A: From the time the regular offering is abolished and an **appalling abomination** is set up will be a thousand two hundred and ninety days. Happy the one who waits and reaches one thousand three hundred and thirty five days. But you, go on to the end; you shall rest, and arise to your destiny at the end of the days.
(Dan. 12:6–13, emphasis added)

The discussion of the "king of the north," the "king of the south," and the "contemptible man, on whom royal majesty was not conferred" entails a lot of history, as we see it retrospectively. The interpretation of this vision by Jewish scholars parallels the vision in Daniel 7 and is fulfilled by the desecration of the temple by Antiochus IV Epiphanes, (See *Il Messia*, by David Casttelli, pp. 152–156.)[188] The abomination of desolation is again mentioned here. Some scholars see similarity to the desecration by the Roman power. Again, some cite a dual fulfillment consistent with the apotelesmatic principle.

It is highly significant that the great messianic application is present here in the personage of Michael. His standing up is implicit with the challenge posed by the abomination of desolation, the time of trouble, and the resurrection of the dead that starts the messianic kingdom. Some Christological scholars see another fulfillment in the future besides the fulfillments by Antiochus IV Epiphanes and the cruel power of pagan Rome. But clearly the Messiah is to make His catastrophic kingly appearance, with Judgment, the Resurrection, and the kingdom of Messiah ben David being ushered in. This messianic kingdom will last forever. The Messiah for these functions must be divine and eternal.

In summary, the whole book of Daniel is steeped in messianic enthrall. The overriding contemplation of Daniel's experiences and visions is the eschatological and catastrophic appearance of the Messiah to start the messianic kingdom after Atonement, Judgment, and the Resurrection. But there is no doubt that in Daniel's third vision Gabriel links up with Isaiah's suffering Servant. He characterizes it by "the Anointed One [who] will disappear and vanish" (Dan. 9:26).

This distinctly and succinctly implies Messiah's death. The *KJV* translates it as "… shall Messiah be cut off," also implying death. Isaiah concurs: "For He exposed Himself to death" (Isa.53:12), and David sees life after this death that the Messiah suffers: "Thou didst not leave His soul in Sheol, nor didst thou suffer Thy Holy One to see corruption" (Ps. 16:10 *KJV*). This messianic event is part and parcel of Gabriel's spoken words to Daniel:

> Seventy weeks have been decreed for your people and
> your holy city until the measure of transgression is filled
> and that of sin complete, **until**
> > [i] **iniquity is expiated, and**
> > [ii] **eternal righteousness ushered in; and**
> > [iii] **prophetic vision ratified, and**
> > [iv] **the Holy of Holies anointed.**
> (Dan. 9:24, emphsis added)

The commentators in the margin of *The Jewish Study Bible* attribute these accomplishments to Judas Maccabee in 164 BC. This is clearly incorrect, since Judas Maccabee is not recognized as a messiah. These accomplishments are what happens with messianic atonement in the symbolism of the blood of the animal without blemish in the sacrifice for Israel's sin during the daily and the yearly Day of Atonement. Judas Maccabee was never considered the Messiah. There is no description in Daniel that fits him.

E. The Appalling Abomination

The word "abomination" provides a recurring theme in Daniel 8, 9, 11, and 12. It is a key word, and its relation to the apocalyptic Messianism of the book is important. It has also been translated as "abomination of desolation." Desmond Ford made this a PhD study, supervised by theologian F. F. Bruce:

> The pattern clearly traced is that of a Gentile oppressor
> whose idolatry displaces the worship of Yahweh, and whose
> physical might destroys the worshippers of the Temple.[189]

Desmond Ford rightly sees these instances of abomination as *anti-Messianism.* He unifies the book of Daniel in the message "The Temple will be Vindicated."

This is not only a simple reference to the temple structure as such, but what the temple service was all about. And this is the sacred essence of redemptive Judaism. This is found in the ideation of the Most Holy Place.

Ford makes Daniel 8:14 pivotal: the inexorable advance of the messianic kingdom is unstoppable by any anti-Messianism. The appalling abomination has multiple applications. It is any pagan power, any rival system, any attempted substitution, any new concoction, and any diversion from the messianic redemption established from eternity, implemented at the gates of Gan Eden and beamed from Sinai. It attempts to *preempt the worship of the true God.* In Gan Eden it was "Thou shalt not surely die." Outside the gates of Eden, it was Cain's "Fruits and vegetables." At Mt. Sinai it was the golden calf. In Solomon's reign, it was the altars he built in the high places around the temple to the gods of his heathen wives. It was the pollution of the plundered holy temple vessels at Belshazzar's feast. It was the desecration of the temple by Antiochus IV Epiphanes. It was pagan Rome (Caligula, Nero, Titus) that did the final desecration before Herod's temple was torched. Desmond Ford expands on the Jewish apocalyptic literature that quoted Daniel as well as noncanonical Jewish writings about this anti-Messianism. He stresses the severity of the condemnation of *anti-Messianism* in the Talmud.[190]

In stupendous significance, Gershom Scholem tied the *true Messianism* to Gan Eden's Tree of Life.[191]

Daniel's message is that the Messiah, His people, and His temple will be finally vindicated. Michael will stand up with Judgment and the Resurrection to usher in the kingdom of Messiah ben David.

Joseph Klausner has beautifully written a conclusion to his evaluation of the book of Daniel. He uses extracts from the Talmud:

> [Daniel's] Messianic idea eventuates in "the Age to Come,"
> and "the World to Come," in which the dead rise and "the
> righteous sit enthroned, their crowns on their heads, and

enjoy the lustre of the Shekinah" (Ber. 17a). The latter idea is already embodied in the words "they that are wise shall shine as the brightness of the firmament."[192]

I add the rest of the words of Daniel:

And they that be wise shall shine as the brightness of the firmament; and they that turn many to righteousness, as the stars *forever and ever.* (Dan. 12:3 *KJV*, emphasis added)

David Castelli wrote in support of the kingdom of Messiah ben David as "The World to Come," indicating a new earth and assuming the existence in it of perfection and immortality. (See *Il Messia*, by David Castelli, pp. 248–251.)[193] The saints, the kingdom, and Messiah the King, the functionality of Elohim, will be around *forever and ever, and forever is a long, long time.* The Messiah cannot under these expectations be only a one-lifetime human. He must be considered as deity. The Mashiach functionality has existed within Elohim from eternity. The Lord our God is one; blessed be He.

CHAPTER 25

The Ha-Mashiach of Habakkuk

Habakkuk was a contemporary of Jeremiah. The name "Habakkuk" means "To caress or embrace." It is interpreted as the symbol of clinging to God, as in Jacob's brook Jabbok experience. It also recalls devekut in Gan Eden—God and humanity mystically clinging to each other.

It has been pointed out by several scholars that Habakkuk *does not* speak to Israel on behalf of God. Instead he speaks to God *on behalf of Israel*. He tells God that Torah is not achieving its stated goals, because God suffers wrong to triumph. There is no justice in the world. The Chaldeans (Assyrians, Egyptians) have too much power over Israel.

This complaint of Habakkuk was amplified in the Talmud. There was a major lamentation about the destruction of the second temple. The complainant, a rabbi, concluded, "Abandon not belief in retribution" (Aboth. I. 7). Abraham Cohen comments on this by reciting a legend about Rabbi Akiba. The Jewish Virtual Library tells the story of Rabbi Akiba, who was martyred by the Romans:

> When Moses ascended to heaven and there beheld Rabbi Akiba (still unborn) expounding the Torah in a wondrous manner, he said to God, "Thou hast shown me his learning, now show me his reward." He was told to turn round, and, on so doing, beheld Akiba's flesh being sold in the market-places. He spake before Him, "Sovereign of the Universe! Such is his scholarship and such is his reward!" God replied to him, ***"Keep silent; so has it come up in thought before Me."*** (Men. 29b). The legend seems to indicate that the problem is beyond human understanding. Events, inexplicable to man, were so determined by God and he must submit resignedly ... It is not in our power to

explain either the prosperity of the wicked or the affliction of the righteous. (Aboth IV. 19)[194]

Habakkuk's message starts out with the searing question "How long shall I cry and Thou wilt not hear?" Surprisingly, the answer comes immediately. It is the assurance that God understands:

But the righteous shall live by his faithfulness. (Hab. 2:4)

Is there messianic import in this verse? We have an answer from Joseph Klausner:

> ... in the three prophetic chapters of Habakkuk it is difficult to find Messianism. Therefore [David] Castelli, for example, considers the book of Habakkuk as lacking Messianic verses altogether (*Il Messia, p. 112* by David Castelli). Yet actually, it contains two or three Messianic verses. Habakkuk prophesies a day of punishment for the Assyrians (or Chaldeans) and says of this day (and not of the day of redemption, as the Talmud interprets): "*Though it tarry, wait for it; because it will surely come, it will not delay*" *(Hab. 2:3)* Along with this, Habakkuk promises that in the day of punishment all the upright and good will be saved: "*But the righteous shall live by his faith*" *(Hab. 2:4)*. Like Isaiah (Isa. 11:9), he too is convinced that the day will come when "the earth shall be filled with the knowledge of the glory of the LORD, as the waters cover the sea." (Hab. 2:14, emphasis added)[195]

The meaning of the two italicized Habakkuk quotes above are subjects of controversy:

1. The Conservative subset of Jews do not agree with Joseph Klausner regarding the application of Habakkuk 2:3 as quoted above, and follow the talmudic application, interpreting it as the delay in arrival of the Messiah.[196] Perhaps both are correct in view of all punishment finally being made on judgment

day, when the messianic kingdom is ushered in. The day of vengeance on Israel's persecutors is surely coming with the arrival of the Day of the Lord.

2. Biblical scholars do not all agree with Klausner's interpretation of Habakkuk chapters 1 and 2, particularly 2:4.[197] There is also contention about Habakkuk chapter 3, which is considered by the majority of Biblical scholars to be a much later interpolation.[198]

The Jewish Study Bible translates this "controversial" verse thus:

> **But the righteous man is rewarded with life for his fidelity.**
> (Hab. 2:4)

Analysis of this translation is clearly congruent with Klausner's interpretation. I wholeheartedly agree with his interpretation of Habakkuk 2:4 as being totally messianic in import. Further elucidation of this controversial verse by *The Expositors' Bible* is rendered as follows:

> Of course it has faith in God as its secret – the verb from which it is derived is the regular Hebrew term 'to believe' – but it is rather the temper which faith produces of *endurance, steadfastness, integrity*. Let the righteous, however baffled his faith be by experience, hold on in loyalty to God and duty, and he shall live ... In face of experience that baffles faith, the duty of Israel is patience in loyalty to God ... Even Job, when most audaciously arraigning the God of his experience ... turned to God in his heart of hearts ... experience notwithstanding ... *"though He slay me, yet will I trust in Him."* [Job 13:15 emphasis added].[199]

Faith in God is born of God and implies confidence in the Almighty in spite of the vicissitudes of life. As with repentance, faith is bolstered by the Holy Spirit. *That faith hangs totally on His promise of final redemption with the restoration of perfection and immortality to humanity.* That was the import of Paul the apostle when he declared, "The just shall live by his faith." Thus the messianic intent of Habakkuk is enormous. There is no other promise in the Tanak on which to more surely hang the endurance of hope and the eternity of God's love. The author of Ecclesiastes stated,

> The sum of the matter, when all is said and done: Revere
> God and observe His commandments! For this applies to
> all mankind: that God will call every creature to account
> for everything unknown, be it good or bad. (Eccl. 12:13)

Since Isaiah declared that our righteousness is as filthy rags, none of our efforts are totally successful, and God requires total perfection for the restoration of immortality. So dependence on Messiah is 100 percent, despite our best efforts. But God is well pleased and honoured by our striving to keep His commandments. It tells Him that we are serious in appropriating messianic provision. Otherwise, we would live our religion in an antinomian attitude. The law stands as God's infinite Torah. But terrestrially it is judgmental and not salvific. In the Messianic Age to come, we will obey it perfectly. For our present mortal and imperfect terrestrial sojourn, *we must depend on grace*, which is unmerited favor bestowed by Ha-Mashiach, totally efficacious. We must tenaciously cling to it. Our faith in it will sustain our clinging to messianic redemption. It is Jacob's brook Jabbok experience that must surely be ours.

Habakkuk goes on in chapter 2, describing a scene of wickedness and crime. But he sees a future where this will be wiped away as he declares the effect of the messianic antidote:

> For the earth shall be filled with awe for the glory of the
> Lord as waters cover the sea. (Hab. 2:14)

Habakkuk explains this further in the next messianic statement found in the last verse of chapter 2. It is the most majestic utterance in the Tanak. Its messianic import is enormous. Terrestrial and cosmic *silence* is observed:

> But the Lord [is] in His Holy Temple; let all the earth *keep silence* before Him. (Hab. 2:20 *KJV*)

> But the Lord in His holy Abode – *be silent* before Him all the earth! (Hab. 2:20)

This declaration follows a dismissal of all other gods as "carved images," "false oracles," "dumb idols," and "inert stones" with "no breath inside." (Hab. 2:18, 19). The prophet is pitting monotheism against all false systems of worship. He is pitting messianic redemption against all other systems of salvation. What is happening in the holy temple, God's abode, is stupendously significant!

Why does God need a temple in heaven? Why does He set up His abode in it? (See Isaiah 6.) God occupies eternity and infinity, and His existence is boundless! But when He is effecting redemption, the restoration of perfection and immortality to His beloved Israel and the human race, He resides in the temple: "*For the Lord has prepared a Sacrifice*" (Zeph. 1:7). Zephaniah is also depicting the heavenly Day of Atonement. This archetypal temple in heaven and its copy on earth are one and the same in effecting redemption, the cleansing of the multiverse of disobedience and mortality. And Elohim does it through His functionalities of Ruach Hakodesh and Ha-Mashiach. Isaiah also saw this heavenly Day of Atonement:

> I beheld my Lord seated on a high and lofty throne, and the skirts of His robe filled the Temple ... Then one of the seraphs flew over to me with a live coal, which he had taken from the altar ... He touched it to my lips and declared ... *your guilt shall depart and your sins be purged away.* (Isa. 6:1, 6–7, emphasis added)

In this hiatus of silence, a span of time in eternity, God positions Himself in the temple, and His messianic functionality is the sacrifice being offered. As portrayed on earth, Messiah has been the expiation on the heavenly temple mount, the celestial Mount Moriah. The multiverse is clean again, and perfection and immortality have been restored after the Ha-Mashiach has atoned for humanity. This is exactly as it happens on Yom Kippur, but in the cosmic sense and dimension in the heavenly temple. His own blood, messianic blood, is accepted by God in silence.

Why is Habakkuk insisting on *silence* when God is in His holy temple? Silence here is more than ordinary reverence. It signifies the recognition of the redemptive work of Ha-Mashiach. It is the active and dramatic presentation of the messianic blood; it is the heavenly messianic Day of Atonement. Moses ordained that in the earthly temple on the Day of Atonement there should be a great silence when the high priest carried the blood of the sacrificial animal without blemish into the Most Holy Place and sprinkled it on the ark of the covenant and the mercy seat in the presence of the Shechinah.[200] In Biblical history, after ten days of penitence, Israel totally shut down on the Day of Atonement, in an observation of national silence on that special Sabbath. The nation stood in awe of the messianic atonement as the high priest carried the blood of the bullock without blemish into the Most Holy Place and sprinkled it on the ark of the covenant and mercy seat. Has Israel forgotten that national and personal silence? This messianic act cleansed them all from all their sin and rendered them perfect before God. Abraham's offering of Isaac is the stupendous enactment of this messianic sacrifice. The heavenly Day of Atonement cleanses the multiverse; God's Creation has been redeemed. It is His redemptive Sabbath. Franz Rosenzweig was enraptured by it.

Habakkuk contains mighty messianic proclamations. He ties it all up with the meaning of his name: His name means "embrace." *God embraces Israel and all humanity in the Ha-Mashiach sacrifice and infinite love,* where, on the heavenly Day of Atonement, in the Most Holy Place of the heavenly temple, *mercy triumphs over justice!* The Talmud swells with this declaration. (See Aboth IV. 29; Ber. 28b; Num. R. III. 2; Gen. R. XXXIII. 3; Gen. R. XII. 15; Gen. R. VIII. 4; Aboth. V. 2; Gen. R. XXXIX; Sanh. III a; Tosifta Sot. IV. I; Pes. 87b; Ber. 7a; Pes. 119a; Sanh. 39b; and Aboth. III. 19.)[201] Torah is immutable and eternal because God made it so, but "The attribute of **GRACE** ... exceeds that of punishment (i.e. justice) by five-hundredfold." (Tosifta Sot. IV. I).[202] In His embracing love, He has saved us. The multiverse is silenced in awe of the grace of God. His caressing and embracing arms are locked around us. He is enjoying this great provision of grace, which His eternal love has provided, but not without His own travail, in silence. That is why God needs a temple in heaven. That is why He wanted one on earth. The one on earth has been destroyed twice. But no earthly power can ever destroy the temple in heaven. No substitution of the practice of benevolence will suffice for messianic redemption. The temple in heaven challenges any substitute: fruits and vegetables, benevolent acts, and deep study of Torah. On looking back at the destroyed temple, let us not conjure a substitute. We must exult with Isaiah and Habakkuk and still see in faith the Lord, high and lifted up, accepting messianic provision in the heavenly temple. The Lord our God is one, blessed be He.

CHAPTER 26

Ezekiel's "Mystic" Messiah

Ezekiel, son of Buzi, was a priest of the House of Zadok. He is said to be a contemporary of Jeremiah and Daniel. They lived through the destruction of Jerusalem and Solomon's temple by the Babylonians in 586 BC. They saw the ends of the reigns of Jehoiachin and Zedekiah, the last kings of Judah. *The Jewish Study Bible* states that Ezekiel was faced with three big questions:

1. Why did God allow the temple and Jerusalem to be destroyed?
2. Why did God allow the exile of His people into Babylonian captivity?
3. What future is there for Israel?

He answers these questions by arguing that it was a divine punishment for the people's sin. But he assures Judah that there is still a future for a *remnant* of them.

The authorship of the book is a matter of controversy, and its acceptance into the Tanak was a matter of consternation to many rabbinic sages. Some modern scholars argue that the book had several editors who inserted several interpolations: the oracles concerning Egypt in chapters 29–32, the prophecy concerning Gog and Magog in chapters 38 and 39, and the vision of the temple in chapters 40–48. Despite these alleged interpolations, the book has a solid theme constructed on *consolation, judgment, resurrection, and induction of the messianic kingdom.*[203] Ezekiel mixes "immediate" and "delayed" predictions for Israel. The "immediate" concerns the return to Canaan from Babylonian captivity and the "delayed" are references to the eternal messianic Kingdom at the "End of Days."

The book is densely misted with a thick veil of mysticism. Ezekiel's visions are the medium in which his messages are imparted, particularly his first and recurring vision within the heavenly temple. This vision takes place by the Chebar Canal in the land of the Chaldeans. In this vision Ezekiel makes major reference to a *divine 'hypostasis'* manifested as a "*voice.*" (See study titled *Hypostasis in the Hebrew Bible*, by Azzan Yadin, which appeared in *The Journal of Biblical Literature* 122/4, 2003, pp. 601–626.) In this cogent study, Azzan Yadin links this "voice" or "hypostasis" (described particularly in Ezekiel 1:24–26; 2:2; 9:1; 40:3; and 43:6) with other Biblical passages (particularly Exodus 19:18–20; 20:18; Numbers 7:89; and Deuteronomy 4:1–40). (The subject of hypostasis is discussed previously in chapter 13, "Messiah in the Wisdom Literature."). Yadin concentrates heavily on the fiery Mount Sinai experience when God descended and the "voice" was heard. He uses the Septuagint and the Masoretic text translations in his comparative discussion of the "voice." The conclusion of his study focuses on this "voice" being a "hypostasis" of God. I draw the conclusions that Yadin notes that the "hypostasis" of God was first manifest to Moses at the burning bush, and then on fiery Mt. Sinai. It is now heard in Ezekiel's vision in the heavenly temple.

Ezekiel 1:26–28 is very revealing. In this passage, there are four "creatures" bearing a throne. (Read Ezekiel 1:1–25.) This scene (in the Kavod) is translated by *The Jewish Study Bible* thus:

> Above the expanse over their heads was the semblance of a throne, in appearance like sapphire; and on top, upon this semblance of a throne, there was the *semblance of a human form* ... There was a radiance all about him ... That was the appearance of the *semblance of the Presence of the Lord.* When I beheld it, I flung myself down on my face. And I heard the *voice* of someone speaking. (Ezek. 1:26–28)

God's socalled "hypostasis" is described as the "semblance of a human form" appearing as "the semblance of the Presence of the Lord" and is the source of the "voice." This human semblance has also been translated as *"The likeness of the image of the Glory of God'* (see A. F. Segal's essay *Conversion and Messianism* in the book *The Messiah* p. 333). So here in the **Kavod** Ezekiel is seeing a human figure he calls the semblance of a human which is also the likeness of the image of the Glory of God. A. F. Segal goes on to say that this idea in the Kavod "has a deep prophetic, apocalyptic, and mystical meaning in Judaism." I conclude that with the prohibition of a "hypostasis" in monotheistic Judaism this could only apply to God's functionality of the Messiah.

Many Biblical scholars are cited by Yadin in the discussion of this "hypostasis" quoted above. The description of such a "hypostasis" is a definite challenge to monotheism. Many rabbinic sages rejected any such thing as a "hypostasis" as a second God. I concur. This challenge can be solved only by the acceptance of this "hypostasis" in the heavenly temple in this "semblance of a human form" as none other than the Ha-Mashiach functionality of God, and not a "hypostasis" or duplication of God. Obviously the Mashiach is seen here in His human form. Here is another proof that the Messiah has existed in eternity as very God. His humanity emphasized here gives deep meaning to His penetration of humanity. Daniel (chapter 7) visualized this socalled "hypostasis" as the Son of Man, in a heavenly setting, in the presence of the Ancient of Days.

The Abrahamic covenant as a mission was entrusted to Israel. Here is its gist, which God declared to Israel:

> And you shall be unto Me a kingdom of priests and a holy nation. (Ex. 19:6)

Gershom Scholem exulted in this text and declared it as the true definition of Zionism. (See *On Jews and Judaism in Crisis*, p. 36.)

David Castelli declared this verse to be the cornerstone of messianic proclamation. (See *Il Messia*, by David Castelli, pp. 41–43.)[204]

When we read Ezekiel 5:5–17 we see how far from this destined holy status Israel had strayed from God. God's punishments are shattering. Ezekiel is very stark in quoting God: ***"Because you defiled My Sanctuary*** with all your detestable things and all your abominations ... One-third of you shall die of pestilence or perish in your midst by famine, one-third shall fall by the sword around you, and I will scatter one-third in every direction and will unsheathe the sword after them." History bears record of the reality of this punishment. How sad! Does modern Israel realize how serious an agreement they have with God in the Abrahamic covenant? They should; they have suffered enough.

As mentioned above, the book of Ezekiel has a definite mystical orientation but is wrongly considered as one of Jewish mysticism's initial foundations. Ezekiel's mysticism is coupled with what is incompatible with "Jewish mysticism." Kabbalah and Hasidism do not endorse the Biblical eschatological apocalyptic future. This is not in tune with Kabbalistic mysticism and its teachings.

Hava Tirosh-Samuelson, one of the contributors to the *Cambridge Guide to Jewish History*, poignantly pointed out that although the actual origins of the Jewish mystical tradition cannot be ascertained, it had ample expression in the sixth century BC. There was a longing to communicate with God. Ezekiel was an exiled priest in Babylonia whose great longing to talk to God resulted in this mystic vision. He saw the "Glory of God" (*kavod*), in the form of a moving chariot (*merkavah*). It was a living entity with four wheels composed of four "living creatures," who were four independent angelic beings with lives of their own.

The *Cambridge Guide* points out that in Ezekiel 8–11, the prophet sees the kavod abandoning the polluted temple in Jerusalem, five years before the temple was actually destroyed. In Ezekiel 40–48 the prophet describes a rebuilt temple to which *God will return to the eschatological future when the people of Israel will be fully purified.*[205]

It is obvious that Tirosh-Samuelson sees that Jewish mysticism is definitely incompatible with the eschatological apocalyptic wrapped in Ezekiel's mystical presentation. All the prophets invested their hopes and dreams in the eschatological apocalyptic. Gershom Scholem insists on that. With the impending destruction of the earthly temple, they steadfastly gazed on the heavenly temple.

Both Ezekiel and Jeremiah sought to orient their messianic prophecies around King Zedekiah, but he disappointed them. They hoped that Israel would indeed be "a kingdom of priests and a holy nation." After the temple was destroyed, they disappointed the Jews in Babylon by proclaiming a lengthy exile. They could not deliver an immediate messianic salvation.[206] As a comfort, they both turned their prophesying to the ***"end of days."*** This was to be the end not of the Babylonian exile but of something further down the line.

Ezekiel offered as a further comfort the oracle against Pharaonic Egypt as retribution for the ill-treatment of Israel. It condemns Egyptian pride. Perhaps it was a prediction also for the future punishment of Babylon for ill-treating Israel. It commences with threatening though flowery, mocking poetic imagery:

> Thus saith the Lord God
> I am going to deal with you, O Pharaoh king of Egypt,
> Mighty monster sprawling in your channels,
> Who said, My Nile is my own;
> I made it for myself.
> I will put hooks in your jaws ...
> And I will fling you into the desert.

But Ezekiel also condemns Judah for her sinfulness. He is scathing: Judah is a rebellious house (see Ezekiel 2:5; 3:9); even heathen Philistia is ashamed of the prevailing gross wickedness in God's people (see Ezekiel 16:27); Sodom is virtuous in comparison (see Ezekiel 16:48); Jerusalem is the pot whose filth is therein (see Ezekiel 24:6).[207] God is utterly displeased with His chosen people. God loathes them.

In the last era of Israel's kings, there was nothing to recommend them to God. Ezekiel's Messiah allows severe punishment. They had let God down. But redemption comes for the protection of God's own reputation:

> I punished them in accordance with their ways and their deeds. But when they came to those nations [in the diaspora] they caused My holy name to be profaned, in that it was said of them, "These are the people of the Lord, yet they had to leave His land." Therefore I am concerned for

> My holy name, which the House of Israel have caused to
> be profaned among the nations to which they have come.
> Say to the House of Israel: Thus said the Lord God: Not
> for your sake will I act, O House of Israel, but for My holy
> name, which you have caused to be profaned ... I will
> sanctify My great name ... And the nations shall know that
> I am the Lord – declares the Lord God – when I manifest
> My holiness before their eyes through you. I will take you
> from the nations and gather you from all the countries, and
> I will bring you back to your own land ... *I will cleanse*
> *you* from all your uncleanness and from all your fetishes.
> And *I will give you a new heart* and put a new spirit into
> you: *I will remove the heart of stone* from your body and
> give you a heart of flesh. (Ezek. 36:19–28, emphasis added)

This latter has not happened as yet, despite Israel being relocated to the land of Israel in 1948. Imperfection and mortality still prevail. Here is therefore the promise of the Messiah ben David's kingdom at the final *"end of days."* Despite the severe punishment predicted, this chapter ends with a great spiritual and material prosperity. This can only come in the messianic kingdom.

Now follows the mystical story of the valley of dry bones, an apocalyptic enactment of the resurrection of the dead and induction of the messianic kingdom:

> And He said to me, "O mortal, these bones are the whole
> house of Israel. They say, Our bones are dried up, our hope
> is gone; we are doomed. Prophesy therefore and say to
> them: Thus saith the Lord God: I am going to open your
> graves and lift you out of the graves, O My people, and
> bring you to the land of Israel ... I will set you upon your
> own soil." (Ezek. 37:11–14)

Ezek. 37:15-28 goes on to describe the eternal kingdom of Messiah ben David.

Rather than an immediate return of the exiles, the rabbinic sages believed this scripture described the last judgment and the resurrection, which usher in the messianic kingdom. (See m. Sanh. 10.1; b. Sanh. 90b.)[208] And so it is. Joseph Klausner is so wrong to imagine that Israel is its own Messiah.[209] How far-fetched! Ezekiel vehemently declares that God does it all in redemption: I will cleanse you and I will give you a new heart and I will remove your heart of stone. It all happens by the power of Messiah ben David.

The thirty-seventh chapter of Ezekiel goes on to predict the unification of the tribes of Judah and Benjamin with the other ten tribes devastated by Assyria when the messianic kingdom is established in the Promised Land. Messiah ben David will be their king.

Ezekiel's oracles against Gog and Magog are seen as an apocalyptic scenario of God's victory over all the nations who have threatened and persecuted Israel. All the wicked are collectively destroyed. (See Ezekiel ch. 39.)

Then, on Yom Kippur, Ezekiel has a vision of the restored temple in Jerusalem. There is a return at this point to the immediate future. The temple is rebuilt:

> ... the hand of the Lord came upon me, and He brought me
> there ... in visions of God, to the land of Israel, and He set
> me down on a very high mountain on which there seemed
> to be the outline of a city on the south. He brought me over
> to it, and there, standing at the gate, was *a man who shone
> like copper* ... (Ezek. 40, emphasis added)

Here Ezekiel is turning attention to the immediate rebuilding of Solomon's temple because a resumption of animal sacrifices occurs. This *man* gives him a detailed tour of the rebuilt temple, measuring it in detail. Ezekiel is instructed to pass on all this information to the House of Israel. Rules regarding this temple are to be strictly enforced. Israel is to do what is right and just. Instruction is given regarding all the sacrificial offerings to be made. The sacrificial animals are to be *without blemish, a symbol of messianic sacrifice for sin.*

But then occurs a return to the apocalyptic *"end of days."* A total admission of the messianic redemption is hereby acknowledged.

Twelve tribal territories are reallotted in the Holy Land. The Holy City is to be renamed "The Lord is There." The Shechinah will never leave the Most Holy Place ever again. God will dwell forever with His people. As a doctrine this description is faithful to the primitive redemptive Judaism of Moses. Some rabbinic sages believed this temple to be the third temple that will be built in the "days of the Messiah" (Seder Olam 26; Rashi; Radak).[210] They did not envision this third temple as that which would be built prior to the second temple.

The significance of the current reclamation of a Holy Land whose territory is much less than was promised in the Abrahamic covenant is a quandary. At the *"end of days,"* all the nations are wiped out and God's chosen people appear to be the only survivors in Ezekiel's messianic kingdom.

Joseph Klausner wrongly sees no hint in Ezekiel of universalism as is prominent in the messianic kingdom described by the other prophets:

> In his vision of the future no foreigner can enter the sanctuary (Eze. 44:6-9). Truly he says: "No alien, uncircumcised in heart and uncircumcised in flesh, shall enter" (Eze. 44:7, 9); thus the uncircumcised in heart, even if he is circumcised in the flesh, will not be acceptable to Him. In any case, in all the Book of Ezekiel we do not find that lofty universalism which we saw in all its majesty and splendor in Amos, Isaiah, Micah, and Zephaniah.[211]

Klausner wonders if this is a backlash because of Israel's vulnerability to idolatry when mixing with and accepting non-Jews in Israel's own land. He worries about Israel's mission to the Gentiles contained in the Abrahamic covenant. The fault lies with Israel and not the Gentiles. Is there a loophole in the statement "No alien, uncircumcised in heart and uncircumcised in flesh, shall enter?" Can the converse be true, so that aliens who are circumcised in heart and flesh (foreskin) gain admission? Can this be the loophole to claim universalism for Ezekiel? Is Ezekiel making ritual circumcision a prerequisite for the messianic kingdom? But circumcision was only a sign of the covenant, not the covenant itself. The covenant will have been already fulfilled in the messianic kingdom. A deeper assessment of Ezekiel's restrictive membership perceived by Klausner could be that every soul in the messianic kingdom has been redeemed by Israel's God. *Ezekiel sees such unity in the final redeemed that he describes them all in the garb of fleshly Israel!*

The identity of the heavenly being described as "a man who shone like copper" is an interesting feature. The phenomenon of a human with authority in heavenly places does point again to the messianic Son, the Ha-Mashiach functionality of God, the divine penetration of humanity by divinity. Moses, David, Isaiah, Daniel, and now Ezekiel all see the divine-human Son of Man who is the Son of God, the Mashiach, who is Elohim Himself.

CHAPTER 27

Haggai's Messiah in His Temple

Haggai's messages are direct from God. There is no temple in Jerusalem. The Babylonians had destroyed it in 587 BC. God had been evicted from His earthly abode. His quest for reinstating perfection and immortality by His messianic functionality had been thwarted. Shechinah, law, mercy, and blood, the essence of primitive redemptive Judaism, the earthquake that rocked the whole world from Mt. Sinai, had been wiped off the map of Judah. Haggai is the prophet who brought the great reproof from God about this calamity.

Joseph Klausner has carefully painted the historical picture of that time.[212] Medo-Persia destroyed the Babylonian power. Cyrus had made the declaration for the rebuilding of Jerusalem and the temple. His son Cambyses succeeded him in a rebellious empire. The powerful Darius I then came to the throne. Haggai names two powerful people to do the job of rebuilding the temple: Zerubbabel, the son of Shealtiel, and Joshua the high priest, son of Jehozadak.

There were gainsayers, people who had lost the messianic vision and hope. They had made a secular return to Judaea:

> Thus said the Lord of Hosts: These people say, The time has not yet come for rebuilding the House of the Lord. (Hag. 1:2)

The rebuke for this complacency was swift:

> Is it time for you to build paneled houses, while this House is lying in ruins? ... While you all hurry to your own houses! That is why the skies above you have withheld [their] moisture and the earth has withheld its yield ... (Hag. 1:4–11)

So what does God do?

> Then the Lord roused the spirit of Zerubbabel ... and
> Joshua ... Who is there left among you who saw this
> House in its former splendor? How does it look to you
> now? It must seem like nothing to you. *But be strong, O*
> *Zerubbabel ... and Joshua ... and act! For I am with*
> *you ... and My spirit is still in your midst. Fear not.* (Hag.
> 1:14–2:9, selected verses, emphasis added)

Selfishness, half-heartedness, uncleanliness, defilement, and
secularism occupy the land. (See Haggai 2:11–19). Here is God's
challenge: "*As long as no stone had been laid on another in the*
House of the Lord" (Hag. 2:15), there will be no prosperity in the
land. But if the temple is rebuilt: "*I will send blessings.*" God promises
great temporal prosperity: "... the seed in the granary, the vine, fig
tree, pomegranate, and olive tree" will be abundant (Hag. 2:19).

But wait! The greatest promise of all is embodied in the temple,
its Most Holy Place, the essence of Judaism. The redemptive
Shechinah, law, mercy, and blood, signifying the messianic sacrifice
and atonement, are not enshrined. God wants them replaced. Their
return comes with mighty power:

> **I am going to shake the heavens and the earth. And**
> **I will overturn the thrones of kingdoms and destroy**
> **the might of the kingdoms of the nations.... On that**
> **day – declares the Lord of Hosts -- I will take you, O**
> **My servant Zerubbabel son of Shealtiel – declares the**
> **Lord -- and make you as a signet; for I have chosen**
> **you – declares the Lord of Hosts. (Hag. 2:21–23)**

Ah! Zerubbabel, the son of Shealtiel, is from the tribe of Judah, a
messianic figure. He will rebuild the earthly house for the restitution
of redemptive messianic Judaism. The prophecy also spells out the
great Judgment and Resurrection to come; history will be destroyed
and the messianic kingdom will commence. The signet here represents
the power of the Messiah ben David, the Divine King.[213]

Is there a parallel today? Israel has returned to the Promised Land. The US and the Soviet Union recognized it as a country in 1948. The Romans had destroyed the second temple in AD 70. God has no dwelling on planet earth. He wants the temple rebuilt. That is Haggai's message to modern Israel: Restore the Most Holy Place with the Shechinah, the ark of the covenant containing the law, the mercy seat, and the bloodstains. Let Mt. Sinai shake again. The people are worshipping another golden calf. They are paneling their own comfortable and grand residences. Technology shines in the land. Israel is prosperous again. But redemptive Judaism is far from their minds. The Lord's house still lies in ruins. Moses, hasten down from Mt. Sinai and grind their secularism and prosperity to powder. God forbid. Aliya Israel and the prosperous voluntary diaspora have built comfortable houses for themselves, but there is no dwelling for God. Is He looking for a modern-day Zerubbabel and Joshua. Where are they?

> But the people of Judah argued stubbornly that a time of perplexity is precisely not "the time that the LORD'S house should be built" Is it a time for you yourselves to dwell in your ceiled houses, while this House lieth waste? (Hag. 1:2, 4)[214]

These excuses are rampant in modern Israel and the voluntary diaspora, whose numbers exceed aliya Jews—nearly seven million in the US alone! The essence of Judaism must return to Israel. God is restless for the proclamation of the Mashiach. The Abrahamic covenant must be fulfilled.

CHAPTER 28

Zechariah: The Messiah of Zion and the Nations

According to many scholars, the book of Zechariah has two authors: one who wrote chapters 1–8, and one who wrote chapters 9–14. But scholars agree the message has unity and purpose. It is all about the rebuilding of the temple and reinstating the messianic atonement.

The Jewish Study Bible commentary notes that many ancient readers found in Zechariah numerous references to messianic times. The rabbinic sages interpreted many of these texts in relation to a messianic time still to come (e.g., Zech. 3:8; 6:12 in the Targum; in relation to Zech. 6:12 see *Num. Rab.* 18.21; for Zech. 9:9 see *Gen. Rab.* 56.2, 98.9; and for Zech. 12:10 as pointing to the Messiah from the house of Joseph, see *b. Sukkah 52a*).[215]

Zechariah starts the book with a statement of God's anger and a call for reform. God laments that He has allowed Jerusalem and the [first] Temple to be destroyed. The glory of Messianism now pours forth from the prophet:

> Turn back to Me – and I will turn back to you … I graciously return to Jerusalem. ***My House shall be built in her*** … For the Lord will again comfort Zion; He will choose Jerusalem again … Jerusalem shall be peopled as a city without walls … so many shall be the men … it contains. And I Myself … will be a wall of fire all around it, and ***I will be a glory insde it*** … Whoever touches you touches the pupil of My own eye. [According to *Mekhilta*, Shirata 6.10, the original text read, "The pupil of My own eye," which is what I have retained here]. Shout for joy, Fair Zion! For lo, I come; and ***I will dwell in your midst*** – declares the Lord. In that day many nations will

attach themselves to the Lord and become His people ...
[Ezekiel, are you listening?]. The Lord will take Judah
to Himself as His portion in the Holy Land, and He will
choose Jerusalem once more.

Be silent all flesh before the Lord!
For He is roused from His Holy Habitation.
(Zech. 2:17, emphasis added)

The context here is clearly the rebuilding of the temple and the
return of the Shechinah to the Most Holy Place. The above verse,
Zech. 2:17, is a duplication of Habakkuk 2:20 and alludes to the Day
of Atonement service, in which *the high priest carries the blood of
the bullock without blemish in silence to the Most Holy Place* of the
temple and sprinkles it on the ark of the covenant and mercy seat. The
heavenly Day of Atonement has aroused God in His holy habitation,
the heavenly temple. The messianic blood is to be offered there.
God reconciles Israel to Himself through this messianic mediation.
Zechariah strongly declares that God wants the temple rebuilt:

**Shout for joy, Fair Zion! For lo, I come, and I will dwell
in your midst – declares the Lord of Hosts.** (Zech. 2:14)

Enter Joshua, the high priest on the Day of Atonement. The
Accuser (In Hebrew ha-Satan) stands at his right hand to accuse him
of sin. He is wearing the ephod with the onyx stones mounted on the
shoulders. They bear the names of the twelve tribes of Israel, and thus
Joshua bears the entire sin of Israel on his shoulders. The Accuser's
accusation is correct. Israel stands before God having broken the
law, which has sentenced them to death. "Now Joshua was clothed in
filthy garments, the sins of all Israel, on the Day of Atonement." The
command comes from God. Joshua is a messianic type as high priest:

The Lord rebuke you O Accuser; may the Lord who has
chosen Jerusalem rebuke you! For this is a brand plucked
from the fire ... Take the filthy garments off him! ... See, I
have removed your guilt from you, and you shall be clothed

in robes ... Let a pure diadem be placed on his head.
(Zech. 3:1–5)

This cleansing is reminiscent of what happened in Isaiah's vision
of the Day of Atonement in the heavenly Temple where a sacrifice
was being offered:

> I beheld my Lord seated on a high and lofty throne;
> And the skirts of His robe filled the Temple ... I cried,
> Woe is me; I am lost!
> For I am a man of unclean lips
> And I live among a people
> Of unclean lips;
> Yet my own eyes have beheld
> The King Lord of Hosts.
> Then one of the seraphs flew over to me with a live coal,
> Which he had taken from the altar with a pair of tongs.
> He touched it to my lips and declared,
> Now that this has touched your lips,
> Your guilt shall depart
> And your sin be purged away.
> (Isa. 6:1–7 selected verses)

Enter the *Messiah Himself* into the Holy of Holies of the heavenly
temple and the glory of Redemption is heightened. Joshua, the high
priest, receives a charge from God:

> Thus said the Lord of Hosts: If you walk in My paths
> and keep My charge, you in turn will rule My House
> and guard My courts ... Harken well, O High Priest
> Joshua, you and your fellow priests sitting before you!
> For those men are a sign that *I am going to bring My
> Servant the Branch*. For mark well this stone, which I
> place before Joshua, a single stone with seven eyes ...
> I will remove that country's guilt in a single day.
> (Zech. 3:7–9, emphasis added)

The message of Zechariah is so much like that of Isaiah and Haggai.

Enter Zerubbabel:

> This is the word of the Lord to Zerubbabel: Not by might, nor by power, but by My Spirit – saith the Lord of Hosts. Whoever you are, O great mountain in the path of Zerubbabel, turn into level ground! For he shall produce that excellent stone; it shall be greeted with shouts of Beautiful! Beautiful! ... Zerubbabel's hands have founded this House and Zerubbabel's hands shall complete it. (Zech. 4:6–8)

Rabbis down through the ages have recognized "My Servant the Branch" as the Davidic messianic figure and linked this reference with Jeremiah 23:5–6; 33:15–16; and Isaiah 11:1–2. Further:

> Thus said the Lord of Hosts: Behold *a Man called the Branch* shall branch out from the place where he is and he shall build the Temple of the Lord. (Zech. 6:12)

And as Haggai associated Zerubbabel, who was of the tribe of Judah as a messianic figure, the association here is established. The magnificent stone here described is likewise a messianic link with Psalm 118:22–24, where "The stone which the builders rejected has become the *Chief Cornerstone.*" It is clear that Joshua and Zerubbabel are both messianic types but not the Mashiach himself, as they merely portend the Man called the Branch, the Chief Cornerstone, and the Prophetic Promise, the Ha-Mashiach Himself.

Joseph Klausner is quite bold and explicit in his interpretation of Zechariah. He comments on the ideas of Haggai that were followed by Zechariah:

> So even little Judah laid plans for becoming an independent kingdom as of old. A king was ready to hand: Zerubbabel was of the house of David ... and he stood at the head of his people as the governor of Judah (Hag. 1:14) ... It was

> necessary, therefore, ... to arouse the people to build the
> Temple, without which *the Prophetic Promises* could not
> be fulfilled, and also to strengthen the Messianic hope for a
> king of the house of David ... We find the very same ideas,
> only amplified and clarified, in the first eight chapters of
> Zechariah ... [216]

And after the temple is rebuilt, and God's dwelling has been restored with His people, the nations will flock to Israel. Jerusalem will be the religious center of the earth. (See Zechariah 8:20–23.) The Most Holy Place will be supreme where law, mercy, and blood will mingle in the presence of the Shechinah. Messianic expiation will provide the blood, as did the bullock without blemish, and mercy will triumph over justice.

Chapters 9–13 of Zechariah, or Deutero-Zechariah, are a matter of controversy among scholars. Many date it much later, to around 400 BC.[217] It presents a turbulence of the nations and Israel. Interpretation of the narrative of the prophecies presents many difficulties and perplexities. Klausner sets it in the post-Babylonian, Medo-Persian, and Greek historical setting.[218]

But the Deutero-Zechariah narrative is penetrated with some of the most highly significant messianic passages in the Tanak. The greatest and most explicit messianic prophecy of the Messianic Age pours from the prophet Deutero-Zechariah's mouth:

> *Rejoice greatly, O daughter of Zion; shout, O daughter*
> *of Jerusalem; behold, thy King cometh unto thee; He is*
> *just and having salvation; lowly, and riding upon an ass,*
> *and upon a colt, the foal of an ass And He shall speak*
> *peace unto the nations; and His dominion is from sea to*
> *sea, and from the river to the ends of the earth.*
> (Zech. 9:9–10 KJV)

Klausner interprets this as "...the Jews wait for One lowly and riding upon an ass who is to come."[219]

> *As for thee also, by the blood of the covenant I have sent*
> *forth thy prisoners out of the pit ... And the Lord, their*
> *God, shall save them in that day as the Flock of His*
> *people; for they shall be like the stones of a crown, lifted*
> *up as an ensign upon His land. For how great is His*
> *goodness, and how great is His beauty?*
> (Zech. 9:11–17, selected verses, *KJV*)

There is no doubt that this messianic passage invokes the Day of Atonement, when the blood of the Messiah of the Abrahamic covenant frees all sinners—not only with forgiveness, but also from eternal death, Sheol, synonymous with the pit. The prisoners of death are out of the pit. God will be proud of them as they are lifted as an ensign of His goodness and they enhance the glory of His salvation. Isaiah states it as follows:

> Out of His anguish He shall see it;
> He shall enjoy it to the full through His devotion.
> My righteous Servant makes the many righteous,
> It is their punishment that He bears;
> Assuredly, I will give Him the many as His portion,
> He shall receive the multitude as His spoil.
> (Isa. 53:11–12a)

> *And I will pour upon the house of David, and upon the*
> *inhabitants of Jerusalem, the spirit of GRACE and of*
> *supplications; and they shall look upon Me whom they*
> *have pierced. In that day there shall be a fountain*
> *opened to the house of David and to the inhabitants of*
> *Jerusalem for sin and for uncleanness.*
> (Zech. 12:10–14; 13:1 *KJV*)

This passage invokes a messianic provision of *grace* and a messianic *fountain for cleansing from sin.* This double messianic provision is associated with a death by piercing. Joseph Klausner gives the reference from the Talmud (Sukkah 52a). Klausner also associates Isaiah here:

The idea of the "suffering Messiah" has its source in this verse in Zechariah together with Isaiah 53.[220]

Abraham Cohen quotes from the same reference from the Talmud in a commentary on this passage from Deutero-Zechariah:

> Mention is made of a rather mysterious figure called Messiah son of Joseph. The passage reads: Messiah son of Joseph was slain, as it is written, "They shall look unto Me whom they have pierced; and they shall mourn for Him as one mourneth for his only son." (Zech. xii: 10) (Suk. 52a) 'Son of Joseph,' like 'son of David,' means a descendant of the ancestor of that name; and its origin seems to be indicated in this citation: 'Our father Jacob foresaw that the seed of Esau would only be delivered into the hand of the seed of Joseph, as it is said, "The house of Jacob shall be a fire, and the house of Joseph a flame, and the house of Esau for stubble, and they shall burn among them and devour them." (Obad. 18) (B.B. 123b).[221]

The talmudic idea that Messiah comes from the tribe of Joseph is erroneous. Messiah comes from Judah. This will be discussed again later.

The final messianic prophecy I perceive in this book is the beginning of the messianic kingdom. The resurrection of the dead will occur, and history will be no more. Gershom Scholem calls it the Utopia.[222] It is the culmination of the triumph of God's mercy over justice. It was accomplished by Isaiah's "Suffering Servant." Zechariah saw it as follows:

> *Lo, a DAY OF THE LORD is coming. On that Day, He will set His feet on the Mount of Olives, near Jerusalem on the east; and the Mount of Olives shall split across from east to west, and one part of the Mount shall split to the north, and the other to the south, a huge gorge. And the Lord my God, with all the holy beings, will come*

to you. And the Lord shall be King over all the earth;
in that Day there shall be one Lord with one Name.
(Zech. 14:1–9, selected verses)

The Lord our God is one. Blessed be His name.

CHAPTER 29

Malachi: The Messiah's Usher

The name "Malachi" is not the real name of the author of the book of Malachi. Some scholars believe Ezra or Mordecai authored it. "Malachi" means "my messenger" in Hebrew. His message from God proclaimed the arrival of both the forerunner of the Messiah and the Messiah Himself. Malachi had an exciting and cosmic agenda.

The practice of the Judaism of Malachi's day was *corrupt beyond measure*. Geza Vermes describes the condition of the priesthood as an endemic clash between prophets and temple personnel. He cites this as the common complaint of the prophets Amos, Hosea, Isaiah, Micah, and Jeremiah. (See *Christian Beginnings*, p. 26.) Corruption of the priesthood with the taking of bribes, blemished animal sacrifices, intermarriage with idolaters, thieving and misuse of the tithes and offerings, and the general arrogance of the people were specific problems Malachi addressed. The challenge he faced was the threat to the very essence of the Judaism beamed to the multiverse from Sinai. There is nothing more sacred than the essence of Judaism, enshrined in the Most Holy Place.

1. Malachi's Accusation about Blemished Sacrificial Animals:

When Moses set up the tabernacle temple and the Aaronic Priesthood at Mt. Sinai, *its most prominent function was the disposal of sin, the transgression of the law.* This was a reiteration of the same mechanism that was enunciated at the gates of Gan Eden. It had incited the first murder on the planet. Abel had died for it. Repentance, mediated by Ruach Hakodesh, was a gift from Elohim. Confession, restitution, forgiveness, expiation, and mediation were achieved by the sacrifice of an *animal without blemish*, signifying the Ha-Mashiach functionality of Elohim. When Solomon's temple was built on the temple mount, *the essence of redemptive Judaism remained in the Most Holy Place of the sanctuary* where the Shechinah dwelled. The law, justice, and mercy came together, mediated by the messianic blood sprinkled on them on the Day of Atonement. The blood dripped on the floor of the Most Holy Place. This was highly significant, as the Most Holy Place was situated on the very spot where Abraham had sacrificed Isaac, the very *Abrahamic symbol of messianic atonement.* All Israel stood perfect before God as a result of the blood sprinkling on the Day of Atonement. No one can disagree with that mighty doctrine of the Tanak.

The most important qualification of the messianic symbol, the sacrificial bullock on the Day of Atonement, was that it be *without blemish.* It signified the perfect Ha-Mashiach functionality of Elohim. This was a requirement of all sacrificial animals at the temple. The priest had to inspect the animal and pass it as being without blemish. On the Day of Atonement, the blood was applied to the holiest item in Judaism—the ark containing the two tables of stone on which God had written the law with His own finger, with the mercy seat above it. The law represented order and justice and the perfect cosmic government of Elohim. Disobedience in Eden had brought eternal death. So here was an invention of the Almighty, cast in eternity before Creation. His Ha-Mashiach functionality would intervene and suffer death for all humanity. The animal without blemish was the symbol. Here was the implementation of grace and mercy. So the mercy seat was constructed to signify that *mercy triumphs over justice* in the salvation of all humanity. This provision is as clear as daylight, and its mighty energy was beamed from Sinai on the same frequency as the law and justice. It was motivated by the most intense love for us, demonstrated by God in the multiverse. Can you call what was beamed from Mt. Sinai cultic? Can you think of a better plan or more fantastic and eternal reason? Can you fathom a greater love? There is none. God said through Moses,

> For the life of the flesh is in the blood, and I have assigned
> it to you for making expiation for your lives upon the altar;
> ***it is the blood, as life, that effects expiation.***
> (Lev. 17:11, emphasis added)

And here is what Malachi said:

> ... Where is the reverence due Me? – said the Lord of
> Hosts to you O priests who scorn My name. But you ask,
> How have we scorned Your name? ... When you present
> a blind animal for sacrifice – it doesn't matter! When you
> present a lame or sick one – it doesn't matter! ... If only
> you would lock My doors, and not kindle fire on My altar
> to no purpose! I take no pleasure in you – said the Lord
> of Hosts – and I will accept no offering from you ... You
> say, "Oh, what a bother!" And so you degrade it – said the
> Lord of Hosts – and you bring the stolen, the lame, and the
> sick; and you offer such an oblation ... A curse on the cheat
> who has an unblemished male in his flock, but for his vow
> sacrifices a blemished animal to the Lord! For I am a great
> King – said the Lord of Hosts – and My name is revered
> among the nations. And now O priests, this charge is for
> you: Unless you obey and unless you lay it to heart, and do
> honour to My name – said the Lord of Hosts – I will send
> a curse and turn your blessings into curses. (Indeed, I have
> turned them into curses, because you do not lay it to heart).
> I will put your seed under a ban, and I will strew dung
> upon your faces, the dung of your festal sacrifices, and
> you shall be carried out to its [heap]. (Mal. 1:6–14; 2:1–3)

There are some things that I find surprising about my God.
This is one of them! To mention another, in Eden after the great
transgression "He drove the man out ..." (Gen. 3:24). The man
naturally ran with his wife, both naked, both frightened out of their
wits, and God chased them together with the threatening cherub
with "the fiery ever-turning sword" till they were outside the garden
at its east gate. Imagine it: Adam and Eve, a pathetic pair, crying,
frightened, naked, running to get away from this angry God chasing
them with fury! And now this unimaginable and shocking spectacle
of my God throwing animal dung in the faces of the corrupt priests!
Imagine it: God picking up dung and hurling it in people's faces!
But that is the measure of God's detestation of the insult to the

purity and perfection of His own character and His justice and mercy, and that immortal love that makes Him go to any lengths in the long run to restore humanity to His bosom. What a God! Great is Jehovah the Lord! Mighty is His power! The Lord our God is one; blessed be He.

The iniquity of the priesthood was great in Malachi's day and continued its acceleration through 450 years to the destruction of the second temple in AD 70. The corruption of the priestly or Sadducee class had reached giddy heights. They were rich from the bribes taken and the money continually stolen from the temple treasury by their "artful" accounting. During the Hellenistic onslaught, Jews had become blind to their redemptive Judaism, both in Judaea and the diaspora. In the Roman domination that followed, the high priest became the stool pigeon of the Romans. Appointed by the Romans, to stay in power they slavishly did the Roman bidding, somewhat covertly. The power and wealth of the priestly class was thus maintained. Some of the high priests were not even Levites. The anger of the lowly Jews toward this corrupt priestly class was reflected later by the slaughter inflicted on them by the Zealots. Simon Sebag Montefiore described it well:

> Annas [AD 30] dominated Jerusalem and personified the rigid, incestuous network of Temple families. Himself a former high priest, he was the father-in-law of the present incumbent Caiphas and no less than five of his sons would be high priests. But he and Caiphas were despised by most Jews as venal, thuggish collaborators, whose servants, complained one Jewish text, 'beat us with staves'; their justice was a corrupt moneymaking scam.

> Young brash brigands [Zealots] now challenged the rule of the priests. They seized the Temple, overthrowing the high priest himself ... The Idumeans [invited by John of Gischala] broke into the city, stormed the Temple, which 'overflowed with blood,' and then rampaged through the streets, killing 12,000. They murdered Ananus [AD 70] and then his priests, stripped them, and stamped on the

naked bodies, before tossing them over the walls to be eaten by dogs.[223]

But the Zealots would not win in the end.

Commenting on the Judaism that existed at the time of the destruction of Jerusalem and the second temple in AD 70, Simon Sebag Montefiore said,

> Jerusalem was just the wilderness of a failed faith.[224]

Sad indeed! Was the Almighty sad? He silenced all His adoring angels as He read Montefiore's words. He cried Himself to a sleep of despair. Only deeply in love jilted lovers will understand God's sadness, if that is possible. Is my anthropomorphism going too far? O for greater devekut with God that we might understand Him. His ways are past finding out. But this we know: He wants us back in His bosom. By way of comfort, could we remind God of Ben-Sira's prayer of hope as an antidote to Simon Sebag Montefiore's pessimism?

> Have mercy on Thy Holy City, Jerusalem, the place of Thy dwelling. Fill Zion with Thy majesty, And Thy Temple with Thy glory. (Ben-Sira, chapter 36)[225]

Isaiah tried to forge an understanding of our relationship with a God who is immeasurable:

> Let the wicked forsake his way, and the unrighteous man his thoughts, and let him return unto the Lord, and He will have mercy upon him; and to our God; for He will abundantly pardon. For My thoughts are not your thoughts, neither are your ways My ways, saith the Lord. For as the heavens are higher than the earth, so are My ways higher than your ways, and My thoughts than your thoughts. (Isa. 55:7–9 *KJV*).

2. Malachi's Accusation about Tainted Bread

> You offer defiled food on My altar. But you ask, "How
> have we defiled you?" By saying, "The table of the Lord
> can be treated with scorn." (Mal. 1:6–7)

At Mt. Sinai the table of showbread was designed as spectacularly as was the ark of the covenant. (See Exodus 25:23–30.) Rabbi Geoffrey Dennis describes this symbol as representing God's sustaining presence in the Holy Compartment. He termed it the bread of the Divine Presence. The showbread consisted of twelve loaves placed there every Sabbath and replaced a week later and then eaten by the priests. (See Leviticus 24:5–9; Numbers 4:7; 1 Samuel 21:4–7; 1 Chronicles 9:32.) Rabbi Dennis sees great significance in that the table is in the antechamber, separated from the Holy of Holies by the curtain. (See Exodus 26:31–35).[226]

The implication by Malachi is that the showbread, which represented God's sustaining presence with the twelve tribes of Israel, was polluted. God makes specific charges:

> Know then that I have sent this charge to you that My
> covenant with Levi shall endure – said the Lord of Hosts –
> I had with him a covenant of life and well-being, which I
> gave to him, and of reverence, which he showed Me. For
> he stood in awe of My name.
> Proper rulings were in his mouth,
> And nothing perverse was on his lips;
> He served Me with complete loyalty
> And held the many back from iniquity.
> For the lips of a priest guard knowledge,
> And men seek rulings from his mouth;
> For he is a messenger of the Lord of Hosts.
> But you have turned away from that course: You have
> made the many stumble through your rulings; you have
> corrupted the covenant of the Levites – said the Lord of
> Hosts. And I, in turn, have made you despicable and vile in

the eyes of all the people, because you disregard My ways
and show partiality in your rulings.
(Hab. 2:1–9)

3. Malachi's Accusation About Idolatrous Marriages

Israelites had divorced their wives en masse and married heathen
women. Marrying heathen women entailed a sexuality which dabbled
with significant idolatry (cf. the golden calf). The sexual immorality
involved with idolatry had tantalizingly bewitched Israel. Divorced
mothers and abandoned children were left in the lurch, entailing
much suffering.

> Judah has broken faith; abhorrent things have been done
> in Israel and in Jerusalem. For Judah has profaned what
> is holy to the Lord – what He desires – and espoused
> daughters of alien gods … So be careful of your life-
> breath, let no one break faith with the wife of his youth.
> For *I detest divorce* – said the Lord, the God of Israel.
> (Mal. 2:10–16, emphasis added)

4. Malachi's Accusation about Stolen Tithes and Offerings

The matter of the corruption of the priests went much deeper. The
priestly class had fast become the rich aristocrats in Israel. There was
only one source of this illicit money that had made them rich. They
were accepting bribes and kickbacks for waiving the important sacred
rules of the temple. A "wicked commonsense" had been applied to
soothe their consciences. After all, the sacrificial animals were to be
killed and burned anyway, so what did it matter if they winked at
blemished animals and unpalatable or leavened showbread. They had
declined to eat parts of the animal of sacrifice and had thrown the
showbread in the garbage. Their pockets became too small to carry
the bribes. Tithes and offerings were diminished because of the cost
to the people of the bribes and kickbacks:

Turn back to Me, and I will turn back to you – said the
Lord of Hosts. But you ask, "How shall we turn back?"
Ought man to defraud God? Yet you are defrauding Me.
And you ask, "How have we been defrauding You?" In
tithe and contribution. You are suffering under a curse,
yet you go on defrauding Me – the whole nation of you.
(Mal. 3:7–9)

5. Malachi's Accusation About Israel's Pride and Arrogance

Israel had become hardened in sin, self-sufficient, and arrogant.
The spiritual filthiness of the temple was commonplace, and they
had hardened to its criminality. They were enjoying the pleasures
and debauchery of their illicit profit from their flouting of the great
principles of God's justice and mercy. They felt they were exempt
from God's oversight:

You have spoken hard words against Me – said the Lord.
But you ask, "What have we been saying among ourselves
against you?" You have said, "It is useless to serve God.
What have we gained by keeping His charge and walking
in abject awe of the Lord of Hosts. And so we account the
arrogant happy: they have indeed done evil and endured;
they have indeed dared God and escaped."
(Mal. 3:13–15)

6. Malachi's Accusation about Multiple Other Crimes

I will step forward to contend against you, and I will act as
a relentless accuser against those who have no fear of Me:
who practice sorcery, who commit adultery, who swear
falsely, who cheat labourers of their hire, and who subvert
the cause of the widow, orphan and stranger, said the Lord
of Hosts. (Mal. 3:5)

Ah! Beware you foolish people! Here comes Malachi's
Ha-Mashiach:

> Behold, I am sending My Messenger to clear the way before Me, and the Lord whom you seek shall come to His Temple suddenly. As for the angel of the covenant that you desire, He is already coming. But who can endure the day of His coming, and who can hold out when He appears? For He is like a smelter's fire and like fuller's lye. He shall act as a smelter and purger of silver; and He shall purify the descendants of Levi and refine them like gold and silver, so that they shall present offerings in righteousness. Then the offerings of Judah and Jerusalem shall be pleasing to the Lord ... (Mal. 3:1–4)

> For lo! That day is at hand, burning like an oven. All the arrogant and all the doers of evil shall be straw, and the day that is coming – said the Lord of Hosts – shall burn them to ashes and leave them neither stock nor boughs. But for you who revere My name a sun of victory shall rise to bring healing. (Mal. 3:19–20a)

For those who would set aside the redemptive nature of primitive Judaism, Malachi has some special advice:

> ***Be mindful of the teaching of My servant Moses, whom I charged at Horeb [Sinai] with laws and rules for all Israel (Mal. 3:22).***

The law resides in the Most Holy Place, within the ark of the covenant. Written by the finger of God, it shall never be void. God requires justice. As long as we shall live, we must try to obey God's law. The law wants us dead, because the primal couple lost their immortality by disobedience, and we all disobey. But, recognizing that we are dust and our righteousness is as filthy rags, God covers the ark with the mercy seat. His mercy triumphs over justice. The Talmud supports this overwhelmingly. (See Sanh. 111a; Joma 69b; Tosifta Sot. 1V. 1; Pes 87b; Ber. 7a; A.Z. 3b; Pes. 119a; p. Kid. 61a; Sanh. 39b; Aboth 111. 19.)[227]

Imagine it! The high priest carries the blood in great silence.[228] He splashes it on the ark and the mercy seat, in the presence of the Shechinah. The blood drips on the floor of the Most Holy Place, the very sacred spot where Abraham offered Isaac.

Imagine it! In the heavenly temple, Elohim sits upon His throne, high and lifted up, and His train fills the temple. The seraphim sing, "Holy, Holy, Holy, is the Lord of Hosts" (Isa. 6:1–8 KJV). The singing stops abruptly. There is a sudden great silence in the multiverse as the heavenly messianic blood is splashed on God's justice and mercy. The blood drips down through space and sky to the earth to cleanse it. The whole earth is filled with His glory! Mercy triumphs over justice. Grace is greater than all our sin. "The attribute of Grace exceeds that of punishment (i.e. justice) by five-hundredfold" (Tosifta Sot. 1V. 1).[229]

> *The Lord is in His Holy Temple.*
> *Let all the earth keep silence before Him.*
> (Hab. 2:20 KJV)

This is the essence of Mosaic primitive redemptive Judaism. "Be mindful of the Teaching of My servant Moses." Do not set him aside. What a thrilling religion is primitive redemptive Judaism! Praise be to Elohim. His love is stupendous and eternal! The Lord our God is one. Blessed be He.

> *Lo, I will send the prophet Elijah to you before the*
> *coming of the awesome, fearful Day of the Lord.*
> (Mal. 3:23, emphasis added)

It must be noted that in the book of Malachi the appellation to God is repeatedly "The Lord of Hosts." It occurs twenty times in this short book. Its prominence shapes in the context of the whole world, and not Israel alone:

> The Lord of Hosts has said: If only you would lock My
> doors, and not kindle fire on My altar to no purpose! I take
> no pleasure in you – said the Lord of Hosts – and I will

accept no offering from you. *For from where the sun rises to where it sets, My name is honoured among the nations, and everywhere incense and pure oblation are offered to My name; for My name is honoured among the nations – said the Lord of Hosts … For I am a great King – said the Lord of Hosts – and My name is revered among the nations.* (Mal. 1:9a–14, emphasis added)

Who were "the nations" where pure oblations were offered and God's name was honoured in Malachi's day? Was God counting His chickens before they were hatched? Was He looking down through the corridors of time? Whatever he was doing, He did not want a worship that was so immensely corrupted in Malachi's day. He was coming as the Mashiach. So Malachi proclaimed. Ah! The terrible corruption of Israel! But God's mercy exceeds His justice by five hundredfold! (See Tosifta Sot. IV. 1.)

God was thinking of Isaiah's prediction: He would see the outcome of the travail of His soul and *He would be satisfied.* The Lord is one; blessed be He.

CHAPTER 30

The Messiah of the Talmud

In this chapter I will try to cull the talmudic description of Ha-Mashiach. It should be understood that there is no such thing as a unanimous opinion in the Talmud. Opposite and variant opinions must be accepted for what they are. The tanakian record of the prophets should be held as the *gold standard,* and the "'Talmudic Messiah" must be viewed simply as a discussion by erudite sages. The redemptive Messiah beamed from Sinai is a unified doctrine of the Tanak that cannot be set aside.

For the uninitiated reader, orientation to the Torah and the Talmud is essential. I will first try to accomplish this. The comparative and contrasting qualities and importance of these texts must be clear.

The Torah

The Torah, or the law of God, has existed in eternity and governs the multiverse and all existence.[230] The wording "Eternal Torah" would be presumptuous, because the Torah does not preexist God. But it can be described as a perfect document in the mind of God. Care must be taken not to define "Eternal Torah" as something that governs Elohim. Rather, it is Elohim that speaks the "Eternal Torah." The essence of the "Terrestrial Torah" as we know it was beamed from Sinai. Terrestrial Torah is what is known to us, and is the earth view. It is our incomplete earthly view of the Eternal Torah, and definitely not the whole story. "The half has never yet been told."

The tanakian "Terrestrial Torah" prevalent on the earth, as we know it, given to Israel at Sinai, has also been in the mind of God from eternity. It is the Torah that governs *our* knowledge and tells the story of *our* human existence. It began in Eden as the Oral Torah and unfolded in God's conversation of devekut with Adam and Eve. It continued to unfold outside Eden after the great disobedience. It evolved with the lives of the patriarchs down to Moses, who wrote it down at Sinai. With a mass of unschooled, idolatrous, unruly, and irreligious ex-slaves who hardly knew their monotheistic God after three hundred plus years in slavery, Moses had a daunting task. Terrestrial Torah "expanded" at Sinai to cover virtually every facet of their lives. God and Moses had a difficult task to fashion them into the "Chosen People" to whom the Abrahamic covenant had been entrusted. This Written Torah was beamed from Sinai and defined primitive redemptive Judaism. The Torah written down by Moses underwent many edits and interpolations. These were mainly effected by the Levitical priests and scribes. There is evidence that these changes made it somewhat severe in its summary judgments which lack mercy. ***But it is a perfect document in its sacred central concepts of God as creator and redeemer.*** We are assured of redemption.

The Sinai document was centered on the tabernacle temple service. Therefore, every facet, every beam of light emanating from Sinai, must be viewed in terms of the functions of the temple. Judaism cannot escape being defined by the temple service. Destroy the temple and you forget Moses and the prophets. Rebuild the temple and you rebuild Moses and the prophets. Blood, symbolic of messianic atonement, splashed in the Most Holy Place, stains the temple and the temple mount and cannot be wiped from Judaism. Eradicate messianic blood from Judaism and you invite abominations, and God will allow the temple to be destroyed, if and when that happens. Moses spoke very clearly: expiation is in the blood (See Exodus 29, 30; Leviticus 16, 17.) In this "Messianic shed blood" the two greatest Jewish festivals are founded: the Passover and the Day of Atonement. Messianism cannot be extracted from these two great blood festivals. Judaism beamed from Sinai is deeply stained with blood. That temple mount, underneath that misplaced and illegal Moslem dome, is deeply stained with symbolic messianic blood of Judaism. Deny it and you deny the temple ever existed there.

Moses is criticized in modern times as extremely severe and too oriented to the minutiae in the discipline of the Israelites. It is declared that the severe summary judgments and punishments he enforced are incompatible with a merciful God we call Rachmana. They are considered harsh in the modern moral world, especially in the treatment of misdemeanors in sexuality and Sabbath keeping. The demand that parents stone to death their own homosexual children is the most heinous and cruel infliction on both parents and children. Scholars describe good evidences of repeated editing, interpolations, and large additions in the context of this severity. This may have occurred in the resultant drastic merciless punishments and rigorous ritual exactions found in the Pentateuch. These harsh "moral" summary *judgments lacking mercy,* and extremely *tedious ceremonial laws lacking worship,* are out of character with a merciful and joyful God. Recognition of this does not deny Sinai. But all in all, the Pentateuch has kept the religious of Israel fully occupied in terms of their day-to-day existence. The Pentateuch is credited with the fashioning of a disciplined, dedicated, moral, God-fearing, generous, and gifted people, despite their historical catastrophic lapses into idolatry. Jews have high principles and great reverence for God. But *they also have feet of clay.* They all have need of mercy. Rachmana, do not leave us.

Our knowledge of the Eternal Torah as it exists on the planet could be functionally summarized in the three dramatic words: creation, redemption, and glorification, designed to fashion and procure a loved object for God. The implementation of this mighty triad was entrusted as the Abrahamic covenant to the chosen people to bring back the perfect Edenic state and immortality, which had been lost by the great disobedience. Land, Torah, and Messiah were the instruments to bring this about. Mashiach blood symbolized by the blood of the animal without blemish provided atonement. The Messianic Age would bring about a redeemed humanity who will be ushered into the world to come, in which they will be glorified. Glorification is the state of primal devekut with God in their redeemed state of perfection and immortality. This ideation constituted the foundation of primitive redemptive Judaism. I challenge any Jew to contradict this plan outlined by Moses.

The Written Torah evolved into the Tanak with the unfolding of the history of Israel and was essentially God's conversation with Israel through the prophets as God continued to guide and instruct them. But this period was a torrid and idolatrous period, during which they squandered post-Edenic devekut. The prophetic era appeared to stop at the tenure of Malachi, about 400 BC. Malachi warned that the next great event would be the arrival of the Messiah, preceded by Elijah's spiritual revival. When the prophetic voice ceased with Malachi, the rabbinic sages who followed in the hiatus jumped to conclusions:

> When the latter prophets, Haggai, Zechariah, and Malachi died, the Holy Spirit departed from Israel (Sanh. 11a) "… From the day the Temple was destroyed the prophetic gift was taken away from the prophets and given to the sages." (B. B. 12a)

> From the day the Temple was destroyed, prophecy was taken away from the prophets and given to fools and children. (B.B. 12b).[231]

These statements from the Talmud are not intrinsically true. Are "the sages" synonymous with "fools and children?" None of "the sages" were given or achieved prophetic standing. There have been no proclamations of "Thus saith the Lord" emanating from "the sages" since Malachi. Most importantly, *the Holy Spirit has not been withdrawn from the earth.* It was a supposition of "the sages," not a proclamation from God. We do not need a Bath Kol. The "Last Days" to come held many surprises:

> I will pour out My Spirit on all flesh.
> Your sons and daughters will prophesy;
> Your old men shall dream dreams,
> And your young men shall see visions.
> I will even pour out My Spirit
> Upon male and female slaves in those days.
> (Joel 3:1, 2)[232]

So the Holy Spirit is still with us awaiting further expression. And the Torah evolved into the Tanak, which expanded to contain the Pentateuch, the Nevi'im, and the Kethuvim. The Sanhedrin closed the Tanak as the written Torah and sacred canon of the Hebrews.[233]

No additions or subtractions are allowed by the Sanhedrin to the Holy Writ of Sinai. The process of closure occurred before the destruction of the second temple by the Romans. As a person dedicated to the sacredness of the Tanak as canon, I accept it as "The Conversation of God with Israel" to assure me of redemption.

The Talmud

The "sages" of Rabbinic Judaism had already been building up their power long before the destruction of the second temple in AD 70. They were powerful in Babylon and in the theology schools in Jerusalem. In the evolution of the Talmud, they became the determiners of religious thought in Jewry. The "sages" fashioned Rabbinic Judaism as a replacement of Sinai, and thereby *consolidated their power* over the rank and file of Jewry. Without the temple, their domination was complete. I define the Talmud as the "non-canonical conversation of the Israelites with each other." The Tanak, as the source of revelation, became reinterpreted to suit their ideas. They superceded Moses and the Tanak as the God-given authoritative source by which to live. Abraham Cohen states unequivocally that the Talmud contains much that has been "added to Sinai." Gershom Scholem states unequivocally that *"The Judaism of today is not the Judaism of Moses."*

The Talmud must be admitted to be a discussion of varying opinions, and is totally nonauthoritative. However, the effort that went into the composition of the Talmud should be recognized as valuable. Abraham Cohen stated that the rabbinic sages who contributed to the Talmud would deny that they were "originators of Jewish thought." He described them as "excavators in the inexhaustible mine of the divine Revelation contained in the Scriptures ..."[234] Cohen believed the Scriptures were "inspired" and that to meditate on and study the Scriptures was the chief privilege and greatest duty of the Jew. But *the rabbinic sages created a new religion.*

How did the Talmud evolve?

The "sages" had begun composing the Mishnah after Solomon's temple was destroyed in 586 BC. Judah was captive in Babylon. Expounding the Tanak became the theological occupation of

Babylonian Jews who had been carried away captive. Almost simultaneously, the same process also began in Jerusalem among the residual Jews. The Mishnah was thus produced and called an "Oral Torah."

The second temple was destroyed in AD 70. The evolving Mishnah was redacted about AD 200 by Rabbi Judah the Prince. The discussion of the Mishnah, already begun in Babylon and Jerusalem as parallel writings, eventually became the Bavli and Yerushalmi Gemara. Eventually Mishnah and Gemara gelled as the Talmud. Although considered "open-ended" by some Jewish scholars, the Talmud is said to have undergone closure about AD 600.[235]

Unfortunately, the Talmud replaced the Tanak as the main focus of study and became the authoritative substitute canon of the religious Jews. Primitive redemptive Judaism was thus replaced by Rabbinic Judaism, a talmudic philosophy, extremely oriented to ritual. Moses continued to be cited as an authority, but his Sinai-declared primitive redemptive Judaism of the blood, which was centered on the temple service, was deserted. Much in the Talmud has no basis in the Tanak.

Five great rabbinic sages came into prominence at the turn of the era (BC to AD)[236]

1. Rabbi Hillel (60 BC–AD 20) was a Babylonian Jew who migrated to Israel, established the School of Hillel, and was president of the Sanhedrin. He was a contributor to the Mishnah.

2. Rabbi Shammai (50 BC–AD 30) was born in Israel. He established the School of Shammai, which was in "opposition" to the School of Hillel. He contributed to the Mishnah.

3. Rabbi Akiva (AD 50–AD 135) lived through the destruction of the second temple in AD 70. He contributed to the Mishnah.

4. Rabbi Yochanan Ben Zakkai (AD 30–AD 90) was a pupil of Hillel. He was trapped in Jerusalem when it was taken by the Zealots. He was pacifistic toward Rome and would have been killed by the Zealots. He escaped by being smuggled out of Jerusalem in a coffin. With permission from Vespasian, he started the School at Yavneh, which became the leading center of Jewish learning for centuries.

5. Rabbi Judah the Prince (AD 135–AD 219) was the redactor of the Mishnah. Because the Mishnaic material was fragmentary and existed in mainly oral form, there was danger that it might be lost. He therefore made it his task to codify it and write it down.

The Tannaim were teachers of the Talmud during the time of Rabbi Hillel and Rabbi Shammai. Six generations of them (AD 10–AD 220) wielded opinion during this period. Their names are listed.[237]

The Amoraim were the interpreters of the Talmud and the opinion leaders from AD 220–AD 500. Their names are also listed.[238]

The Tannaim and the Amoraim are mentioned separately here because their opinions are qualitatively different. The Tannaim lived closer to the destruction of the second temple and were more stressed by the destruction. The Amoraim were more affected by the prominent emergence of messianic ideas in the Christianity of their era to which they were averse.[239]

So now to discuss the Messiah of the Talmud:

Amora R. Hillel (not Rabbi Hillel) stated that Hezekiah was the Messiah and there was no other to come in the future. Amora R. Joseph reprimanded him for this statement. Amora R. Hillel explained that he did not believe in a future *human* Messiah but was expecting the Holy One, blessed be He, would Himself come and redeem His people. He saw that God Himself must accomplish the Redemption of Israel. *He felt that only deity was qualified to do the job of redemption.* I totally agree. No "human only" Messiah can do the job.[240] Did Amora R. Hillel believe in the deity of the Messiah? If he did, he would be in agreement with the Tanak, but he would be wrong if he denied the penetrance of humanity by deity. I sincerely believe that only deity can create, redeem, and glorify humanity as spoken by Moses, David, Isaiah, and the prophets. It is God's eternal prerogative. He cannot share this work. Because of it, the Redeemer demands sole and total worship by humanity. Because of God's creative and redemptive acts, we cannot and do not have any other God. There is no other God.

347

Some rabbinic sages were outstandingly perceptive. They identified the Messiah as the central subject of the religious discussion of the Jews:

> *From the beginning of the Creation of the World King Messiah was born, for He entered the mind (of God) before even the World was created. (Pesikta Rab. 152b) Every prophet only prophesied for the days of the Messiah and the penitent (Ber. 34b) Great is repentance because it brings the Redemption near.* (Joma 86b)

These sages focused their thinking on the Yahwistic Levitical priesthood's commandment-keeping theology, which centralized and gelled in the Jerusalem temple. There is a collaboration with the rival Elohistic worship system, which was the spirituality of the northern Israelite kingdom. It should be noted that Yahweh and Elohim are the same God. There is no doubt that sages consider the prophets of the Tanak as the authoritative direction of Judaism and its central messianic hope. Scholars divide the prophets arbitrarily into pre- and post-exilic prophets, with application to the Assyrian and Babylonian exiles. Their pre-exilic message was full of foreboding. Their post-exilic stance had to cope with frustration and the misery of bondage.

Prophets were essentially messengers to the north or the south, but application was to all Jews. These prophets are a cluster of God's organized effort to bring the Jews back to Yahwistic theology and enforce the Abrahamic covenant. All Israel's kings were involved with idolatry, with the exception of David. Even Josiah and Hezekiah were weak or partial in the fight against idolatry. David's magnificent understanding of Messiah was Israel's highest kingly achievement. He understood repentance and the atonement for sin as no other Israelite ever did. He rejoiced in the perfection and immortality that was to come in Messiah ben David's eternal kingdom. The prophets of the Tanak battled the corruption of the kings of Israel. Their messages were packed with a doom-and-gloom punishment, but the sheer force of messianic deliverance shone through. The Talmud very perceptively declares, *"Every prophet spake for the Messiah and the penitent."*

Max Weber, in his book *Ancient Judaism*, sees the prophets as demagogues. Weber correctly states that they all were absolutely religious and had no political agenda other than the coming kingdom of Messiah ben David, their ideal future state. There was not total clarity in their perception of Israel's eschatology. They had difficulty relating and separating the immediate politiconational future of Israel from the *Day of Yahwe*, wherein were Judgment and Resurrection leading to the eternal kingdom of Messiah ben David. For Judah's exile in Babylon, Jeremiah had predicted a return after seventy years. The prophets did not push a political program but championed the cause of the poor. They condemned the corruption of the priesthood and saw the uselessness of the sacrificial system *only in its corrupt status.* They were strict Yahwists and condemned the temple harlotry, orgiastic fertility cults, and Baal shrines that had crept into Israel's places of worship. Their theology was drawn from Moses and David. They saw Messiah as a succession in the royal line of David, installed only by God's own anointing. Isaiah's Immanuel prophecy contained the legitimacy of the zenith of David's kingdom. It foretold the coming Messiah as an incarnation of deity. This "represented the climax of national history ... That the political aspirations of Israel would only be realized through a miracle of God." This would be accomplished with the messianic Day of Yahwe. (See *Ancient Judaism*, by Max Weber, pp. 277–335.) Many of the rabbinic sages of the Talmud expressed similar ideas, but others got sidelined by confused ideas of Messianism. They saw redemption by lawkeeping: practicing the minutae of halakah and the magnification of ritual. Messiah was not their redeemer.

Many rabbinic sages generally felt the need to define the Messiah as an exceptionally gifted purely human being. But the massive tasks expected of the Messiah—such as Judgment, Resurrection, and the establishment of the eternal kingdom of Messiah ben David—required the power and longevity of deity. They saw that perfection and immortality waited in the wings, but these sages could not give a mechanism or a chronology for the implementation of these desired qualities. Some rabbinic sages embraced the impractical alternative of world domination by Israel in the status quo. They failed to see that the idea of a one-human-lifetime messiah does not fit in with the prophets' apocalyptic predictions. (For these rabbinic opinions cited by Abraham Cohen, see p. Ber. 5a; Lam. R. 1. 51; Sanh. 90a, 90b, 96b, 97a & b, 98b, 99a, 110b; Gen. R. XLII. 4; Meg.IIa; A.Z. 9b; p. Taan. 64a; Keth IIIb; Shab. 30b; Ex. R. xv. 21; Lev. R. xxv. 8; Gen. R. xcv. 1; Tanchuma Noach S 11, 19; Lev. R. xxxvI. 2; Tanchuma Reeh S 4; A.Z. 3b; Tosifta Sanh. xIII. 12; Pes. 79a, 88a; Midrash to Esth. i. 8; Sifre Deut. $ 306, 352, 132a 145b; Gen. R. xcvIII. 2; Midrash to Cant. Iv. 4; Cant. R. to 11. 13; Tanchuma Ekeb S 7; Cant vii. 9, and so on.)

Instead of making a sole attempt of my own to decipher and interpret the Messiah in the Talmud, I will rely on eminent Jewish scholars to assist with this. But I will demand congruence with the Tanak in acceptance of talmudic ideas. The following ideas of talmudic Messianism in this chapter are sourced mainly from the writings of four great modern Jewish thinkers and one great contemporary German thinker:

1. Abraham Cohen (AD 1887–1957, born in Britain): *Everyman's Talmud*
2. Joseph Klausner (AD 1874–1958, born in Lithuania): *The Messianic Idea in Israel*
3. Franz Rosenzweig (AD 1886–1929, born in Germany): *Star of Redemption*
4. Gershom Scholem (AD 1897–1982, born in Germany): *The Messianic Idea in Judaism* and *On Jews and Judaism in Crisis*
5. Peter Schafer (b. AD 1943 in Germany): *The Jewish Jesus: How Judaism and Christianity Shaped Each Other*

These prolific writers are relatively contemporary. Schafer has the advantage of the writings of the others. In this chapter I will pay special attention to Messianism in the above-listed books, in their treatment of the Talmud. All of them, more or less, rely heavily on talmudic writings but also seek a foundation in the Tanak. Use of the Tanak must be in harmony with the great concepts of Creation and Redemption emanating from Sinai. The Tanak must be the *Gold Standard.* Will any Jew dare to contradict this, if he has respect for Sinai? The question that must dominate is, does our conclusion agree with the essence of Judaism as found in the Most Holy Place of the temple, where Shechinah, law, mercy, and messianic blood comingle to effect the Redemption?

Abraham Cohen's book *Everyman's Talmud: The Major Teachings of the Rabbinic Sages* is the best source to hand in English of talmudic teachings. An entire chapter, the last in this book, is titled "The Hereafter" and is descriptive of the Messiah and the Messianic Age. Some of the ideas expressed are controversial and contradictory, but they reflect the varying and sometimes opposite views of the rabbinic sages. The sages were by no means unanimous. Some rabbinic sages followed tanakian ideas; some conjured up their own from misinterpreted and farfetched conclusions that do not fit into the tanakian conceptual messianic centrality and unity. Cohen tries desperately to unify variant talmudic ideas but at the same time exposes contradictions. Sometimes he will cull the tanakian idea first, or emphasize it as a summary.

Joseph Klausner's book *The Messianic Idea In Israel From Its Beginning to the Completion of the Mishnab* makes a great effort to differentiate between "Messianic Expectation" and "Belief in Messiah." He believes in a progressive improvement of history culminating in the triumph of the national and political ambitions of Israel.[241] He sees a Jewish *universalism* taking place within the status quo with advancement toward this end in the formations of the League of Nations and the United Nations.[242] He is not able to fit the Judgment and the Resurrection neatly into his messianic scheme. He leans very heavily on the apocrypha, pseudepigrapha, and talmudic Baraitha of the Tannaim, and lesserly the Amoraim. He puts great weight on his conclusion that

> In the course of the long evolution of the Jewish Messianic idea, two different conceptions were inseparably woven together: *politico-national salvation* and *religio-spiritual redemption* .... The Messiah must be both *king* and *redeemer.* He must overthrow the enemies of Israel and rebuild the Temple; and at the same time he must reform the world through the Kingdom of God, root out idolatry from the world, proclaim the one and only God to all, put

an end to sin, and be wise, pious, and just as no man had
been before him or ever would be after him.[243]

Klausner does not envision the kingdom of God as an apocalyptic
establishment on a brand-new earth. He ignores Isaiah's insistence
on a new heaven and a new earth. Isaiah was emphatic:

> For as the new heavens and new earth which I will make,
> Shall remain before Me, saith the Lord,
> So shall your seed and your name remain.
> And it shall come to pass that,
> From one new moon to another,
> And from one Sabbath to another,
> Shall all flesh come to worship before Me, saith the Lord.
> (Isa. 66:22–23 KJV)

Klausner's conclusions are contrary to Isaiah and Daniel's
apocalyptic framework. The Tanak teaches that history will end.
Participation in Isaiah's new earth is the reward of those deemed
righteous. New moons and Sabbaths are a hallmark of planet earth.
The new earth will be a cleansed planet. King Messiah will reign
from the New Jerusalem eternally. (See Psalm 2:7, 8; Daniel 7:13,
14.) Perfection and immortality are restored.

Klausner is unable to visualize the catastrophic apocalyptic of the
prophets. He does not envisage a Messiah who comes from eternity
and goes on into a future eternity in perfection and immortality. He
envisages no mechanics for the messianic atonement. He gives his
"mere human" Messiah enormous divine tasks without investing
Him with divine power.

Franz Rosenzweig's book *Star of Redemption* is a very difficult
book to read because he employs his own, somewhat mystical,
theological jargon. It is of significant depth and is challenging to
understand. However, he summarizes his book clearly at the end,
with his conviction that *personal piety is the Messiah that redeems
us*. But sparsely distributed throughout his book is a less-than-
subtle, very dramatic unveiling of a marvelous personal divine
Messiah with a preexisting eternity and an everlasting kingdom for

the future. I discuss Rosenzweig's fantastic but solid redemptive Messiah throughout this book. It is clear that he wants it both ways, redemption by lawkeeping and redemption by Messiah.

Gershom Scholem's books discussed are *The Messianic Idea in Judaism and Other Essays on Jewish Spirituality* and *Jews and Judaism in Crisis, Selected Essays.* Scholem is much closer to tanakian theology. While Klausner and Rosenzweig (halfheartedly) reject the catastrophic apocalyptic of the Tanak, Scholem embraces it with the greatest enthusiasm. He exults in it. He criticizes Rosenzweig and Martin Buber for rejecting the apocalyptic:

> Buber's sharp turn against the revolutionary element in Jewish Messianism is connected with another important point, his striking aversion to the apocalyptic. Buber is among those – no less than Franz Rosenzweig and a long line of liberal Jewish thinkers – who, at least in his later period, represent a tendency to remove the apocalyptic sting from Judaism. I have discussed this tendency in detail in my lecture, *"Toward the Understanding of the Messianic Idea in Judaism."*[244]

No other modern Jewish writer known to me is as tanakian and thrilling to read as Scholem. He firmly believes in the catastrophic and apocalyptic character of the Messianic Age. His love for the apocalyptic declarations of Moses, David, Isaiah, and Daniel knows no bounds. His theology sees a dramatic demise of history, and a messianic restorative accomplishment before the Utopian era can take place.[245] I stand in awe of his comprehension of the tanakian Messiah. But occasionally he tries to accommodate the talmudic sages by a halfhearted espousal of personal piety as deserving of redemption.

Peter Schafer, a German scholar, is in my opinion the most knowledgeable and erudite non-Jew in the contemporary era, with the widest and deepest familiarity with Jewish writings. He is widely accepted and respected by Jewish scholars as an authority in the Tanak and Talmud.

Now follows a discussion of the Messiah through the eyes of these five outstanding and gifted men who were or are influenced greatly by the Tanak and Talmud. Their ideas will be intertwined so as to create a discussion to evaluate the "contemporary" talmudic Jewish identity of the Messiah. The basis of the discussion and gold standard naturally will be the Tanak.

Abraham Cohen: The first segment of Cohen's chapter on the hereafter is titled "The Messiah." The first paragraph is as follows:\

> Whereas other peoples of antiquity placed their Golden Age in the dim and remote past, the Jews relegated it to the future. The prophets of Israel repeatedly allude to 'the latter days', still unborn, *as the period when the national greatness would reach its zenith.* This hope took a firm grip of the popular mind and grew not only in intensity but, as time proceeded, likewise in the marvels which its realization would bring to the world. The glorious future centred around the person of a Mashiach, *"an Anointed One"* who would be deputed by God to inaugurate this new and wonderful era."[246]

Cohen links the past golden age of King David with the golden age of Messiah ben David. This is a grand entry into the central vista of the Tanak, the central vista of the Jewish longing, the desire of all those to whom the beauty of this life is enormous, but who still long for something more that will fill their unsatisfied yearning for greater adoration of the God we love and worship. Those who have suffered all their lives; whose share of misery has been disproportionate; whose sensibilities have been cruelly blunted by people, circumstances, and paths they mistakenly chose or which were thrust upon them—they wait in painful agony. The Jews, no matter how enormous their frailties, have suffered disproportionately and wait patiently for that great day. But Cohen, speaking for the Talmud, also had great hopes for the political and *national triumph of Israel in the planetary status quo.* He wanted to satisfy the political and national yearnings of Jews. Little emphasis was laid on the achievement of atonement,

354

perfection, and immortality because he could not fit them squarely into his scheme of the envisioned national aggrandizement of "the latter days."

The Ha-Mashiach is the balm the world needs to heal its suffering in all the mayhem. Man's inhumanity to man has reached higher than the heavens. Ruach Hakodesh-assisted "Groanings which cannot be uttered" reach the sensibility of almighty God, and He longs to fill the great void where only peace, perfection, and immortality will satisfy our longings. His longings and our longings are the same; we want that devekut we had with Him in Gan Eden. And so, *in the tanakian Messiah He pours out heaven with Himself.* He will first fulfill His plan in the Torah for atonement and then reclaim His precious treasure in a perfect eternal happiness in a new earth.

There is no definition of and no mechanism for the "spiritual work" the Messiah has to do to give us *peace, perfection, and immortality* in Cohen's grand trumpeting of the arrival of Ha-Mashiach. If Ha-Mashiach comes just to give us political relief from our oppressors within the status quo for His one human lifetime, he might as well not come. We do not want to continue in the state we are in now, dying after a short life lived in frustration and regret—the regret of things done and things left undone. Our life record is one of broken laws, despite our own innate desires to love and obey our God. God will not waste His time with a prolonged "Investigative Judgment" for He and the multiverse know we are all sinners. Our common condition needs no investigation. The Law wants us dead. We want perfection and immortality, because that is what we lost in Gan Eden. We need an immortal Messiah to bequeath immortality to us. The rabbis, according to Cohen, were unanimous that Ha-Mashiach is a mortal human being exactly like the rest of us:

> On one point the Rabbis were unanimous, viz. he would
> be just a human being, divinely appointed to carry out an
> allotted task. The Talmud nowhere indicates a belief in a
> superhuman deliverer as the Messiah ... The prevailing
> belief was that the Messiah would be a descendant of
> the king, and a common designation for him in rabbinic
> literature is "the son of David." Biblical passages which

were interpreted in a Messianic sense afforded a variety
of names which he would be called. Certain Rabbinic
students even exercised their ingenuity to discover for him
a name similar to that borne by their teacher.[247]

First of all, ***the rabbinic sages were not unanimous*** in this
belief, as Cohen thinks. Rabbi Judah the Prince believed in the
divine "Suffering Messiah," as we have seen. Rabbi Judah's
Messiah was a divine-human person, born on the planet. He did
not subscribe to Israel as the suffering Servant. Cohen was blind
to Daniel's discussion of the Son of Man and the Ancient of Days.
Many rabbinic sages delved deeply into that topic with conclusions
of messianic divinity.

The Messiah portrayed by Franz Rosenzweig is unmistakably
divine. He accepted the portrayal by Isaiah that the Messiah was
not a "mere human." This belief that "he would be just a human"
and "not a superhuman deliverer as the Messiah" is un-tanakian and
a gross error. A human being like us, limited to one short lifetime,
will not be able to accomplish more than King David, His "type,"
accomplished. And then if He were just an ordinary human, He
would die a terrestrial death, and we would bury him and create
another "Holy Site" in Jerusalem. And who would ensure that the
reforms He brought would be guaranteed for eternity? The status
quo of sin and suffering will continue. But the Messiah cannot die
an ordinary human death unless He can come alive again, because
He has to be there for the duration of the messianic kingdom, which
must last forever and ever in an "Earth made New." He has to
bestow immortality to us, so He had better be immortal himself. The
prophet Daniel said that the Son of Man is to perform Judgment and
preside over the Resurrection. What is the point of a resurrection
into the same status quo which we left! No "human-only" can enable
a resurrection into perfection and immortality. Franz Rosenzweig
believed in an eternal Messiah without a doubt.[248] This will be
discussed further.

Returning to the rabbinic students' suggestions for names for the
Messiah:

- The school of Rabbi Sheila named him "***Shiloh***," as it is written, "until Shiloh come" (Genesis 49:10).
- The school of Rabbi Jannai named him "***Jinnon***," as it is said, "His name shall be continued as long as the sun" (Psalm 72:17 [Here is an eternity that cannot be denied]).
- The school of Rabbi Channina named him "***Chaninah***," as it is said, I will show you no favour" (Jeremiah 16:13).
- Others contended that his name is "***Menachem***," son of Hezekiah, as it is said, "The comforter that should refresh my soul is far from me" (Lamentations 1:16).[249]

And here follows a major talmudic contradiction where the Ha-Mashiach now presents as the suffering Servant, a very welcome contradiction indeed:

> The Rabbis maintain that his name is *'the leprous One'* of the School of R. Judah the Prince', as it is said, 'Surely He hath borne our griefs and carried our sorrows; yet we did esteem Him stricken, smitten of God, and afflicted'. (Isa. 53;4)[250]

By connecting to the "Suffering Servant" of the messianic passage in Isaiah, the messianic utterances therein with which these rabbinic sages agree—the birth, death, and resurrection of the Messiah—are there declared in Isaiah. I have outlined these in chapter 18, "The God Messiah of Isaiah." Isaiah 9:6 declares He was "the Mighty God planning Grace" and "the Everlasting Father, a Peaceable Ruler." It is a distinct assertion that the messianic passages in Isaiah declare the Messiah to be superhuman since he is deity, who is born, dies, and returns from the dead. Isaiah plainly declares His deity. And David had already declared his affirmation of this vital characteristic of the Messiah (Ps. 2;1–12). More than that, there is messianic propitiation here, as Isaiah declares:

> My righteous servant makes the many righteous,
> *It is their punishment that He bears;*
> Assuredly, I will give him the many as his portion,

He shall receive the multitude as his spoil.
For he exposed himself to death
And was numbered among the sinners,
Whereas *He bore the guilt of many*
And made intercession for sinners.
(Isa. 53:11b–12, emphasis added)

Joseph Klausner also makes a great effort to fashion a purely "human" Messiah despite Isaiah's solid assertion of Messiah's deity. Klausner twists the Baraitha that states that the Messiah existed before Creation. (See Peshahim 54a; Nedarim 39b.) He calls this Tannaitic Baraitha "strange" and "unusual" in order to dismiss it. He grasps the thesis of Maurice Vernes and Meir Friedman[251] to imply that this reference to Messiah was simply *"the idea of redemption through the Messiah*, which idea did precede Creation, but only as an idea. And then he goes on to make this most astounding statement:

> Before Creation, Israel was predestined to produce from itself a Messiah, to be redeemed by him, and through him to redeem all mankind from the evil in the world.[252]

What a massive task, which demands omnipotence, to be laid on the shoulders of a "mere human!" This idea of Klausner, because it denies messianic deity, is not tanakian and is designed to deny Messiah eternal preexistence and deity, oneness with God—God's functionality that is God Himself. Read again Franz Rosenzweig's statement:

> Yet no one knows better than he that being dear to God is only a beginning, and that man remains unredeemed so long as nothing but this beginning has been realized. Over against Israel, *eternally loved by God and faithful and perfect in eternity, stands he who is eternally to come, he who waits and wanders, and grows eternally – the MESSIAH.*[253]

In this instance Rosenzweig is solidly with Isaiah; Messiah has been named *"The Mighty God, planning Grace, the Everlasting*

Father" (Isa. 9:6). Both Cohen and Klausner are way out of line here. Klausner cannot substitute this mighty tanakian declaration with "Israel was predestined to produce *from itself* a Messiah." That Messiah was eternally waiting in the wings to redeem His people. Sure, He will come through the loins of Jacob and David, for so they joyfully declared, but He will be more than a "mere human." Abraham entertained Him under the terebinths, Jacob wrestled with Him at the brook Jabbok, and David declared His eternity in Psalms 2, 16, 22, 23, 110, and others. And Isaiah will irresistibly insist He is *the mighty God planning grace.* A mighty redemption indeed!

> Rabbi Nachman asked R. Isaac, 'Have you heard when Bar Naphle ('son of the fallen') will come?' He said to him, Who is Bar Naphle? He answered, the Messiah. The other asked, Do you call the Messiah Bar Naphle? He replied, I do because it is written, In that day will I raise the tabernacle of David that is fallen.' (Amos 9:11; Sanh. 96b)

This idea is congruent with the condescension of the Messiah into shame and pity:

> He had no form or beauty that we should look at him;
> No charm that we should find him pleasing.
> He was despised, and shunned by men,
> A man of suffering, familiar with disease
> As one who hid his face from us,
> He was despised, we held him of no account
> Yet it was our suffering that he was bearing.
> (Isa. 53:2b, 3)

King David heard the God of Israel describe the condescension of Himself thus:

> But I am a worm, less than human;
> Scorned by men, despised by people
> (Ps. 22:7)

359

What condescension! The Pesiqta Rabbati regarded Psalm 22 as the travail of the suffering Messiah!

David danced naked before the ark of the covenant and mercy seat, stained with blood to depict messianic shame and condescension, and death. He recognized the Mashiach as Bar Naphle. Years later Isaiah confirmed David.

The names of the Mashiach are synonymous with "redeemer." *God has sole ownership of the title of Redeemer.* In chapter 2, "The Eternal Pre-existence of the Ha-Mashiach," the Redeemer's names are listed. These names are excerpted from the Tanak and are applicable here. Messiah is God in His functionality of Redeemer.

There is solid evidence that the Mashiach, when he comes, must atone for our sins in order to give us perfection and immortality and restore us to Elohim's bosom. Mashiach must take us through Judgment and the Resurrection, a massive task equal only to deity. Many talmudic rabbis had lost sight of the redemptive function of the Messiah. The Jews who do not understand this feel their political burden more than their burden of sin and guilt. They see their temporal political needs as greater than their spiritual needs.

Cohen states, quite rightly, and goes on to interpret the Talmud:

> The hope for the coming of the Messiah naturally became more fervent in the time of national eclipse. When the oppression of the conqueror grew intolerable, the Jews instinctively turned to the Messianic predictions contained in their Scriptures. Josephus records how, in the years immediately preceding the destruction of the Temple, men came forward claiming to be the Redeemer foretold by the prophets.[254]

> The time of his [Messiah's] advent will be particularly marked by political unrest, culminating in bitter warfare. 'If you see the kingdoms contending with each other, look for the foot of the Messiah … ' (Gen. R. 42. 4). "This strife is symbolized under the term 'wars of Gog and Magog' (See Ezekiel chapter 38)." "Attempts to calculate 'the end', i.e. the time of the Messiah's coming, were

deprecated by the majority of rabbis on the grounds that they raised hopes which were ultimately falsified. There is the emphatic warning: 'Cursed be they who calculate "the end," because they argue that since "the end" has arrived and the Messiah has not come, he never will come; but wait for him, as it is said, "Though it (the appointed time) tarry, wait for it (Habakkuk 2:3).
(Sanh. 97b)[255]

Some rabbis felt that personal holiness, repentance, good deeds, and proper Sabbath keeping (especially keeping two Sabbaths perfectly in a row) could hasten the Messiah's coming. But some believed God had a set fixed time.

The Talmud indulges in the conditions that the Messiah will institute in the Messianic Age. Briefly they are as follows:

1. He will illumine the world. The talmudic mechanics and venues for this are not clear, except in world domination by Israel and unusual prosperity generated by a magnified productivity of the natural world. The light will have healing power. Mass proselytizing to Judaism appears to take place. (Isa. 60:19)
2. He will cause running water with healing powers to issue from Jerusalem. (Ezek. 47:9)
3. He will cause trees to bring forth fruit more frequently. (Ezek. 47:12)
4. All ruined cities will be rebuilt, and there will be no waste places in the world. (Ezek. 16:55)
5. He will rebuild Jerusalem with sapphires. (Isa. 54:11; 60:3)
6. Peace will reign throughout nature. The cow and the bear will feed together. (Isa. 11:7)
7. The animal kingdom and humans will live at peace. (Hos. 2:18)
8. Weeping and wailing will cease in the world. (Isa. 65:19)
9. *There will be no more death.* (Isa. 25:8)
10. There will be no more sighing or groaning or anguish, but all will be happy. (Isa. 35:10); (Ex. R.15. 21 emphasis added).

In the "World to Come" one will only have occasion to say

Blessed is he who is good and doeth good. (Pes. 50a)

Israel's oppression by a hostile world will end:

So striking will be the change in Israel's fortune that many non-Jews will attempt to join the community but will be rejected. No proselytes will be accepted in the days of the Messiah (A.Z. 3b).[256]

Some rabbis disagreed with this exclusion of the Gentiles. Some rabbis believed that the lost ten tribes of Israel would be restored (see Tosifta Sanh. 8:12), while others opposed that view (see Isaiah 27:13; Jeremiah 3:12; Sanh. 110b). Jerusalem (see Tanchuma Noach:11) and the temple will be rebuilt (see Sifre Deut. 352; 145b; Midrash to Cant. 4: 4). The temple service will no longer need the sacrificial system, since *sin will be abolished.* Only thanksgiving offerings will be offered (Pesikta 79a).[257]

The method or mechanism for the eradication of sin and death is not elaborated in talmudic discussion of the end time, but it is assumed that it has miraculously happened. The question arises, was this by messianic atonement, and how was it made? Isaiah answers that question succinctly: "Surely, He hath borne our griefs and carried our sorrows, the chastisement of our peace was upon Him, and with His stripes we are healed" (Isa. 53:4, 5 KJV). *The eradication of sin and death means that perfection and immortality are restored,* but how did it happen in order to procure renewed access to Gan Eden? The assumption is that Messiah did accomplish atonement, but when, how, and where was the atonement made, and how will it be accomplished? Will this be possible by a "merely human" Messiah? These unanswered questions must be answered, especially if the Messiah is to be a mere human.

Cohen then moves on to the talmudic discussion of the Resurrection and the Judgment. The Judgment must decide who is worthy for perfection and immortality, and who is not, and on what basis or standard that decision is made.

In the above discussion, it is noted that good deeds, Sabbath-keeping, etc. have merit. It leads to the questions as to who qualify and why they qualify to partake of the messianic kingdom and the new earth where there is an abolition of sin and death.

Cohen focuses on the resurrection, declaring that the Talmud states the following:

> No aspect of the subject of the Hereafter has so important a place in the religious teaching of the Rabbis as the doctrine of the resurrection. It became with them an article of faith the denial of which was condemned as sinful; and they declared: 'Since a person repudiated belief in the resurrection of the dead, he will have no share in the resurrection'.
> (Sanh. 90a).[258]

The Sadducees did not believe in the resurrection:

> [The Sadducees] taught that the soul became extinct when the body died and death was the final end of the human being (Sanh. 90a; Ber. ix. 5; Sifre Deut. $ 306, 132a).[259]

It is true that the soul has no separate existence when the body dies. A living soul is a living person. A dead soul has no existence. But death is not the final end of a redeemed human being. The Sadducees claimed that the resurrection is not taught in the Pentateuch. The Pharisees maintained that it is (See Deuteronomy 31:16; 32:39; Numbers 14:1; 15:31.) There is no question that the entire Pentateuch is fashioned on the principle of the atonement and the promise of immortality and a hereafter involving a restored devekut. The translation of Enoch and Elijah and the resurrected Moses into heaven stand as proof that death is not the end of everything in Judaism. The entire Tanak teaches the resurrection.

The rabbinic sages disagreed on the resurrection of the physical body. Some taught that earthly blemishes and deformities of the body will be retained.

Talmudic disunity is quite clear here. Cohen depicts the world to come thus:

> In the eschatological doctrine of the Talmud a clear ***divergence of opinion*** may be traced. The earlier generations of the Rabbis identified the Messianic era with the World to Come. The promised Redeemer would bring the existing world-order to an end and inaugurate the timeless sphere in which the righteous would lead a purely spiritual existence freed from the trammels of the flesh. Subsequent teachers regarded the Messianic period as but a transitory stage between this world and the next. That this life is only preliminary to another and higher life was universally accepted by the Rabbis.[260]

This passage, of course, does not refer to the Sadducee's beliefs. It presumes that the Messiah as a "mere human" will also be resurrected. There is a clear admission here of the catastrophic apocalyptic: "The promised Redeeemer would bring the existing world-order to an end and inaugurate the timeless sphere." These sages read Isaiah and the prophets correctly.

The "vestibule/hall" (this life/the "World to Come") metaphor was believed by some rabbis. They considered that this life is only preliminary to another and higher life:

> This world is like a vestibule before the World to Come;
> prepare yourself in the vestibule that you may enter into
> the hall. (Aboth IV. 21; see also Ber. 34b)

David's declaration "I shall be satisfied when I awake with Thy likeness" (Ps. 17:15) is interpreted as the state in which the inhabitants of the "World to Come" would find themselves. Awakening with "Thy likeness" is an immortal state.

Some rabbis envisaged stages of increasing spirituality in the "World to Come."

Entry into and exclusion from the "World to Come" was arbitrarily assigned by the rabbis. There is not one standard or qualification in these rabbinic discussions.[261] Abraham Cohen, in considering these inclusion/exclusion criteria, appears a little embarrassed as he dismisses these talmudic criteria, as "They are nothing more than a hyperbolic expression of approval or disapproval." Regarding a second set of inclusion/exclusion criteria set out by R. Akiba and Abba Saul (Sanh. 10:1), Cohen says, "It is an error to read into the first sentence in this declaration ['All Israel has a share in the World to Come'] any idea of favouritism on the part of God for Israel."[262]

Cohen considers the following as the *locus classicus:*

> The School of Shammai declared, There are three classes with respect to the Day of Judgment: the perfectly righteous, the completely wicked, and the average people. Those in the first class are forthwith inscribed and sealed for eternal life. Those in the second class are forthwith inscribed and sealed for Gehinnom ... The third class will descend to Gehinnom and cry out ... and then ascend, as it is said, "I will bring the third part through the fire, and will refine them, as silver is refined, and will try them as gold is tried; they shall call on My name and I will answer them" (Zech. 8:9).[263]

While everyone will admit that there is a bell curve of people from very good to very bad in the general population, I challenge the school of Shammai that there are no perfect people. So this division of people is illogical and does not work. The cutoff point between the second and third groups would indeed be extremely difficult. I would say to God, "All three classes of people are guilty of breaking the law. Send them all to Gehinnom and refine the whole lot? Is Your name not Rachmana?" If such is true God should be embarrassed at His poor judgment.

"On the question whether Gentiles will share in the Hereafter there was not an agreed opinion." R. Eliezer excluded all Gentiles, whereas R. Joshua disagreed and allowed some Gentiles in (Tosifta Sanh. 13:2). The rabbinic argument is not conclusive about whether or not the innocent children of wicked Gentiles will or will not be allowed in.[264]

The entirety of the inclusion/exclusion criteria in the Talmud is a shambles. The Tanak needs to be consulted in the qualification of who is allowed into the Messianic Age and World to Come, where perfection and immortality are universal.

The need remains to define what messianic atonement and Redemption mean. There is no clarity in the Talmud about atonement per se, although the Day of Atonement is so vital in Judaism.

Before considering that topic, the talmudic opinion on the Last Judgment should be re-evaluated.

The Last Judgment

The talmudic idea of judgment appears to be one of retribution. In other words, it is to punish people for their bad lives, rather than to select the ones worthy of entering into immortality:

> The doctrine of Retribution ... was a cardinal belief of the Rabbis. Apart from the fact that it was a necessary corollary of their trust in Divine Justice, it afforded the only solution to the problem, which was created by the unhappy plight of their people. Gentile nations could not oppress God's elect with impunity, and a day of reckoning had to come" (Mechilta ad loc. 39a; Tanchuma Kedoshim $ 1; A.Z. 2a, b; Mechilta to xvi. 25, 50b; Ber. 58b; Aboth. Iv 29; Erub. 19a; Eccles. R. to iii. 9, are talmudic details cited by Cohen concerning the Judgment). [265]

Exodus 15:7, "Thou overthrowest them that rise up against Thee," is quoted by Abraham Cohen in support of retribution. Idolatrous Israel does not appear to be included here, although Jewish history bears out that they were very wicked and were severely punished for it.

The rabbinic sages, Cohen explains, came to a consensus that the Judgment is primarily to punish the Gentiles for persecuting Israel. This is a little difficult for some to understand, since it is presumed by the prophets that God allowed the Gentiles to punish idolatrous Israel. There is no doubt that Israel suffered inhuman persecution and people will be punished for it. But all born on the planet will face Judgment. All have broken God's law, both persecuted and persecutors.

It appears that the "Elders" of Israel will be some of the judges sitting in judgment with God to punish the Gentiles. This belief is based on a misinterpretation of Isaiah 3:14, which is quoted as

> The Lord will enter into judgment with the elders of His people.
> (Isa. 3:14)

The particular translation of Isaiah 3:14 used here is not credited. But Cohen gives the rabbinic argument for using this text:

> It is not written 'against the elders' but 'with the elders,' which indicates that the Holy One, blessed be He, will sit with them and judge the gentile nations ... (Tanchuma Kedoshim:1).[266]

In this third chapter of Isaiah, the context discusses the national disintegration of Jerusalem and Judah. God is fed up with sinful Judah. It reaches a height in verse 8:

> For Jerusalem is ruined, Judah is fallen, because their tongue and their doings are against the Lord, to provoke the eyes of His glory. The show of their countenance doth witness against them, and they declare their sin like Sodom; They hide it not. Woe unto their soul! For they have rewarded evil unto themselves. (Isa. 3:8–9 KJV)

The Jewish Study Bible translation is more scathing:

> Ah, Jerusalem has stumbled,
> And Judah has fallen,
> Because by word and deed
> They insult the Lord,
> Defying His majestic glance.

Their partiality in judgment accuses them;
They avow their sins like Sodom,
They do not conceal them.
Woe to them!
For ill have they served themselves.
(Isa. 3:8–9)

The crucial verse 14 translation by *The Jewish Study Bible* does not support the rabbinic sages' interpretation of "the elders" being co-judges with God:

The Lord will bring this charge against the elders and officers of His people: 'It is you who have ravaged the vineyard; that which was robbed from the poor is in your house. How dare you crush My people and grind the faces of the poor.
(Isa. 3:14–15)

The rabbis were in this instance more than a little careless in their exegesis. Following this fallacious interpretation, the Talmud details the judgment. Rome and Persia are singled out for particular punishment.

God is the Judge of all the earth, and Cohen is more inclusive of all humanity:

Not only Israelites, however, but every human being is called to account.[267]

Cohen proceeds to quote a particularly vital passage from the Talmud:

They that are born are destined to die; and the dead to be brought to life again; and the living to be judged, to know, to make known, and to be made conscious that He is God, He the Maker, He the Creator, He the Discerner, He the Judge, He the Witness, He the Complainant; He it is that will in the Hereafter judge, blessed be He, with

whom there is no unrighteousness, nor forgetfulness, nor
respecter of persons, nor taking of bribes ... you will in
the Hereafter have to give account and reckoning before
the supreme King of kings, the Holy One, blessed be He
(Aboth. 4:29).[268]

Cohen says:

In many other passages the terms used are 'righteous' and
'wicked' without restriction of creed or nationality.

He then quotes the Talmud again:

... Lord of the Universe! rightly hast Thou judged, rightly
hast Thou acquitted, rightly hast Thou condemned, rightly
hast Thou instituted Gehinnom for the wicked and Gan
Eden for the righteous (Erub. 19a).[269]

To further clarify the difference between the "righteous" and the
"wicked," Cohen quotes another passage from the Talmud:

... If a person is meritorious and righteous, he takes his
share and that of his fellow in Gan Eden; and if he incurred
guilt and is wicked, he takes his share and that of his fellow
in Gehinnom. (Chag. 15a)
In preparation for the day of judgment a record is kept of
all that the human being does while on earth. 'All your
deeds are written in a book (Aboth. 2. 1)
What does the text mean, 'When iniquity at my heels
compasseth me about' (Psalm 49:5)? The iniquities which
a man treads down with his heels [meaning to disregard
as of no importance] in this world will compass him about
in The Day of Judgment (A.Z. 18a, emphasis added).[270]

Using this logic of the Talmud, the question must be asked, is
there any human who faces the Day of Judgment with a perfect
record of goodness in his life? Do the good deeds recorded in his

book cancel out the bad deeds? If no one has a 100 percent mark on the Day of Judgment, what is the pass mark to qualify for Gan Eden? Isaiah has the answer to that question:

> But we are *ALL* as an unclean thing, and *ALL* our righteousness is as filthy rags; and we *ALL* do fade as a leaf, and *OUR* iniquities, like the wind, have taken *US* away. (Isa. 64:6 KJV, emphasis added)

Isaiah is quite clear. Eating of a fruit was such a minor misdemeanor on the part of the primal couple. Its major significance was its disobedience to Elohim. So it is with any tiny sin in the life—it is disobedience to Elohim. It is obvious to the honest in heart that the most pious person has at some time or other in his or her life slighted God by a sin of commission or omission. No one stands at the judgment bar of God with a 100 percent pure and clean record. So no one qualifies for Gan Eden. We can get into paradise only by getting our passport stamped by a messianic 100 percent pass mark. The Talmud has the identity of that divine stamp necessary to qualify for Gan Eden. Many questions asked in the Judgment are posed by the rabbinic sages, but the most important one has to be, *"did you hope for the salvation of the Messiah?"* (See Shab. 31a.)[271]

The dictum of the school of Shammai will not suffice during the Day of Judgment. "Perfectly righteous" people do not exist. "Average" people do not exist as a category. We are *all* as filthy rags. The only categories in the judgment will be *"The Redeemed"* and the *"Unredeemed."* What need is there for a Redeemer if the rabbis believed that the three categories of people named by them is the standard of judgment? Why call God Rachmana?

The rabbinic sages had almost overlooked the messianic atonement for sin and guilt, which is written in everyone's record who gets into Gan Eden. The stamp necessary to pass the Judgment is *"REDEEMED."*

The events in the Judgment are the same as on the Day of Atonement: Law, mercy, and messianic blood must comingle in the presence of the Shechinah in the Most Holy Place of the heavenly temple on behalf of those directed to Gan Eden. That is messianic Redemption.

The Abrahamic covenant, proclamation of messianic redemption to the Gentiles, will be fulfilled by Israel. Reformation is needed to make that happen. The redemptive Messiah will be uplifted in Jerusalem. Entrance through the gates of Gan Eden will be by redemption and not by the measurement of personal good deeds. Degrees of 'goodness' and 'badness' simply place people on the bell-curve, but are not the standard in the Judgment. The only pass mark is messianic redemption, *"the salvation of the Messiah."*

The fate of the wicked in Gehinnom occupied much of the rabbinic sages' time. Eternal damnation is just that—eternal. Our merciful God will not permit everlasting hellfire. As soon as the body is burned, the candidate will turn to ash, and there is no existence or further suffering in ash. Such an idea is a cruel excess in a human-devised vengeance. Hellfire is everlasting only in that there is no recovery.

The reward of the "Redeemed" in Gan Eden will be eternal *devekut*. The experience of God's love will be our enjoyment throughout eternity. He will dwell with us forever. That is what messianic Redemption does for humanity. God created us, God redeemed us, and now we are glorified in His presence. We are perfect and we are immortal. Great is Jehovah the Lord. Mighty is His redemptive power!

I now pay attention to Joseph Klausner's discussion of the messianic idea. He prefaces it in a very exciting way:

> What could be more Hebraically original than the Messianic idea, which absorbed into itself the most *splendid national-humanitarian ideals of Israel!* And what is more closely linked with the land of Israel than this idea, in which even Hugo Gressmann detected "the odour of the soil of Palestine?" Indeed, in the Tannaitic period the Messianic idea had not yet become *solely imaginative and spiritualized.* It still had a definite *political side* along with its exalted *spiritual side;* and the exuberant Oriental imagination had not yet made it merely a religious delusion embroidered with a spate of colours. It still remains in this period an exalted outlook upon *its own future and the*

> *future of the human race* – the outlook of a people closely
> linked with its own land and looking forward to both
> political and spiritual rulership – an outlook still retaining
> the remnant of a nation's strength and the remnant of the
> freshness of its soil. This is the great and unchanging value
> of the Tannaitic Messianic views for the Jews who look
> forward to redemption.
> Dated April 24, 1953[272]

In this preface Klausner emphasizes the Abrahamic covenant,
which invokes the "blessedness of all nations." He phrases this as
"the splendid national-humanitarian ideals of Israel." He decries any
post-Tannaitic change to a "solely imaginative and spiritualized"
quality, further described as "merely a religious delusion embroidered
with a spate of colours." No doubt he had in mind what has become
the messianic idea in the hands of the Kabbalists, Hasids, and the
Reform Jews. And then he recedes into the tanakian blueprint when
he courageously states that the Tannaitic belief was a future for
both Israel and the human race who look forward to a Messiah who
will bring both "political and spiritual rulership." I enthusiastically
endorse Klausner if in this he sees the catastrophic apocalyptic
ushering in of the messianic world to come. But he unfortunately
does not, as he does not endorse the catastrophic apocalyptic future.

Klausner closes the period of the Tannaim dated with the
redaction of the Mishnah, about 200 AD. He states that the period
of the Amoraim and Geonim followed. He describes a boundary
between the Tanna and the Amora that was fixed and unchanging.
This appears to be a boundary of authority. No Amora could disagree
with a Tanna unless he had the support of another Tanna. An Amora
could not disagree with the Mishnah.[273]

In a discussion of the Messiah, Klausner is dogmatic in defending
the Tannaim:

> It is obvious, therefore, that in describing the Messianic
> idea we must distinguish between the Messianic sayings
> of the Tannaim and those of the Amoraim; for the Tannaim
> are earlier, *more original,* and rightly regarded as greater

authorities. This is the case also, of course, from the purely historical point of view; for if we put before ourselves the Tannaitic period and observe the course of Jewish history during that period, we see immediately that the historical events of that period *must* have influenced, *and in fact did influence in a very special way,* the nature and form of the Messianic idea of the Jewish people.[274]

Klausner goes on to emphasize further the idea in the Tanak that the Messiah is a very powerful person who will accomplish cosmic tasks. He is not to be spiritualized into a mystical sensation, as the Kaballists and Hasidim treat him:

… two different conceptions were [are] inseparably woven together: *politico-national salvation* and *religio-spiritual redemption.* These two elements must walk arm in arm. The Messiah must be both *king* and *redeemer.* He must overthrow the enemies of Israel, establish the kingdom of Israel, and rebuild the Temple; and at the same time he must reform the world through the Kingdom of God, root out idolatry from the world, proclaim the one and only God to all, put an end to sin, and be wise, pious, and just as no man has been before him or ever would be after him … This idea of the twofold nature of the Messiah was current in the best Pharisaic circles, led by the Tannaim, even before the destruction of the Second Temple.[275]

It warms my heart that here are the messianic redemptive events taking place that are necessary to achieve the messianic kingdom depicted as "arm in arm" by Klausner. I am ecstatic that he sees the temple being rebuilt. But he is not being realistic. In 1948 Israel achieved political independence. Israel has overthrown all the enemies who have invaded since. With its reestablishment as a nation, Israel has all the power to rebuild the temple. With modern engineering, the illegal Muslim structure on the temple mount can be moved to another location. Zerubbabel and others rebuilt the temple in weaker times, so it is not beyond the purview of modern Israel, the mightiest of the smaller nations in the world today. So part of the Messiah's work listed above is already done or achievable without Him. *Rooting out idolatry and putting an end to sin* in the world are gargantuan tasks, which I would say without fear of contradiction are beyond the power of any Messiah born only as an ordinary human being. To look for such a person, we are whistling in the wind. God said He Himself would redeem, and *He will, by His messianic functionality.* Messiah must come as deity penetrating humanity. Gershom Scholem saw an *acute Messianism,* which is catastrophic and apocalyptic and will bring an end to history, invoke the resurrection, and usher in the messianic world to come in an earth made new. (See Isaiah 66:22.) Perfection and immortality will be restored, and King Messiah will reign forever and ever. All the prophets predicted this tanakian scenario. As Franz Rosenzweig envisioned it, it must be cosmic:

> Thus the soul must pray for the coming of the kingdom. God once descended and founded His kingdom. The soul prays for the future repetition of this miracle, for the completion of the once-founded structure, and nothing more. ***The soul cries out: Oh that you would part the heavens and descend.***[276]

It is quite apparent that Rosenzweig is looking up into the heavens and longing for a divine Messiah to descend. In this context, Klausner must be obliged to answer the question, what is the ultimate goal of the Redeemer? Klausner will admit that whatever Messiah does will lead to the world to come—that is, Gan Eden regained. But in the interim he wants a gifted but mere human Messiah to give Israel political rulership of the world in the status quo. He does not see this as the work of the Abrahamic covenant, which we have agreed is to bring blessedness to the nations by propagation of the messianic Redemption. Rather, he sees it as a correction of all the evils in the world by this gifted but human-only Messiah. He is unable to transit this gifted but purely human Messiah into the perfect and immortal world to come in his planning. Klausner states,

One of the most difficult problems in connexion with the Jewish Messianic idea is this: In what manner and to what extent can we distinguish the Messianic Age from the World to Come in its broader sense?[277]

Klausner desperately grapples with implementing a judgment and a resurrection in this period of Israel's political/national domination of the world, which he places in his Messianic Age.[278] He comes to a sort of conclusion with which we sense that he is still not comfortable:

> Jewish eschatology, to be sure, has its beginning in the prophecies of the first Isaiah ... For the Messianic idea is primarily the hope for the fulfilment of the political expectations of the Jewish people; and these expectations remained by nature more or less mundane. Yet, because of afflictions and persecutions, there was to come a time when the Jews perforce would dream of a *"kingdom of heaven"* and *"a kingdom not of this world."*[279]

To be fair to Klausner, he was assessing the messianic hope in a historical setting, but nonetheless he was stating what he felt was the true thrust of the redemptive process. *His "final" assessment of the redemption as a kingdom of heaven, a kingdom not of this world is enormous!* Was this the Messiah that he really was looking at? This is what redemption of the Tanak is about—the restoration of perfection and immortality of humanity in the mighty God Elohim's bosom in pure devekut, made possible by His own redemptive power and sacrifice. Symbolic of this was the blood splashed on the ark of the covenant and mercy seat in the presence of the Shechinah in the Most Holy Place. And as that blood dripped down on the temple mount, the very spot where Abraham had sacrificed Isaac, there was cosmic silence in the multiverse. God was in His holy temple with His head bowed in that cosmic silence. He was watching the messianic blood, *His very own divine-human blood,* dripping down from its splash on the ark of the covenant and mercy seat in the heavenly temple Most Holy Place. Indeed, *it was dripping down through cosmic space onto the temple mount*, Mount Moriah, where Abraham offered Isaac. That blood was the stamp of redemption. He was weeping tears of joy at the success of the redemption of His most precious prize in the entire multiverse—humanity. We must stand in awe:

> For Thou, Lord, hast made me glad through Thy work;
> I will triumph in the work of Thy hands.
> O Lord, how great are Thy works!
> And Thy thoughts are very deep. (Ps. 92:4–5 KJV)

> You have gladdened me by Your deeds, O Lord;
> I shout for joy at Your handiwork.
> How great are Your works, O Lord,
> How very subtle Your designs. (Ps. 92:4–5)

David exulted in that blood dripping down from the Most Holy Place of the heavenly temple through cosmic space upon a sinful earth in redemption. But Klausner's ideas of the Messiah are concussed. He is also tied to *redemption by human piety in a world of the status quo.* He has no mechanics to present of the redemptive act. He assumes that the gifted merely human Messiah can accomplish miracles in a political/national setting on an earth in status quo. He denies the apocalyptic of Isaiah and Daniel by not dealing with it, except to admit that a "Jewish eschatology" exists. He then resorts to the mysterious realization that there is "a kingdom not of this world," an idea he had discarded previously by defining a purely human Messiah in the status quo.[280] As the Amoraim declared, this "kingdom not of this world" was anathema. It did not suit their aspirations. They did not embrace an atonement. They wanted an aggrandizement of the nation of Israel in the status quo, in the absence of perfection and immortality, which contrarily to their thinking, will exist in the new earth of Isaiah.

And now I turn to Gershom Scholem. He is the most tanakian in his concept of the Messiah. In his excellent essay *The Crisis of Tradition in Jewish Messianism,* he makes Isaiah 2:3 pivotal in his definition of Torah. In this chapter Isaiah is describing the apocalyptic end time. Isaiah 2:3 states, "From Zion goes forth the Torah and the word of the Lord from Jerusalem." Scholem interprets this verse as referring to messianic Torah. He qualifies it as follows:

> It is simply Torah, not old Torah and not new Torah. It is *untouched* Torah, which has not known any crisis and which in the prophetic vision is seen in its full development. Related to this is the notion, widely found in Rabbinic literature, that the Torah of the Messianic Age will solve the contradictions and difficulties which now exist in regard to several points. On this issue the sources of Jewish tradition are nearly all clear. There is progress in the understanding of the Torah which in the Messianic Age reaches its height. But the idea of a radical change or a questioning of the traditional element was eliminated and was not even perceived as a real possibility.[281]

Scholem quotes from W. D. Davies's *Torah in the Messianic Age:*

> Since the Days of Messiah represent the religious and political consummation of the national history and, however idealized, still belong to the world in which we live, it is only natural that in the Messianic Age the Torah not only retain its validity but be better understood and better fulfilled than ever before.[282]

So, Scholem strongly links Messiah to the tanakian blueprint. The dream, the beauty, and the completeness of the messianic description is found in the Tanak, as I have shown in this book. More than any other modern Jewish writer, to my knowledge, Scholem takes great pains to decipher the messianic revelation in the Tanak.

It must be acknowledged that there is a kind of unintentional fudging or mixing of the various portrayals of messianic functions and their chronology by the writers of the Tanak. Overawed and overwhelmed, they let separate "suffering" and "majestic" events of messianic actions run together. Max Weber, in his book *Ancient Judaism*, writes eloquently about this "fudging" of the events of the

Day of the Lord by all the pre-exilic and post-exilic prophets. (See pp. 297–335.)

Thus the prophets were not clearly comprehended by the general Jewish rabbinic readership of the Tanak. Perhaps the tanakian writers expected everything messianic to be accomplished in one swoop, when the Messiah appeared.

Two roles for Messiah are prominent in the Tanak, and Scholem perceives them. The Ha-Mashiach is depicted both as a "Suffering Redeemer" and as "a Glorious Conquering King." These separate inexorable acts by Messiah have been planned by Elohim from eternity, are basic to the Judaism of Abel and Moses, and are supported by parts of the Talmud. They also perfectly fit into Scholem's scheme of *acute Messianism.* Scholem has a preamble to his acute Messianism:

> Revelation in Judaism is considered *the voice, which resounds from Sinai throughout the world,* a voice which, although it can be heard, is not immediately meaningful ...

> In juxtaposition to all of this in the history of Judaism stands *Messianism in its manifold facets.* It expresses the intrusion of a new dimension of the present – redemption – into history which enters into a problematic relation with tradition. The Messianic idea required a long period of time until it could emerge in post-biblical Jewish literature as the product of very diverse impulses, which, in the Hebrew Bible still exist side by side without connection or unity. Only after the Bible did such varying conceptions as that of an ideal state of the world, of a catastrophic collapse of history, of the restoration of the Davidic Kingdom, and of the "Suffering Servant" [of Isaiah] merge with the prophetic view of the "Day of the Lord" and "A Last Judgment." ...

> *Two elements* are combined in the Messianic idea and they determine the historical configurations, which Messianism has assumed in Judaism. These two elements are the *restorative* and the *utopian.*[283]

This "merging" of the two elements by the prophets was always there but not clearly perceived. Scholem clearly sees it and highlights the two messianic roles as "The Suffering Servant" and "The Davidic King." He sees them as temporal roles of Ha-Mashiach. The *restorative* redemptive act of the suffering Servant must of necessity come before the superbly triumphant catastrophic apocalyptic arrival of the Davidic King to usher in the *Utopian* era. Clearly and thunderously, Scholem is endorsing the tanakian redemptive work of the Ha-Mashiach functionality of Elohim, which must come before His triumphant entry as the eternal Davidic King. Messianic atonement must occur between the two.

It is very useful to outline Scholem's factors of Acute Messianism:

1. The Conservative Factor—Here he names the Jewish body of Halakah, which came into prominence after the second temple destruction. The Mishnah, redacted by Rabbi Judah the Prince, was combined with the Bavli and Yerushalmi Gemara, which had developed and followed, eventually forming the Talmud. These took shape as a 'conversation among the Jews.' This document, as previously described was in contradistinction to the Tanak, which was Israel's conversation with God.

Scholem sees the Body of Halakah as a cleansing agent, a necessary factor, which indeed it is, if one is describing a healthy life style and sanctification of the person, but not redemption. He describes tension between Halakah and Messianism:

> The opposition between restorative and purely utopian,
> radical elements in the conception of the Messianic Torah
> brings an element of uncertainty into the Halachah's attitude
> to Messianism. The battle lines are by no means clearly drawn.
> Unfortunately, a penetrating and serious study of this
> relationship of the medieval Halachah to Messianism is
> one of the most important yet unfulfilled desiderata of
> the scientific study of Judaism …
> As long as Messianism appears as an abstract hope, as an
> element totally deferred to the future which had no living
> significance to the life of the Jew in the present, the

> opposition between the essentially conservative rabbinic and never completely defined Messianic authority, which was to be established from entirely new dimensions of the utopian, could remain without real tension; indeed, there could be attempts to create a certain harmony between such authorities.
>
> But whenever there was an actual eruption of such [messianic] hope … the tension, which exists between these two forms of religious authority immediately became noticeable.[284]

I strongly suspect that besides seeing tension between the two, Scholem sees Messianism as superior to Halakah.

There is no doubt that Utopia achieved by Messiah is superior to Halakah in the status quo, which the Jew strives after but does not perfectly perform. Halakah does not inaugurate the eternal kingdom of Messiah ben David.

Gershom Scholem names the Edenic Tree of Life as messianic. His "restorative" and "utopian" roles of Messiah comprise pure tanakian theology. Nowhere does the Tanak teach that a redemptive Messiah has been superceded by Halakah. Scholem freely admits that humanity is unable since the great disobedience to keep Halakah perfectly (a fallen and sinful state). Messiah is therefore an absolute necessity to provide redemption from sin. All humanity is weak in Halakah, and since the law requires perfect obedience, Halakah does not redeem. The messianic Redeemer is needed.

2. The Restorative Factor—Here we see the role of the "Suffering Servant" as outlined by Scholem. Scholem is in agreement with Rabbi Judah the Prince in seeing the messianic role in Isaiah's chapters 52 and 53. It must be noted that this restorative factor is implicit with and happens after the Immanuel phenomenon, where "The Mighty God planning Grace" is born on the planet as predicted by Isaiah. Modern scholar Thomas Cahill extolls the messianic utterances of the prophets, especially Isaiah's preamble to the suffering Servant. (See *The Gifts of the Jews*, by Thomas Cahill, pp. 218–221.) Here is outlined the messianic atonement:

> For He was cut off from the Land of the living,
> Through the sin of My people, who deserved the punishment.
> And His grave was set among the wicked,
> And with the rich in *His death.*
> (Isa. 53:8–9)

But Isaiah does not leave Him dead in the grave:

> My Righteous Servant makes the many righteous
> It is their punishment that He bears;
> Assuredly, I will give Him the many as His portion,
> He shall receive the multitude as His spoil.
> For He exposed Himself to death
> And was numbered among the sinners,
> Whereas *He bore the guilt of many*
> And made intercession for them.
> (Isa. 53:12)

Years before Isaiah described "The Suffering Servant," King David, as a messianic figure, grappled with this redemptive Messiah's condescension to bear his guilt, shame, and death. David fights the death of his own body in Psalms 4 and 6. He finds denouement of his agony in this condescension in Psalm 16, where he names his body parts and pleads for their preservation. We all know that King David died and was buried, and his body turned to dust, but in this triumphant messianic Psalm 16 he proclaims,

> So my heart rejoices, my whole being exults,
> And my body rests secure.
> For you will not abandon me to Sheol,
> Or let your faithful One see the Pit.
> (Ps. 16:9–10)

In the Masoretic text, the Hebrew words "cha-si-yd-kha" must be translated as "Your Holy One," instead of "Faithful One." The messianic intent in this Psalm 16 is very secure. More appropriately, Messiah is the Holy One. The Tanak insists that death must be conquered to regain immortality, and Elohim designates Himself as the Ha-Mashiach to do this. The "Suffering Servant" does indeed taste of death, to vanquish it for humanity's redemption. But He does not stay in Sheol. He must enjoy His "spoil," the booty He has triumphantly captured by dying for them. *In His Messianic power all Israel—indeed all humanity—can leave the pit.* Isaiah is perfectly clear about this; and so is David, who saw his own personal salvific atonement in it.

David understood the condescension of Mashiach and His atonement. He knew this would cost a great deal of suffering. Psalm 22 clearly delineated messianic suffering long before Isaiah wrote about the suffering Messiah. Some rabbinic sages saw this clearly, as will be discussed later in this chapter.

3. The Utopian Factor—Here Scholem clearly sees the success of the restorative or redemptive factor, because he endorses it and describes its fruition in the apocalyptic events. He recognizes the catastrophic end of history. He calls this Utopian because he sees the old sinful order totally wiped away. He sees a new perfect world and immortality ushered in by Messiah. Scholem labels all forms of Ha-Mashiach denial as "anarchic" and describes their methods as *denial, dilution, and liquidation* of the Messiah of the Tanak. He names Kabbalah, Hasidism, and The European enlightenment as deniers of the Messiah of the Tanak. Speaking as a Jew, he says:

> The Nineteenth Century and nineteenth century Judaism, have bequeathed to the modern mind a complex of ideas about Messianism that have led to **distortions and counterfeits** from which it is by no means easy to free ourselves. We have been taught that the Messianic idea is part and parcel of the idea of the progress of the human race in the universe, is achieved by man's unassisted and continuous progress, leading to the ultimate liberation of all goodness and nobility within him. This, in essence, is ... the result of an attempt to adapt the Messianic conceptions of the prophets and of Jewish religious tradition to the ideals of the French Revolution.

Traditionally, however, the Messianic idea in Judaism was not so cheerful; *the coming of the Messiah shakes the foundations of the world.* In the view of the prophets and Aggadists, redemption would only follow upon a revolutionary disturbance, unparalleled disasters in which history would be dislodged and destroyed. The nineteenth century view is blind to this catastrophic aspect. It looks only to progress toward infinite perfection. In probing into the roots of this new conception of the Messianic ideal as man's infinite progress and perfectability, we find surprisingly, that they stem from the Kabbalah ...

History was not a development toward any goal. History would reach its terminus, and the new state that ensued would be the result of a totally *new manifestation of the divine.* In the prophets this stage is called "The Day of the Lord." ... Accordingly, upon the advent of The Day of the Lord, all that man has built up in history will be destroyed.[285]

Ah Scholem! How marvelous and tanakian are your assertions, your assessment of the true status of redemptive Judaism! Your perception of what the Most Holy Place of the temple declares is enormous!

Scholem calls the messianic interference a "totally new manifestation of the divine." Is he admitting the deity of the Messiah? Of course he is, whether he is conscious of doing so or not. *Redemption, like Creation, is an act of Deity.* No merely human being can perform such a powerfully divine act. Scholem believes in the tanakian doctrines of the Judgment, Resurrection, and the new heaven and new earth. He calls to witness the great rabbinic sages of the Talmud:

Classical Jewish tradition is fond of emphasizing the catastrophic strain in redemption. If we look at the tenth chapter of the Sanhedrin, where the Talmudists dicuss the question of redemption at length, we see that to them it was a colossal uprooting, destruction, revolution, disaster, with nothing of development of progress about it. "The Son of David will come only in a generation wholly guilty or wholly innocent" – a condition beyond the realm of human possibility ... *Liberation of Israel is the essence, but it will march in step with the liberation of the whole world.*[286]

Scholem did not see Israel enjoying the Messiah as their sole aggrandized earthly king. He saw the Messiah as a universal savior. Scholem clearly perceived that Halakah (the law) could not be kept perfectly throughout a human lifetime. He saw that repentance, confession, and messianic absolution were essential elements of a heavenly redemption and applies to all humanity. This is humanity's "daily bread and tears." Scholem desperately embraced the restorative redemptive expiation as a prerequisite to the apocalyptic ushering in of his utopia, a perfect new earth where sin was totally eradicated and history was totally destroyed. I salute him as a giant in Israel for his magnification of the Tanakin Messiah. He no doubt saw that repentance was absolutely essential. He saw that expiation was indeed necessary. Messianic blood must be splashed on the ark of the covenant containing the law, and on the mercy seat in the presence of the Shechinah. In recognizing that the Messiah's blood splashed in the Most Holy Place, performing expiation, he found the essence of primitive redemptive Judaism. Mercy triumphs over justice. The Judaism beamed by Moses from Sinai is indeed a gloriously satisfying and saving religion. What a triumphant and stupendous religion the Jews have to offer the world! It thrills me beyond measure. Rejoice! Our God is King Messiah ben David, penetrating humanity with His divinity to redeem us. The Lord our God is one; blessed be He.

Now we will consider Peter Schafer's research in the Talmud, which elucidates the birth and sufferings of the Messiah. Many rabbinic sages and Jewish scholars deny that Messiah will be born on the planet as a penetration of humanity by divinity. There is in modern Rabbinic Judaism a denial of the substitutive suffering by the Messiah for the sins of the world. But these important ideas of messianic deity, birth, and suffering are well supported by some sages of the Talmud, and seen in some second- to fourth century AD tannaim and later amoraim discussions.

There is a strong tendency in modern Rabbinic Judaism to attribute salvation to the "merit of the Fathers," thus diminishing "messianic merit" in redemption. Relying on the "merit of the Fathers" is similar in principle to relying on the Messiah, that is, there is a personal reliance on something outside one's self. But it must be considered a substitution of relying on the Messiah. It is no different to "fruits and vegetables" and "benevolent acts." These are all abominations. Rabbinic Judaism is strongly resistant to the "Atonement by the Blood" that occurs in the Most Holy Place Day of Atonement ritual. Instead the law and Halakah are emphasized as the salvific elements. The "merit of the Fathers" is not what God ordained as His redemptive act in His eternity.

The Birth of Messiah in the Talmud

Schafer cites the Palestinian (Yerushalmi) Talmud's tractate *Berakhot (Blessings or Benedictions)*. The Messiah in this case is named *Menahem,* meaning "comforter," (see Lamentations 1:16) by *Rabbi Yudan* in the name of Rabbi Aibo. (See y Ber 2:4/12; parallel in EkhaR 1:16 S 51 ed. Buber, p. 89f.) The Messiah Menahem's mother is very prominent in the story. Hezekiah is named as the father. The birth occurs in Bethlehem, and Micah 5:1 is cited. This gives the Berakhot a very serious tanakian quality, lifting it above humour, which some scholars see in it. The story of the birth is very involved and has several very unusual details, some of which are humorous. The mystery in the story is that the baby Messiah is snatched up by a whirlwind and disappears. The proximity of the birth to its causative destruction of the second temple is emphasized. But this Messiah Menahem, despite having disappeared as a baby, apparently rebuilds the temple.

Menahem, as son of Hezekiah, is also mentioned in the Bavli (b Sanh 98b). The reason for naming Hezekiah as the Messiah Menahem's father is unclear and somewhat confusing. King Hezekiah had a son named Manasseh, whom many consider the worst king in Israel's history and who is held responsible for the destruction by Babylon of the first temple. (See 2 Kings 24:3).

Other Menahems are mentioned in the Talmud.

Schafer cites an account by Josephus of the Jewish Revolt of 66–73 AD, where a certain Menahem, described as son of Judas, son of Hezekiah, was prominent in the Masada story but was killed by the Zealots when he entered the temple in "royal attire." (See Anna Maria Schwermer's *Elija als Araber*, pp. 118, 132.) The connection of these other Menahems with the birth of the Messiah Menahem in Bethlehem is unclear. Schafer cites mention of the warrior mother of the Davidic Messiah in the seventh-century Sefer Zerubbabel (Apocalypse of Zerubbabel) who is named Hephzibah and who was prominent in the "last war between the Jews and Armilos."

This Yerushalmi Berakhot does not have clear edges despite its being extraordinarily messianic in its description. What I feel is most significant in this Berakhot is that it *recognizes a birth of the Messiah, born of a woman, in Bethlehem,* the royal city. Modern Rabbinic Judaism does not endorse a messianic birth, despite this Berakhot. Schafer evaluates this somewhat "garbled" story put together by Rabbi Yudan, and concludes that Rabbi Yudan has attempted to discredit Christianity's messianic belief. (See *The Jewish Jesus*, by Peter Schafer, pp. 268–271). Schafer infers that this story is perhaps presented as a parody of the birth of Yeshua, son of Mary, to nullify any authenticity the birth of Yeshua might possess. This conclusion may or may not be correct. Rabbi Yudan's motives are not explained by him and there is a very serious subject being considered here. Rabbi Yudan's motives must be presumed honorable.

Nonetheless, that Messiah exists pre-Creation in eternity is firmly Talmudic with some rabbis. To get Him to earth as a redeemer, a birth mechanism is defined. It is clear that *the birth of the Messiah is ingrained in primitive Judaism* long before Christianity became a 'separate' religion. David, Isaiah, and Micah strongly attest to it. Some sages and modern rabbis may be blind to Judaism's committal to messianic birth, if indeed this Berakhot is being presented as a parody. In the next section it will be shown that the Talmud envisioned the Messiah to be in the Guf beneath God's throne, *waiting to be born* on the planet. Being in the Guf means "waiting to be born" in talmudic literature. The existence of a Guf is not a tanakian doctrine. But messianic birth certainly is.

The Suffering Messiah in the Talmud

I would like to point out again that Rabbi Judah the Prince, redactor of the Mishnah, recognized messianic suffering in the expiation in Isaiah 53 (b Sanh 98b).

Messianic suffering is carefully researched by modern scholars Peter Schafer and Daniel Boyarin. Schafer shows two talmudic messianic traditions:

1. The original Messiah from the tribe of Judah, the Messiah ben David. He is a kingly Messsiah.
2. The later supplemental from the tribe of Joseph, the suffering Messiah ben Joseph / Ephraim (*Targum Pseudo-Jonathan; Bavli – b Suk 52a*; see also BerR 75:6, MidrTeh 60:3, cf. MidrTeh 87:6; see also Apocalypse of Zerubbabel).

This appears to be a deduction from Jer. 31:9. (See David C. Mitchell's book *Messiah ben Joseph: A Sacrifice of Atonement for Israel*, RRJ 10, 2007, pp. 77–94.)

In addition there is named in the Midrash Pesiqta Rabbati a Messiah Ephraim without the "ben" (see below). It is reasonable to conclude that the two are one and the same. This Midrash has been dated to the sixth or seventh century AD.

In the Bavli reference above, the story is told by *Rabbi Dosa*, a fourth-generation tanna of the second century AD. The Messiah ben Joseph / Ephraim preceeds Messiah ben David and will be killed in battle (see *Targum Tosefta* on Zech. 12:10; Rimon Kasher, *Targumic Tosefot to the Prophets*, Jerusalem) against Gog and Magog (see Targum Cant. 4:5, 7:4). Zechariah 12:10 is used as evidence: "And they will look at the one whom they have pierced, they shall mourn for him, as one mourns for an only child" (NRSV). The Rabbis state that *in the celestial scene,* when Messiah ben David sees that Messiah ben Joseph / Ephraim has been killed, He asks God to spare Him that fate, and God grants His request. So, in this rabbinic tradition, Messiah ben David does not suffer or die.

387

The Jewish Study Bible translates Zechariah 12:10 differently, leaving out the piercing. In any case, Zechariah chapter 12 in *The Jewish Study Bible* is presumed to be about the Messiah ben David and does not mention Messiah ben Joseph / Ephraim.

The Rabbi Dosa tradition cited above is not consistent with Psalm 22 and Isaiah 53, where the Messiah ben David suffers and dies. Neither King David nor Isaiah spoke of Messiah ben Joseph / Ephraim. Although Joseph was his favorite son, Jacob had determined that Judah, not Joseph, was the God-ordained royal line from which the root/stem/branch of Jesse gives rise to the Messiah ben David.

Schafer points out that in the "second" tradition, a "Messiah Ephraim" (without the "ben") is found in the *Midrash Pesiqta Rabbati*, homilies 34, 36, and 37. It must be concluded they are one and the same. Schafer uses the writings of several Jewish scholars in the discussion, prominently Arnold Goldberg's *Erlosung durch Leiden, on* PesR 34, 36, and 37, Rivka Ulmer's *Pesiqta Rabbati: A Synoptic Edition of Pesiqta Rabbati*, William G. Braude's *Pesiqta Rabbati: Discourses*, and some others. These writers are highly respected scholars.

Schafer is at his best in this revealing discussion. I will try to summarize his masterful lengthy research. I will compare *The Jewish Study Bible* comments on the texts used in the Pesiqta Rabbati alongside:

Pisqa 34: Central to this homily are several Biblical texts:

1. Zechariah 9:9: Rejoice greatly, O daughter of Zion! Shout aloud, O daughter of Jerusalem! Lo, your king comes to you; triumphant and victorious is he, humble and riding on a donkey, on a colt, the foal of a donkey. (*The Jewish Study Bible* margin emphasizes the messianic nature of this verse.)
2. Jeremiah 31:9: For I am ever a Father to Israel. Ephraim is My first-born. (*The Jewish Study Bible* makes no marginal comment on this verse. I suspect Jeremiah is magnifying Ephraim in a first-born-grandson relationship. Reuben was Jacob's firstborn son from Leah, and Joseph was his firstborn son from Rachel, whom he loved more than Leah. Jeremiah does not actually define Ephraim as a Messiah.)

3. Zephaniah 3:8: Therefore wait for me, says the Lord, for the day when I arise as a witness. (*The Jewish Study Bible* margin makes no specific comment on this verse.)

4. Isaiah 57:15: (I am) with the one who is of a contrite spirit. (*The Jewish Study Bible* makes a highly significant marginal messianic comment here. Messianic condescension is summarized as "the highest of all beings desiring to dwell among the lowest, the Lord voluntarily accepting human roles out of love for the people." Cf. Isaiah 52:6; 58:9; 65:1.).

The homily describes *Torah keeping* as very important but emphatically ranks it secondary to *messianic redemption*. (See Rivka Ulmer PesR 34, S 6; Braude PesR., pp. 665f; and Goldberg pp. 71f.) Peter Schafer points out that this is a bold statement and deviates from the accepted standards and conventions of Rabbinic Judaism, which extol law-keeping as salvific, and use the messianic idea mainly for political aggrandizement. The homily criticizes the neglect of the messianic expectation. Since Messiah is to come as a human, herein is also a definite condescension of deity into humanity, unusual for Rabbinic Judaism.

Pisqa 36: Again several Biblical texts are central to the discussion:

1. Isaiah 60:1: Arise, shine; for your light has come, and the glory of your Lord has risen upon you. (*The Jewish Study Bible* sees a magnificent messianic meaning in this sixtieth chapter, which may be summed up in the marginal comment. Deutero-Isaiah is noted to borrow royal vocabulary from texts that are concerned with the Davidic dynasty [Isaiah 11 and Psalm 72]. Strangely however, the commentator decides to ignore the presence of messianic definition here because the words City of the Lord, Zion of the Holy One of Israel [verse 14] are used. He insists that it is talking about the Israelite nation as a whole and not about a Messiah. But it is reassuring that he states that God will rule the nation directly in the future, and the whole nation will enjoy royal status. It should be remembered that this section of Isaiah is talking

about the eternal kingdom of Messiah ben David in an earth made new, where all flesh come before Him to worship. The implication that Israel qualifies for messianic status in Isaiah's new earth is farfetched.)

2. Psalm 36:10: For with you is the fountain of life, in your light we see light. This light is referred to in Genesis 1:4 as the light of the Messiah hidden beneath God's "Throne of Glory"(cf."Guf") to be released at the appointed time. (*The Jewish Study Bible* margin comments for Ps. 36:10 are highly messianic.)

3. Jeremiah 31:9: For I am ever a father to Israel. Ephraim is my first-born. This text is pivotal again, from which is deduced that Ephraim is the Messiah. See comments above in Pisqa 34 on this text.

4. Jeremiah 31:18: Indeed I heard Ephraim pleading: You disciplined me and I took the discipline. I was like a calf untamed. (*The Jewish Study Bible* margin comment on this verse sees no messianic meaning for Ephraim. Instead it states that Ephraim refers to the northern kingdom, which did indeed behave as a calf untamed.)

5. Psalm 22:16: My strength is dried up like a potsherd, my tongue sticks to my palate. (*The Jewish Study Bible* sees in this Psalm the terrible state of suffering of the Jews in the diaspora. It makes no reference here to messianic suffering as the Pisqa 36 strongly asserts [see discussion below]).

This Pisqa also addresses the tension between *Torah obedience* in Rabbinic Judaism and *messianic Redemption*. The author of the Pisqa invokes Genesis 1:4, indicating that Messiah and "the human race waiting to be created" were hidden away beneath the "Throne of Glory" in heaven (cf. "Guf"). (See Ulmer, PesR 34, S 7; Braude, PesR, p. 677; Goldberg, *Erlosung durch Leiden, p. 73*.) The implication of hiding the Messiah with "uncreated humanity" underneath the "Throne of Glory" is considered of massive significance, as shown by the development of the Pisqa in *a celestial scene*. Here an altercation between God, Messiah, and the angelic host occurs, with some very incomprehensible drastic consequences. After first interpreting Isaiah

60:1 as Torah obedience leading to salvation (which is Rabbinic Judaism's doctrinal exegesis), the homily strongly asserts that the light of messianic Redemption waits beneath God's throne for the appointed time to be unleashed, a time determined by God, and ultimately independent of Israel's Torah obedience. The foreseen problem was that disobedience to Torah *would be rampant and necessitate messianic atonement.* And it was at this point that the atonement by Messiah would be activated and would incur messianic birth, suffering, and death. The Pisqa thus poses an inexplicable problem for rabbis who deny the substitutive suffering of the Messiah for the expiation of the sins of the world.

In this celestial scene, two important events take place:

1. **God consults the angels about Creation.** A segment of those angels advise Him not to proceed with the creation of humanity because they will sin. Since He has long since in His eternity decided to create humanity even though He knows they will all sin, God goes ahead anyway. God gets extremely upset with this angelic adverse advice, and He casts some angels down into the abyss, and others He burns up! (See Ber8:4f; b Sanh 38b; BerR 1:4.) The classical rabbinic tradition is that the existence of humanity is made possible, despite their impending sinfulness, because from eternity He had planned repentance (teshuah) to be gifted to humans. But here in God's plan in this celestial scene, atonement by the Messiah is the next step.

2. **God consults the Messiah.** What follows is astounding. I have already quoted Arnold Golberg's response to this tannaitic "incident" in the eternity of God. Here it is again:

   In a unique way the Messiah is put (here) into the centre
   of creation; all future life depends on him. (Goldberg's
   Erlosung durch Leiden, p. 186.)

Pisqa 36 gives a revealing account of this most unusual consultation between God and Messiah. This is as follows:

391

> At that time the Holy One, blessed be he, began negotiating
> with him [the Messiah] the terms (*matneh*) and said to him:
> ***Those that are hidden with you [in the Guf], it is their***
> ***sins that will bend you some day under a yoke of iron*** and
> make you like that calf whose eyes grew dim, and they will
> choke your spirit as with a yoke. Because of their sins your
> tongue will stick to your palate. ***ARE YOU WILLING***
> ***TO ENDURE THIS?*** (*Midrash Pesiqta Rabbati* 36 S 4,
> emphasis added)

The Holy One informs the Messiah that he will suffer for seven
years (b Sanh 97a). In this pressure on the Messiah to accept the
suffering, God is threatening that if Messiah is not prepared to do
so, He will revoke His decision to create mankind. Jeremiah 31:18
is used to indicate the acceptance of the messianic suffering, and
Psalm 22 is used to outline the intensity of the suffering. It could
be inferred here that Messiah's "humanity" is defined by His status
of being lumped with the rest of humanity waiting to be born (cf.
"Guf") beneath God's "Throne of Glory." Messianic death is not
mentioned in this Pisqa, but it is in Psalm 22:16: "*You commit me to
the dust of death.*" Despite the suffering Servant of Isaiah 52–53 not
being mentioned in this homily, there is no doubt of the similarity.
One wonders whether Isaiah got his theology from David! I feel that
he did indeed.

There are other aspects in this Pisqa in which Peter Schafer
sees Isaiah 53 clearly as a significant coincidence—in particular the
"Aramaic Testament of Levi":

> ***And He will atone (yekhapper) for all….***
> (Qumran fragment 4Q541)

And in the "Self-Glorification Hymn":

> Who bears all sorrows (tze'arim) like me?
> And who suffers evil like me?
> (Qumran fragment 4Q491c)

392

Schafer shows this in the prerabbinic Qumran fragments: 4Q541, 4Q274-11Q31, 4Q47B, RdQ17/65-68, and 4Q491c, fragment 1. These studies are cited also in other scholars. (See *The Jewish Jesus*, by Peter Schafer, pp. 243–261, 321–322). Schafer is superb in the meticulous depth of his research and culling of the messianic evidence in the Talmud. He notably cites Israel Knohl's *The Messiah Before Jesus: The Suffering Servant of the Dead Sea Scrolls.*[287]

Schafer feels that the Messiah's expiatory suffering in Pisqa 36 transcends the boundaries of traditional Rabbinic Judaism, and indeed it does. Substitutive messianic expiatory suffering cannot be denied. He quotes Goldberg's marvelous words, which exalt and exult in the suffering of Messiah in the Redemption:

> The amplification (*Uberhohung*) of the Messiah's expiatory suffering in PesR 36-37 is unique in the Rabbinic literature. It expresses itself here all the more forcefully as all this is being said with a high degree of authority, as if there couldn't be any doubt about it. It is not the opinion of one teacher that is rendered **but something that happens in heaven,** something that is not qualified by "as if" or "probably." (Goldberg's *Erlosung durch Leiden*, p. 195, emphasis added).

In this Pisqa, the messianic answer to the Holy One who warned Him about the suffering involved in being the Messiah is absolutely stupendous:

> Master of the Universe, with joy in my soul and gladness in my heart I take (this suffering) upon myself so that not one person in Israel shall perish. That not only those who are alive be saved in my days but also all those who are dead, who died from the days of Adam up until now ... Such are the things I desire, and for these I am ready to take upon myself *(Whatever You decree).* (*Pesiqta Rabbati* 36, S 4, emphasis added)

The Messiah accepts *God's decree in the suffering.* Psalm 22 is the major scripture used by the homily to describe the agony of the Messiah in the expiation. One has to ask when and where all this is going to happen. It emphasizes messianic humanity and the omnipotence of divinity to endure the condescension and go through the agony alone. David's Psalm 22 reveals both *messianic humanity and divinity* in the suffering. The similarity to Isaiah 53 is unmistakably striking. It is painfully sad but gloriously triumphant reading:

> My God, my God, why have You forsaken me. O my God, I cry and weep, by day and night and You do not answer ... I am a worm, less than human; scorned by men, despised by people. All who see me mock me, they curl their lips, they shake their heads ... You drew me from the *womb* ... I became Your charge at *birth*; From my mother's *womb* You have been my God. Do not be far from me, for trouble is near, and there is none to help. Many bulls surround me, mighty ones of Bashan encircle me. They open their mouths at me like tearing, roaring lions. My life ebbs away: All my bones are disjointed; my heart is like wax, Melting within me; my vigour dries up like a shard; My tongue cleaves to my palate; *You commit me to the dust of death*. Dogs surround me; a pack of evil ones closes in on me, Like lions [they maul] my hands and feet. I take account of all my bones while they look on and gloat. They divide my clothes among themselves, casting lots for my garments But You, O Lord, be not far off; my strength, hasten to my aid. Save my life from the sword, my precious life from the clutches of a dog. Deliver me from a lion's mouth; from the horns of wild oxen rescue me. (Psalm 22 abbreviated, emphasis added)

David did indeed know his messianic theology as he beheld the substitutive messianic suffering in the expiation. In it he saw the atonement for his sins. Isaiah's suffering Servant matches it. The substitutive messianic suffering is not only symbolic as in the blood splashed on the Day of Atonement, but is real and cast in heaven—an agreement between God and the Messiah, according to this Pisqa. It has a tremendous place in primitive redemptive Judaism, matching the wondrousness of the Day of Atonement's messianic blood being splashed on the ark of the covenant, the mercy seat, and on the Shechinah. Imagine that! God having messianic blood splashed on Himself. He suffers and dies in the messianic functionality! Many ancient and modern Jewish scholars of Rabbinic Judaism would deny the substitutive expiatory messianic suffering. The Midrash *Pesiqta Rabbati* embraces and extols it. It is undeniably primitive redemptive Judaism, the Judaism of Sinai.

Pisqa 37: Again biblical texts are central to this homily:

1. Isaiah 61:10: Rejoicing I will rejoice in the Lord, my soul shall be joyful in my God; for he has clothed me with garments of salvation. He has covered me with the robe of righteousness. (*The Jewish Study Bible* margin comment ascribes this verse quite broadly, with some messianic intent to the prophet, to Zion and to the whole nation of Israel. It is satisfying to note that Israel is covering herself with the garments of salvation, the robe of messianic righteousness. It is not their law-keeping, but a gift from God who has clothed them. And so must all humanity cover themselves with the messianic robe of righteousness. Their "filthy garments" as described by Isaiah will not suffice. This is marvelously a substitutive messianic provision which they have not earned by law-keeping. It is pure *grace* in action: the Mighty God planning Grace [Isa. 9:6].)

2. Micah 7:8: Do not rejoice over me O my enemy! Though I have fallen I rise again; Though I sit in darkness, the Lord is my light. (*The Jewish Study Bible* margin comment does not ascribe any messianic intent to this verse.)

3. Lamentations 4:8b: Their skin is shriveled on their bones, it has become dry as wood. (*The Jewish Study Bible* margin does not indicate any messianic intent here.)

4. Psalm 22 is used again in this homily and recites elements of messianic suffering. (There is a veiled messianic intent here in the margin comments of *The Jewish Study Bible*, but the

Midrash Rabbati use of this psalm to describe substitutive messianic agony is not mentioned. Perhaps the commentators did not know of the existence of this Midrash.)

The merit of the fathers (*zekhut avot*) comes to the fore again in a conversation with the Messiah. The homily declares that the Messiah's merit exceeds their own because he has taken upon Himself the sins of all humanity. The Messiah unleashes all His earthly wretchedness, quoting Psalm 22 to them. The psalm clearly states that he was *committed to the dust of death* (verse 16).

The messianic resurrection is clearly recognizable: *"At this hour the Holy One, blessed be He, will lift the Messiah up to the heavens and will cloak him in something of the splendor of his own glory."* (See PesR 37, S 3; Braude, PesR, 686; Goldberg, *Erlosung durch, Leiden*, p. 269.)

Several conclusions may be drawn from this Midrash Pisqa Rabbati:

1. Messiah exists before the creation of the world. The Holy One consults him about undertaking the redemption and gets his commitment before the final decision to go ahead and create humanity. He is installed as a redeemer before He gets to be a creator, that is, before the creation of the universe.

2. God suffers with the Messiah: Now after the fact God states He suffered with the Messiah: "Ephraim, my Messiah of righteousness, ever since the six days of creation you did take this (ordeal) upon yourself. *Now your pain is like My pain.*" At this hour he will reply: "Master of the universe, now I am reconciled. The servant is content to be like his master" (Manuscript Parma, *editio princeps;* Goldberg; *Erlosung durch Leiden*, p. 152). Schafer notes that God reminds Messiah that he has accepted this unbearable suffering before the creation of the world but He comforts the Messiah with the fact that ultimately *he takes on himself God's own grief.*

3. Messiah comes to earth in human form: Am I not flesh and blood? (Ps. 22:6). From this Pesiqta this appears to have

come about by His being placed in the Guf beneath God's throne of glory. In addition, he will be born on earth by a woman.

4. Messiah comes to earth via a woman's *womb*. (See PesR 37, S 8; Braude, PesR, p. 689; Goldberg *Erlosung durch Leiden*, p. 2740.) This is stressed by David, Isaiah, and Micah.

5. The messianic suffering (and death) is superior as a redemptive agent to "teshuah" or "merit of the fathers" or lawkeeping and is urgently necessitated because of rampant failure in lawkeeping.

6. The messianic suffering provides expiatory redemption. Schafer endorses Arnold Goldberg's *Erlosung durch Leiden* statement (p. 199): "Essentially, the Messiah does not redeem through an open, liberating act but by creating through his suffering, the precondition for this act. *We are dealing with a truly redemptive act by Messiah.*" Schafer concludes that such a statement is unheard of within the taxonomy of Rabbinic Judaism.

7. There is a culmination to the Messiah's suffering and death: At this hour the Holy One, blessed be he, will appoint the Messiah four creatures (cf. Ezekiel 1) who will carry the Messiah's "Throne of Glory" (PesR 36, S 4; Braude, PesR p.679; Goldberg *Erhlosung durch Leiden*, p. 151). Schafer feels that here God has His Messiah take a seat on His own "Throne of Glory." This has implications for messianic resurrection from the death implicit in Psalm 22. I have no problem with this, because Messiah is God's functionality, one and the same substance with God. This is implicit in Psalm 22. I see no problem here. "This concept" of messianic exaltation, Schafer states, "goes far beyond what we can expect from classical Rabbinic Judaism."

8. The *Midrash Pisqa Rabbati* is a unique document in the talmudic writings, contrary to the usual rabbinic doctrine of salvation by lawkeeping. It clearly extols messianic redemption as being superior. Its depiction of messianic substitutive expiatory suffering is convincing. The use of Psalm 22 to describe it is astounding. Isaiah 53 duplicates it, a remarkable feature.

In Summary: The tanakian Messiah is defined as Messiah ben David. The rabbinic sages have accepted Him as a kingly figure. They have invented a competing suffering Messiah with the peculiar name Joseph/Ephraim who will be the atoning one. The idea of an atoning Messiah is contrary to Rabbinic Judaism and to many modern Jewish scholars who see redemption by lawkeeping. The concept of the redemption by the suffering Messiah Joseph/Ephraim's atonement in this talmudic study is stated to be far superior to lawkeeping and the "Merit of the Fathers." In this Midrasch Pesiqta Rabbati, the suffering Messiah is the result of a conference of the Holy One, the Messiah, and the angels in a scene in paradise that determines creation and redemption.

This Messiah comes as a human who is present with the Holy One in eternity but is somehow relegated to the Guf beneath the "Throne of Glory," to await the Holy One's elected time to appear on earth, to be born from a woman's womb. But after the expiatory suffering (and death), he is exalted to the "Throne of Glory." The nomenclature "Messiah Joseph/Ephraim" is a farfetched idea that may be a measure by rabbinic sages to prevent Messiah ben David from suffering and dying in the fulfillment of Psalm 22.

For reasons unknown, these rabbis were averse to Messiah ben David being the suffering Servant, atoning (and dying) for the sins of the world. Some modern Jewish authors and rabbis resist the interpretation of the suffering Servant being Messiah ben David or even this talmudic Messiah Joseph/Ephraim, insisting rather that all Israel is the suffering Servant of Isaiah. The second- and sixth-century rabbinic sages cited in this study push the messianic atonement as the substitutive suffering Messiah of Psalm 22 (and coincidentally Isaiah 53) as the messianic atonement for sin, albeit by the wrongly conjured-up untanakian Messiah Joseph/Ephraim.

Peter Schafer feels that these rabbinic sages were being influenced by Christianity. He is mistaken because messianic expiatory suffering is clearly apparent in the Tanak, before the Christian era commenced. Moses, David, Isaiah, Micah, and without doubt every prophet spoke of the salvation by the Messiah ben David. There is no Messiah Joseph/Ephraim spelled out in the Tanak. Messiah Joseph/Ephraim is a fiction, but if taken as the suffering outlined for Messiah ben David, this is a magnificent redemption, totally congruent with the Tanak. The splashing of the blood of the animal without blemish on the Day of Atonement is implicit with the expiation, the atonement, the suffering and death of the Messiah. It is the raw messianism of Sinai.

In concluding this chapter, there is not a clear and unified Messiah in the Talmud. But many elements are there if the tanakian blueprint is stringently applied. Gershom Scholem, Peter Schafer, and Daniel Boyarin, all painstakingly defined the Messiah according to the Tanak. Daniel Boyarin, a stalwart Jew, has also written about "Gospel Judaism" as being primarily a Jewish idea. He discourages the interpretation of the suffering Servant of Isaiah as the Jewish people as a whole. "The suffering Messiah who atones for our sins was a familiar idea throughout the history of the Jewish religion … The idea of a suffering Messiah is present in ancient, medieval, and early modern Judaism."[288] The tanakian provision of grace by messianic Redemption is definitely the product of primitive redemptive Judaism. Arnold Goldberg, Rivka Ulmer, William G. Braude, and others should also be mentioned as those who envisioned the tanakian suffering Messiah who atones. These authors present ideas quite contrary to modern Rabbinic Judaism but quite consistent with the Tanak.

Remember, *"Every prophet spake for the Days of the Messiah and the penitent."* The Lord our God is one. Blessed be He.

Praying at the Western Wall

CHAPTER 31

The Messiah(s) of Modern Jewry

The previous chapter presents a discussion of the messianic ideas of the Talmud. In the last hundred years, great Jewish scholars like Abraham Cohen, Joseph Klausner, David Castelli, Franz Rosenzweig, Gershom Scholem, and Daniel Boyarin have expressed their ideas and research on the concept of the Mashiach. Current modern sects and subsets of Jews have developed concepts of the Messiah from a mixture of tanakian and Talmudic ideas, and some unique ideas of their own. In this chapter I will give an account of the prevalent current beliefs of these sects and subsets. Most are "doctrinal" expressions of Messiah, and range from the secular to the ultra-Orthodox in the Jewish spectrum.

1. The Messiah of Kabbalah and Hasidism

These are dealt with together because they share some unique characteristics. The mystic element in these two systems makes the Messiah appear quite ethereal and un-tanakian. Gershom Scholem also sees significant common elements. I will take it for granted that the reader knows about the rise, variant theological beliefs, and history of these two movements. I will use Scholem's excellent analysis.

The "neutralization" of tanakian Messianism in Kabbalah and Hasidism presents two related examples of major variance with basic tanakian theology. Scholem's essay "Neutralization of Messianism in Early Hasidism" tells the whole story. The fact that Scholem uses the word "neutralization" indicates the evolution that took place in basic Kabbalah and its Lurianic branch, and in early Hasidism, shaped by Israel Baal Shem. In the writings of both Hasidism and Kabbalah, there is a dedication to *tikkun* (the reestablishment of the harmonious condition of the world) being achieved by devekut (close communion with God). Scholem's opinion is quite clear that errors occurred in Kabbalah, Hasidism, and the Sabbatian heresy regarding their definition and use of the words "tikkun" and "devekut." Scholem also castigates the scholars who wrote that "The Enlightenment" was a messianic fulfillment. He states that it had borrowed its errant messianic idea from Kabbalah:[289]

> What these changes have in common is precisely that element, which concerns us here, namely the elimination of the acute Messianic tension or Messianic reference which it had in the primary [tanakian] sources and its transference onto another plane where *the sting of Messianism has been neutralized.*[290]

I see a great significance in Scholem's reference to "primary sources" and his use of the word "sting" to define Messianism. It is consistent with his belief that the messianic apocalyptic of the Tanak brings catastrophe to the existing order of things on the planet. Lurianic Kabbalists believe that there was a dramatic event when sin entered the world, which they describe as "the scattering of the sparks." But Kabbalism shrinks away from the tanakian catastrophic apocalyptic of messianic intervention, which manifests as a latter-day *"Day of the Lord."*

The first Scholem dictum concerns Lurianic Kabbalah and its "sparks." He describes this erroneous doctrine as follows:

> This non-Messianic meaning of devekut is brought out with utmost clarity by the highly significant qualification which is given to the Lurianic doctrine of "lifting up of the sparks." In its original conception there is no connection between this notion and devekut ... To lift up the scattered sparks of light and to restore them to the place they were intended to occupy had not catastrophe intervened – this is the essential task of man in the process of tikkun. To fulfil this task is the preparation for Messianic Redemption in which each of us plays his part ... The soul of all mankind was originally contained within Adam. Now, its sparks

were scattered throughout the terrestrial universe, and the continued existence of sin has evermore increased their dispersion. They are in exile and must be led home and restored to their primordial spiritual structure, which is at the same time the structure of Adam and the structure of Messiah. Everybody must work at this task ... of collecting the sparks ... from the husks in which they are held captive by the dark power of the "other," or demonic side.[291]

There is no doubt that the Kabbalists in this description deny the tanakian catastrophic apocalyptic appearance of Messiah at the "End of Days." In discussing Lurianic Kabbalah, Scholem spoke quite plainly:

> ... for the Kabbalists have no special need of a personal Messiah.[292]

The second Scholem dictum concerns Hasidism:

> Of course, the Hasidim speak of tikkun too but its meaning has been qualified ... into the strictly personal sphere of man, where tikkun is achieved by devekut ... Luria is primarily interested in ... sparks ... whereas Baal Shem and his followers emphasize the mystic connection between man and his immediate environment ... Only the Zaddik is granted the privilege of meeting the sparks of his own soul.[293]

The Zaddik is he who attains the state of devekut, a charismatic spiritual leader believed to maintain a channel to God. To further understand these two dicta of Scholem, I reference his criticism of a critique by Isaiah Tishby of an essay written by Rivka Shatz on Hasidism. (Isaiah Tishby wrote much on Hasidism, principally the work *Messianic Mysticism: Moses Hayim Luzzatto and the Padua School*. In his criticism of Rivkah Shatz, Tishby denied that there is a weakening of the messianic concept in Hasidism. Scholem took him to task with the following:

Rivka Shatz who quite correctly had underlined this process [in Hasidism] of replacing acute Messianism by a personal and mystical salvation ... he [Tishby] quotes several passages stating that the Zaddik is empowered to bring about the coming of the Messiah, i.e., there is in him a potential to bring on redemption. Tishby goes so far as to argue that "the bringing on of the national redemption is considered here as the principal function of the outstanding Zaddik." The truth of the matter is quite different. The stressing of this potential capacity of the Zaddik is by no means accidental – for he is expressly forbidden to use it. But this decisive point is not even mentioned by Tishby. The Zaddik has the power to annihilate the forces of severity and rigour by getting down to their root and "sweetening" them at their original place ...

But the Rabbi of Lizensk warns the Zaddik that he should not exert himself to annihilate the unclean power altogether, because by this he would cause the immediate coming of the Messiah (No'am Elimelekh, Lvov, 1786, f. 54b). In other words: Messianic exertion is forbidden ... To see in such an idea proof of acute Messianic tension seems strange to me. It is precisely what I call neutralization of the Messianic element ... ***But redemption of the soul WITHOUT redemption of the social body, i.e., of the nation from its historical exile, of the outward world from its broken state, has never had a Messianic meaning in Judaism.***[294]

Scholem railed against the anti-eschatological orientation of Kabbalah and Hasidism. It is quite clear that Scholem defended the tanakian concept of a personal intervention of the Messiah in an apocalyptic Day of the Lord that brings about the catastrophic final end of history:

Messianic terms were transformed and neutralized. The one and unique great act of final redemption was thrown out. Let us not forget that while Hasidism brought about an

unheard of intensity and intimacy of religious life, it had
to pay dearly for its success. It conquered in the realm of
inwardness, but it abdicated in the realm of Messianism.[295]

It is quite clear that Scholem considered the ideas of Messianism
in these two Jewish religious subsets as grossly erroneous when
he measured them by the yardstick he labeled "revelation" in the
"primary sources." Unmistakably, he placed himself on the side of
tanakian theology when he labeled Messianism as *"The one and
unique great act of final redemption."* This "act" is steeped in the
catastrophic apocalyptic Messianism of Moses, David, Isaiah, and
Daniel, and indeed all the prophets. *In conclusion Hasidism and
Kabbalah deny the Tanakian Messiah.*

2. The Karaites' Messiah

In my reading of the literature in Karaism, I found that the most
prominent feature is that their sole accepted Torah is the Tanak. I
applaud this greatly; they discuss the Talmud, but they subordinate all
their belief systems to the Tanak only. They do not allow the Talmud
to trump the Tanak.

It is alleged by critics that there are two Messiahs in Karaism.
There is some evidence for this in their multiple "centrally unedited"
writings. The basis for this two-Messiah assertion by critics appears
to be the following scripture:

> And he shall build the Temple of the Lord, and shall
> assume majesty, and he shall sit on his throne and rule.
> And there shall also be a priest seated on his throne, and
> harmonious understanding shall prevail between them.
> (Zech. 6:13)

To my understanding of Zechariah here, he is emphasizing the
priestly mediation of atonement and the majesty of King Messiah,
both of which are messianic tasks. Messiah ben David the eternal
king, and Messiah—the one who atones, as noted in the Aaronic
ministration of the priesthood (sometimes interpreted by Karaism

405

as Elijah the forerunner)—appear to be differentiated by Zechariah. Basic to this is the liturgical prayer in Karaism: "… for the restoration of the priesthood and the Davidic kingdom." Some of their writers assign some of the messianic actions to Elijah, giving the impression that he also is a Messiah.[296] I will assert here that Zechariah is not speaking of two Messiahs but of the atoning priestly and kingly functions of the one Messiah. He is following the theology of Moses beamed from Sinai. Zechariah is interpreted by some to credit Messiah to be the High Priest, who bears His own blood on that cosmic Day of Atonement into the Most Holy Place of the heavenly temple. Considering the functions of Messiah in the Aaronic Priesthood, this is not at all a farfetched idea. The high priestly function on the Day of Atonement in the earthly temple was a type of what was to happen in the heavenly temple.

There is no connection made by Karaism to the two Messiahs of the Midrash Pesiqta Rabbati: the Messiah Ephraim and the Messiah ben David. Here are two messiahs named in Rabbinic Judaism, to which Karaism makes no homage.

I do not profess an exhaustive knowledge of Karaism. However, I am inclined to believe that there is a wide range of interpretation by a wide range of writers in Karaism, without reference to their centrally adopted system of beliefs. Some statements are conceptually unclear, and some are confused. Considering the tanakian scriptures from which they draw, all references are conceptually and contextually messianic in the single messianic sense. I mean that the tanakian texts they use do not indicate two Messiahs. Karaism appears to be quite aware of only one tanakian Messiah, Messiah ben David. Therefore, the idea that two different Messiahs exist in Karaism is unjustified. Their desires to have the temple rebuilt, the Aaronic priesthood restored, and the messianic sacrifice symbolized by the animal without blemish emphasized expands the messianic function into two broad roles. These roles are the accomplishment of the atonement (as in the High Priestly act on the Day of Atonement) and the establishment of the eternal King Messiah ben David's kingdom. The Tanak clearly describes these two messianic roles, but both are accomplished by Messiah ben David. Therefore the correct orientation is "One Messiah, two roles." This is perfectly compatible with tanakian theology. It stands up to Scholem's own "Restorative" and "Utopian" elements of apocalyptic "Acute" Messianism. In conclusion Karaism expects the Messiah to be high priest officiating in the atonement, and the Davidic king. This is quite congruent with the Tanak.

3. The Messiah of the Messianic Zionists

Rabbi Abraham Kook (HaRav) and his followers form the bulwark of the Messianic Zionists and have a nationalist ideology encapsulating their Messiah:

> The great ingathering of the exiles is a revelation of the light of the Messiah, which does not depend on our teshuah [repentance, turning back to God] but on the decree "This people I have formed for Myself, *that they might declare My praise."*
> (Isa. 43:21)[297]

This verse quoted from Isaiah can be considered a paraphrasing of the Abrahamic covenant, which is Israel's duty commissioned by God. This is a remarkable perception of HaRav.

Aviezer Ravitsky, current chairman of Jewish Thought at Hebrew University, has made a remarkable study of the Messianic Zionists titled "The Revealed End: Messianic Religious Zionism." I quote from him:

> Unlike the traditional Kabbalist sages, who saw redemption as hinging on spiritual rectification and the fulfillment of a mystical cosmic mission, this activist school gives precedence to perfecting this world and achieving historical, political fulfillment. For them it is a Zionist undertaking, in all its concreteness, that embodies the needed collective rectification, and truly reflects the Jewish people's response to the divine call. And it is Zionism that, in the last analysis, prepares the way for universal personal redemption as well. Thus Kook wrote, "The end is being

revealed before our very eyes, and there can be no doubt
or question that would detract from our joy and gratitude to
the Redeemer of Israel ... The End is here." (See Shlomo
Aviner, "Am ke-lavi," Jerusalem, 1983, 2:192; Uriel Tal,
"Mithos u-tevunah be-yahadut yamenu,"
Tel Aviv, 1987, p. 102)[298]

Aviezer Ravitsky showed great perception when he realized that
in the two generations since Rabbi Abraham Isaac Kook's death, his
messianic hopes had come much closer to realization in the ***material***
than in the ***spiritual*** realm. Ravitsky goes on to say:

> Independence, the enormous growth of the Yishuv [the
> Jewish community in the land of Israel], success in making
> the land productive, military power and victory, all these
> material achievements have given encouragement to the
> belief in the revealed End. But the spiritual picture is rather
> different: a nonreligious majority that stubbornly refuses
> to heed the Call and ground its national identity in faith ...
> In sum, the visible elements of salvation have become
> more visible, while the invisible ones have become more
> deeply hidden ... Why has faith not yet surfaced on the
> level of personal conscious affirmation, as expected? ...

> But what he [Rabbi Abraham Kook] hoped for was a gradual
> convergence of the outward and the inward, an imminent
> merging of outward historical salvation with the inward
> religious awakening. He firmly believed that when the
> secularism achieved their worldly goals – legitimate goals,
> in his view – they would quickly realize that what they had
> really wanted all along was something more, something
> higher, a return to the Jewish soul and the commandments.
> He thus foresaw a process of perfection taking place in both
> realms, matter and spirit, land and Torah.[299]

There is no doubt that the Messianic Zionists are expecting
to create the messianic advent themselves, by achieving material

and national possession of land and hoping for the law to be kept perfectly. But the latter is not happening, because the gap between the religious minority and the secular majority in Israel is widening. The Messianic Zionists are not looking for a personal Messiah who will atone for sin, bring an apocalyptic catastrophic end to history, and usher in the kingdom of Messiah ben David. I emphasize here that the Tanak expects every Jew to strive to the utmost to keep the law. But realizing a failure to do so perfectly, Jews must totally rely on personal messianic redemption. The Messianic Zionists are to be highly commended for their striving, but their efforts do not constitute the tanakian Redemption. The strength of modern material Israel is considered, as far outstripping Israel's spirituality, a great divergence in their messianic hopes. It seems their Messiah will therefore never be realized in the light of modern trends.

3. The Messiah of the Religious Zionists (Modern Orthodox Jews)

It is extremely difficult to describe Jewish orthodoxy, because there are so many branches and subsets. The general definition composes it as Jews who traditionally believe in Torah (the Tanak) and Talmud as the collective canon. But the Talmud has come to be its main ideological base. With the prolific variant rabbinic leadership and divergent opinions over the last three centuries, there is no discernible unity of messianic belief. Orthodox Messianism hopes for a better future, a more perfect existence at death or in a possible resurrection. "My Jewish Learning" declares the following:

> The immortality of the soul, the World to Come, the resurrection of the dead, and the Messianic Age all feature prominently in Jewish tradition, but their details are fuzzy. The belief in a Messiah, a person who will redeem the people Israel and usher in a better, more perfect era – the Messianic Age – is often thought of as one of Judaism's defining Characteristics.[300]

The Tanak does not teach the immortality of the soul. "The soul that sinneth, it shall die" (Ezek. 18:20). Apart from that, the above statement is in line with the Tanak. But the next claim of Orthodox Messianism is erroneous, confusing, and misleading—the claim that the Tanak does not use the word "Messiah" to refer to an eschatological redeemer.[301] All the prophets and David would totally disagree. And Scholem vehemently disagrees with this alleged absence of an eschatological Messiah in the Tanak. Some clarity is forthcoming in the admission that the word "Messiah" is derived from the Hebrew "*mashah*," meaning "to anoint."[302] The Tanak and the Talmud clearly declare that the Ha-Mashiach has been in the mind of God from eternity. Orthodox Messianism does make the further admission that though Messianism is rarely discussed in the Mishnah, it is very much present in the Gemara and Midrash.

> Here the Redeemer is called Messiah, … a military, political figure, … a being with supernatural abilities … [who] dresses like a blighted beggar, sitting at the gates of Rome, awaiting Jewish repentance.[303]

Modern Orthodox Judaism leans heavily on Rambam to define the Messiah for them. Their core messianic beliefs are found in Rambam's thirteen principles of faith, the twelfth of which defines the coming of the Messiah.[304]

On Chabad.org, Orthodox Judaism provides a good discussion under the title "Who is Moshiach?" Here the messianic Redeemer will be ushered in as a person, a human leader, a descendent of Kings David and Solomon who will reinstate the Davidic royal dynasty. Orthodox Judaism predicts that if at any moment the Jews are worthy of redemption, this person would be directed from above to assume the role of the redeemer. Moshiach is perceived as a monarch in the Messianic Era *ruling over all humanity* with kindness and justice, and upholding the law of the Torah. Maimonides stated that if a Jewish leader (1) toils in the study of Torah and is meticulous about the observance of the mitzvoth [fulfillment of the commandments of the Jewish law], (2) influences the Jews to follow the ways of the Torah, (3) wages the "battles of God," (4) rebuilds the holy temple in Jerusalem, and (5) facilitates the ingathering of the Jews to the Land of Israel, *then he is certain to be the Messiah.*

This set of criteria is highly reflective of the longing of the Jews, but it is not a blueprint from the Tanak. It is dependent on all the Jews keeping the law perfectly, which will never happen. It could be interpreted that the Moshiach will be chosen by a committee, by observation of his behavior and lifestyle. This picture is restricted to gifted humans in a temporal setting, with no atonement for sin and no apocalyptic end of history. Presumably this Messiah will last only for his lifetime, since he is only an ordinary, though gifted, human. *The tanakian plan* for atonement for sin, the apocalyptic catastrophic end of history, the occurrence of the Judgment and Resurrection, and the ushering in of the Messiah's reign over a perfect and immortal people *has been abandoned.*

4. The Messiah of the Messianic Jews

The Messianic Jews believe that Yeshua of Nazareth, the son of Mary, is the Ha-Mashiach of Israel. They are currently estimated at 30,000 living in Israel, 250,000 living in the United States, and 1 million worldwide. To my knowledge there are two messianic synagogues in Toronto, Canada. They live as religious Jews, attend their own synagogues, keep the Jewish Sabbath, celebrate all the Jewish festivals, and practice circumcision as a sign of the Abrahamic covenant. Like the Karaite Jews, they believe that the Messiah fulfills two major roles: atonement and the King Messiah of the new earth. They believe that Yeshua fulfilled the role as Isaiah's "Suffering Servant" and David's suffering Messiah of Psalm 22. His expiatory death on the cross of Calvary was the atonement for the sins of the whole world. They look forward to Yeshua's return as Judge and King ben David to implement an apocalyptic end to history, the Judgment and Resurrection, and the establishment of a perfect and immortal new creation. They do not identify as Christians, but they accept the B'rit Hadashah, an eminently Jewish document, as their expanded Torah. They do not carry the non-tanakian baggage that the vast majority of Christians do.[305]

I spoke at length with a young Messianic Jew in Jerusalem and was highly impressed by his positive and exciting outlook. This young man is ablaze with hope for the redemptive future of Israel and the whole world. He is thrilled by his Messiah and is excitedly waiting for Yeshua's return. But it should be noted that the powerful rabbinate in Israel, a major player in government policy, rejects the Messianic Jews as a part of Judaism.

5. The Messiah of Conservative Judaism

The Conservative camp of Judaism makes up the vast majority of worldwide Jewry, enumerated at 4.5 million adherents and constituted mainly by American Jews. Arising in Europe around 1886 as Masorti Judaism under the inspiration of Zecharius Frankel, they have a belief system based on the Tanak and Talmud. Their headquarters are now in New York City. Judging from their literature, Conservative Jews see themselves occupying the space between the ultraliberal Reform Jews and the traditional Orthodox Jews. As such a large group, it is not truly unified under a specific body of doctrine. There are several branches with variations in beliefs. It is therefore difficult to arrive at a definition of the concept of Messianism in this very large group.

Nonetheless, the Emet Ve-Emunah, the Conservative movement's Statement of Principles, inspired by Frankel, is as follows:

> Since no one can say for certain what will happen in the Messianic Era each of us is *free to fashion* personal speculation. Some of us accept these speculations as literally true, while others understand them as elaborate metaphors ... For the world community we dream of an age when warfare will be abolished, when justice and compassion will be axioms of all, as it is said in Isaiah 11: "...the land shall be filled with the knowledge of the Lord as waters cover the sea." For our people we dream of the ingathering of all Jews to Zion where we can again be masters of our own destiny and express our distinctive genius in every area of our national life. We affirm Isaiah's prophecy (2:3) that "...Torah shall come forth from Zion, the word of the Lord from Jerusalem."
>
> We do not know when Messiah will come, nor whether he will be a charismatic human figure or is a symbol of

the redemption of humankind from the evils of the world. Through the doctrine of a Messianic figure, Judaism teaches that every individual human being must live as if he or she, individually, has the responsibility to bring about the Messianic Age. Beyond that we echo the words of Maimonides based on the prophet Habakkuk (2:3) that though he may tarry, yet do we wait for him each day.[306]

It seems a pity that such a large group of Jews are not able to visualize that they themselves continue the exile, now as a voluntary exile, considering they "dream of the ingathering of all Jews to Zion." As well Jews are now "masters of their own destiny" since 1948. It is certain that Conservative Judaism does not go along with Scholem's tanakian, catastrophic, apocalyptic Messiah. They do not see the blueprint in the Tanak.

6. The Messiah of Reform Judaism

Originating in Germany, Reform Judaism sought to adapt the prevailing Jewish beliefs to modern times. This commenced in the AD 1800s. As a movement it grew in America, and it now has over 1.5 million adherents. Reform-oriented rabbi Joseph Meszler gave a lecture in 2006 at the Temple Sharon in Massachusetts, US, on Rosh Hashanah. It is as follows, in a very abrrevited form. I do not think the abbreviation distorts his thesis:

> One of the first things that the early Reform rabbis did was cut out any reference to the theological belief in the Messiah, ... Resurrection, ... [and] rebuilding of the Temple in Jerusalem. In the 19th Century, these early Reform rabbis found these beliefs in the supernatural to be too fantastic to be true [thus] reject[ing] ... a personal Messiah, resurrection, and the restoring of the sacrificial rite of a Third Temple ... *the Reform Jewish belief is that humanity must and can save itself.*

In his sermon he fashioned Reform Judaism as a partnership with God, where each person has a role to play in making the world a better place, and not waiting for divine intervention. Every Jew starts his spiritual journey in the process of teshuah, of repentance. Then the adherent must give tzedakah—that is the practical support of benevolent causes. Finally, by this method the Jews will collectively become advocates as a light to the nations. In his sermon, Rabbi Meszler finally dealt a mortal blow to the tanakian concept of the Messiah:

> ***There is a potential piece of the Messiah in each of us, and the Messianic Age can be had, if we all do our part.***[307]

This reform-conjured messianic idea is not from the Tanak. This is a do-it-yourself religion. It is not primitive redemptive Judaism. It is not what was beamed from Sinai. Moses has been set aside. The essence of Judaism in the Most Holy Place of the temple has been discarded. Passover and the Day of Atonement have no significance. Torah scrolls are to be danced with in the synagogue. The actions of teshuah and tzedakah are certainly laudable, but they do not constitute messianic deliverance. Isaiah's new heaven and new earth have been abandoned. Perfection and immortality are "too fantastic to be true." Messiah ben David's eternal kingdom is a figment of the imagination. Sad!

7. The Messiah of the Secular Jews

This group comprises the majority of Israeli Jews, and there is likely a large number in the voluntary diaspora as well. Thomas Friedman sums up the Secular Jews of Israel well:

> Being back in the Land of Israel, erecting a modern society and army, and observing Jewish holidays as national holidays all became a substitute for religious observance and faith ... For them, coming to the Land of Israel and becoming "normal" meant giving up religious ritual as the defining feature of their Jewish identity. Science, technology, and turning the desert green were their new Torah.[308]

The identification in the Tanak of a personal Messiah has been amply and convincingly described in this my book. The Talmud firmly attests in its pages to the eternal preexistence of the Messiah in the mind of God. More than any other writer in the world of Jewish scholars, Gershom Scholem has described the tanakian Messiah and His apocalyptic catastrophic interference in the affairs of His world, His creation. He created, He redeems, and He will glorify us with His perfection and immortality. The essence of Judaism, contained in the Most Holy Place of the temple, is stained with centuries of symbolic messianic blood. *Humans cannot atone for themselves.* We are not messianic bits and pieces. As "messianic bits and pieces" we pollute God's temple as much as did Solomon when he built the altars of the gods of his idolatrous foreign wives around the temple mount. With such an ideology as messianic bits and pieces, we are as much of an abomination as Antiochus IV Epiphanes. We have stopped the daily sacrifice for sin. We have rendered useless the Day of Atonement. We have substituted for the Ha-Mashiach of Israel. We have become idolatrous and worship ourselves. The greatest longing in the Jewish heart has been eclipsed. Hope is gone from Israel.

But the Ha-Mashiach is inexorable, and as idolators we will be swept away. The Ha-Mashiach promised to Abraham is eternal. Blessed be He; the Lord our God is one.

CHAPTER 32

Hastening and Delaying the Coming of Ha-Mashiach

Desire for the Mashiach is the greatest longing in the Jewish heart. The arrival of the messianic kingdom brings back Eden. Perfection and immortality become ours. Sin and death are vanquished. In Israel's history, this longing was heightened during the periods of personal and national stress. It started outside the gates of Gan Eden and had its keenest expression in Eve's life. In Israel's history, the losses of national status when the captivities occurred were periods of intense agony. Its expression in the Babylonian captivity was heartrending:

> By the rivers of Babylon, there we sat and wept, as we thought of Zion. There on the poplars we hung up our lyres, for our captors asked us there for songs, our tormentors, for amusement, Sing us one of the songs of Zion. How can we sing a song of the Lord on alien soil? If I forget you, O Jerusalem, let my right hand wither, let my tongue stick to my palate if I cease to think of you, if I do not keep Jerusalem in my memory even at my happiest hour. (Ps. 137:1–6)

This lamentation for the loss of the homeland was prolonged from 586 BC to 1948 AD. Most Jews did not accept the Hasmonean dynasty as national independence. The Hasmoneans were not from the tribe of Judah. Every last Jew in the diaspora felt that national independence would come only with the renewal of the Davidic dynasty and the arrival of the Messianic Age. They thought of Messiah as a political leader who would rule Israel and the world. But lo! National independence was achieved after 2,500 years without the arrival of the Messiah. Ingathering of many diasporic Jews has occurred since 1948, but now a voluntary diaspora keeps over 7 million of them clinging tenaciously to this voluntary exile. Currently more Jews are in the diaspora than in Israel. In the USA alone there are nearly seven million Jews, a million and a half more than in Israel. Is this a limiting factor preventing the arrival of the Messiah? For what do the Jews now need the Messiah? More Jews now prefer the new Egypt, since they are no longer slaves. Is there still a longing in the Jewish heart anywhere in the voluntary diaspora? There must be.

With regard to the "great ingathering" from the diaspora, Rabbi Abraham Isaac Kook (HaRav) felt it would usher in the Messianic Age. The Messianic Zionists pinned their hopes on it. HaRav wrote,

> The great ingathering of the exiles is the revelation of the light of the Messiah, which does not depend on our teshuvah [deliverance, salvation] but on the decree that 'this people I formed for Myself' (Isa. 43:21)[309]

Are these now empty words? Has the "Great Ingathering" now been rendered meaningless? Rabbi Kook's statement indicates the belief that God is firmly in command as to when Messiah will appear, and it is now no longer hinged to the "Great Ingathering." A lever to bring the Mashiach has been lost. Is there to be a "Greater Ingathering" or do we now look for other means? Has that romantic yearning "If I forget thee O Jerusalem!" now become an empty shell?

In discussing whether one may "press for the End" when Messiah will appear, Gershom Scholem recalls the deep division among the talmudic teachers about this. Was it right or wrong to try to force the coming of the Messiah "by one's own activity?" Scholem concludes,

> … in the Biblical [tanakian] texts … it is nowhere made dependent upon human activity."[310]

This is a startling statement. Piety and law-keeping are always lauded in the Talmud as instruments to bring the Messiah. I agree with Scholem that there is no requisite injunction set out in the Tanak whereby the arrival of Messiah could be hastened or delayed. But because of the largeness of God's heart, He wants the maximum number of people to avail of being redeemed. It is a *big investment* He has made, and He wants a *big return* for it. The longing for Mashiach continued from Eve through the line of patriarchs to Noah, and then to 1948 AD. Were Theodor Herzl and Ben Gurion merely romantics? Has longing for Jerusalem and Messiah now been dissipated?

Scholem further discusses the deduction from Song of Songs 2:3:

> I adjure you, daughters of Jerusalem ... do not awaken or
> stir up love until it is ready.

This may have a strong sexual connotation, but Rabbi Helbo interprets this scripture as a warning not to try to force the coming of the Messiah. Scholem asks and answers the question,

> Can man master his own future? And *the answer of the*
> *apocalyptist would be: No.* But the enticement to action,
> the call to fulfilment, is inherent in this projection of the
> best in man upon his future, which is just what Jewish
> Messianism in its utopian elements so emphatically set
> forth.[311]

Believers in the practicality of the Abrahamic covenant feel they have a mission to fulfill that was assigned by God. All God's promises to the *chosen people in the Promised Land* were dependent on their fulfillment of that covenant. Abraham and Jacob placed their signatures to this covenant. It was a business investment indeed, and God wanted the Jewish people to be the intermediaries for its accomplishment. There is no other agreement between God and the Jews. The blessedness of all nations was the task. That blessedness was the sharing of the messianic deliverance, the redemption instituted at the gates of Gan Eden and beamed mightily from Sinai. How many times should it be repeated? *Redemption is the essence of Judaism residing in the Most Holy Compartment of the temple.* Disobedience to the law, in which all humanity shares, is met by mercy and is expiated by the application of messianic blood. The great reminder of this expiation is the *Day of Atonement*, Israel's holiest day of the year. The question to be asked is quite legitimate: Can Israel and all diasporic Jews hasten the coming of the messianic kingdom? Can we force the earth made new by propagation of the messianic redemption? Israel's corruption of the temple (see Malachi's message) and the placement of the abomination of desolation in God's holy house led God to allow its destruction. In God's plan, *no substitution or rival redemption is allowed. He is both Creator and Redeemer.* He will not share it with any "do-it-yourself" religion or other gods. That is why idolatry is so repugnant to Elohim. Is the conclusion, then, that Israel is delaying the coming of Ha-Mashiach by not implementing the Abrahamic covenant?

Would conditions prevailing on the earth, either friendly or hostile, facilitate the coming of the Messiah to hasten it? Gershom Scholem cites the Talmudists' discussion of this in the tractate Sanhedrin:

> The Son of David will come only in a generation wholly guilty or a generation wholly innocent" [argued the Talmudists, but Scholem disagreed, concluding]– a condition beyond the realm of human possibility.[312]

Lurianic Kabbalism felt it would be dangerous to initiate Messiah's arrival in the apocalyptic sense. Kabbalism does not advocate a Messiah from above but prefers a messianic orientation of the individual by devekut, to take place in the human soul. Kabbalists believe that the individual initiates and generates his own Messianism by his actions. Kabbalism has "cancelled" apocalyptic Messianism. This will be discussed later in this chapter in another setting.

Setting dates for the arrival of the Messiah was anathema in Israel. But the Tanak refers to various auspicious "times" for certain events:

1. "The *time* drew near" (Gen. 47:29)
2. "Cut down out of *time*" (Job 22:16)
3. "Reserved against the *time* of trouble" (Job 38:23)
4. "And at that *time* shall Michael stand up …" (Dan. 12:1)
5. "For there is yet a prophecy for a set term, a truthful witness for a *time* that will come. Even if it tarries, wait for it still; for it will surely come, without delay" (Hab. 2:2–3)

419

These last three tanakian statements are deemed messianic. They indicate that there may be an auspicious time set by God for the arrival of the Mashiach to which we are not privy and of which we have no control, unless we believe that Israel can speed it up by fulfilling the Abrahamic covenant.

But then we are told that God is not committed to time because He lives in eternity:

> ... before You brought forth the earth and the world, from eternity to eternity You are God ... For in Your sight a thousand years are like yesterday that has passed, like a watch of the night.
> (Ps. 90:2–4)

Nonetheless, we would hope that He would "wrap things up" in the apocalyptic catastrophe that will start the messianic kingdom.

The recognition that patience is required in awaiting the Messiah is generally accepted. Impatience is nonetheless a common and desirable manifestation. Why should we not be impatient for the arrival? It emphasizes our dedication to Mashiach and the catastrophic but yearned-for new order to be ushered in with the resurrection. All those harrowing problems on earth will be solved. Israel should have no greater desire or yearning than the advent of the Messiah.

Conservative Judaism is the largest segment in religious Jewry (4.5 million Jews, mostly living in the USA). In the Emet Ve-Emunah, the Conservative Movement's statement of principles, it is stated,

> We do not know when Messiah will come, nor whether he will be a charismatic human figure or is a symbol of the redemption of humankind from the evils of the world. Through the doctrine of a Messianic figure, Judaism teaches us that every individual human being must live as if he or she, individually, has the responsibility to bring about the Messianic Age. Beyond that, we echo the words of Maimonides based on the prophet Habakkuk (2:3) that though he may tarry, yet we do wait for him each day.[313]

With all the tanakian evidence of messianic definition, this ignorance ("we do not know") on the part of an official body in Judaism is staggering. A doctrinal statement of such a large and august body of *Jews must decipher the characteristics and qualifications of the Mashiach from the Tanak,* if there is still any longing in the heart. Eve had God's word to go on and longed for the One to put them back in Gan Eden. The Tanak holds the answer, and it is the ancient canon of the Hebrews. There is much in the Talmud that agrees with the Tanak, and the reverse of that statement is also true. But the very admirable fact in this statement by the Conservative Jewish Movement is the recognition that the Jews have been and are a very patient people. Their commitment is colossal. It is fantastic to hear the words "though he may tarry we will wait for him." What inestimable joy it will be when Ha-Mashiach does appear! Franz Rosenzweig expressed it so longingly:

> The soul cries out: Oh that You would part the heavens and descend.

CHAPTER 33

Messianic Denouement

The *"Day of the Lord"* is the prophetic statement of the redemptive messianic intervention. In straightforward or modified dark and foreboding tones, sometimes tinged with promise, mixing judgment and mercy, *all the prophets spoke of it:*

Moses:

> The Lord your God will raise up for you a prophet from
> among your own people, like myself; Him you shall heed ...
> And if anybody fails to heed the words He speaks in My
> name, I Myself will call him to account.
> (Deut. 18:15, 19)

Joel:

> Alas for the day! For the Day of the Lord is near ...
> Let all dwellers on earth tremble,
> For the Day of the Lord has come ...
> And the Lord roars aloud ...
> For great is the Day of the Lord ...
> I will pour out My Spirit ...
> Before the great and terrible Day of the Lord comes ...
> For the Day of the Lord is at hand.
> (Joel 1:15; 2:1, 11; 3:1, 3; 4:14)

David:

> Thou art My son, this Day have I begotten thee. (Ps. 2)
> My God, My God, Why have You forsaken Me?
> Do not be far from Me,

For trouble is near,
And there is none to help. (Ps. 22, excerpt)
Though I walk through a Valley of Deepest Darkness
[Valley of the Shadow of Death (KJV)],
I fear no harm, for You are with me. (Ps. 23:4)

Isaiah:

In that Day,
The stock of Jesse that has remained standing ...
In the Day, my Lord will apply His hand again
To redeeming the other part of His people ...
For the Lord of Hosts has ready a Day
Against all that is proud and arrogant ...
For the Day of the Lord is near ...
Lo! The Day of the Lord is coming ...
On the Day of His burning wrath
For I had planned a Day of Vengeance
And My Year of Redemption arrived.
(Isa. 2:12; 11:10, 11; 13:6, 9; 63:11)

Micah:

But thou Bethlehem Ephrathah ...
Out of thee shall come forth ...
He that is to be ruler of Israel,
Whose goings forth have been
From of Old, from Everlasting.
(Mic. 5:2 KJV)

Zephaniah:

For the Day of the Lord is approaching ...
On the Day of the Lord's wrath,
In the fire of His passion,
The whole land shall be consumed.
For the Lord has prepared a Sacrifice.
(Zeph. 1:7, 18)

Haggai:

I am going to shake the heavens and the earth,
and I will overturn the thrones of kingdoms ...
on that Day declares the Lord of Hosts.
(Hag. 2:21, 22)

Jeremiah:

But that Day shall be for the Lord God of Hosts
A Day when He exacts retribution ...
(Jer. 46:10)

Obadiah:

Yea, against all nations
The Day of the Lord is at hand.
(Obad. 15)

Daniel:

But there is a God in Heaven ... Who has made known ...
What is to be at the End of Days
At that Time, the great Prince, Michael ... will appear ...
Your people will be rescued.
(Dan. 2:28; 12:1)

Ezekiel:

A Day of the Lord is near.
It will be a Day of cloud.
(Ezek. 30:3)

Amos:

Ah, you who wish for the Day of the Lord!
Why shoud you want the Day of the Lord ...

> Surely the Day of the Lord shall be not light but darkness,
> Blackest night without a glimmer.
> (Amos 5:18–20)

Hosea:

> And Israel will thrill over the Lord
> And over His bounty in Days to come.
> (Hos. 3:5)

Zechariah:

> Lo, a Day of the Lord is coming … On that Day
> He will set His feet on the Mount of Olives.
> (Zech. 14:1)

Malachi:

> But who can endure the Day of His coming …
> And on that Day that I am preparing …
> They shall be My treasured possession …
> For lo! That Day is at hand, burning like an oven
> Lo I will send the prophet Elijah to you
> Before the coming of the awesome, fearful Day of the Lord.
> (Mal. 3:1, 19)

Assigning a chronology to the important sequence of events, which must occur in the eschatology of the Tanak, is difficult. The dogmatic placing of an order of events borders on a prediction of the date of the Messiah's arrival. This the rabbis considered anathema. The following are important:

1. The "Birth Pangs" of Messiah
2. The days of the Messiah
3. The end of days
4. The Messianic Age
5. King Messiah's eternal kingdom
6. The world to come

To some scholars the above are neatly packaged periods of events during which certain fulfillments of predictions occur. The above categories are difficult to define, and they seem to be somewhat synonymous and seem to occur together when tracking them in the Tanak. At the least they run into each other. In my current understanding, items 1 to 4 constitute one envelope, and King Messiah's kingdom and the "world to come" are one and the same in a second envelope. But many scholars keep these "demarkations" separate.

Listing a package of prerequisites to the coming of the Messiah is tantamount to saying that He cannot come till all the conditions in the list are fulfilled. Klausner cites a talmudic controversy about this (Sanh. 97b and 98a) that occurred between two disciples of Rabbi Johann ben Zakkai: R. Eliezer ben Hyrcanus and R. Joshua ben Hananiah. It is one of the most erudite dialogues in the Talmud as it quotes and discusses the relevant passages in the Tanak. R. Joshua's opinion prevailed: "That the redemption of Israel must *inevitably* come in any case."[314]

This is indeed a far cry from Kabbalah.

Among very religious Jews, there is a burning desire to know the signs of the messianic arrival:

> *When and how will the Mashiach atone for sin?*
> *When and how will the Mashiach destroy sin and death?*
> *When and how will the Day of Atonement be accomplished in the Heavenly Temple?*
> *When and how will the Resurrection and Judgment occur?*
> *When and how will Mashiach restore perfection and immortality?*
> *When and how will we reaccess Gan Eden?*[315]

After all, this package was promised to Eve, to all the patriarchs, and to Abraham, Jacob, Moses, and David. It is the tanakian eschatology. Apocalyptic is dependent on this provision, to be accomplished by God's Ha-Mashiach functionality. It is the deepest longing of my soul.

There is a paucity of Jewish scholarly discussion of the anatomical mechanics of messianic atonement, although the Day of Atonement is the biggest event on the Jewish calendar. Why was blood sprinkled on the ark of the covenant and mercy seat? Messianic atonement must be given a place in the Day of the Lord. *All Jews must face up with the use of blood on the Day of Atonement in the Most Holy Place.* Judaism screams for an explanation. How and when does the messianic expiatory atonement occur?

Psalm 22 and Isaiah 53 need to be deciphered by all Jews. The notion that entire Israel of all time is the "Suffering Servant," who atones for the sin of the entire world, does not theologically hold water. It is ridiculous when considered within the idolatrous and wayward history of the Jews. Jews who believe this are worshiping idols – themselves. Do they forgive themselves for their sins because they have suffered so incredibly? Sinai has not beamed such an idea, and it is not present in any of the tanakian sacred writings. The notion that Israel is her own Messiah is extremely unsound and was not in Elohim's mind from eternity. It borders on blasphemy. All three Isaiahs (if one adds Trito-Isaiah) have a personal Mashiach, God's messianic functionality, embedded in the declarations of the book. The Mashiach depicted in Isaiah comes from eternity and is anxious to redeem Israel and carry her on into eternity. Isaiah says He will shortly electrify the whole world with Judgment, Resurrection, and the establishment of the new earth. When will Messiah ben David set up this kingdom, which will last forever? After the "Suffering Servant" is "crushed" for the iniquities of the world (Isa. 53), we are promised an end of history as we know it. Then He must establish a new heaven and a new earth. (See Isaiah 66:22–23.) If Israel was collectively the "Suffering Servant," have they not suffered enough? Or is there more to come, God forbid? They have never been more comfortable in the world since King David than they are today, especially in the voluntary diaspora, a self-chosen exile. But Israel is not her own redeemer. No sensible rabbi will assail Gershom Scholem's personal apocalyptic Messiah who will bring utopia. In the Jewish dispensation, it is high time for the Mashiach ben David to appear.

Some scholars talk of the Messianic Age as the period enclosing all the messianic events discussed. Others refer to the period commencing with the catastrophic destruction of history and the installment of the perfect new heaven and new earth. Isaiah declared,

> For as the new heaven and the new earth
> Which I will make
> Shall endure by My will – declares the Lord …
> And Sabbath after Sabbath,
> All flesh shall come to worship Me.
> (Isa. 66:22, 24d)

This is a "back to Eden" description. *We all long for this.*

❖ *Talmudic Prerequisites to the Coming of the Messiah*

The rabbinic discussion here is interesting. Joseph Klausner quotes Rabbi Simeon ben Yohai:

> If Israel were to keep two Sabbaths according to the laws thereof, they would be redeemed immediately, for it is said (Isa. 56:4-7), "Thus saith the LORD concerning the eunuchs that keep My Sabbaths"; and following that is written (Verse 7), "Even them will I bring to My holy mountain," and so on. (Shabbath 118b).[316]

The above is a summary condition, which is considered to be able to immediately bring Messiah. This is not a tanakian doctrine. The consensus is that Israel is unable to keep one Sabbath perfectly, let alone keep two Sabbaths in a row perfectly.

Klausner goes on to quote other prerequisite characteristics of Jewish religious life in statements by Tannaitic rabbis as follows:

1. **Charity**—Rabbi Jose emphasized this. (See Baba Bathra 10a.) This is based on Isaiah 56:1: "Keep ye justice and do charity, for My salvation is near to come, and My favour to be revealed."

2. **Repentance**—Rabbi Jose the Galilean spoke to this. (See Yoma 86b; Yalkut on Isaiah 59.) It is a given that all Israel will not be repentant and thus will not fulfill this prerequisite. (See note above on talmudic controversy.)

3. **Expungement**—Our rabbis have taught that proselytes and those that play with children ("They that marry girls too young to bear children" [Niddah 13b]) need to be expunged from Jewry before Messiah can come. My opinion is that this is not a problem in Israel today. Another interpretation is "Those that emit semen to no purpose." This statement has no tanakian support. It is a given in Jewish family life that the emission of semen in spousal lovemaking is for both procreation and pleasurable conjugal relations. Onanism or coitus interruptus is not defined as masturbation.

4. **Guf**—The Son of David will not come until all the souls in the Guf are disposed of. (According to Rashi, Guf is "the treasury of souls," a storage tank established at the creation of the world.) This is based on Isaiah 57:16. Klausner discusses Guf in his treatment of the pseudepigraphic fourth book of Ezra, quoting Abodah Zarah 5a.[317] *The Jewish Study Bible* margin commentary states that the meaning of Isaiah 57:16 is uncertain, and makes no interpretive comment on it. The Guf concept is not a tanakian teaching.

5. **The Temple**—Miscellaneous other prerequisites listed have more or less to do with the destruction of the second temple and the Roman domination and its overthrow, mostly political in nature. These are now passé.

6. **Forerunner**—This refers to the arrival of Elijah the Forerunner. See below.

7. **Birth Pangs**—These are the occurrence of the "Birth Pangs of the Messiah." See below.

❖ Arrival of Elijah the Forerunner

Behold, I am sending My Messenger to clear the way before Me ... Lo, I will send the prophet Elijah to you before the coming of the awesome, fearful Day of the

Lord. He shall reconcile parents with children and children with parents, so that when I come, I do not strike the whole land with destruction. (Mal. 3:1a, 23)

Malachi felt Elijah was necessary to reconcile fathers and sons in discordant families. This was interpreted to apply also to discordant rabbis and rabbinic schools in their disputes. (See Eduyyoth 8:7.) Both Klausner[318] and Scholem[319] wrote extensively about this. It is a topic that needs a book to be written for its discussion. Discordance in family life is much more prevalent than is recognized.

Elijah would actually announce the messianic arrival. Elijah would also perform ritual cleansing of families with problems (e.g., illegitimate children [it is the parents who are illegitimate], temple slaves, mixed marriages, and forbidden unions). Those who had been wrongfully excluded from the Jewish community would be welcomed, and those who were mistakenly included would be expelled as unfit.

The rabbis found other functions for the forerunner:[320]

- restoration of the flask of manna
- restoration of the flask of water for purification
- restoration of the flask of oil for anointing (This is an ancient oil that was used for anointing Aaron and his sons, and Elijah will personally anoint the Messiah with this oil.)

❖ **Birth Pangs of the Messiah**

This idea stems from several Biblical texts and talmudic discussions of the Tannaitic rabbis (see Sotah 49b):[321]

1. **Malachi** 4:1 (3:19) states, "For lo! That day is at hand, burning like an oven. All the arrogant and all the doers of evil shall be straw, and the day that is coming – said the Lord of Hosts – shall burn them to ashes and leave of them neither stock nor branch." This is more congruent with the final fire that will consume all the wicked and imperfection. See also

the quote below from Flavius Josephus concerning "the flood of fire at the end of time."

2. **Isaiah** 2:19 states, "And men shall enter caverns in the rock and hollows in the ground – before the terror of the Lord and His dread majesty, when He comes forth to overawe the earth." (See *The Jewish Study Bible* margin commentary.)

3. **Daniel** 9:24–26; 12:1 states, "Desolation is decreed ... It will be a time of trouble, the like of which has never been since the nation came into being."

4. **Rabbi Nehemiah** said, "In the generation when the Son of David comes, impudence will increase and esteem will be perverted ... And the whole empire will be converted to heresy ..." (Sanh. 97a; Derekh Eretz Zuta, Chap. 10; Song of Songs R. 2.13).

5. **Rabbi Judah** said, "... [there will be] harlotry ... Galilee will be laid waste ... Gablan be made desolate ... scribes become foolish ... this generation is as the face of a dog, and truth is lacking ..." (Sanh. 97a).

6. **Rabbi Nehoral** said, "... the young will insult their elders ... daughter rise up against her mother ... a son does not feel ashamed before his father" (Sanh. 97a; Pes. Rabbathi, Chap. 15).

7. **Rabbi Simeon ben Yohai** said, "... cause it not to rain ... arrows of hunger ... famine ... the Law will be forgotten ... In the fifth year the Law will return ... In the seventh year, wars; and at the end of the seventh year, the Son of David will come" (Sanh. 97a; Pes. Rabbathi, Chap. 15; etc.).

Gershom Scholem states:

> To be sure, the predictions of the prophets do not yet give us any kind of well-defined conception of Messianism. Rather we have a variety of different motifs in which the much emphasized utopian impulse – the vision of a better humanity at the End of Days – is interpenetrated with restorative impulses like the reinstitution of an ideally conceived Davidic Kingdom.[322]

I totally agree with Scholem in this respect. He has further erudite insights:

> Here God no longer shows the seer individual instances of historical occurrences or only a vision of history's end; rather he sees all of history from beginning to end with particular emphasis on the arrival of that new aeon which manifests itself and prevails in the Messianic events. The Pharisee Josephus had already seen in Adam, the first man, as a prophet whose vision encompassed not only the flood in Noah's day *but also the flood of fire at the end of time* and thus included all of history[323] The Talmudic Aggadah saw things very much the same: God shows Adam – but also Abraham or Moses – the entire past and future, the current and the final aeon (*Midrash Tanhuma,* Section *Mas'e* Paragraph 4; *Midrash Bereshit Rabba,* ed. Theodor, p. 445).[324]

Scholem feels that the prophets (e.g., Hosea, Amos, and Isaiah) magnified the Jewish world. The status of Israel was important to them, but nonetheless dominant elements of very wide cosmic application transcended the national scene. Scholem speaks to this in distinct and discerning terms:

> Their eschatology is of *a national kind*: it speaks of the re- establishment of the House of David, now in ruins, and of a future glory of an Israel returned to God ... In contrast, apocalypticism produced the doctrine of the two aeons which follow one another and stand in antithetical relationship: *this world* and *the world to come*, the reign of *darkness* and the reign of *light.* The national antithesis between Israel and the heathens is broadened into a cosmic antithesis in which the realms of the holy and of sin, of purity and impurity, of life and death, of light and darkness, God and the anti-divine powers stand opposed. A wider cosmic background is superadded to the national content of eschatology and it is here that the final struggle

between Israel and the heathens takes place. There arise the conceptions of the Resurrection of the Dead, of reward and punishment in the Last Judgment, and of Paradise and Hell, in which notions of individual retribution at the End of Days occur. ... All these are conceptions which are now closely tied to the ancient prophecies.[325]

The above is the clearest description of the messianic future that I have been pleased to read from the pen of a Jewish scholar. It is in my opinion absolutely tanakian. Scholem now defines the "Birth Pangs of the Messiah":

The elements of the catastrophic and the visions of doom are present in peculiar fashion in the Messianic vision. On the one hand, they are applied to the transition or destruction in which the Messianic redemption is born – hence the ascription of the Jewish concept of "birth pangs of Messiah" to this period. But, on the other hand, it is also applied to the terrors of the Last Judgment ...[326]

Scholem goes on to try to work out a chronology of events but he does not exactly place it clearly before us. My own view conforms to his idea of the conservative or revelatory event, which is followed by his restorative event, which is followed by the Utopia. In other words, the Revelation occurs in the Tanak, atonement is then made by the Messiah, and there finally follows the "birth pangs" and Judgment. The Judgment is simultaneous with the Resurrection. The Resurrection happens simultaneously with the reward to the "Righteous" and the punishment of the "Wicked." There is a catastrophic end of history in all this, and the creation of a new earth where there will be perfection and immortality. This new creation is the commencement of King Messiah ben David's eternal reign. Some scholars label the entire denouement of these events as the Messianic Age. It matters not to dispute about it, because Ha-Mashiach is involved with atonement, the catastrophic end of history, Judgment and the Resurrection, and the new earth where *He is the Eternal King Messiah ben David.*

Scholem very bluntly discards any kind of rapprochement with the redemptive process being a progress in the enlightenment of humanity:

> The Bible and the apocalyptic writers know of no progress
> in history leading to the redemption.[327]

❖ The Judgment

At the outset of this discussion, the idea that the organism is composed of body and spirit, a living soul, is to be recognized. It is my belief that the Tanak accounts for the soul or spirit as the breath of God that gives the body, made of the "stuff of the earth," life. The Tanak has no evidence to support a Guf. The Creative energy is in the "nostrils" of the Creator. On the death of the organism, that life or breath goes back to God. "The stuff of the earth" returns to the earth. That individual awaits the resurrection. (See Ezekiel's valley of dry bones, etc.) The organism ceases to have an existence when there is no more breath. There is evidence that some rabbinic sages believed in the immortality of the soul. The spirit or soul came from a "tank or reservoir" of souls (the Guf) and when the body dies the soul or spirit flits "somewhere." This non-tanakian idea may have come from Rabbi Judah the Prince:

> "… the Holy One, blessed be He, will (in the Hereafter)
> take the soul, cast it into the body and judge them as one"
> (Sanh. 91a, b).[328]

I would rather believe that Rabbi Judah perceived that God breathes again into the nostrils of humanity His breath of life to enable the resurrection. I do not believe in the immortality of the soul. There is no evidence in the Tanak for it. "The soul that sinneth, it shall die" (Ezek. 18:20). And death is eternal unless there is messianic intervention.

Every individual faces the judgment bar of God in the hereafter and will be apportioned the reward of the just, or the damnation of the wicked. The law is the standard by which judgment is made.

Messianic redemption is an intervention or rescue. Abraham Cohen described it thus:

> On the theory that justice must rule in the divine government of human beings, one is obliged to believe that God rewards the good according to their merits and punishes the wicked according to their deserts.[329]

Since *all humans have broken the law* and have some wickedness in their lives, they do not qualify for immortality on their records. But the good who qualify are the ones who have availed of mercy. With God, mercy triumphs over justice because of the splashing of messianic blood in the Most Holy Place. And the rabbinic sages declared that the question asked in the Judgment is,

> *Did you hope for the Salvation of the Messiah?*
> (Shab. 31a).[330]

The righteous are those who have messianic salvation. An excellent account of the Last Judgment is found in *Everyman's Talmud* by Abraham Cohen.[331]

❖ The Resurrection

There is ample tanakian evidence for the resurrection of the dead. The righteous rise to immortality, and therefore the new earth creation is standing in the wings!

Abraham Cohen declares,

> No aspect of the subject of the Hereafter has so important a place in the religious teaching of the Rabbis as the doctrine of the Resurrection. It became with them an article of faith the denial of which was condemned as sinful; and they declared: "Since a person repudiated belief in the Resurrection of the dead, he will have no share in it (Sanh. 90a)."[332]

The tanakian proclamation for the resurrection is exceedingly strong:

Moses:

> The machinery of the Most Holy Place was designed to provide expiation and release from death so that resurrection was possible.

Job:

> For I know that my Redeemer liveth, and that He shall stand at the latter day upon the earth; And though after my skin worms destroy this body, yet in my flesh shall I see God, Whom I shall see for myself, and mine eyes shall behold, and not another. (Job 19:25–27 KJV) Oh, that Thou wouldest hide me in Sheol, that Thou wouldest conceal me until Thy wrath be past; that Thou wouldest appoint me a set time, and remember me! If a man die shall he live again? All the days of my appointed time will I wait, till my change come. Thou shalt call and I will answer Thee. (Job 14:13–15 KJV)

David:

> As for me, I will behold Thy face in righteousness; I shall be satisfied when I awake with Thy likeness. (Ps. 17:15 KJV)

Isaiah:

> Oh, let your dead revive! Let corpses arise! Awake and shout for joy, you who dwell in the dust! – For your dew is like the dew on fresh growth; you make the land of the shades come to life (Isa. 26:19).

Ezekiel:

> Thus said the Lord to these bones: I will cause breath to enter you and you shall live again. And you shall know that I am the Lord … I am going to open your graves, and lift you out of the graves, O My people and bring you to the land of Israel (Ezek. 37:11).

Daniel:

> Many of those that sleep in the dust of the earth will awake, some to eternal life, others to reproaches, to everlasting abhorrence. (Dan. 12:2).

❖ The Final Destruction of Evil

The creation of a new heaven and a new earth must mean that the old are no longer in existence:

> For lo! That Day is at hand, burning like an oven. All the arrogant and the doers of evil shall be straw, and the day is coming – said the Lord of Hosts – that shall burn them to ashes and leave of them neither stock nor boughs. (Mal. 3:19)

Scholem reinforces this in the stark words of Josephus, written in *Antiquities*:

> The Pharisee Josephus had already seen Adam, the first man, as a prophet whose vision encompassed not only the flood in Noah's day but also *the flood of fire at the end of time* and thus included all of history.[333]

❖ King Messiah's Eternal Kingdom

There is much in the Talmud and the pseudepigraphic writings about the transition from Judgment, resurrection, destruction of the wicked and all evil, and Satan, to the creation of the new earth and the installment of the eternal King Messiah. The fourth book of Ezra abounds in details. Since these writings are not canon, I cannot endorse their accounts. Joseph Klausner provides an excellent account of the messianic details therein. In a discussion of Fourth Ezra, he states,

> These "signs" are already known to us in large part from the Book of Enoch and the Syriac Book of Baruch, and from the talmudic Baraithas about "the footprints of the Messiah" and "the seven year cycle at the end of which the son of David will come," ... But the "Fourth Ezra" presents many more "signs of Messiah."[334]

I prefer to draw attention to Daniel's account. I am seconded by James Drummond:

> And in the time of those kings, the God of Heaven will establish a kingdom that shall never be destroyed, a kingdom that shall not be transferred to another people. It will crush and wipe out all these kingdoms, but shall itself last forever – ... (Dan. 2:44)[335]

Daniel is very succinct:

> As I looked on, in the night vision,
> One like a human being
> Came with the clouds of heaven;
> He reached the Ancient of Days
> And was presented to Him.
> Dominion, glory, and kingship were given to Him;
> All peoples and nations of every language must serve Him.
> His dominion is an everlasting dominion that shall not pass away,
> And His kingship shall not be destroyed.
> (Dan. 7:13–14)

Note that this latter account of Daniel follows upon a Judgment scene:[336]

> Thrones were set in place,
> And the Ancient of Days took His seat …
> The court sat and the books were opened.

Had he lived in our day, Daniel would have said "the computer was opened." Perhaps he should have said "God's omniscience knew already who were His children."

Daniel has more to say:

> At that time, the great Prince, Michael, who stands beside the sons of your people, will appear. It will be a time of trouble, the like of which has never been seen since the nation came into being. At that time your people will be rescued, all who are found inscribed in the book. Many of those that sleep in the dust of the earth will awake, some to eternal life, others to reproaches, to everlasting abhorrence. (Dan. 12:1–2)

In summary, the messianic tasks within the Messianic Age, synonymous with the *Day of the Lord*, are Atonement, Judgment, Resurrection, and the creation of the new heaven and new earth. Those looking for a "Golden Age" for the Jewish nation within the status quo will be surely disappointed. Disobedience, sin, and death cannot be allowed to continue eternally. History must end catastrophically by messianic intervention. Atonement must be made, for that is what empowers the establishment of perfection and immortality, absolute qualities of Messiah ben David's kingdom.

CHAPTER 34

The Glory and Triumph of Israel

I now conclude this tanakian blueprint of the Ha-Mashiach. I have tried to be true to its intended meaning. This meaning is envisioned within the great concepts of Creation, Redemption, and Glorification—the restoration of primal devekut in God's bosom. This is the Jewish legacy to humanity. There is no other grand solution to the woes of humanity. God is a Spirit, and we will one day commune with Him in an unprecedented closeness. The Ha-Mashiach is the central theme of the Tanak, Israel's ancient sacred canon. Messiah is the basis of Judaism, and provides the escape from the consequences of breaking the law. Rabbinic Judaism has betrayed the Messiah. Primitive redemptive Judaism is the most vibrant and exciting religion on the planet, the redeeming message beamed from Sinai. The Ha-Mashiach is the glory and triumph of Israel.

Well-meaning rabbis and political and religious leaders have created distractions to Mashiach redemption. Halakah has concentrated on one article of the essence of Judaism, the law. The importance of mercy has been diminished. Religious Jews feel they earn their way into paradise by Torah study and benevolent acts. Shechinah is discussed peripherally, and God's Mashiach presence is distorted. Mashiach must be cultivated. Israel must rest in the redemption by Ha-Mashiach. Franz Rosenzweig said,

> Redemption is his [God's] day of rest, his great Sabbath, the day, which is but adumbrated in the Sabbath of creation ... Redemption redeems God by releasing him from his revealed name.[337]

This is a stupendous concept. I see in it the great responsibility that God felt on His own shoulders for the redemption of humanity, preplanned before the great disobedience. And He redeems Himself by the messianic provision; He is assured He has reclaimed humanity through His functionalities of Ruach Hakodesh and Ha-Mashiach. As the Australians put it in their apt common live lingo, "*He done it Himself!*" This statement is not sacrilege. So He rests in that accomplishment. I accept Rosenzweig's claim that "Redemption redeems God." The responsibility has been met. Creation and Redemption were fashioned in bygone eternity, and the substance of God has been demonstrated by His functions we perceive as the Holy Spirit and Messiah. What a God! Blessed be He; the Lord our God is one, and we adore Him.

But Mashiach has been evicted from the majority of the synagogues of Conservative and Reform Jews as too mystical, unreal, and impractical. The *blood* of the animal without blemish, which the high priest carried into the Most Holy Place in silence, is totally ignored. The blood has been dumped down the drain of Israel's modern religious abattoir and runs into the sewer of things "too fantastic to be true." That bloody spot on the temple mount has been dry for two thousand years. Turn around and look back at the temple mount and cry with Rabbi Joshua, the disciple of Rabbi Jochanan ben Zakkai, "*Woe to us! The place where Israel obtained atonement for sins is in ruins!*" (ARN 1v).[338] Ah! Alas! The place where Israel obtained atonement for sins is still in ruins! Weep and gnash your teeth with the young Rabbi Joshua! In its ruinous place there stands a symbol devoid of Messiah, a building the God of Israel has not ordained. It is an affront to Jews who long for messianic redemption. No religion without a Messiah can redeem us to perfection and immortality and to the bosom of our gracious God. The practice of benevolence is demonstrative of our love for our "neighbor," but it is not redemptive. It is a humbug, an abomination, if we intend it to be salvific. Where is Israel's Mashiach, the Redeemer? Where is His splashed blood that dripped from the ark of the covenant and the mercy seat on to that bloody spot on the temple mount, that bloody rock of all ages, sacred to every Jew that ever lived? I stood at the Western Wall and wept at the spectre of the dripping blood, now dried up.

Primitive redemptive judaism has been devastated over the past 2,400 years. The corrupt priests of Malachi's day accepted bribes to sacrifice blemished animals. "Benevolent acts" are "blemished animals" now being accepted by a corrupt modern priesthood. There has been no *accepted* prophetic guidance for 2,400 years, and the messianic messages of the prophets are not deciphered and celebrated. The temple has not been rebuilt after sixty-eight years of strong political and national independent sovereignty. Sinai is invoked by rabbis and scholars, but the Sinai message is garbled and distracting because it is restricted to legalism. Ritual dancing with the Torah scrolls has replaced identification of the Mashiach in those scrolls. Circumcision is magnified, but the Abrahamic covenant, for which it was only a ritual sign restricted to males, has been forgotten. Every Jew today is a priest in the eyes of God, a priest who is responsible to bless the Gentiles with the supreme messianic redemption. Their message must be the "Circumcision of the Heart." Israel was chosen to be a holy nation, a royal priesthood.

The return of the exiles is only partially realized while the voluntary diaspora grows and thrives. An assimilated Jewish identity stamped with *secularism* consumes the majority of diasporic Jews and the majority of Israelis. Striving for material prosperity is the new idolatry. Proselytizing has no motivation or power, because Jews do not have a clear messianic redeeming message to offer. The world hungers for it. The Abrahamic covenant has no meaning anymore. The Passover and Day of Atonement are hollow rituals without *the blood and the cosmic silence.* And many Christians who believe they have inherited the job from the Jews run around with nonsensical baggage, beating drums that do not proclaim the eternal music of messianic redemption.

The Tanak declares that the Mashiach functionality of Elohim has an inexorable progress. He will first atone. The angel at the gates of Eden will fell Him with that fiery sword to shed His blood for the expiation of *our* sin. We will walk back in resplendent immortality into Eden, naked and barefoot, with our feet wet with that messianic blood shed at that gate. It is the same symbolic blood that the high priest carried into the Most Holy Place in silence on the Day of Atonement. And it is the same blood that will be accepted in the heavenly temple in cosmic silence. God will splash Himself with His

442

own messianic blood and sit in cosmic silence. He will celebrate His Sabbath of Redemption. His teardrops of blood will drip down on humanity through cosmic space. He will redeem humanity. He will redeem Himself. This is the glory and triumph of Israel! It is achieved by their Mashiach.

Listen to the prophet:

> Is it nothing to you, all ye that pass by?
> Is there any agony like Mine,
> When the Lord afflicted Me
> On the Day of His wrath? (Lam. 1:12)

Messiah suffers in His divinity and humanity and redeems from that dreadful Edenic calamity of disobedience.

> Who is this coming from Edom,
> In crimsoned garments from Bozrah –
> Who is this, majestic in attire,
> Pressing forward in His great might?
> It is I, who contend victoriously,
> Powerful to give *triumph.*
> Why is your clothing so red,
> Your garments like his who treads grapes?
> I trod out a vintage *alone;*
> Of the peoples no man was with Me.
> I trod them down in My anger,
> Trampled them in My rage;
> Their life-blood bespattered My garments,
> And all My clothing was stained.
> For I had planned a Day of Vengeance,
> And *My year of Redemption arrived.*
> Then I looked, but there was none to help;
> I stared, but there was none to aid –
> *So My own arm wrought the triumph,*
> And My own rage was My aid.
> (Isa. 63:1–5, emphasis added)

443

Read Isaiah 40:9–12, Genesis 49:9–12, and Isaiah 53. These scriptures are all accepted by the Talmud as messianic utterances. They all describe the messianic atonement. Habakkuk recorded the cosmic Day of Atonement in the Most Holy Place of the heavenly temple thus:

> But the Lord is in His Holy Temple
> Let all the earth keep silence before Him.
> (Hab. 4:20 KJV)

The Jewish Study Bible translates this as a vehement command and follows on to declare the coming of the Messiah in glorious and mighty language:

> But the Lord [is] in His holy Abode
> Be silent before Him all the earth!
> O Lord! I have heard of Your renown;
> I am awed, O Lord, by Your deeds.
> ***Oh, make them known in these years!***
> Though angry, may You remember compassion.
>
> God is coming from Teman,
> The Holy One from Mount Paran.
> His majesty covers the skies,
> His splendor fills the earth:
> It is a brilliant light
> Which gives off rays on every side –
> And therein His glory is enveloped.
> Pestilence marches before Him,
> And plague comes forth at His heels.
> When He stands, He makes the earth shake;
> When He glances, He makes nations tremble.
> The age-old mountains are shattered,
> The primeval hills sink low.
> His are the ancient routes:
> As a scene of havoc I behold …
> Yet will I rejoice in the Lord,

> **Exult in the God who delivers me.**
> My Lord God is my strength:
> He makes my feet like the deer's
> And lets me stride upon the heights.
> (Hab. 2:20; 3:1–7a, 18–19)

Why must we keep silence when the Lord is in His holy temple? It is because God is celebrating His redemptive Sabbath. He rested after Creation; now He will rest again after the messianic task is complete—after the blood has been splashed on the law and mercy seat. God is in His temple as the cosmic Shechinah and will get splashed with that blood. Mercy is granted to the human race when the cosmic Day of Atonement is observed. The blood that is offered is His own. Now He can rest. Franz Rosenzweig was so right. Now God can observe His redemptive Sabbath! Let all mortal flesh keep silent in awe of the redemption. Immortality is imminent!

The messianic kingdom follows the atonement. In Scholem's nomenclature, the Utopia will follow the restoration. In the preceding chapter of this book, the events were described: The birth pangs of the Messiah, the catastrophic apocalyptic end of history, the Judgment and Resurrection. The restoration of perfection and immortality in a "New Heavens and a New Earth" will be established after sin and death and all impurity in the multiverse is burned up. The Messiah has His hand in all this, and His kingdom will be forever. The Messiah is the human penetration by deity to redeem. He is Elohim. Devekut in His bosom is restored. The Lord our God is one; blessed be He.

In his *Star of Redemption*, the much-admired Franz Rosenzweig said,

> … over against the first, who draws about him the mantle
> of divine love, the last, from whom salvation issues forth
> to the ends of the earth; over against the first miracles, the
> last, which – so it is said – will be greater than the first.

The first miracle was the Creation. The last, as recounted by Rosenzweig, is the redemption, by none other than the Messiah, God Himself.[339]

Franz Rosenzweig was a reformer. As a deep spiritual thinker, he realized that there was no Messiah in the Judaism of his day. He was almost converted to Christianity to satisfy his longings for a personal Mashiach. But then he decided to concentrate on Halakah and make a substitute for the Messiah. The star in his book *Star of Redemption* is Halakah, although there are occasional glimpses of the personal Messiah in it. I joyfully repeat the above quotation from him—beautiful, glorious words coming from the hidden depths of his soul, where there was an intense longing for the personal Messiah, the one existing from eternity. These immortal words will resound through the corridors of time as long as time lasts, and will be celebrated in eternity. These words of Rosenzweig incorporate the great love of God, in whose likeness we are made so we can love our fellow humans:

> Over against Israel, eternally loved by God and faithful and perfect in eternity, stands he who is eternally to come, he who waits and wanders, and grows eternally – *the Messiah.* Over against the man of earliest beginnings, against Adam the son of man, stands the man of endings, the son of David the king. Over against him who was created from the stuff of the earth and the breath of the mouth of God, is the descendant from the stem of anointed kings; over against the patriarch, the latest offspring; over against the first, who draws about him the mantle of divine love, the last, *from whom salvation issues forth to the ends of the earth;* over against the first miracles, the last, which – so it is said – will be greater than the first.[340]

Here is the glory and triumph of Israel! What a stupendous discovery of the Mashiach. Rosenzweig utterly believed in Mashiach redemption, though he kept retreating into the rabbinic Judaism of the Talmud. This was incoherent devekut, because it did not contain Messiah. He saw the brilliance of devekut in Eden as the primal couple ate of the Tree of Life and resided in the bosom of the Father, our great and glorious God, the Great Spirit. That was pure "unfallen" devekut. Rosenzweig joyfully proclaimed that he *"was already with the Father."* He decided that he would continue that devekut by doing the will of the Father and turned his attention to redemption by law-keeping. But he lost sight of the fact that *"in Adam"* he had been *evicted from Gan Eden and the Father's bosom.* And at times he also failed to perceive that despite being an ardent law-keeper, he broke that law by sins of commission and omission every day. He lost sight of the fact that Isaiah had said that his "righteousness was as filthy rags" (Isa. 64:5–6). He lost sight of the blood that was provided for expiation. In dominant and transcendant rare moments, however, as cited above, he saw the Ha-Mashiach in all His redeeming splendor. God be praised!

Gershom Scholem analyzed Franz Rosenzweig's thinking and found him to be antiapocalyptic; in other words, Rosenzweig did not endorse the apocalyptic interference of the Mashiach in the affairs of the planet. Gershom Scholem embraced that same desired apocalyptic Messiah that lay deep in the soul of Franz Rosenzweig. Here is what Scholem summarized about Rosenzweig's book *Star of Redemption:*

> Apocalypticism, as a doubtlessly anarchic element, provided some fresh air in the house of Judaism; it provided a recognition of the catastrophic potential of all historical order in an unredeemed world. Here, in a mode of thought deeply concerned for order, it underwent metamorphosis. The power of redemption seems to be built into a clockwork of life lived in the light of revelation, though more as restlessness than as potential destructiveness.[341]

Rosenzweig's "restlessness" needed to confront the coming destructiveness of messianic interference. *The Mashiach must demolish our past.* The physical, spiritual, and environmental record must be wiped clean. Rosenzweig could only be restored to the Father's bosom and pure devekut *by messianic power.* Having no access to the messianic Tree of Life in Gan Eden, Rosenzweig needed to activate the messianic blood waiting to be shed at Gan Eden's gate. Renewed access to the Father's bosom could be achieved only by messianic expiation. Be reminded that that is exactly what Moses set up at Sinai in the service in the temple, where Shechinah, law, mercy, and blood comingled on the Day of Atonement. *Beam it again to the world. Beam it from the third temple standing on the temple mount in Jerusalem!* Relocate the Most Holy Place on that bloodiest spot on the planet, dried up in the past two thousand years, that very spot where Abraham sacrificed Isaac. Here is the glory and triumph of Israel and the world. There is no other way of redemption. Cain's substitute was not accepted. Abel was murdered for it. The loss of the second temple has resulted in a talmudic substitution of benevolent acts for the essence of Mashiach redemption defined in the Most Holy Place:

> Rabbi Joshua asserted: *Since the day that the Temple was destroyed there has been no day without its curse, and the dew has not fallen in blessing and the fruits have lost their savour.* (Mishnah, Sotah 9.12).[342]

This tragedy is reflective of the post-destruction aftermath of the second temple period, which includes the years since AD 1948. It is ameliorated by Isaiah's prophecy of messianic intervention:

> Comfort, O comfort My people, Says your God.
> Speak tenderly to Jerusalem, And declare to her
> That her term of service is over,
> That her iniquity is expiated …
> The presence of the Lord shall appear,
> And all flesh, as one, shall behold __
> For the Lord Himself has spoken …
> Announce to the cities of Judah:
> *Behold your God.*
> (Isa. 40: selected verses, emphasis added)

I focus attention on the four great intellects in modern Jewish history, the Judaism described in the chapter on the talmudic Messiah. They are all great students of the Talmud—monotheists in the extreme, but with different views of the climax of the faith that is Judaism. The cacophony of the Talmud perplexed every one of them, but they were imbued with the great longing in Jewish hearts, much more extreme in their own, for messianic intervention—primarily in the Jewish world but embracing all humanity. What I will now write about them will be brief in the extreme because they live(d) very vast lives in their concept of Judaism. Some are tainted (or governed) by their inclination to believe that the entirety of talmudic writings (beginning with the Mishnah, Bavli, and the Yerushalmi Gemara, to the writings of the Tannaim and Amoraim and subsequent rabbinic sages) were "beamed from Mt. Sinai." That is the great watershed of their belief system. But be apprised, *only the Pentateuch* was beamed from Sinai, and the essence of the Pentateuch was the messianic redemptive structure standing in the Most Holy Place of the temple. The power of messianic blood has been amplified by the prophets and writers of the Tanak, as I have shown in this book. There can be no setting aside of any part of Sinai. Any incongruent talmudic deviations must be discarded.

In my own humility I respectfully call on them to refocus retrospectively on exactly what indeed was "beamed" by God and Moses from that fiery mountain. Moses was the author of that first "Jewish Halakah," but halakah was only a fractional part of Sinai. The Talmud ran with halakah, and when we lost the second temple, we made a substitution for the messianic redemption with benevolent acts. We lost sight of that essence of Judaism that resided with the *Shechinah* in the Most Holy Place: *law, mercy, and messianic blood.* And because these talmudic sages magnified halakah, which magnification grew into an entire confused religious culture, we lost the most invigorating and exciting entirety of redemptive Judaism: messianic Redemption, culminating in God's own redemptive Sabbath. *How dare we?* Since then, bogus beams have emanated from Mt. Sinai, and worldwide Jewry has been led astray.

And so, with this background, these great men did their best to describe their religion as reflected by the Talmud; they used what suited their independent thoughts, but with highly significant references to the tanakian record. They all have a background in the diaspora, which contained the greatest sensitivity to the loss of political and national independence and pride. Dominated by 430 years of Egyptian slavery, there was a brief respite in the zenith of the magnificent physical and spiritual achievements of King David. And since King David's glorious reign, Jews have dwelled in political and national limbo, idolatry, diaspora, and the cruel Nazi death camps, with a continued sense of slavery, subjugation, and massive vulnerability of murderous anti-Semitism. It has been a period of immense suffering of almost 3,000 years, hopefully ending in AD 1948. But now let it be known that *Judaism owns the temple mount*, that bloodiest spot in the multiverse. Israel *must possess it*. The unity of Jerusalem, the eternal city, *must be preserved*. It is the bastion of the Abrahamic covenant. Jewry has a work to do! Splash again the Mashiach blood on the law and the mercy seat! Watch it drip down in silence on the temple mount and cleanse all humanity! The Lord is in His holy temple!

It is with great respect that I now summarize the thoughts of these eminent authors. I purposely describe them in the present tense because their writings continue to speak loudly to us. Some see halakah as a redemptive agent, but the idea that halakah and Messiah are synonymous does not hold tanakian water.

Scholem regards halakah as a redemptive agent very reservedly and halfheartedly. He palpably prefers a catastrophic apocalyptic "acute" messianic redemption, which he clearly and neatly describes as conservative, restorative, and utopian in its denouement. His restorative factor clearly embraces messianic redemption by atonement. He sees Messiah as an eternal king in a new heaven and new earth. A "purely human" Messiah does not satisfy or fulfill Scholem's expectations of the apocalyptic redemption. Scholem is a giant in tanakian Judaism. His messianic redemption is indeed inexorable. After Judgment and the Resurrection, his Messiah restores perfection and immortality in the eternal kingdom of Messiah ben David.

Cohen, in his attempted faithful and honest dissection of the Talmud, gives lip service to both "Halakic" and "messianic" redemption. Cohen's vision of God and the universe is enormous, and he generates a remarkable and exhilarating messianic excitement. His understanding of Elohim in Creation and Redemption will lift any worshipful soul into the tender and forgiving arms of his or her

Father-God. The tone of his writings of talmudic interpretation is subtly swayed by his reverence for the tanakian redemption.

Klausner is a studious "scientific" researcher, but he quietly and grudgingly admits a longing deep down for an individual, personal "human only" but "very gifted" Messiah who he hopes will, within the status quo, transform the world. He hopes that through this "human only" Messiah, Israel will dominate a changed, "purified" world, politically and nationally and eternally. This is a tall order for a "purely human" Messiah. Sometimes Klausner is almost at the point of admitting that redemption must be accomplished by the power of deity. But he is unable to express how that messianic intervention could impart perfection and immortality. He almost embraces a *"Kingdom not of this World."*

Rosenzweig produces a mystical longing in his own invented language of his admired cosmic view. Bypassing the great disobedience in Eden, he bowed to the idea that he "was already with the Father," and all he needed was to do the Father's will in order to be redeemed. But he had a sense that his obedience to the law was not perfect and it produced a "restlessness," which Scholem identified in a great empathy. Scholem stated about Rosenzweig, "A thinker of Rosenzweig's rank could never remain oblivious to the truth that redemption possesses not only a liberating but a destructive force – a truth which only too many Jewish theologians are loathe to consider and which a whole literature takes pains to avoid."[343] Rosenzweig's restlessness destabilized his own sense of security. He realized his piety was a tarnished, imperfect piety. I have already described his welcome lapses, of escape into reliance on the redemption by a personal Mashiach, in all the splendor of that Mashiach's eternity and divinity. Rosenzweig wrote as if he disallowed an apocalyptic Messiah, but he reluctantly exposed his deeply and longingly desired redemptive Mashiach. Can you not detect this deep longing in the following dramatic vision?

> Thus the soul must pray for the coming of the kingdom.
> God once descended and founded His kingdom. The soul

prays for the future repetition of this miracle, for the completion of the once-founded structure, and nothing more. ***The soul cries out: Oh that you would part the heavens and descend!***[344]

In their heart of hearts, Scholem and Rosenzweig clung tenaciously to the tanakian Mashiach of Jacob, Moses, David, Isaiah, and Daniel. I am thrilled to repeat again Rosenzweig's immortal words, which I cherish by reading again and again and again. Every sentence is an earthquake within me:

> Yet no one knows better than he that being dear to God is only a beginning, and that man remains unredeemed so long as nothing but this beginning has been realized. Over against Israel, eternally loved by God and faithful and perfect in eternity, stands he who is eternally to come, he who waits, and wanders, and grows eternally – ***THE MESSIAH.*** Over against the man of earliest beginnings, against Adam the son of man, stands ***the man of endings, the son of David*** the king. Over against him who was created from the stuff of the earth and the breath of the mouth of God, is the descendant from the stem of anointed kings, over against the patriarch, the latest offspring, over against the first, who draws about him the mantle of divine love, ***the Last, from whom salvation issues forth to the ends of the earth;*** over against the first miracles, the last, which – so it is said – will be greater than the first.[345]

Schafer writes lucidly about the suffering Messiah, citing his research of the Bavli and other para-Hebraic noncanonical writings. The crucial and most sublime message from the talmudic, Tannaitic, and Amoraitic writings come from the Midrash Pesiqta Rabbati, homilies 34, 36, and 37, dated to the sixth or seventh centuries AD. The sages erred in naming Messiah Ephraim as the Suffering Messiah. But this story of messianic expiatory suffering in the Redemption is here revealed. In these homilies, envisioned celestial happenings in past eternity of the planned redemption are revealed, where God's messianic functionality must suffer and die in turmoil and great agony. Arnold Goldberg qualifies that great pre-Creation event as follows: *"In a unique way the Messiah is put [here] into the centre of creation; All future life depends on Him."* Goldberg further summarizes, and I repeat: *"The amplification (Uberhohung) of the Messiah's expiatory suffering in PesR 36-37 is unique in the rabbinic literature. It expresses itself here all the more forcefully as all this is being said with a high degree of authority, as if there couldn't be any doubt about it. It is not the opinion of any one teacher that is rendered but something that happens in Heaven,* something that is not qualified by 'as if' or 'probably.'"[346]

This defines Messiah as present in eternity and not just someone who is purely human and comes to earth for one mortal lifetime. As well, it succinctly declares that there will be a big celestial cost measured in terms of messianic suffering and death—a death that will vanquish all death and restore perfection and immortality. Daniel Boyarin declares that the suffering Messiah who atones for sin is a familiar idea throughout the history of the Jewish religion and is part and parcel of Jewish tradition from antiquity to modernity. (See *The Jewish Gospels*, pp. 150,151.)

* * *

This chapter is titled "The Glory and Triumh of Israel." I have tried in this book to show the "glory" residing in the Tanak, the glory in Elohim's choice of Israel to fulfill the mission of the Abrahamic covenant. It is a covenant to bring messianic redemption to all humanity. The "triumph" is in the achievement of the Messiah in enabling a restoration of perfection and immortality in the eternal King Messiah ben David's kingdom, in a new heaven and a new earth.

I hope this book has achieved the exposition of the Ha-Mashiach of the Tanak: His cosmic eternity and deity as the redemptive functionality of Elohim. God Himself is the redeemer, and just as His refusal to share worship is ingrained in monotheistic Judaism, *I see His absolute refusal to share the redemptive act.* No fruits and vegetables, no benevolent acts, no deep study of Torah, no halakic filthy rags, and no enlightenment can substitute for Elohim's own apocalyptic redemptive power. These are all sanctifying agents, but if given salvific efficacy, these substitutions are the abomination. They are the same as Antiochus IV Epiphanes' and the pagan Roman emperors' images being erected in the temple, aimed to annul the typical messianic daily sacrifice of blood for sin, and the Day of Atonement. Any do-it-yourself religion is the abomination of desolation, as verily declared by Daniel about the pagan powers.

And so God penetrates humanity with His deity by His functionality as Redeemer, in similar fashion to His assumption of the Ruach Hakodesh functionality as the Provider of repentance and power. A gifted "purely human" Mashiach cannot provide the massive miracle of bringing back Eden and devekut in Rosenzweig's "Father's bosom." Franz Rosenzweig can only be "already with the Father" by messianic propitiation, of which he spoke so eloquently. Ah, surely Rosenzweig's eternal Messiah will bring the redemption and perfection and immortality to the human race.

And all this symbolism of the Most Holy Place of the earthly temple reflects, extremely dramatically, what takes place in the heavenly temple's Most Holy Place, where on the heavenly Day of Atonement there is a great cosmic silence. God bows His head in the great satisfaction that He Himself, as Elohim, has redeemed us. He is enjoying His own private Sabbath of Redemption. His first terrestrial Sabbath was after Creation. Now He celebrates another cosmic Sabbath as He sees Redemption as *His own finished job, His Re-Creation.* His blood is splashed on His eternal Torah; His justice is mitigated by the triumphant mercy of His great love for humanity. That blood drips down through limitless space on the temple mount where Abraham sacrificed Isaac. *On this, His glorious private Sabbath of completed Redemption, the world is healed and perfection and immortality are restored in the multiverse.* Judgment has been rendered. All heaven is enveloped in the rapturous music of the eternal kingdom of Messiah ben David. The Lord our God is one. Blessed be He. Great is Jehovah the Lord; mighty is His power!

When those cosmic blood drops fall on the temple mount, they cleanse the earth, and there will be heard the *cosmic song of Moses:*

> Give ear, O ye heavens, and I will speak,
> And hear O earth, the words of my mouth.
> My doctrine shall drop as the rain,
> My speech shall distil as the dew,
> As the small rain upon the tender herb,
> As the showers upon the grass,
> Because I will proclaim the name of the Lord;
> Ascribe ye greatness unto our God.
> He is the Rock, His work is perfect,
> For all His ways are Justice;
> A God of truth and without iniquity,
> Just and right is He ...
> For the Lord's portion is His people;
> Jacob is the lot of His inheritance,
> He found him in a desert land ...
> He kept him as the apple of His eye.
> (Deut. 32 KJV, selected verses)

Israel's triumph is just ahead. It is at the gates of the heavenly Jerusalem. Habakkuk and Zechariah saw the cosmic offering made in silence in that heavenly temple, where Isaiah saw God's robe fill the temple. They were electrified with the vision of King Messiah ben David establishing His eternal kingdom:

> Rejoice greatly, O daughter of Zion,
> Shout, O daughter of Jerusalem;
> Behold thy King cometh unto thee ...
> He is the righteous Saviour ...
> And He shall speak peace unto the nations.
> (Zech. 9:9–10 KJV)

In talmudic thinking, "Daughter of Zion" and "Daughter of Jerusalem" signified the communities dependent on Zion and Jerusalem. Let it be known that these communities signify the whole Gentile world, for the King comes to them as well. The Gentiles are the daughters of Zion and Jerusalem. But the word "daughter" must also have a dual application, which includes a female application.

Male Jews can take credit and responsibility upon themselves by the ritual circumcision signifying the duty to accomplish the Abrahamic covenant. This ritual has become the main message, although it was only meant to be a sign of the commitment to the Abrahamic covenant. *In the other sense, it is by the womb of the woman that the Messiah penetrates the humanity of the planet earth.* Most Jewish men think they are special because their foreskins are gone. They must now feel the responsibility left behind on their shoulders of the great mission for the achievement of the blessedness of the Gentiles. **But it is by the womb of the woman that Messiah comes to earth.** David, Isaiah, and Daniel trumpeted this occurrence:

> The Lord will stretch forth from Zion Your mighty Scepter ... In majestic holiness *from the womb, from the dawn,* Yours was the dew of youth. (Ps. 110:2, 3)

Although recognizing this psalm as messianic, the chauvinist rabbis ignored this declaration, which God also made to Eve at the gates of Gan Eden. Zechariah perceived it when he exulted in the exhortation to "rejoice greatly O **daughter** of Zion, and shout, O **daughter** of Jerusalem." God keeps His promise to Eve. It is by the woman's womb that entrance of divinity occurs when Elohim redeems the planet. *This divinity arrives in the humanity of the perfect first Adam, but as the Second Adam,* **a unique implant into a surrogate woman's womb.** He is Franz Rosenzweig's "The Last," the functionality of Elohim. Behold, thy King cometh unto thee! He is the righteous Saviour! He shall speak peace unto the nations. What a glorious and thrilling religion is primitive redemptive Judaism! It is soul-satisfying! It is our greatest exultation! There is no more glorious exultation for the Jew, male or female. Praise the Almighty that He loves us so deeply that He has made messianic provision to have us back in His bosom. The Lord our God is one; blessed be He forevermore.

I recall that glorious day in my life when I viewed Jerusalem for the first time. It was from the Mount of Olives. I panicked as I saw the burning of the holy house by the Roman soldiers in AD 70, and the Zealots, brave souls, dying in a frantic attempt to extinguish the flames. My heart cried in anguish, "Woe to us! The place where Israel obtained atonement for sins is in ruins!" Then I looked again through my moistened eyes: "What promise AD 1948 holds! Jerusalem rebuilt, modern, **unified,** looking eternal, and standing resplendent in the morning sun as I beheld Israel's glory—but you are still empty! The ashes of the holy house have long since blown away. Where is our temple? Where is the Shechinah? Where is Ha-Mashiach?"

Be warned, Jerusalem! Be warned by what was beamed to the multiverse from Mount Sinai! Be warned by the silence that occurs in heaven when on that heavenly Day of Atonement the Lord is in His holy temple and His train fills the temple. He is celebrating His mighty redemption that has been accomplished. Elohim does it all Himself, so He bows His head in His solitary satisfying silence. That is why we must also bow our heads in cosmic silence. And if we build the new third temple on the temple mount, be warned! If we do not recognize our atonement by the messianic blood of Elohim, splashed all over the ark of the covenant and the mercy seat, in the presence of the Shechinah, where *God's mercy far exceeds His justice in a love He has had for us in eternity*, our future is doomed. If we do not see that blood dripping down from that heavenly Holy of Holies, penetrating cosmic space, and dripping down on that bloodiest spot of the ages, where Abraham offered his son Isaac, that third temple we build will also be destroyed. *But fear not!* Ha-Mashiach ben David will establish His inexorable eternal kingdom in the new heaven and the new earth, wherein dwelleth righteousness. And we will dwell eternally with Him in that heavenly Jerusalem, and worship in that celestial temple, because of the expiation of the Lord our Righteousness. That is the glory and triumph of Israel. There is none other. The Lord our God is one; blessed be He forevermore. Amen.

CHAPTER 35

Epilogue

When Moses arrived with his motley crew at Mt. Sinai, he did not say to himself, "Now I am going to start a new religion called Judaism." He had the education acquired as a prince of Egypt and the memorized Oral Torah that had come down from Gan Eden. These two components were the preparation for the tasks that were given him at Mt. Sinai by God. The dual tasks were intertwined. God desired Moses to:

1. *Transform* those suffering miserable idolators and fornicators He love so dearly into His "Chosen People" according to His covenant with Abraham and Jacob.
2. *Prepare* those "Chosen People" to be the bearers of His messianic mission to redeem humanity to fulfill that covenant.

God was in a prolonged state of frustration. He had created a perfect and immortal humanity, a couple who squandered that marvelous state of being. He was their Creator, and now He was their Redeemer. The law they broke was His request to not eat of the Tree of Knowledge of Good and Evil. But this disobedience was disastrous and brought sin and death. God had a plan, already well thought out from eternity. He was their Creator and He would Himself be their Redeemer. To redeem them from death He would die for them. They needed repentance and atonement. Elohim would provide both Himself: repentance gifted by His Ruach Hakodesh functionality and atonement by His Ha-Mashiach functionality, both eternally preexistent in Him. *Elohim is indivisible in these functionalities chanelling His omnipotence.* He is the only God He will allow us to worship, and He is the only God He will allow to redeem us. The Lord our God is one; blessed be He.

And so God took Moses up into the Sinai mountain and gave him the machinery for this redemptive plan. It was not new. Indeed He already had outlined His plan to the weeping sinful couple outside the gates of Gan Eden. The blood of the sacrificial animal without blemish would be the symbol of messianic redemption. Abel died because of the attempted substitution of that blood. The great institution thought up by God Himself, the earthly temple, was built according to the pattern He had set up in heaven. The Ruach Hakodesh would convict the heart of the sinner and gift him with repentance. His sin would then be expiated by the symbolic Ha-Mashiach blood. Individual sin was disposed of on a *daily* basis in the Holy Compartment. A national day of repentance and expiation became the special *yearly* Day of Atonement in the Most Holy Compartment. The temple was thus structured to implement God's expunging of sin and death (the results of disobedience to His *law*) from the multiverse by the triumph of His *mercy over justice.* Both the daily and yearly forgiveness of sin was by the *blood of the animal without blemish, a symbol of God's messianic self.* This is the demonstration of the greatness of God as the Redeemer. Once a year that symbolic messianic blood was brought into the Most Holy Place and splashed on the Ark and mercy seat and dripped onto the temple mount where Abraham had offered Isaac. The broken law had pronounced death in judgment. But God's mercy exceeded that sentence by the expiation by His blood. This *grace* provided personal and national atonement. Sin and death would be expunged from the multiverse when the heavenly Day of Atonement was accomplished.

Law, mercy, and messianic blood also comingle in God's presence in His heavenly temple to bring the Redemption. It is quite clear in the tanakian writings from start to finish that the Ha-Mashiach functionality is to come to the earth by a penetrance of humanity by deity. First promised to Eve, Ha-Mashiach will be born of a woman and suffer the death depicted by Moses, David, Isaiah, and Daniel. Moses beamed this symbolic temple machinery from Sinai. Abraham, Jacob, Moses, David, Isaiah, Daniel, and Micah were in the forefront of the proclamation of the reality of the penetrance of humanity by divinity for the price He had exacted and would pay. These prophets expanded on the catastrophic apocalyptic of the restoration of perfection and immortality accomplished by Elohim. Atonement, Judgment, and the Resurrection will preceed the establishment of the eternal kingdom of Messiah ben David. Here is a re-Creation, a new heaven and a new earth. This is the beautiful and saving religion of primitive redemptive Judaism that was beamed from Sinai. By this redemption, humanity is restored into Elohim's bosom in primal devekut.

What a far cry from rabbinic Judaism, so fixed on ritual, with no dynamic Messiah to offer for the redemption! Israel is not redeemed by the practice of ritual. Judaism has no hope without Messiah. Jewishness has no soul without Messiah. Primitive redemptive Judaism restores the highest value and gives the Jew an inheritance in Messsiah ben David's eternal kingdom. Elohim, the messianic kinsman-redeemer, gets it done. This is the *glory and triumph of Israel.*

NOTES

Preface

[1] Cited in Klausner, *The Messianic Idea in Israel*, 458, 466.

[2] See *Judaism 101*, (available online: judaismabout.com)

[3] See Klausner, *Jesus of Nazareth*, 196–198.

[4] Scholem, *The Messianic Idea in Judaism*, 38, emphasis added.

[5] Klausner, *The Messianic Idea in Israel*, 113–134.

Introduction

[6] Ber. 34b (https://books.google.ca/books?isbn).

[7] See Scholem, *The Messianic Idea in Judaism*, preface and chapter titled "The Science of Judaism," 304–313.

[8] See Klausner, *The Messianic Idea in Israel*, introduction dated 1926, 5.

[9] See Scholem, *The Messianic Idea in Judaism*, chapter titled "Revelation and Tradition as Religious Categories in Judaism" 304–313.

[10] Ibid., 26.

[11] Ibid., 264.

[12] Quoted in Montefiore, *Jerusalem: The Biography*, 157–158. See also Josephus, *Antiquities: The Jewish Wars*.

[13] Ibid., 159.

[14] Scholem, *The Messianic Idea in Judaism*, 56.

[15] See Cohen, 124.

[16] Chabad.ORG: Ranam's views (www.chabad.org).

[17] See Klausner, *Jesus of Nazareth*.

[18] Scholem, *The Messianic Idea in Judaism*, 56.

[19] See Ford, *The Abomination of Desolation in Biblical Eschatology*, 11–13. See also Ford, *Daniel*, 12, 21, 23, 30, 59.

[20] Scholem, *The Messianic Idea in Judaism*, 4–12.

Chapter 1: Modern Jewish Scholarly Attitudes to Judaism

[21] Baskin and Seeskin, 1–5.

[22] Scholem, *On Jews and Judaism in Crisis*, by Gershom, 42, emphasis added.

[23] Ibid., 2.

24 Ibid., 4–5, emphasis added.
25 Ibid., 6, emphasis added.
26 Ibid., 7–18.
27 Seeskin, Kenneth, Essay on"Jewish Philosophy" in *The Cambridge Guide* pp. 381–398.
28 Ibid., 393–394.
29 Ibid., 394, emphasis added.
30 Ibid., 396–398.
31 Scholem, *The Messianic Idea in Judaism*, 8–9.
32 Baskin and Seeskin, 4–5, emphasis added.
33 Laqueur, 394–403. Also see Juriansz, *The Fair Dinkum Jew*, 155–156.
34 Friedman, 474–475.
35 *Emet Ve-Emuneh: Statement of Principles (www.bjpa.org/Publications/details.cfm)*.
36 Scholem, *On Jews and Judaism in Crisis*, 261–297.
37 Ibid., 281, emphasis added.
38 Rosenzweig, *Star of Redemption*, xii.
39 Ibid., 410–411.
40 Scholem, *Messianic Idea in Judaism*, 322–323, emphasis added.
41 Rosenzweig, *Star of Redemption*, 185, emphasis added.
42 Ibid., 307, emphasis added.
43 "The Religion of the Bible," essay in *The Jewish Study Bible*, 2021–2040.

Chapter 2: The Eternal Preexistence of the Ha-Mashiach

44 Cohen, 347.
45 Rosenzweig, *Star of Redemption*, 383.
46 Scholem, *The Messianic Idea in Judaism*, 5, emphasis added.
47 See Juriansz, "Origin of Evil," in *King David's Naked Dance*
48 Wilson, 44.
49 Rosenzweig, *Star of Redemption*, 383, emphasis added.

Chapter 3: The First Terrestrial Messianic Promise

50 See Juriansz, chapter "The Tanak," in *King David's Naked Dance*
51 Cited in Scholem, *The Messianic Idea in Judaism*, 298.
52 Cohen 123–5, emphasis added.
53 Ibid., 45–46.
54 Ibid., 56.

55 Quoted in Klausner, *The Messianic Idea in Israel*, 26.

56 Cited in Cohen, 104.

57 Ibid., 347–348. See also Juriansz, *King David's Naked Dance*, 126–27.

58 Scholem, *The Messianic Idea in Judaism*, 1–36.

Chapter 4: The Murder of Abel

59 Berlin, Brettler, and Fishbane, eds., *The Jewish Study Bible*, 19.

60 Daniel Grossberg, margin commentary, in *The Jewish Study Bible*, ed. Berlin, Brettler, and Fishbane, 1591.

Chapter 5: Does God Have a Plan?

61 Cohen, 360–361.

Chapter 6: The Patriarchal Messiah

62 Cohen 114.

63 *The Jewish Encyclopaedia*, available online.

64 See Juriansz, "Malachi, the Messiah's Usher," in *King David's Naked Dance*.

65 Cohen, 385.

Chapter 7: Abraham's Messiah

66 Jewish Roots.net on Psalm 110: (www.jewishroots.net/library/prophecy)

67 See comments by Robert Hayward, University of Durham (www.templestudiesgroup.com).

68 Chazalic references in Talmudic literature voicing opposition to Christian beliefs (en.wikipedia.org/wiki)

69 *The Jewish Encyclopaedia on Targums* (www.jewishencyclopedia.com/articles/14248-targum).

70 See "Epistle to the Hebrews" *B'rit Hadashah*, (*The New Testament)*

71 Cited in Cohen, 48, 50.

72 Omri Boehm, "The Binding of Isaac: An Inner-Biblical Polemic on the Question of 'Disobeying' a Manifestly Illegal Order, *Vitus Testamentum* 52, Fasc. 1, January 2002.

73 Boehm, *The Binding of Isaac*.

74 Ibid., p. 347.

75 Daniel Grossberg, margin commentary, in *The Jewish Study Bible*, ed. Berlin, Brettler, and Fishbane, 798.

Chapter 8: Jacob's Messianic Dream

76 See David Castelli, *Il Messia*, 38–41, quoted in Klausner, *The Messianic Idea in Israel*, 30. See also Daniel Grossberg, margin commentary, in *The Jewish Study Bible*, ed. Berlin, Brettler, and Fishbane, 798.

77 See *Midrash Rabah* commentary on the following texts: Genesis 49:8–10; Psalm 72:8–11; Daniel 7:14; 2:35.

Chapter 9: The Messiah of the Prince of Egypt

78 Daniel Grossberg, margin commentary, in *The Jewish Study Bible*, ed. Berlin, Brettler, and Fishbane, 1502.

79 Cohen, 146, emphasis added. See also Weber 47–51, re: seventh sabbatical year of the land and remission of debts; also the theological circles of literati.

80 See David Castelli, *Il Messia*, 103, quoted in Klausner, *The Messianic Idea in Israel*, 74.

81 Cohen, 18–20.

82 Ibid., 375, emphasis added.

83 Scholem, *The Messianic Idea in Judaism*, 38, emphasis added.

84 Baskin and Seeskin, 288–289.

85 Rosenzweig, *Star of Redemption*, 365.

86 Ibid., 367, emphasis added.

87 Daniel Grossberg, margin commentary on Deuteronomy 18, in *The Jewish Study Bible*, ed. Berlin, Brettler, and Fishbane, 408.

88 Rosenzweig, *Star of Redemption*, 307.

89 Ibid., p. 307.

Chapter 10: The Messianic Utterances of Joel

90 Scholem, *On Jews and Judaism in Crisis*, 42.

91 Berlin, Brettler, and Fishbane, eds., *The Jewish Study Bible*, 1166.

92 Klausner, *The Messianic Idea in Israel*, 208.

93 MacArthur, 10, 1267.

94 Daniel Grossberg, margin commentary, in *The Jewish Study Bible*, ed. Berlin, Brettler, and Fishbane, 1167–1168.

Chapter 12: King David's Messiah for Sinners

95 Ibid., 1280–1284.

96 Cohen, 143.

97 David Castelli, *Il Messia*, quoted in Klausner, *The Messianic Idea in Israel*, 219–20.

98 *Avoda Zara 3b*, cited in Santala.

99 See William W. Hallo, "Translator Hallo," in Rosenzweig, *Star of Redemption*, vii.

100 See Nahum N. Glatzer, foreword, in Rosenzweig, *Star of Redemption*. Emphasis added.

101 Ibid.

102 Rosenzweig, *Star of Redemption*, 307.

103 See *Stanford Encyclopaedia of Philosophy* (www-iep.utm.edu/). See also Benjamin Pollock (www.religiousstudies.msu.edu/index.php/faculty/benjamin-pollock).

104 Quoted from Cohen, 347–48.

105 Rivca Ulmer's *Pesiqta Rabbati*, in Biblical Hermaneutics Beta *A Synoptic Edition Based Upon All Extant Hebrew Manuscripts and the Editio Princeps vol 2, pp.* 34–37.

106 See "Messiah Son of Ephraim" by Charles C. Torrey in *Journal of Biblical Literature* 66, no. 3, September 1947 (www.mythicistpaprs.com/tag/messiah). See also "Moshiach Ben Ephraim/Ben Joseph," in *Teshuahs HaMinim*, September 2013.

107 See Lamentations by *Jewish Virtual Library* online (www.jewish virtuallibrary.org/source/Biblical/Lamentations/.html)

108 Cited in Vermes, *Jesus the Jew*, 139–40, 197–98.

109 See Sumner.

Chapter 15: Jonah's Messianic Mission

110 Ehrman, 64–70, emphasis added.

111 Alan F. Segal, *Two Powers in Heaven: Early Rabbinic Reports About Christianity and Gnosticism* (Leiden: E. J. Brill, 1977).

112 Klausner, *The Messianic Idea in Israel*, 493.

113 Philo, *On Rewards and Punishments*, chapter 16, sections 95–97.

114 Klausner, *The Messianic Idea in Israel*, 523.

115 Ehrman, 72–75. All translations of Philo are from C. D. Yonge, *The Works of Philo* (Peabody, MA: Hendrickson, 1993), emphasis added. See also Klausner, *The Messianic Idea in Israel*, 528.

116 Ariel Bloch and Chana Bloch, translators, *Song of Songs:* (New York: Random House, 1995).

[117] Klausner, *The Messianic Idea in Israel*, 8.

[118] See Ehud Ben Zvi, commentary, in *The Jewish Study Bible*, ed. Berlin, Brettler, and Fishbane, 1199.

Chapter 16: The Messianic Utterances of Amos

[119] Berlin, Brettler, and Fishbane, eds., margin commentary in *The Jewish Study Bible*, 1176.

[120] Ibid. 1176–1177. See also Klausner, *The Messianic Idea in Israel*, 36–51.

[121] Ibid, 1189.

[122] See David Castelli, *Il Messia*, quoted in Klausner, *The Messianic Idea in Israel*, 48.

Chapter 17: The Sad Ha-Mashiach of Hosea

[123] See Berlin, Brettler, and Fishbane, eds., margin commentary in *The Jewish Study Bible*, 1143.

[124] Klausner, *The Messianic Idea in Israel*, 51.

Chapter 18: The God Messiah of Isaiah

[125] See MacArthur, 952. See also Berlin, Brettler, and Fishbane, eds., margin commentary in *The Jewish Study Bible*, 781.

[126] Berlin, Brettler, and Fishbane, eds., margin commentary in *The Jewish Study Bible*, 781.

[127] See Berlin, Brettler, and Fishbane, eds., margin commentary in *The Jewish Study Bible*, 980.

[128] MacArthur, commentary, 952.

[129] Cohen, 30.

[130] Berlin, Brettler, and Fishbane, eds., margin commentary in *The Jewish Study Bible*, 798–799.

[131] Berlin, Brettler, and Fishbane, eds., margin commentary on Isaiah 7:10-17, in *The Jewish Study Bible*, pp. 797-799

[132] See Klausner, comments on David Castelli and J. Wellhausen, in *The Messianic Idea in Israel* 29–31.

[133] Quoted in Klausner, *The Messianic Idea in Israel*.

[134] Berlin, Brettler, and Fishbane, eds., margin commentary in *The Jewish Study Bible*, 1326–27.

[135] David Castelli, *Il Messia*, 98, quoted in Klausner, *The Messianic Idea in Israel*, 64.

136   Berlin, Brettler, and Fishbane, eds., margin commentary in *The Jewish Study Bible*, 807.

137   Cohen, 347–48. See also Sanh. 98b, 96b.

Chapter 19: Micah's Messiah from Bethlehem Ephrath

138   Weber, 373.

139   Berlin, Brettler, and Fishbane, eds., margin commentary in *The Jewish Study Bible*, 1213.

140   Klausner, *The Messianic Idea in Israel*, 77.

141   Avram Yehoshua, *Micah 5:2 and Messianic Deity (http://Seedof Abraham.net)*.

142   Klausner, *The Messianic Idea in Israel*, 77.

143   Ibid., 79.

144   Written by R. C. Freeman.

Chapter 20: The Comfort and Consolation of Nahum

145   Klausner, *The Messianic Idea in Israel*.

Chapter 21: The Messiah of Zephaniah

146   Ibid., 85–87.

147   Scholem, *The Messianic Idea in Judaism*, 4–48.

148   Juriansz, *King David's Naked Dance pp. 334–369*.

149   Cohen, 375.

Chapter 22: Messiah in the Oracles of Jeremiah

150   Berlin, Brettler, and Fishbane, eds., margin commentary in *The Jewish Study Bible*, 917.

151   MacArthur, commentary, 1059–60, emphasis added.

Chapter 23: The Messianic Vision of Obadiah

152   Klausner, *The Messianic Idea in Israel*, 135.

153   Berlin, Brettler, and Fishbane, eds., margin commentary in *The Jewish Study Bible*, 1193.

154   See Ford, *The Abomination of Desolation in Biblical Eschatology*. See also Ford, *Daniel 8:14, The Day of Atonement and the Investigative Judgement*, 345.

155   Berlin, Brettler, and Fishbane, eds., margin commentary in *The Jewish Study Bible*, 1193–94.

Chapter 24: The Messianic Visions of Daniel

156   MacArthur, commentary, 1225.

157   Berlin, Brettler, and Fishbane, eds., margin commentary in *The Jewish Study Bible*, 1640. See also Heim, *Jesus, the World's Perfector*, quoted by Ford in *Daniel*, 22–23.

158   For a discussion of this topic of authorship, see Ford, *The Abomination of Desolation in Biblical Eschatology*, 113–14.

159   Ibid.

160   See *Hebrew Streams* online (www.hebrewstreams.org/).

161   See Daniel 3—Hebrew/English translation Masoretic Text online (www.mechon-mamre.org/p/pt/pt0.htm).

162   See Bible.org re: "Elohim" online (https://bible.org/question/does-ielohimi-gen-11-me.

163   See Collins, *Daniel: A Commentary on the Book of Daniel*, 291.

164   See Vermes, *Jesus the Jew*, 185–88.

165   Ibid., 172.

166   Ibid., 160–222.

167   Klausner, *The Messianic Idea in Israel*, 228.

168   Ibid., 229.

169   Ibid., 230, emphasis added.

170   Cited in Cohen, 385.

171   Ibid., 4.

172   Ibid., 30.

173   Ibid., 50.

174   *Jewish Encyclopaedia* on Michael (www.jewishencyclopedia.com/articles/10779-michael).

175   Cohen, 50.

176   Ibid., 30.

177   Berlin, Brettler, and Fishbane, eds., margin commentary in *The Jewish Study Bible*, 1665.

178   Ibid, 1658.

179   MacArthur, xxxi.

180 See *A Measure of Faith* (www.gotquestions.org/measure-of-faith.html). See also David Malick, "An Argument of the Book of Daniel," Bible. org, June 21, 2004, https://bible.org/article/argument-book-daniel.

181 See Schwartz, *Antiochus IV Epiphanes in Jerusalem.*

182 Berlin, Brettler, and Fishbane, eds., margin commentary in *The Jewish Study Bible*, 1660.

183 See John F. Walvoord, "The Prophecy of the Seventy Weeks," Bible.org, January 1 2008, https://bible.org/seriespage/9-prophecy-seventy-weeks.

184 Berlin, Brettler, and Fishbane, eds., margin commentary in *The Jewish Study Bible*, 1660.

185 See comments by Rabbi Baruch in *Torah Class Podcasts on Daniel chapter 9*, (www.torahclass.com/.../411--daniel-924-27-daniel-and-the-messiah-part). Note that this source is a Messianic Jewish one and not Rabbinic.

186 See Ford, *Daniel 8:14, The Day of Atonement and the Investigative Judgment.* See also Ford, *The Abomination of Desolation in Biblical Eschatology.* See also Theophilus.

187 See Klausner, "Political Conditions," in *Jesus of Nazareth*, 135–73.

188 David Castelli, *Il Messia*, 152–56, cited in Klausner, *The Messianic Idea in Israel*, 234.

189 Ford, *The Abomination of Desolation in Biblical Eschatology*, 118–19.

190 Ibid., 26–27.

191 See Scholem, *The Messianic Idea in Judaism*, 22, 40, 68–73, 130, 149, 157, 261, 274.

192 Klausner, *The Messianic Idea in Israel*, 236.

193 David Castelli, *Il Messia*, 248–51, cited in Klausner, *The Messianic Idea in Israel*, 408, 414.

Chapter 25: The Ha-Mashiach of Habakkuk

194 Cohen, 114, emphasis added.

195 Klausner, *The Messianic Idea in Israel*, 87.

196 See Gordis, Robert, *Emet Ve'emunah, the Statement of Principles of Conservative Judaism*, 1990, http://masortiolami.org/wp-content/uploads/2014/03/Emet-VEmunah-Statement-of-Principles-of-Conservative-Judaism.pdf.

197 See Wilson, 41, 121.

198 Klausner, *The Messianic Idea in Israel*, footnote, 88.

199 See *Expositor Klausner in Israel*, available online.

200 Berlin, Brettler, and Fishbane, eds., margin commentary in *The Jewish Study Bible*, 1050, 1089, 1230, in commentary on Ezek. 3:22–26, 24:25–27, Zeph. 1:7, Zech. 2:17 [2:13 in KJV], regarding the "silence."

201 Cohen, 16–20.

202 Ibid. Quoted by Cohen on p.18, emphasis added.

Chapter 26: Ezekiel's Mystic Messiah

203 Berlin, Brettler, and Fishbane, eds., margin commentary in *The Jewish Study Bible*, 1042–1044.

204 David Castelli, *Il Messia*, 41–43, cited in Klausner, *The Messianic Idea in Israel*, 34.

205 See "Jewish Mysticism," essay by Hava Tirosh-Samuelson in *The Cambridge Guide to Jewish History, Religion, and Culture*, 400–401

206 See Klausner, *The Messianic Idea in Israel*, 115–118.

207 Ibid., 119.

208 See Berlin, Brettler, and Fishbane, eds., *The Jewish Study Bible*, 1114.

209 Klausner, *The Messianic Idea in Israel*, 230.

210 Berlin, Brettler, and Fishbane, eds., margin commentary in *The Jewish Study Bible*, 1118.

211 Klausner, *The Messianic Idea in Israel*, 134.

Chapter 27: Haggai's Messiah in His Temple

212 Ibid., 185–93.

213 Berlin, Brettler, and Fishbane, eds., margin commentary in *The Jewish Study Bible*, 1248.

214 Klausner, *The Messianic Idea in Israel*, 190.

Chapter 28: Zechariah: The Messiah of Zion and the Nations

215 Ehud Ben Zvi, margin commentary, in Berlin, Brettler, and Fishbane, eds., *The Jewish Study Bible*, 1250.

216 Klausner, *The Messianic Idea in Israel*, 191–93.

217 Ibid., 197–202.

218 Ibid. 201–206.

219 Ibid. 203–204.

220 Ibid. 204.

221   Cohen, 347–50.
222   Scholem, *The Messianic Idea in Judaism*, 15.

Chapter 29: Malachi, The Messiah and His Usher
223   Montefiore, *Jerusalem: The Biography*, 124, 151.
224   Ibid., p. 159.
225   Klausner, *The Messianic Idea in Israel*, 253.
226   Berlin, Brettler, and Fishbane, eds., margin commentary in *The Jewish Study Bible*, 167, 179, 201, 267, 1124. See also Dennis, *The Encyclopedia of Jewish Myth, Magic, and Mysticism*.
227   Cohen, 16–20.
228   See article "The Day of Atonement" in the *Times of Israel*. See also S. David Sperling, "Day of Atonement," in *The Jewish Virtual Library: www.jewishvirtuallibrary.org/jsource/.../ejud_0_04999.html*, http://www.jewishvirtuallibrary.org/jsource/judaica/ejud_0002_0005_0_04999.html.
229   See Jacob Milgromi, *"Forgiveness,"* in *The Jewish Virtual Library*, https://www.jewishvirtuallibrary.org/jsource/judaica/ejud_0002_0007_0_06619.html. See also Cohen, 18.

Chapter 30: The Messiah of the Talmud
230   Cohen, 342.
231   Ibid., 124.
232   Ibid., 180.
233   http://www.sanhedrin.org.
234   Cohen, 125.
235   See Jacob Neusner, preface, in Cohen, x, xi.
236   See *Jewish Virtual Library*, http://www.jewishvirtuallibrary.org. See also *My Jewish Learning*, http://www.myjewishlearning.com.
237   See *The Jewish Encyclopedia*, http://www.jewishencyclopedia.com.
238   Ibid.
239   Klausner, *The Messianic Idea in Israel*, 391–407.
240   See Rashi, Sanhedrin 99a.
241   Klausner, *The Messianic Idea in Israel*, 386.
242   Ibid., 377–79, 384–86, 475–82.
243   Ibid., 392.
244   Scholem, *On Jews and Judaism in Crisis: Selected Essays*, 162.

245 Scholem, *The Messianic Idea in Judaism*, 1–36.

246 Cohen, 346, emphasis added.

247 Ibid., 347.

248 Rosenzweig, *Star of Redemption*, p. 307.

249 Cohen, *Everyman's Talmud*, 347–48.

250 Ibid.

251 Vermes, *Histoire des idees messianiques*, 168–169. See also Vermes, *Introduction to Seder Eliyahu*, 114.

252 Klausner, *The Messianic Idea in Israel*, 460–61.

253 Rosenzweig, *Star of Redemption*, 307, emphasis added.

254 Cohen, 348–49.

255 Ibid., 350–51.

256 Ibid., 352–54.

257 Ibid., 355.

258 Ibid., 357.

259 Ibid., 357.

260 Ibid., 364.

261 Ibid., 368.

262 Ibid., 368–69.

263 Cohen, 377.

264 Ibid., 369.

265 Ibid., 370.

266 Ibid., 371.

267 Ibid., 372.

268 Ibid., 372–73.

269 Ibid., 373.

270 Ibid., 373.

271 Ibid., 375.

272 Klausner, *The Messianic Idea in Israel*, 389–91.

273 Ibid., 391.

274 Ibid. 391–92.

275 Ibid., 393.

276 Rosenzweig, *Star of Redemption*, 185.

277 Klausner, *The Messianic Idea in Israel*, 408.

278 Ibid., 408–409.

279 Ibid., 418, emphasis added.

[280] Ibid., 10, 526.

[281] Scholem, *The Messianic Idea in Judaism*, 53, emphasis added.

[282] Ibid., 53.

[283] Ibid., 50–51 emphasis added.

[284] Ibid., 21–22.

[285] Ibid., 37–38, emphasis added.

[286] Ibid., 38.

Chapter 31: The Messiah(s) of Modern Jewry

[287] Israel Knohl, *The Messiah Before Jesus: The Suffering Servant of the Dead Sea Scrolls* (Berkeley: University of California Press, 2000).

[288] Boyarin, *The Jewish Gospels*, 150.

[289] Juriansz, *King David's Naked Dance,* 346–48. See also Scholem, *The Messianic Idea in Judaism*, 1–36, 48.

[290] Scholem, *The Messianic Idea in Judaism*, 184–85, emphasis added.

[291] Ibid., 186–187.

[292] Ibid., 48.

[293] Ibid., 191–192.

[294] Ibid., 192–194.

[295] Ibid., 200–202.

[296] See online *What do the Karaite Jews Believe About the Messiah? (roshpinaproject.com/.../karaiti-jew-messianic-judais-created-b-rabbinic).* See also Shawn Lichaa, Nehemiah Gordon, and Meir Rakhavi, *As It Is Written: A Brief Case For Karaism* (Grand Prairie, Texas: Hilkiah Press, 2006).

[297] See Zvi Yehuda Kook, *Le-netivot Yisrael* (Tel-Aviv: Menorah, 1967), emphasis added.

[298] Ravitsky, "The Revealed End: Messianic Religious Zionism," chapter in *Messianism, Zionism, and Jewish Religious Radicalism*.

[299] Ibid.

[300] My Jewish Learning, http://www.myjewishlearning.com.

[301] Ibid.

[302] Ibid.

[303] Ibid.

[304] Jewish Virtual Library, http://www.jewishvirtuallibrary.org.

305 See online www.messianic_jews.info/general/faq.html, www.israel today.co.il/Topics/tabid/194/catid/7/Default.aspx?article. Also the following online:

1. Motel Boleston
2. Boleston following online:library.
3. Torah Messiah
4. Nazarene.net, http://nazarene.net/
5. P. E. Goble, trans. *The Orthodox Brit Hadasha...net/ine:l*
6. Union of Messianic Jewish Synagogues / Union of Messianic Judaism, http://www.umjc.org/

306 See Gordis, Robert, *Emet Ve'emunah, The Statement of Principles of Conservative Judaism*, 1990, http://masortiolami.org/wp-content/uploads/2014/03/Emet-VEmunah-Statement-of-Principles-of-Conservative-Judaism.pdf.

307 Rabbi Joseph Meszler, *"Do Reform Jews Believe in a Messiah?"* address on Rosh Hashanah 5767/2006, emphasis added (Huffington Post).

308 See Friedman, 288.

Chapter 32: Hastening and Delaying the Coming of the Ha-Mashiach

309 Zvi Yehuda Kook, *Le-netivot Yisrael* (Tel-Aviv: Menorah, 1967).

310 Scholem, *The Messianic Idea in Judaism*, 14.

311 Ibid., 15, emphasis added.

312 Ibid., 38.

313 *Beliefs of Orthodox Jews and Maimonides* (www.chabad.org).

Chapter 33: The Messianic Denouement

314 David Castelli, *Il Messia*, 185, cited in Klausner, *The Messianic Idea in* Israel, 428–29.

315 Klausner, *The Messianic Idea in Israel*, 240–41.

316 Ibid., 427.

317 Ibid., 332, 355.

318 "Elijah, the Forerunner" in ibid., 451–57.

319 Scholem, *The Messianic Idea in Judaism*, 300–303.

[320] Klausner, *The Messianic Idea in Israel*, 455.

[321] Ibid., 427–57.

[322] Scholem, *The Messianic Idea in Judaism*, 5.

[323] Josephus, 1, 70.

[324] Scholem, *The Messianic Idea in Judaism*, 5–6, emphasis added.

[325] Ibid., 6.

[326] Ibid., 8.

[327] Ibid., 10.

[328] Cohen, 238.

[329] Ibid., 109–11.

[330] Ibid., 376.

[331] Ibid., 110–20, 370–78.

[332] Ibid., 357.

[333] Josephus, 70.

[334] Klausner, *The Messianic Idea in Israel*, 272–384. See also Drummond, 1–132.

[335] See Drummond, 6–10, 337–44.

[336] Ibid., 360–61.

Chapter 34: The Glory and Triumph of Israel

[337] Rosenzweig, *Star of Redemption*, 383.

[338] Cohen, 157.

[339] Rosenzweig, *Star of Redemption*, 307, emphasis added.

[340] Ibid., 307.

[341] Scholem, *The Messianic Idea in Judaism*, 323.

[342] Klausner, *The Messianic Idea in Israel*, 438.

[343] Scholem, *The Messianic Idea in Judaism*, 323.

[344] Rosenzweig, *Star of Redemption*, 185, emphasis added.

[345] Ibid., 307, emphasis added.

[346] Arnold Goldberg, *Erlösung durch Leiden* (Frankfurt am Main: Gesellschaft zur Förderung Judaistischer Studien, 1978), 195.

TALMUDIC, TANNAITIC, AND AMORAITIC REFERENCES CITED

Preface

Ber. 34b; Midrash Tanhuma, Section Mas'e, Para. 4; Midrash Bereshit Rabba, ed. Theodor, 445; Midrash Shirha Shirim Rabba, vi, 10; Sanh. 97a; Ex. Rabba, XXV, 16; Midrash Tehillim to Ps. 53; Sanh. 98a; Midrash Tehillim to Ps. 45.

Introduction

Ber. 34b; Joma 86a et seq.

Chapter 2 The Eternal Preexistence of the Messiah

BerR 1:3; 3:8; 8:3, 4, 8; PesR 14:9; b Sanh 38b, 98b; Dead Sea Scroll fragments 4Q541, 4Q274 –11, 4Q471B and 4Q491; Pes. 54a; Pesikta Rab. 152b; Aboth III. 19; (Ex. 20:5): Joma 69b; Tosifta Sot. IV. I; Pes. 87b; Ber. 7a; A.Z. 3b; Pes. 119a; p. Kid. 61d; Sanh. 39b; Lam. R. I. 45; BerR 8:4f; b Sanh 38b; BerR 1:4; PesR 34. 36. 37; PesR 37, S 8; Braude, PesR, p. 689.

Chapter 3 The First Terrestrial Messianic Promise

Avodat Ha–Kodesh; Ex. R. 28:6; Meg. 14a; Lev. R. XV. 2; Sanh. 11a; Ber. 34b; Ber 7a; A.Z. 3b; Pes. 119b; p. Kid 61d; Aboth III. 19; Gen. R. XII. 15; Gen. R. VIII. 4; B.B. 16a; Pes. 54a; Sanh. 96b; Sanh. 96a; Ber. 5a.; Tosifta Ber. 3.20; Yerushalmi Ber. 9a.

Chapter 4 The Murder of Abel

Aboth III. 19.

Chapter 5 Does God Have a Plan?

Ber. 61a; ARN xxxvi; Tosifta Sanh. XIII; Hil. Teshubati III. 5; Lam. R. I. 16; Lam. R. I. 45.

The Hebrew Messiah

Chapter 6 The Patriarchal Messiah
Ber. 7a; b Hag 15; 3 Enoch; Hekhalot Rabbati; Merkhavah Rabbah; Yoma 4a; Pesikta Rabbah 20:4; Shab. 31a; b Sanh 38b; ShemR 32:4

Chapter 7 Abraham's Messiah
Midrash Book One, 19.29; Midrash Rabbah Gen. LXXXV. 9; Num. XVIII, 23; Midrash Yelamdeim; Ber. 4b; Maimonides: Guide to the Perplexed, II 24, 42; Ex. R. 11. 5; Pes. 54a; Pesikta Rab. 152b; Gen. R. LVI. 4.

Chapter 8 Jacob's Messianic Dream
Midrash Rabah (commenting on Gen. 49:10). Pesiqta Rabbati.

Chapter 9 The Messiah of the Prince of Egypt
Joma. 69b; Pes. 87b; Aboth. III. 19; Shab. 31a.

Chapter 11 The Messianic Love Stories of Ruth and Esther
Esth. Rab. On 1:11

Chapter 12 King David's Messiah for Sinners
Midrash Shemoth. Par. Va-era 8; Midrash Tehillim 21; Sanh. 97a; Sanh. 38a; Mikraoth Gedoloth; Peshahim 118b; Avoda Zara 3b; Sukka 52a; Zohar, part III p. 307, Amsterdam Edition; Lament. R. I. 51; Pesiqta Rabbati 34–37.

Chapter 13 Messiah in the Wisdom Literature
b. Shab. 30b; m. 'Ed. 5.3; b. Meg. 7a; Gen. Rab. 1. 2, 5; Rashi to Gen. 1:1

Chapter 14 The Supreme Messianic Lover
b. Sanh. 101a

Chapter 15 Jonah's Messianic Mission
b.Meg. 31a; m.Ta'an. 2:1; b.Ta'an. 16a, cf. Rambam, Mishneh Torah; b.Ta'an. 4:2; Mishneh Torah, Laws of Repentance 7:5

Chapter 18 The God Messiah of Isaiah
Chag. 12a, 12b; Sanh. 98b, 96b; PesR 37 S 8; PesR 36 S 2; m Sanh 4:5;
t Sanh 8:7; b Sanh 38a, b, a Baraitha; b Hag 12a; BerR 8:1,10; WaR 18:2.

Chapter 19 Micah's Messiah from Bethlehem Ephrath
b. Sanh. 98b.

Chapter 21 The Messiah of Zephaniah
Shab. 31a.

Chapter 24 The Messianic Visions of Daniel
b.Sanh. 98a; Num. Rab. 13:14; Aggadat Ber'eshit 14:3, 231; Shab. 31a; Gen.R. I. 3; Chag. 12a; Ber. 4b; Num. Rab. 11. 16; Ex. R. 11. 5; "Re'uyot Yehezqel" p. 101, Hekhalot Literature; b Hagiga 12b, Seder Rabba di −Bereshit (Synopse zur Hekhalot Literature S 772); 1 Macc 1. 54; 2Macc. 6. 5; Ber. 17a.

Chapter 25 The Ha-Mashiach of Habakkuk
Aboth. 1. 7; Aboth. IV. 19; Aboth. IV. 29; Ber. 28b; Num. R. III. 2; Gen. R. XXXII. 3; Gen. R. XII. 15; Gen. R. VIII. 4; Aboth. V. 2; Gen. R. XXXIX; Sanh. IIIa; Tosifta Sot. IV. 1; Pes. 87b; Ber. 7a; Pes. 119a; Sanh. 39b; Aboth. III. 19.

Chapter 26 Ezekiel's Mystic Messiah
m.Sanh. 10. 1; b.Sanh. 90b; Seder Olam 26. (See Rashi, see Radak.)

Chapter 28 Zechariah: The Messiah of Zion and the Nations
Num. R. 18:21; Gen. Rab. 56.2. 98. 9; Sukkah 52a; B.B. 123b.

Chapter 29 Malachi: The Messiah's Usher
Sanh. IIIa; Joma 69b; Tosifta Sot. IV. 1; Pes. 87b; Ber. 7a; A.Z. 3b; Pes. 119a; Kid. 61a; Sanh. 39b; Aboth. III. 19; Tosifta IV. 1.

Chapter 30 The Messiah of the Talmud

Sanh. 11a; B.B. 12a; Persikta Rab. 152b; Ber. 28b, 34b; Joma 86b; Ber. 5a, 28b, 58b; Lam. R. 1. 51; Sanh. 10:1, 90a, 90b, 96b, 97a, 97b, 98b, 99a, 110b; Gen. R. XLII. 4; Meg. IIa; A.Z. 3b, 9b, 18a; p. Taan. 64a; Keth. IIIb; Shab. 30b; Ex. R. xv. 21; Lev. R. xxv. 8; Gen. R. xcv. 1; Tanchuma Noach $ 11, 19; Peshahim 54a; Nedarim 39b; Gen. R. 42.4; Ex. R. 15:21; Pes. 50a, 79a, 88a; A.Z. 3b; Tosifta Sanh. 8:12; Tanchuma Noach: 11, 19; Lev. R. xxxvi. 2; Tanchuma Reeh S 4; Tosifta Sanh. xIII. 12; Midrash to Esth. 1. 8; Sifre Deut. 132a, 145b, 306, 352; Gen. R. xcviii. 2; Midrash to Cant. iv 4; Cant. R. to 11. 13; Tanchuma Ekeb. S 7; vii. 9; Midrash to Cant. 4:4; Pesikta 79a; Tosifta Sanh. 13:2; Tanchuma Kedoshim:1; Aboth. 2:1, 4:29; Erub. 19a; Chag. 15a; Aboth. 2:1; A.Z. 2a, b, 18a; Shab. 31a, 152b et seq; Mechilta ad loc. 39a; Mechilta to xvi. 25, 50b; Ber. 8:4f; BerR 1:4; Qumran fragments: 4Q541, 4Q274 –11Q31, 4Q47B, RdQ17/65 –68, 4Q491c; Erub. 19a; Eccl. R. to iii. 9; 1Taan. 11a; Targum Pseudo–Jonathan; y Ber 2:4/12; parallel in EkhaR 1:16 S 51 ed. Buber, p. 89f; BerR 75:6; MidrTeh 60:3; b Suk 52a; Targum Cant. 4:5, 7:4; Targum Tosefot to the Prophets, Jerusalem; Midrash Pesiqta Rabbati, Homilies 34, 36, 37.

Chapter 33 Messianic Denouement

Sanh. 97b; Sanh. 98a; Shabbath 118b; Baba Bathra 10a; Yoma 86b; Yalkut on Isa. 59; Aboda Zara 5a; Eduyyoth 8:7; Sotah 49b; Sanh. 97a; Derekh Eretz Zuta, chap. 10; Song of Songs R. 2. 13; Sanh. 97a; Pes. Rabbathi, chap. 15; Midrash Tanhuma, Section Mas'e Para 4; Midrash Bereshit Rabbah, ed. Theodor. p. 445; Sanh. 91a; Sanh. 91b; Shab. 31a; Sanh. 90a.

Chapter 34 The Glory and Triumph of Israel

Mishnah, Sotah 9:12; Midrash Pesiqta Rabbati 34, 36, 37.

BIBLIOGRAPHY

Baskin, Judith R. and Seeskin, Kenneth, Editors. *The Cambridge Guide to Jewish History, Religion, and Culture*. Cambridge: Cambridge University Press, 2010.

Berlin, Brettler, and Fishbane, Editors. *The Jewish Study Bible*, Oxford: Oxford University Press, 2004.

Boehm, Omri. *The Binding of Isaac: A Religious Model of Disobedience*. New York: Bloomsbury Publishing, 2007.

Bonhoeffer, Dietrich. *Lectures on Christology*. Translated by Edwin Robertson. London: Collins Fount Paperbacks, 1978.

Boyarin, Daniel. *The Parables of Enoch and the Foundation of the Rabbinic Sect: A Hypothesis*. Paper presented at the Third Enoch Workshop in Tuscany, Italy, 2005. http://nes.berkeley.edu/Web_Boyarin/BoyarinArticles/127%20Parables%20of%20Enoch%20%282005%29.pdf.

———*Beyond Judaism: Metatron and the Divine Polymophy of Ancient Judaism*. Journal for the Study of Judaism 41, 2010

———*The Jewish Gospels: The Story of the Jewish Christ*. New York: The New Press, 2012.

Breitman, Richard, and Lichtman, and Allan J. *FDR and the Jews*. Cambridge, Massachusetts: The Belknap Press of Harvard University Press, 2013.

B'rit Hadashah, The (The Hebrew name for the New Testament)

Buber, Martin. *I and Thou*, Translated in 1937 by Ronald Gregor Smith. Edinburgh: T. and T. Clark, 2nd ed. New York: Scribner, 1958.

———. *On Judaism*. Edited by Nahum Glatzer. Translated by Eva Jospe, et al. New York: Schocken Books, 1967.

———. *Prophetic Faith*. Translated by Carlyle Witton-Davies. New York: Harper-Row Publishers, 1949.

Cahill, Thomas. *The Gifts of the Jews*. New York: Doubleday / Random House, 1998.

Castelli, David. *The Messiah According to the Hebrews (Il Messia Secondo gli Ebrei)*. Florence, Italy: 1874.

Charlesworth, James H., Editor. *The Messiah: Developments in Earliest Judaism and Christianity*. Minneapolis, MN: Augsburg Fortress, 2010.

Cohen, Abraham. *Everyman's Talmud*. New York: Schocken Books, 1995.

Collins, John J. *Daniel: A Commentary on the Book of Daniel*. Minneapolis, MN: Augsburg Fortress, 1993.

Danby, Herbert, trans. *The Mishnah*. Peabody, MA: Hendrickson, 2012.

———. *The Sefer Ha-Zohar* www.servantsofthelight.org/QBL/Books/zohar_1.html/.

———. *The Mishneh Torah* by Moses Maimonides www.myjewishlearning.com>...>HalakhicTextsintheMiddleAges

Dennis, Rabbi Geoffrey W. *The Encyclopedia of Jewish Myth, Magic and Mysticism*. Woodbury, MN: Llewellyn Publications, 2007.

Drummond, James. *The Jewish Messiah: A Critical History of the Messianic Idea*. London: Longman, 1877.

Ehrman, Bart D. *How Jesus Became God*. New York: Harper Collins, 2014.

Ford, Desmond. *The Abomination of Desolation in Biblical Eschatology*. Lanham, MD: University Press of America, 1972.

———. *Daniel 8:14: The Day of Atonement and The Investigative Judgment*. Cassellberry, FL: Evangelion Press, 1980.

———. *Daniel*. Nashville, TN: Southern Publishing Association, 1978.

Friedlander, Saul. *Nazi Germany and the Jews 1933–1945*. Abridged by Orna Kenan. New York: Harper Collins, 2009.

Friedman, Thomas. *From Beirut to Jerusalem*. New York: Harper Collins, 1998.

Gaebelein, Frank E. *The Expositor's Bible Commentary*. 5 vols. Grand Rapids, MI: Zondervan, 1982.

Heim, Karl. *Jesus, The World's Perfecter*. Philadelphia, PA: Philadelphia Muhlenberg Press, 1961.

Maimonides, Moses, *Guide to the Perplexed* vol.2 University of Chicago Press, 1974

Martinez, Florentino Garcia, and Tigchelaar, Elbert, Editors, *The Dead Sea Scrolls – Study Edition,* 1999, William B. Eerdmans Publishing Company, Michigan, USA/Cambridge, UK.

The Holy Bible, Authorized King James Version New York. Oxford University Press 1967

The Holy Bible, *New King James Version.* Grand Rapids, MI: Thomas Nelson, 1979.

The Holy Bible: English Standard Version. Wheaton, IL: Crossway, 2001.

The Holy Bible, *Revised Standard Version.* Oxford: Oxford University Press, 2002.

The Holy Bible, *God's Word Translation.* Iowa Falls, IA: World Publishing, 1995.

The Holy Bible, *Good News Translation.* Grand Rapids, MI: Zondervan, 2001.

The Jewish Encyclopedia. http://www.jewishencyclopedia.com.

Jewish Virtual Library. http://www.jewishvirtuallibrary.org.

Josephus, Titus Flavius. *Antiquities, The Jewish Wars.*

The Journal of Biblical Literature

Judaism 101, http://www.jewfaq.org/index.shtml.

Juriansz, Allan Russell. *The Fair Dinkum Jew: The Survival of Israel and the Abrahamic Covenant.* Bloomington, IN: iUniverse, 2012.

———. *King David's Naked Dance: The Dreams, Doctrines and Dilemmas of the Hebrews.* Bloomington, IN: iUniverse, 2013.

Klausner, Joseph: *The Messianic Idea in Israel, From its Beginning to the Completion of the Mishnab.* Translated by W. F. Stinespring. New York: Macmillan Company, 1955.

———. *Jesus of Nazareth.* Translated from the Hebrew by Herbert Danby. New York: Macmillan Company, 1925.

The Living Bible. Carol Stream, IL: Tyndale House Publishers, 1971.

Laqueur, Walter. *A History of Zionism.* New York, Schocken Books, 2003.

MacArthur, John. *The MacArthur Study Bible.* Grand Rapids, MI: Thomas Nelson, 1997.

Maimonides, Moses. *Mishneh Torah* Halakhic Texts in the Middle Ages

----------, *Guide to the Perplexed II*

Marx, Karl. *Critique of Hegel's 'Philosophy of Right'*. Translated by Joseph O'Malley and Annette Jolin. Cambridge: Cambridge University Press, 1977.

McDowell, Josh. *The New Evidence*. Grand Rapids, MI: Thomas Nelson, 1999.

Montefiore, Claude Goldsmid. *The Hibbert Lectures*. London: Williams and Norgate, 1893.

———. *The Old Testament and After*. London: Macmillan, 1923.

Montefiore, Simon Sebag. *Jerusalem: The Biography*. London: Weidenfield and Nicolson, 2011.

My Jewish Learning. http://www.myjewishlearning.com.

Neubauer, Adolf. *The Fifty-Third Chapter of Isaiah According to the Jewish Interpreters*. 1877. https:/books.google.ca/books?isbn=5880852334 Available online.

Pollock, Benjamin: *Franz Rosenzweig and the Systematic Task of Philosophy,* Cambridge University Press, 2009

Ravitsky, Aviezer. *Messianism, Zionism, and Jewish Religious Radicalism*. Chicago: University of Chicago Press, 1996.

Rosenzweig, Franz. *Atheistic Theology*. Translated by Robert G. Goldy and H. Frederick Holch. 1914. Stanford Encyclopedia of Philosophy, Stanford University Press

———. *Star of Redemption*. Translated from 1930 edition by William W. Hallo. Notre Dame, IN: University of Notre Dame Press, 1970.

Santala, Risto. *Messiah in the Old Testament in the Light of Rabbinical Writings*. Jerusalem: Keren Ahvah Meshihit, 1992.

Schafer, Peter. *The Jewish Jesus: How Judaism and Christianity Shaped Each Other*. Princeton, NJ: Princeton University Press, 2014.

———. *Jesus in the Talmud*. Princeton, NJ: Princeton University Press, 2009.

Scholem, Gershom. *The Messianic Idea in Judaism and other Essays on Jewish Spirituality*. New York: Schocken Books, 1995.

——— *On Jews and Judaism in Crisis, Selected Essays*. Philadelphia, PA: Paul Dry Books, 2012.

Schwartz, Daniel R. *Antiochus IV Epiphanes in Jerusalem.* Department of Jewish History, Hebrew University of Jerusalem. Undated study.virtualreligion.net/iho/Antiochus_4.html

Steinsaltz, Adin. *The Essential Talmud.* Translated from the Hebrew by Chaya Galai. New York: Harper Collins, 1976.

Sumner, Paul. *Hebrew Streams.* 2009. www.hebrew-streams.org/works/hazak/thatsubject.htmlAvailable online.

Michael P. Theophilus. *The Abomination of Desolation in Matthew 24:15.* London: T & T Clarke, 2012.

Vermes, Geza. *Scripture and Tradition in Judaism: Hagadic Studies.* Leiden, Netherlands: E. J. Brill, 1961.

———. *Jesus the Jew: A Historical Reading of the Gospels.* Glasgow: William Collins Sons & Co. Ltd., 1973.

———. *The Complete Dead Sea Scrolls in English.* London: Penguin Books, 1962.

———. *Christian Beginnings, from Nazareth to Niceae.* New Haven, CT: Yale University Press, 2013.

Vermes, M. *Histoire des idees messianiques.* Paris: Sandoz et Fischbacher, 1874.

———. *Seder Eliyahu* en.wikipedia.org/wiki/Tanna_Devei_Eliyahu

Weber, Max. *Ancient Judaism.* New York: The Free Press, 1967.

Wellhausen, Julius. *Prolegomena to the History of Israel,* Paperback edition, 2004, Kessinger Publishing

Wilson, A. N. *Paul: The Mind of the Apostle.* New York: Pimlico, 1998.

Wilson, Barrie. *How Jesus Became Christian.* New York, St. Martin's Press, 2007.

Zeitlin, Irving M. *Ancient Judaism: Biblical Criticism from Max Weber to the Present.* Cambridge: Polity, 1986.

BIOGRAPHICAL SKETCHES
OF SELECTED AUTHORS

Daniel Boyarin

An orthodox American Jew born in Ashbury in1946, New Jersey, Boyarin is also a citizen of Israel. He was educated at Goddard College, the Jewish Theological Seminary, and Columbia University. He has taught in several universities, including Ben Gurion University of the Negev, the Hebrew University of Jerusalem, Yale, and Harvard. Currently he is Taubman Professor of Talmudic Culture and Rhetoric at the University of Southern California, Berkeley.

In my view, he is the living Jewish scholar with the widest and deepest views of the religious spectrum called Judaism. But I do not see his political acumen as very correct, as he does not seem to grasp the precarious security of the nation of Israel in a sea of Arab rage. I would evaluate his idea of Israel's security as less than apt.

His numerous books bridge Judaism and primitive Christianity, and his view that the latter is a Jewish sect is very perceptive, in my opinion. It resonates with many Christians, as noted in blogs on his works. His perceptions do not always fit into the full recognition of the Tanak as sole Hebrew canon, perhaps as expected from an Orthodox Jew. His religious experience appears to wander into the area he dubs a Jewish sect. A question that comes to mind when reading his well researched books is, will he discuss the veracity of the messianic claim of Jesus? His Messianism is very Tanakian and akin to that of Gershom Scholem.

David Castelli

(1836–1901) An Italian Jew born in Tuscany, Castelli was educated at the Rabbinical College of Leghorn and became a teacher there. In 1876 he was appointed professor of Hebrew at the Instituto di Studi Superiori Pratici edi Perfezionamento in Florence, a position he occupied until his death. He wrote much in Italian, notably *Il Messia secondo gli Ebrei* (The Messiah According to the Hebrews), published in Florence in 1874. I have as yet been unable to obtain an English translation. My knowledge of this book comes from Joseph Klausner, who quotes him considerably in *The Messianic Idea in Israel.* Klausner leans very heavily on Castelli throughout his book, citing him forty times. My admiration for Castelli is great because the majority of his opinions cited by Klausner are in tune with Tanakian theology.

Abraham Cohen

(1887–1957) Born in Britain, Cohen was educated at London University and the University of Cambridge. He was appointed rabbi at the Birmingham Hebrew Congregation in 1933. He was an ardent Zionist and participated in the World Jewish Congresses. His major works are *Everyman's Talmud: The Major Teachings of the Rabbinic Sages*, and *The Parting Of The Ways: Judaism and the Rise of Christianity. Everyman's Talmud* was published first in 1949 and reprinted in 1975 and 1995. Jacob Neusner, who wrote the foreword for the 1995 printing, spoke very highly of him: "Cohen's *Everyman's Talmud* is the right place to begin, not only to learn about Judaism in general but to meet the substance of the Talmud in particular." This spectrum encompasses both primitive Judaism and the esoteric nature of Talmudic philosophy. He eerily relies on the Tanak in what may be deciphered as his personal beliefs. *The Hebrew Messiah* takes every advantage Cohen has afforded me in understanding the Talmud.

Desmond Ford

Born in 1929, in Australia, Ford started his theological tertiary education at Avondale College, a prestigious Seventh-day Adventist university in Australia. He was ordained a minister in the Seventh-day Adventist Church. He obtained a PhD from Michigan State University in 1961 for his dissertation *The Rhetorical Analysis of*

Paul's Letters. His second doctorate was from the University of Manchester in Britain in 1972 for his dissertation *The Abomination of Desolation in Biblical Eschatology*, a work on the apocalyptic of the Tanak. He spent fourteen years as professor and chairman of the Theology Department at Avondale College. He became a reformer in the SDA Church, from which he was ejected in 1980 for refuting the "Biblical basis" of the SDA doctrine of the "Investigative Judgment." He has numerous publications, notably commentaries on the biblical books of Daniel and Revelation—thirty books at last count. He connects the Tanak and the B'rit Hadashah in the apocalyptic eschatology. His biography, written by Milton Hook, details the illustrious nature of his studies, the doctrinal controversies within the SDA Church, and the injustice of Ford's treatment by the powerful hierarchy of the administrative leaders of the SDA Church. Their meager doctrinal knowledge took a backseat to Ellen White's supremacy. Ellen White is the SDA prophetess.

As my friend since I met him in 1957, Ford had a great influence on me. This book is dedicated to him.

Thomas Friedman

Born in 1953 Friedman is an American Jew educated at the University of Minnesota, Brandeis University, and St. Anthony's College, Oxford. His outstanding book *From Beirut to Jerusalem* was written after his experiences of five years in the Middle East as bureau chief, first in Beirut and then in Jerusalem, for the *New York Times*. This is one of six best-selling books he has written from his experience as a reporter and columnist for the *New York Times*. He has won three Pulitzer Prizes and is very knowledgeable about Israel and the diasporic Jews. I have paid tribute to him in my book *The Fair Dinkum Jew: The Survival of Israel and the Abrahamic Covenant*. His brilliant mind has made him an expert on many topics, and he sways opinion through his op-eds in the *New York Times*. His regular columns educate people who want to stay in touch with what is going on in the world at a level deeper than ordinary news. His background knowledge is enormous. It is rumoured that he has been an adviser of the Obama administration.

Joseph Klausner

(1874–1958) Klausner was a Lithuanian Jew educated in Odessa and Germany, where he obtained his PhD. As a close friend of Theodor Herzl, he became involved with Zionism and moved to Israel, where he became professor of Hebrew literature at the University of Jerusalem. He wrote many books and essays, importantly

- *The Messianic Idea in Israel*,
- *Jesus of Nazareth: His Life, Times, and Teachings*,
- *The Hebrew University in Jerusalem*, and
- *A History of Modern Hebrew Literature.*

He was a controversial figure in both Jewish and Christian circles. He did not identify as an Orthodox Jew but was very observant and devout in Rabbinic Judaism. He did not define and restrict inspiration to the Tanak as the sole canon of the Hebrews. He developed his ideas of Messianism from all the sources he could find. He divided his book by the sources he used, as follows:

- Part I—The Messianic Idea in the Period of the Prophets
- Part II—The Messianic Idea in the Books of the Apocrypha and Pseudepigrapha
- Part III—The Messianic Idea in the Period of the Tannaim

I find his ideas that are congruent with the Tanak very inspiring indeed. But he did not espouse the eschatological apocalyptic of the Tanak, choosing rather to build the messianic future on the status quo of what he expected was the future of the planet as a continuation of history. However, it would not be fair to restrict him to such a situation, since he appeared to personally expect more. He admired Dr. Judah Leon Magnes immensely and dedicated the second edition of *The Messianic Idea in Israel* to him. He said in the preface to the third edition, "I had hoped that I would be privileged to gladden him with the third edition. I was not so privileged. On the 14th of Tishri, 5709 [October 17, 1948], Dr. Magnes, of blessed memory, went to his eternal reward." Therefore, I would conclude that he expected

Dr. Magnes and perhaps all "noble spirits" to have a future after death, possibly in paradise. But Klausner did not define that future succinctly. It is my conviction that he did believe in the resurrection to which he gives significant attention in his book. (See his comments on Ezekiel's valley of dry bones, page 125, the ingathering of the exiles of Israel, page 183, and yet again when he discusses Daniel chapter 12 and "eschatology," pages 235–36). But I understand him only vaguely, when he treats the resurrection and "the world to come" as ideas only and not the future reality. He did not espouse the Utopia after the resurrection as did Gershom Scholem, which I regard with Scholem as the Tanakian future of the planet.

In the concluding paragraph of his book, he summarizes the messianic idea, whose spiritual intonation was something that "came forth from an essentially political aspiration." There is some doubt whether this was indeed his personal opinion, because he ends the book with "For the kingdom of the Jewish King-Messiah was and remained – at least as far as the Tannaitic period is concerned – *a kingdom of this world*" (*The Messianic Idea in Israel* by Joseph Klausner, p. 517).

Walter Laqueur

Born in 1921 to Jewish parents in Germany, Laqueur was educated at the Breslau Johannes Gymnasium. In 1938 he left Germany for Palestine, where he lived on a kibbutz as a laborer for a year. He then moved to Jerusalem and worked as a journalist. He moved to London, where he was editor of *Survey* from 1955 to 1964. He then was director of the Wiener Library from 1964 to 1993. He became the founder and editor of the *Journal of Contemporary History.* He was a visiting professor to four universities: Chicago, Johns Hopkins, Harvard, and Tel Aviv. He served as professor of history of ideas at Brandeis University from 1967 to 1971, then as a professor at Georgetown University from 1980 to 1991. He is the author of several books, the most important considered to be *The History of Zionism*, which is instructive for any student of Judaism. It is not only a history of modern Zionism but also covers centuries of the torrid experiences of the Jews. This book is perhaps the most analytic of the Hebrew experience that I have had the great joy to read.

Simon Sebag Montefiore

Born in 1965 Montefiore comes from the famous Lithuanian Jewish family pioneered by Sir Moses Montefiore, banking partner of N. M. Rothschild and Sons. Simon was born in Britain and was educated at Caius College, Cambridge, where he read history. He was a popular writer and historian and became a fellow of the Royal Society of Literature. He was active as a foreign affairs journalist but moved on to work as a banker. He wrote many books, such as *Catherine the Great and Potemkin*, *Stalin*, and *The Young Stalin.* His most recent book is the outstanding *Jerusalem: The Biography.* In this he makes the great survey of the Holy City from its beginning to beyond history! He is perhaps unaware of the deep spiritual events his story has uncovered. One cannot deny after reading this book that Jerusalem is regarded by God as His Holy City and has a future on this planet like no other.

Franz Rosenzweig

(1886–1929) Franz Rosenzweig is perhaps the most enigmatic of modern Jewish philosophers. To many, he straddles Judaism and Christianity in a most intriguing and unique way. On the brink of baptism into Christianity he decided to remain in Judaism because he envisioned that he "was already with the Father" and did not need a savior, so it is said. His most famous book, *Star of Redemption*, raises important questions about the so-called divide between Judaism and Christianity. *Star of Redemption* is a most difficult but thrilling book to read. Its concepts are electrifying. He is openly hostile to the Tanakian apocalyptic of Isaiah and Daniel. But he perhaps unconsciously demonstrates a duality in his interpretation of messianic redemption. He expects redemption through the piety of lawkeeping but also has a personal Messiah he enjoys on the side. He grappled with the idea that this Messiah was both human and divine. I have repeatedly pointed this out in this book, repeatedly quoting the most marvelous language in his book.

Fiercely Jewish, Rosenzweig also saw himself as a German. He was born and educated in Germany and studied medicine, history, and philosophy. His doctoral thesis, *Hegel und der Staat* (a thesis on Hegel's *The State and Civil Society*), was published in Munich in 1920. He was greatly influenced by Hermann Cohen and Martin Buber. Gershom Scholem studied *Star of Redemption* very analytically and wrote a revealing essay titled "On the 1930 Edition of Rosenzweig's Star of Redemption" in his book *The Messianic Idea in Judaism.*

In 1920 Rosenzweig founded *Das Freie Judische Lehrhaus* (The Free Jewish House of Teaching). Rudiger Lux enthusiastically wrote in *The Jewish Virtual Library* about this house of teaching:

> The curriculum at the *Lehrhaus* embraced the whole spectrum of Jewish life: philosophy and politics, law and ethics, art and metaphysics, the experience of God in everyday life, and the experience of personal liberation, letter writing, and the laying of a banqueting table. When one looks at the programs and curriculum and tries to sense this living learning and learning life, one cannot help but dream and wish the things to happen also among Christians. In view of so much estranged Christian behavior [*Christlichkeit*] one wonders if a Free Christian *Lehrhaus* could not be the place for a renewed community of learning – a house of teaching not commited to just one theological or denominational stance, but ecumenically open, without preconditions, where teachers are not experts but fellow learners.

Rosenzweig participated with Buber in the translation of the Hebrew Bible into modern German. His death was like Mozart's -- untimely and a great tragedy. Considering his immense talent, the world lost out.

Peter Schafer

Schafer was born in 1943 in Germany and educated at the University of Bonn in theology and philosophy. He then moved to Hebrew University in Jerusalem, where he focused in Jewish

Studies and Semitic languages. In 1968 he obtained his PhD, summa cum laude, from the University of Freiburg. Subsequently he was appointed professor of Jewish studies at University of Tubingen and University of Colonge. From 1983 to 2008 he was professor of Jewish studies at Freie Universitat Berlin. He then was appointed professor of religion and Ronald O. Perelman professor of Judaic studies at Princeton University. Since 1993 he has been coeditor of *Jewish Studies Quarterly.* In a recent review by Mark Nussberger, he was hailed as a great scholar of the Talmud, and for his understanding and distinguishing between the Palestinian and Babylonian sociohistorical contexts as they exist in the Bavli and Yerushalmi. Many Jewish scholars regard him as an expert par excellence in the Bavli. He has authored thirty-two books (at last count) and multiple articles of study. He is highly regarded for the very popular books *Jesus in the Talmud, The Origin of Jewish Mysticism*, and *The Jewish Jesus.* He brings a fresh, thorough, and unambiguous interpretation of the Jewish writings, and his critical evaluation of other scholars' works is honest and deserved. This is possible because of his deep and wide knowledge of Jewish and Christian sources, which are amply displayed in his writings. He has a style that can disagree with some sharpness that belies his gentleness and charity. In September 2014 he was appointed director of the Jewish Museum in Berlin. He is billed as a Christian expert on Judaism, and in my opinion he has a more extensive knowledge of the spectrum in the practice of both ancient and modern Judaism than most Christian and many Jewish scholars.

Gershom Scholem

(1897–1982) Scholem was born in Berlin with the first name of Gerhardt, to an "assimilated" Jewish couple. His father had become a German nationalist. At the age of fourteen years he rejected his father's politics and espoused Zionism. It is told that his departure from his father's influence was hailed by his mother, who bought him a portrait of Theodor Herzl. Having had no Jewish education prior, he started learning Hebrew and studied the Talmud and Kabbalah. Judaism became the center of his life. He tried some religious observation, but by his own estimation it was unsuccessful. In his biography of his early life, *From Berlin to Jerusalem,* he appears commited to secularism. It is alleged he looked at Jewish history and Kabbalah "from the outside." He was turned out of his home by his father. He changed his first name to Gershom (which means "I have been a stranger in a foreign land" [Ex. 2:22]). He began a friendship with Zalman Shazar, who later became the third president of Israel. He loudly expressed disapproval for the start of World War I but was drafted into the German army. A mere two months later he was discharged from the army, labeled as a psychopath "temporarily unfit for duty." He then entered the University of Berlin and began the study of pure mathematics. During this time he met Martin Buber and Walter Benjamin, who influenced him considerably, but it became apparent later that he did not see Judaism through their eyes. He transferred to the University of Munich, where he translated and annotated the *Sefer ha-Bahir* (The Kabbalistic Book of Illumination) as his dissertation, graduating summa cum laude.

He soon after migrated to Palestine, where he obtained the position of librarian of the Hebrew section of the newly opened National Library. While there, he produced highly critical reviews and essays on Kabbalistic authors, which were published in the German-Jewish journal *Der Jude* and in the Hebrew journal in Jerusalem, *Keriat Sefer.* His dissertation *Das Buch Bahir* was published in Leipzig in 1923. He then published numerous books and articles on Kabbalah and Judaism. He dissected and criticized Kabbalistic theory and history. He wrote succinctly on topics in Judaism, notably Messianism. In the latter he chose to stick close to Tanakian theology rather than the opalescent Talmudic portrayal, though he did not spurn the Talmud. I find his Tanakian "acute Messianism" and his espousal of the apocalyptic of Isaiah and Daniel enthralling. His highly critical review of Sabbatianism is extraordinary in the analysis of the disastrous effect that heretical movement had on Jews and Judaism. He felt the desire of the Hebrews for the Messiah very keenly, and his opinions revealed his own commitment to and yearning for the Messiah. He wrote thirty-two books. He is the primary subject of eighteen books and forty-four articles published about him. The admiration other scholars had for him is enormous, and I consider him a giant in Judaism. More than a lifetime is needed to study his works. He was appointed the first Professor of Mysticism at Hebrew University in Jerusalem. His many awards include the Israel Prize, Yakir Yerushalayim, and the Bialik Prize for Jewish Thought. In my view, his greatest accomplishment is the preservation of messianic redemptive Judaism, so neatly packaged in "Classical," "Restorative," and "Utopian" terminology. His love for the apocalyptic of Isaiah and Daniel is very palpable. He correctly defines Jewish mysticism and its place, and severely criticizes Kabbalah and Hasidism for "diluting" and "neutralizing" Messianism. The Ha-Mashiach expected by him is real and will determine Israel's future in the fulfillment of Tanakian apocalyptic eschatology.

Geza Vermes

Vermes was born in 1924 in Hungary to Jewish parents. When he was seven years of age, his parents were baptized into the Roman Catholic Church. But this did not prevent them from perishing in the Holocaust. Geza escaped this fate. He studied Asian history and languages in Budapest and then in the Catholic University in Louvain, Belgium. He became a Roman Catholic priest. He obtained a doctorate in theology for his dissertation on the historical framework of the Dead Sea Scrolls. He left the Catholic Church in 1957, reasserted his Jewish identity, and moved to Britain, where he joined the Liberal Jewish Synagogue of London. He taught at the University of Newcastle-upon-Tyne and then at Oxford University, where he is currently professor emeritus of Jewish studies.

His most important work is likely *The Complete Dead Sea Scrolls in English* (1962). He renounced Christianity and adopted the mantle of a "Scholarly Historian" so he could explain his exit. Unfortunately he has not written sufficiently to clarify his own personal Jewish stance to the redemptive Judaism of Moses beamed from Sinai. He cursorily dismisses the basis of the Day of Atonement and the sacrificial system of the temple as cultic. He very skillfully sifts ideas and labels them acceptable or nonacceptable according to criteria he personally chooses. An example of this is his handling of the Didache and Barnabus documents. By wearing the personal noncommittal garb of a "historical" scholar, he rejects what he personally considers "nonhistoric" Jewish writings that support Messianism. He makes a welter of what he considers "interpolations" without a close scrutiny of these interpolations and their congruency or otherwise with Scripture. He developed a reputation as a Jesus scholar with his notable publications *Scripture and Tradition in Judaism* (1961), *Jesus the Jew* (1973), *Jesus and the World of Judaism* (1983), *The History of the Jewish People in the Age of Jesus Christ* (1987), and *Christian Beginnings* (2013). These writings are all governed by his own set criteria, slanted as a "historical" sifting, so that he can reject at will what he does not personally value. He is yet to come up with the definition and theology of Judaism as beamed from Sinai. Having left Christianity, he has not clarified what he personally has embraced in Judaism. His evasion of such an admission clearly avoids revealing the direction of his own personal religious life. This undermines an authoritative stance in his writings as a Jew. In my opinion he presents a pseudoscholarly attitude, picking and choosing sets of machined criteria to suit his arguments, which he applies to each concept he considers. He ignores certain facts that do not coincide with his opinions. In my opinion he most eloquently provides insight into the sacrifice by Abraham of Isaac. If regarded as the Jewish point of view, these insights are surprising and very enlightening. It is more symbolic than what I felt he was prepared to admit about the Messiah and the "cultic" shedding of blood on the temple mount. His so-called rejected Christianity is still detectable despite his scathing anti-Christian rhetoric. But he still embodies a lovable personality.

INDEX

E

Eli 150

Elijah 44, 72, 227, 235, 339, 344,
  363, 406, 425, 429, 430

Elohim xv, xvi, xxi, xxxiii, 4, 7, 11,
  19, 21, 24, 26, 28, 35, 36, 38,
  40, 46, 49, 50, 53, 60, 72, 74,
  78, 84, 90, 97, 100, 119, 125,
  142, 145, 158, 164, 174, 177,
  178, 183, 184, 202, 211, 218,
  222, 240, 245, 246, 248, 270,
  272, 274, 278, 280, 284, 286,
  288, 302, 307, 318, 330, 339,
  341, 348, 360, 370, 375, 378,
  382, 419, 427, 442, 445, 450,
  453, 454, 456, 458, 460

El Shaddah 33

Enoch xxviii, xxx, 70, 72, 74, 169,
  176, 178, 235, 273, 275, 276,
  363, 438

ephod 152, 154, 157, 205, 232, 323

Esau 57, 74, 93, 94, 96, 98, 100, 102,
  155, 263, 265, 266, 268, 328

eschatology, eschatological xix, xx,
  xxvi, xxxiv, 46, 138, 225, 236,
  299, 313, 349, 364, 375, 376,
  404, 410, 425, 426, 432, 489,
  490, 491, 496

Esther 8, 44, 114, 131, 137, 138, 186

Eve xxviii, 25, 37, 40, 42, 47, 48, 50, 52,
  54, 56, 58, 60, 65, 70, 82, 101,
  109, 114, 159, 160, 185, 186, 207,
  211, 235, 266, 271, 332, 341,
  416, 418, 421, 426, 456, 459

expiation, expiate xxix, 7, 41, 57, 60,
  89, 91, 116, 121, 122, 130, 142,
  144, 150, 154, 179, 185, 196,
  209, 219, 220, 232, 234, 236,
  307, 326, 330, 342, 384, 387,
  391, 394, 399, 418, 436, 442,
  447, 457, 459

F

faith xv, 4, 69, 82, 86, 113, 115, 155,
  166, 190, 247, 304, 306, 309,
  334, 336, 363, 408, 410, 414,
  435, 448

flesh 44, 77, 90, 97, 111, 115, 121,
  123, 129, 148, 164, 180, 191,
  197, 209, 219, 220, 228, 235,
  239, 240, 246, 303, 315, 317,
  323, 331, 344, 352, 364, 390,
  396, 428, 436, 445, 448

Ford, Desmond xxiii, xxvi, xxxiv,
  300, 488

free will 28, 48, 78, 114, 204, 250,
  252, 263

functionality, function xv, xvi, xvii,
  xviii, xxiv, xxxiii, 4, 19, 21, 24,
  28, 30, 32, 34, 37, 38, 40, 48,
  50, 53, 56, 61, 65, 68, 79, 84,
  86, 89, 90, 101, 110, 119, 122,
  125, 126, 133, 135, 142, 145,
  154, 163, 164, 171, 178, 183,
  184, 187, 191, 194, 201, 204,
  209, 217, 218, 219, 222, 224,
  233, 251, 272, 273, 274, 278,
  280, 286, 288, 296, 299, 302,
  307, 312, 318, 330, 342, 358,
  360, 374, 377, 379, 395, 397,
  404, 406, 426, 430, 441, 442,
  453, 454, 456, 458

G

Gabriel 286, 290, 294, 296, 299, 300

Gan Eden, garden of eden xiv, xix,
  xxviii, 4, 17, 18, 22, 30, 37, 42,
  47, 48, 55, 58, 61, 70, 77, 82,
  85, 97, 101, 111, 142, 159, 160,
  196, 204, 210, 223, 233, 250,
  266, 278, 301, 303, 330, 355,
  362, 369, 370, 374, 416, 418,
  421, 426, 447, 456, 458

Y

Z